THE ULTIMATE

GREEN MOUNTAIN

WOOD PELLET GRILL

COOKBOOK

550 TASTY AND HEALTHY RECIPES AND TECHNIQUES FOR THE MOST FLAVORFUL AND DELICIOUS BARBECUE

KAREN TURK

CONTENTS

VEGETABLES RECIPES 116

POULTRY RECIPES 146

BEEF LAMB AND GAME RECIPES 180

APPETIZERS AND SNACKS 215

COCKTAILS RECIPES 225

RECIPE INDEX..**241**

INTRODUCTION

What the Green Mountain Wood Pellet Grill is

A wood pellet grill — also known as a wood pellet smoker — is a special type of grill that uses indirect, pellet-generated heat and smoke to cook food in several different ways. With a pellet grill, you can enjoy traditionally grilled favorites or leave the meat to cook slowly on low smoke throughout the day. You can also use a pellet grill like a type of outdoor oven.

Like other grills, a pellet smoker makes an excellent addition to a campout, tailgating party and your own backyard.

How Does the Green Mountain Wood Pellet Grill Work?

So now you know what they do, but how do pellet grills work?

Much of what a pellet grill does is automated, meaning there's a very small learning curve on figuring out how to operate it correctly. Wood pellets are loaded into a storage chamber called the hopper, where a motor and combustion fan ignite the pellets and circulate that smoky wood flavor throughout the main cooking chamber.

Once they're going, pellet grills work basically like a gas grill or kitchen oven, trapping heat under the hood to cook your food, all while the hopper continues to circulate the aroma and flavor of your choice of wood pellets. Air fans ensure that heat and smoke are evenly dispersed during the cook time, and temperature control dials give you the option to cook either low and slow or hard and fast, depending on the taste and texture that you're trying to achieve.

The Pros of the Green Mountain Wood Pellet Grill

1.   Laid-Back Approach

If you're not the type of person to babysit your grill, opting for a pellet grill can be a far better option. Compared to gas, pellet grills cook slowly and thoroughly with minimal intervention and safety concerns. You'll even find that many have easy-to-use features that allow you to monitor the cooking process remotely.

For example, some pellet grills are equipped with digital controllers that allow you to set specific cook times. You can even use a smartphone app to adjust the grill settings. The only maintenance you'll have to consider with a wood pellet grill vs propane grill is making sure the hopper has enough pellets.

2. Minimal Maintenance

Because pellet grills typically cook for longer, most of the fats and grease will be burnt away, compared to gas grills. At most, you'll have to clean the firepot and any juices and drippings that are collected. You could also opt to season the smoker after cooking to burn away any traces of food.

3. Superior Flavor

The number one reason why people suggest pellet grills are better than gas grills is their flavor profiles. With pellet grills, you will have a diverse selection of different types of wood that you can cook with.

Instead of using regular flavorless gas, these appliances allow you to inject different flavors into the meat. A few of the most popular flavored pellets on the market include pecan, mesquite, hickory, and apple. There are plenty of manufacturers that have an extensive product list of fabulously flavored wood pellets. If you buy them in bulk, you're likely to get better discounts than you would with gas canisters.

Another exciting aspect of the flavors from wood pellets is you can customize them to your liking. You could mix apple and mesquite pellets for a unique flavor for ribs and brisket.

4. Versatility

Interestingly enough, pellet grills are far more versatile than gas grills because they give you several different ways to cook. You can easily set the temperature low, close the lid for smoking, or use it as a traditional grill. Some of the higher-end models even allow you to sear and braise, as well.

5. Enhanced Moisture and Meat Quality

Most people who opt for gas grills search for a quick and efficient outdoor appliance for everyday meals. With a pellet smoker, you have more control over how your meat cooks, especially if you want juicier cuts.

Since this appliance cooks for longer times and at lower temperatures, you'll find the inside of meat will be more moist. You might also find that it's a preferable option for higher-quality cuts of meat that need more attention.

Better to Use Your Green Mountain Wood Pellet Grill

1. Use Lighter-Flavored Wood

Switching up your hardwood changes the flavor of what you're cooking.

You'll want to leave the big smoke flavors for meat and veggies and use a lighter-flavored wood for your baked goods.

You simply want the wood flavor to lightly touch your baked goods. Go ahead and experiment to see which flavors you like the best. Go ahead and combine them, too.

2. Prep Your Ingredients

Just like with baking in the house, you want to prep your ingredients ahead of time. Then, put it all together so it's ready to cook when you are.

For example, if you're having an evening party, put your dessert together in the morning, so you just have to slip it into your grill when you're ready to cook.

3. Keep It Simple

Whether you're a novice baker or a seasoned expert, let the flavor of your hardwood season your baked goods and give it a light smoky flavor.

So, keep your dessert simple and let the grill do the work. There's no reason to over complicate your dessert. After all, the fun of having a party is hanging out with friends and family.

Think cookies, cake, crumbles, and even fruit. Grilled fruit is delightful and refreshing when you put some cool whip on the side.

4. Use a Recipe You Know

A great tip is to use a recipe you know and are comfortable with. You can basically make anything you'd like on your pellet grill. So, pull out your favorite cookie, brownie, cake, pie, or cheesecake recipe. You don't really have to make any modification to cook on your grill.

Do note, though, that recipes may cook a bit faster, so you'll want to check often for doneness.

Cleaning Approaches for Your Green Mountain Wood Pellet Grill

To prove to you just how easy it can be let's review the common methods of cleaning.

1. The Obvious Approach: Brushing

This method works best if it is done immediately after grilling while the grate is still hot. Before the grates cool off, scrape each grate with a brush, both top and bottom sides. You can also dip the brush in water which will create a steam that loosens the grease. Not only will this make cleaning time shorter, but it will discourage insects from hanging around your grill. Depending on your grate you may need to wipe them down with a cloth after scrapping.

2. The Lazy Approach: Burning

The idea behind this method is simple, get the grate super hot (550° F) until all the caked on grease burns up. You can throw the grates in a self-cleaning oven or simply place some aluminum foil down on top of the grate, close the lid and light up the grill. After about 10-15 minutes all of the grease should be a white powder, simply brush it off and you're done.

3. The Neat Freak Approach: Soaking

Although, brushing and burning are the standard methods for cleaning, all grates should be soaked at least a couple times a year.

Just fill up the sink or a large bucket with water and a bunch of dish soap. Add a little baking soda and let the grates soak for an hour. Afterward, scrub and rinse.

4. The DIY Approach

You can easily make your own scrubber with a block of hardwood. Use the block to scrub the grates after grilling, eventually, you will carve grooves into the block that fit perfectly onto your grate.

Aluminum foil is another easy DIY scrubber and also a lifesaver if you have to use a lazy person's grill. Simply heat up the grates, then wad up some foil and scrub away. Let's jump into some do-it-yourself methods to cleaning up those nasty grates.

BAKING RECIPES

Ultimate Baked Garlic Bread

Servings: 4

Cooking Time: 20 Minutes

Ingredients:

- 1 baguette
- 1/2 Cup softened butter
- 1/2 Cup mayonnaise
- 4 Tablespoon chopped Italian parsley
- 6 Clove garlic, minced
- salt
- chile flakes
- 1 Cup mozzarella cheese
- 1/2 Cup Parmesan cheese

Directions:

1. Supply your smoker with wood pellets and follow the start-up procedure. Preheat the grill, with the lid closed, to 375° F.

2. Lay baguette on a cutting board and cut it in half lengthwise.

3. In a bowl, add butter, mayonnaise, parsley, garlic, salt and chile flakes. Mix well.

4. Spread butter mixture on baguette halves and top with mozzarella and Parmesan cheese.

5. Place baguette on the grill (if you like the bread crisp, do not use foil and if you like it soft, wrap with foil). Grill for approximately 15 to 25 minutes. Serve warm. Enjoy! Grill: 375 °F

Baked Chocolate Coconut Brownies

Servings: 4

Cooking Time: 25 Minutes

Ingredients:

- 1/2 Cup gluten-free or all-purpose flour, such as Bob's Red Mill
- 1/4 Cup unsweetened alkalized cocoa powder
- 1/2 Teaspoon sea salt
- 4 Ounce semisweet chocolate, coarsely chopped
- 3/4 Cup unrefined coconut oil
- 1 Cup raw cane sugar
- 4 eggs
- 1 Teaspoon vanilla extract
- 4 Ounce semisweet chocolate chips, optional

Directions:

1. Supply your smoker with wood pellets and follow the start-up procedure. Preheat the grill, with the lid closed, to 350° F.

2. Grease a 9x9 inch baking pan and line with parchment paper.

3. Combine the flour, cocoa powder and salt in a medium bowl. Set aside.

4. In a double boiler or microwave, melt the chopped chocolate and coconut oil. Let cool slightly.

5. Add the sugar, eggs and vanilla. Whisking until well combined.

6. Whisk in the flour mixture and fold in the chocolate chips. Pour into the prepared pan.

7. Place on the grill and bake until a toothpick inserted in the center of the brownies comes out clean, about 20 to 25 minutes. This will yield a somewhat gooey brownie. Continue to bake for 5 to 10 minutes if you prefer a drier brownie. Grill: 350 °F

8. Let the brownies cool completely, then cut into squares. Store in an airtight container at room temperature for up to 3 days. Enjoy!

Italian Herb & Parmesan Scones

Servings: 8

Cooking Time: 20 Minutes

Ingredients:

- 2 1/2 Cup all-purpose flour
- 2 Teaspoon baking powder
- 1 Teaspoon baking soda
- 1/2 Teaspoon garlic salt
- 1 Tablespoon Italian Seasoning
- 1 Cup Parmesan cheese, grated
- 2 Large eggs
- 1 1/2 Cup buttermilk
- 1/4 Cup olive oil

Directions:

1. In a large mixing bowl, combine flour, baking powder, baking powder, soda, garlic salt, Italian seasoning, and 1/2 cup of the cheese. Make a well in the center.

2. In a smaller bowl, whisk together eggs, buttermilk, and olive oil.

3. Pour into the well in the dry ingredients, and stir batter just until it's combined. It will appear lumpy.

4. Oil 12 muffin cups, spray with cooking spray, or line with disposable paper liners.

5. Divide the batter evenly between the cups. Sprinkle the tops of the muffins with the remaining Parmesan cheese.

6. Supply your smoker with wood pellets and follow the start-up procedure. Preheat the grill, with the lid closed, to 400° F.

7. Arrange the muffin tin directly on the grill grate and bake the muffins for 20 to 25 minutes, or until a toothpick inserted in the center of the muffin comes out clean.

8. Cool for several minutes before removing from the muffin tin. Serve warm with butter or olive oil. Enjoy!

Caramelized Bourbon Baked Pears

Servings: 4

Cooking Time: 30 Minutes

Ingredients:

- 3 Whole Pears, fresh
- 1/4 Cup brown sugar
- 1/4 Cup bourbon
- 2 Tablespoon butter, melted
- 1 Teaspoon vanilla extract
- 1/2 Teaspoon salt

Directions:

1. Supply your smoker with wood pellets and follow the start-up procedure. Preheat the grill, with the lid closed, to 325° F.

2. Peel and core the pears. Arrange them in a buttered baking dish.

3. In a small bowl, combine the brown sugar, bourbon, butter, vanilla, cinnamon and salt. Pour the bourbon mixture over the pears.

4. Place the baking dish on the grill grate, close the lid and bake for 30-35 minutes or until the pears are fork tender. Grill: 325 °F

5. Transfer to a serving plate and spoon the caramelized bourbon mixture over the pears.

6. Serve warm over vanilla ice cream. Enjoy!

Vanilla Cheesecake Skillet Brownie

Servings: 2

Cooking Time: 30 Minutes

Ingredients:

- 1 Box Brownie Mix
- 1 Package Cream Cheese
- 2 Egg
- 1/2 Cup Oil
- 1 Can Pie Filling, Blueberry
- 1/2 Cup Sugar
- 1 Tsp Vanilla
- 1/4 Cup Water, Warm

Directions:

1. Combine all brownie ingredients and mix. In a separate bowl, combine cream cheese, sugar, egg and vanilla and mix until smooth. Grease skillets and pour in brownie batter. Top with cheesecake and cherry pie filling, using a knife to blend to give it that marbled look.

2. Supply your smoker with wood pellets and follow the start-up procedure. Preheat the grill, with the lid closed, to 350°F and bake for about 30 minutes.

3. Let cool for about 10 minutes and enjoy!

Donut Bread Pudding

Servings: 8

Cooking Time: 40 Minutes

Ingredients:

- 16 Cake Donuts
- 1/2 Cup Raisins, seedless
- 5 eggs
- 3/4 Cup sugar
- 2 Cup heavy cream
- 2 Teaspoon vanilla extract
- 1 Teaspoon ground cinnamon
- 3/4 Cup Butter, melted, cooled slightly

- Ice Cream

Directions:

1. Lightly butter a 9- by 13-inch baking pan. Layer the donuts in an even thickness in the pan. Distribute the raisins over the top, if using. Drizzle evenly with the butter.

2. Make the custard: In a medium bowl, whisk together the sugar, eggs, cream, vanilla, and cinnamon. Whisk in the butter. Pour over the donuts. Let sit for 10 to 15 minutes, periodically pushing the donuts down into the custard. Cover with foil.

3. Supply your smoker with wood pellets and follow the start-up procedure. Preheat the grill, with the lid closed, to 350° F.

4. Bake the bread pudding for 30 to 40 minutes, or until the custard is set. Remove the foil and continue to bake for 10 additional minutes to lightly brown the top. Grill: 350 °F

5. Let cool slightly before cutting into squares. Drizzle with melted ice cream, if desired. Enjoy!

Vanilla Chocolate Bacon Cupcakes

Servings: 12
Cooking Time: 120 Minutes

Ingredients:

- 1 Lb Bacon
- 1 1/2 Tsp Baking Powder
- 1 1/2 Tsp Baking Soda
- 1 Cup Cocoa, Powder
- 2 Egg
- 1 3/4 Cups Flour
- 1 Cup Milk, Whole
- 1/2 Cup Oil
- 1 Tsp Salt
- 2 Cups Sugar
- 2 Tsp Vanilla

Directions:

1. Supply your smoker with wood pellets and follow the start-up procedure. Preheat the grill, with the lid closed, to 250° F.

2. Once your grill is preheated, place bacon strips on the grates. Smoke for 1hr-1 ½ hours or until desired crispiness is achieved.

3. Remove the bacon from the grill and set aside.

4. Increase set the temperature to 350°F and preheat.

5. Mix the rest of the ingredients in a bowl with an electric mixer until it is nice and smooth.

6. Pour the mixture into a cupcake tin.

7. Transfer the tin to your grill and bake for about 20 - 25 minutes.

8. Allow the cupcakes to cool on a wire rack. Once cooled, top with your favorite premade icing and a half of strip of the bacon. Serve and enjoy!

Spiced Carrot Cake

Servings: 10
Cooking Time: 35 Minutes

Ingredients:

- 1/2 Cup Apple Sauce, Unsweetened
- 2 Tsp Baking Powder
- 1 Tsp Baking Soda
- 1 1/2 Cups Brown Sugar
- 1/2 Cup Butter, Room Temp
- 3/4 Cup Canola Oil
- 3 Cups Carrot, Grated
- 1 1/2 Tsp Cinnamon, Ground
- 2 (8-Ounce) Packages Cream Cheese, Room Temperature
- 4 Egg
- 2 Cups Flour, All-Purpose
- 1/2 Tsp Ginger, Ground
- 1/4 Tsp Nutmeg, Ground
- 1/2 Tsp Salt
- 1/2 Cup Sugar
- 3 Cups Sugar, Icing

Directions:

1. Supply your smoker with wood pellets and follow the start-up procedure. Preheat the grill, with the lid closed, to 350° F.

2. Line the bottom of 2 9-inch cake pans with parchment paper and spray the sides with cooking spray. Set aside.

3. In a large bowl, combine flour, baking powder and soda, spices and salt.

4. In a smaller bowl, combine oil, eggs, sugars, and applesauce and whisk together. Add carrots and stir until well combined.

5. Pour the wet ingredients into the dry. Stir until combined but take care not to over mix. Pour the batter evenly between the two cake pans. Bake for about 35 minutes in your Grill, rotating the cake pans halfway between the cook. Remove once a toothpick is inserted in the middle of the cake and comes out clean.

6. While the cake is cooling, prepare the frosting. Beat the cream cheese until smooth with a hand mixer. Add the butter and icing sugar and mix until fully combined.

7. On a clean plate or cake stand, place one half of the cake and top with a good layer of cream cheese frosting. Place the second half on top and cover with the remaining frosting. Icing tip: try not to lift your knife while icing. Instead make long, smooth strokes. Lifting the knife often make cause crumbs to get into your icing. Top with pecans if desired.

Spiced Lemon Cherry Pie

Servings: 6-8
Cooking Time: 60 Minutes

Ingredients:
- 1/2 Teaspoon Cinnamon, Ground
- 1/2 Teaspoon Cloves, Ground
- 1/2 Cup Cornstarch
- 1 Pound Frozen Sweet Dark Cherries, Thawed
- 1 Teaspoon Water (Beaten With Egg) 1 Egg
- 1 Lemon, Juice
- 1 Lemon, Zest
- 2 Prepared Store Bought Or Homemade Pie Crust
- 1 Teaspoon Hickory Honey Sea Salt Seasoning
- 1 Cup Sugar, Granulated
- 1 Teaspoon Vanilla Extract

Directions:
1. In a large bowl, mix together the thawed cherries and their juices, sugar, cornstarch, lemon zest, lemon juice, cinnamon, clove, vanilla extract and Hickory Honey Sea Salt. Allow to sit for 30 minutes.

2. Flour a work surface and roll out one of the prepared pie crusts so that it fits a 9 inch pie tin. Fill with the cherry pie filling and refrigerate. When the pie is chilled, roll out the second pie crust, brush the edge of the first pie crust with the egg mixture, top with the second pie crust, crimp the edge with a fork, and chill. Alternatively, cut the second pie crust into strips and form a lattice pattern, attaching the strips with the egg mixture. Chill the pie for 15-30 minutes, or until the dough is very cold and firm. Brush the top of the pie with the remaining egg mixture.

3. Supply your smoker with wood pellets and follow the start-up procedure. Preheat the grill, with the lid closed, to 350° F and grill for 45 minutes to 1 hour, or until the pie crust is golden and firm and the filling is bubbly. Remove from the grill and allow to cool at room temperature for at least 4 hours to set the filling, then serve and enjoy!

Pretzel Rolls

Servings: 6
Cooking Time: 20 Minutes

Ingredients:
- 2 3/4 Cup Bread Flour
- 1 Quick-Rising Yeast, envelope
- 1 Teaspoon salt
- 1 Teaspoon sugar
- 1/2 Teaspoon celery seed
- 1/2 Teaspoon Caraway Seeds
- 1 Cup hot water
- As Needed Cornmeal
- 8 Cup water
- 1/4 Cup baking soda
- 2 Tablespoon sugar
- 1 Whole Egg White
- Coarse salt

Directions:
1. Combine bread flour, 1 envelope yeast, salt, 1 teaspoon sugar, caraway seeds and celery seeds in food processor or standing mixer with dough hook and blend.

2. With machine running, gradually pour hot water, adding enough water to form smooth elastic dough.

Process 1 minute to knead. (You could also knead it by hand for a few minutes.)

3. Grease medium bowl. Add dough to bowl, turning to coat. Cover bowl with plastic wrap, then towel; let dough rise in warm draft-free area until doubled in volume, about 35 minutes.

4. Flour a large baking sheet. Punch dough down and knead on lightly floured surface until smooth. Divide into 8 pieces. Form each dough piece into a ball.

5. Place dough balls on prepared sheet, flattening each slightly. Using serrated knife, cut X in top center of each dough ball. Cover with towel and let dough balls rise until almost doubled in volume, about 20 minutes.

6. When ready to cook, start the smoker on Smoke with the lid open until a fire is established (4-5 minutes). Turn temperature to 375 F (190 C) and preheat, lid closed, for 10 to 15 minutes.

7. Grease another baking sheet and sprinkle with cornmeal. Bring water to boil in large saucepan. Add baking soda and sugar (water will foam up). Add 3 rolls (or however many will fit comfortably in the pot) and cook 30 seconds per side.

8. Using slotted spoon, transfer rolls to prepared sheet, arranging X side up. Repeat with remaining rolls. Brush rolls with egg white glaze. Sprinkle rolls generously with coarse salt.

9. Bake rolls until brown, about 20 to 25 minutes. Transfer to racks and cool 10 minutes. Serve rolls warm or at room temperature. Enjoy!

Crescent Rolls

Servings: 8
Cooking Time: 12 Minutes

Ingredients:
*   1 Crescent Dough, Can

Directions:
1. Supply your smoker with wood pellets and follow the start-up procedure. Preheat the grill, with the lid closed, to 375° F.
2. Unroll the dough and separate into triangles. Roll up the triangles and place on an ungreased nonstick cookie sheet. Bake for 10 -12 minutes on your Grill. You will know that they are finished when the rolls are golden brown.

Mexican Black Bean Cornbread Casserole

Servings: 6
Cooking Time: 30 Minutes

Ingredients:
*   1 Lb Beef, Ground
*   1 15Oz Drained Black Beans, Can
*   1 Box Corn Muffin Mix
*   1 15Oz Enchilada Sauce, Can
*   1 Onion, Chopped
*   1 15Oz Drained Pinto Beans, Can

Directions:
1. Supply your smoker with wood pellets and follow the start-up procedure. Preheat the grill, with the lid closed, to 300° F.
2. Mix corn muffin mix according to directions.
3. Place cast iron skillet over flame broiler and heat for a few minutes, leaving Grill lid open.
4. Add onion and ground beef/sausage to skillet and break up
5. Cook until meat is done about 5 to 10 minutes.
6. Add both cans of beans, and enchilada sauce, stir to combine.
7. Bring mixture to a simmer.
8. Carefully close flame broiler and turn Grill up to 400 degrees.
9. Spread prepared corn muffin mix over top of meat and bean mixture and bake for 15 minutes until cornbread mixture is lightly browned.
10. Let sit 15 minutes before serving.

Chocolate Almond Cake

Servings: 8
Cooking Time: 50 Minutes

Ingredients:
*   7 oz good quality dark chocolate; melted
*   5 eggs; separated
*   Pinch salt

- 6.5 oz caster sugar
- 7 oz butter; cubed at room temperature
- 7 oz ground almonds
- 1 oz cocoa powder
- 1 tsp. baking powder
- Icing sugar; for dusting

Directions:

1. Supply your smoker with wood pellets and follow the start-up procedure. Preheat the grill, with the lid closed, to 347 °F.

2. Beat together the butter and sugar until light and fluffy. Then beat in the yolks, one at a time.

3. Gently fold in the almonds.

4. Add the melted chocolate and mix well.

5. Beat the egg whites with a pinch of salt in a separate bowl until stiff.

6. Sift the baking powder and cocoa powder into the cake mix and fold in gently, then fold in the egg whites.

7. Pour the mix into an 8.5" round spring form cake tin (greased and lined), smooth over, and bake in the center of the grill for about 50 minutes. If the top starts to dry out after 25-30 minutes, cover with foil.

Smokin' Lemon Bars

Servings: 8-12

Cooking Time: 60 Minutes

Ingredients:

- 3/4 Cup lemon juice
- 1 1/2 Cup sugar
- 2 eggs
- 3 Egg Yolk
- 1 1/2 Teaspoon cornstarch
- Pinch sea salt
- 4 Tablespoon unsalted butter
- 1/4 Cup olive oil
- 1/2 Tablespoon lemon zest
- 1 1/4 Cup flour
- 1/4 Cup granulated sugar
- 3 Tablespoon Confectioner's Sugar
- 1 Teaspoon lemon zest
- 1/4 Teaspoon Sea Salt, Fine
- 10 Tablespoon Unsalted Butter, Cut Into Cubes

Directions:

1. When ready to cook, set grill temperature to 180°F and preheat, lid closed for 15 minutes.

2. In a small mixing bowl, whisk together lemon juice, sugar, eggs and yolks, cornstarch and fine sea salt. Pour into a sheet tray or cake pan and place on grill. Smoke for 30 minutes whisking mixture halfway through smoking. Remove from grill and set aside.

3. Pour mixture into a small saucepan. Place on stove top set to medium heat until boiling. Once boiling, boil for 60 seconds. Remove from heat and strain through a mesh strainer into a bowl. Whisk in cold butter, olive oil, and lemon zest.

4. To make a crust, pulse together the flour, granulated sugar, confectioners' sugar, lemon zest and salt in a food processor. Add butter and pulse until just mixed into a crumbly dough. Press dough into a prepared 9" by 9" baking dish lined with parchment paper that is long enough to hang over 2 of the sides.

5. When ready to cook, set the smoker to 350°F and preheat, lid closed for 15 minutes.

6. Bake until crust is very lightly golden brown, about 30 to 35 minutes.

7. Remove from grill and pour the lemon filling over the crust. Return to grill and continue to bake until filling is just set about 15 to 20 minutes.

8. Allow to cool at room temperature, then refrigerate until chilled before slicing into bars. Sprinkle with confectioners' sugar and flaky sea salt right before serving. Enjoy!

Chicken Pot Pie

Servings: 6

Cooking Time: 60 Minutes

Ingredients:

- 2 Chicken, Boneless/Skinless
- 1 Cream Of Chicken Soup, Can
- 1 Tsp Curry Powder
- 1/2 Cup Mayo
- 1 1/2 Cups Mixed Frozen Vegetables
- 1 Onion, Sliced
- 2 Frozen Pie Shell, Deep

* 1/2 Cup Sour Cream

Directions:

1. Supply your smoker with wood pellets and follow the start-up procedure. Preheat the grill, with the lid closed, to 425° F.

2. Cut the onion in half and place on the grates of the grill. If you"re using fresh chicken breasts, barbecue the chicken at the same time as the onions. The chicken is fully cooked when the internal temperature reached 170F. While the onion and chicken are cooking, prepare the pie crust by putting one crust in a pie plate. When the chicken and onions are done, shred chicken and chop onion into small pieces and place in the prepared pie plate along with the mixed vegetables.

3. Combine cream of chicken soup, mayo, sour cream, and curry powder in a bowl. Pour into the pie crust with the chicken and mix to combine. Wet the sides of the bottom crust with a small amount of water and top with the second pie crust. Push gently along the sides of the crust to seal the two pie crusts together.

4. Place in the and bake for 40 minutes, or until the crust is golden brown. Serve hot.

Baked Potatoes & Celery Root Au Gratin

Servings: 2
Cooking Time: 60 Minutes

Ingredients:

* 5 Tablespoon butter, softened
* 2 Large leeks, white parts only, cleaned and sliced into half moons
* kosher salt
* freshly ground black pepper
* 5 Small Yukon Gold potatoes, sliced 1/4 inch thick
* 2 Whole celery root, peeled and sliced 1/4 inch thick
* 2 Cup cream
* 1 Tablespoon minced sage
* 1 Cup shredded Gruyere or other hearty Swiss cheese, divided

Directions:

1. Supply your smoker with wood pellets and follow the start-up procedure. Preheat the grill, with the lid closed, to 400° F.

2. Butter a 9x13 baking dish with 1 tablespoon of the softened butter. In a medium frying pan over medium heat, melt the remaining butter. Add the leeks and a generous pinch of salt and pepper and cook, stirring often until softened, about 5 minutes.

3. Remove from the heat and allow to cool. Place the potato and celery root slices into a large mixing bowl. Add the cream, leek mixture, minced sage, 1 teaspoon salt, 1/2 teaspoon pepper and 1 cup cheese. Stir gently to coat.

4. Arrange a layer of potato and celery root slices so they're slightly overlapping in the prepared baking dish. Repeat two more times so there are three layers of potatoes. Pour remaining cream from the bowl over the gratin, then sprinkle the top with the remaining cup of cheese.

5. Cover the dish loosely with foil and bake on the grill for 45 minutes. Remove the foil and continue baking until the top is golden and bubbly and the potatoes are tender when pierced, about 30 to 45 minutes longer. Let stand for 10 minutes before serving. Enjoy!

Chocolate Lava Cake With Smoked Whipped Cream

Servings: 4
Cooking Time: 45 Minutes

Ingredients:

* 1 Pint heavy whipping cream
* 9 Tablespoon Butter
* 220 G Semisweet Chocolate
* 1 1/4 Cup powdered sugar
* 2 Large eggs
* 2 egg yolk
* 6 Tablespoon flour
* 1 Tablespoon Bourbon Vanilla
* Powdered Sugar
* cocoa powder

Directions:

1. Supply your smoker with wood pellets and follow the start-up procedure. Preheat the grill, with the lid closed, to 180° F.

2. For the Smoked Whipped Cream: Add cream to a shallow, aluminum baking pan. Place the pan on the grill and smoke for 30 minutes.

3. Pour the smoked cream into a large mixing bowl and refrigerate for later use. Grill: 180 °F

4. Increase the grill temperature to 375°F and preheat. Grill: 375 °F

5. Brush 4 small soufflé cups with 1 tablespoon melted butter.

6. Melt the chocolate and remaining butter in a heatproof bowl over simmering water, stir until smooth.

7. Stir in powdered sugar. Add eggs and egg yolks, stirring continuously. Whisk in flour until blended completely.

8. Pour batter into the prepared soufflé cups. Place them on the Traeger and bake for 13-14 minutes, or until the sides are set. Grill: 375 °F

9. For the Whipped Cream: Remove the chilled smoked cream from the refrigerator, add the bourbon vanilla and whip until airy.

10. Add confectioners sugar and continue whipping until whipped cream forms stiff peaks.

11. Dust lava cakes with confectioners sugar and cocoa, top with a dollop of smoke-infused whipped cream. Enjoy!

Marbled Brownies With Amaretto & Ricotta

Servings: 4
Cooking Time: 30 Minutes

Ingredients:

- 1 Cup Ricotta Cheese
- 1 eggs
- 1 Tablespoon Amaretto Liqueur
- 1/4 Cup sugar
- 2 Teaspoon cornstarch
- 1/2 Teaspoon vanilla extract
- 1 Brownie Mix

Directions:

1. Coat a 9- by 13-inch nonstick baking pan with cooking spray or softened butter and set aside. (If you do not have a nonstick pan, line a regular one with buttered foil or parchment paper.)

2. In a medium bowl, combine the ricotta, egg, amaretto, sugar, cornstarch, and vanilla and whisk together thoroughly. Set aside.

3. Prepare the brownie mix according to the package directions. Spread the brownie batter evenly in the prepared pan. Randomly drop dollops of the ricotta mixture over the batter. Run a plastic knife through the ricotta mixture to give the brownies a marbled look. (A plastic knife is less likely to scratch your pan's nonstick surface.)

4. Supply your smoker with wood pellets and follow the start-up procedure. Preheat the grill, with the lid closed, to 350° F.

5. Put the pan with the brownie mixture directly on the grill grate and bake, about 25 to 30 minutes. Insert a bamboo skewer or toothpick in the center of the brownies to determine if they are done: the batter should not be wet. Grill: 350 °F

6. Transfer the brownies to a wire cooling rack to cool completely. Cut into squares.

Baked Cast Iron Berry Cobbler

Servings: 6
Cooking Time: 35 Minutes

Ingredients:

- 4 Cup Berries
- 12 Tablespoon sugar
- Cup orange juice
- 2/3 Cup Flour
- 3/4 Teaspoon baking powder
- 1 Pinch salt
- 1/2 Cup butter
- 1 Tablespoon Sugar, raw

Directions:

1. Supply your smoker with wood pellets and follow the start-up procedure. Preheat the grill, with the lid closed, to 350° F.

2. In a 10-inch (25-cm) cast iron or other baking pan, mix together the berries, 4 Tbsp sugar and the orange juice.

3. In a small bowl, mix together the flour, baking powder and salt. Set aside.

4. In a separate bowl, cream together the butter and granulated sugar. Add the egg and vanilla extract and mix to combine. Gradually fold in the flour mixture.

5. Spoon the batter on top of the berries and sprinkle raw sugar on top.

6. Bake the cobbler for approximately 35-45 minutes. Cool slightly and serve with whipped cream. Enjoy! Grill: 350 ˚F

Baked Brie

Servings: 6
Cooking Time: 8 Minutes

Ingredients:

- 16 Ounce (16 oz) brie wheel
- 1/3 Cup honey
- 1/4 Cup pecans
- Crackers
- apple, sliced

Directions:

1. Supply your smoker with wood pellets and follow the start-up procedure. Preheat the grill, with the lid closed, to 350° F.

2. Line a rimmed baking sheet with a piece of parchment or aluminum foil. Using a sharp serrated knife, slice top—the white rind—off the brie. (Le the ave the rind on the sides and bottom intact.)

3. Put the brie, cut side up, on the prepared baking sheet and drizzle with the honey. Sprinkle nuts on top.

4. Bake the brie until it is soft and oozing, but not melting, 8 to 10 minutes. Let it cool for a couple of minutes and transfer to a serving plate. Grill: 350 ˚F

5. Serve with crackers and sliced apple wedges. Drizzle with more honey, if desired. Enjoy!

Smoked, Salted Caramel Apple Pie

Servings: 4
Cooking Time: 60 Minutes

Ingredients:

- 1 Cup cream
- 1 Cup brown sugar
- 3/4 Cup Light Corn Syrup
- 6 Tablespoon butter
- 1 Teaspoon sea salt
- 1 Pastry for Double-Crust Pie
- 6 Granny Smith Apples, Cut Into Wedges

Directions:

1. Supply your smoker with wood pellets and follow the start-up procedure. Preheat the grill, with the lid closed, to 180° F.

2. Fill a large pan with ice and water. Pour the cream into a smaller, shallow pan. Place the pan with the cream in the ice bath and place them both on the Traeger to smoke for 15-20 minutes. Grill: 180 ˚F

3. To make the caramel, combine the sugar and corn syrup in a saucepan and cook over medium heat, stirring constantly until it coats the back of your spoon and starts to turn a copper color, then stir in butter, salt, and smoked cream.

4. To assemble the pie, gather the pie crust, salted caramel, and apples. Place one of the pie crusts into the pie plate and fill with apple slices. Pour caramel over the apples. Lay the top crust over the filling, then crimp the top and bottom crusts together.

5. Make slits in the top crust to release the steam and finish by brushing with egg or cream. Sprinkle with raw sugar and sea salt.

6. When ready to bake, set the Traeger to 375˚F and preheat, lid closed for 15 minutes.

7. Place the pie on the grill and bake for 20 minutes. Grill: 375 ˚F

8. Reduce heat to 325˚F and cook for 25 more minutes. When ready, the crust should be golden brown and the filling, bubbly. Grill: 325 ˚F

9. Remove the pie from the grill and let cool. Serve with vanilla ice cream. Enjoy!

Smoked Vanilla Apple Pie

Servings: 6
Cooking Time: 45 Minutes

Ingredients:

- 1 1/2 cups of self-raising flour
- 3/4 cup of sugar
- 0.3 lbs of butter melted
- 1 tsp of vanilla extract
- 1 egg
- 0.9-lb tin of pie apples
- sugar & cinnamon for dusting

Directions:

1. Supply your smoker with wood pellets and follow the start-up procedure. Preheat the grill, with the lid closed, to 350° F.
2. Combine the self-raising flour, sugar, melted butter, vanilla, and egg in a large bowl until a golden dough texture is formed.
3. Spread half the mixture in a pie dish and press the bottoms and up the sides of the dish.
4. Pour pie apple tin into the pie and spread out evenly.
5. Sprinkle the remaining mixture over the top of the apple evenly and place in the smoker.
6. Leave for 45 minutes or until the golden crust forms on the top.
7. Dust with cinnamon and a little sugar if desired.
8. Serve warm with custard, ice cream, or both.

Sweet Cheese Muffins

Servings: 3
Cooking Time: 15 Minutes

Ingredients:

- 1 package butter cake mix
- 1 package Jiffy Corn Muffin Mix
- 1 cup self-rising or cake flour
- 12 tablespoons (1½ sticks) unsalted butter, softened, plus 8 tablespoons (1 stick) melted
- 3½ cups shredded Cheddar cheese
- 2 eggs, beaten, at room temperature
- 2¼ cups buttermilk
- Nonstick cooking spray or butter, for greasing
- ¼ cup packed brown sugar

Directions:

1. Supply your smoker with wood pellets and follow the start-up procedure. Preheat, with the lid closed, to 375°F.
2. In a large mixing bowl, combine the cake mix, corn muffin mix, and flour.
3. Slice the 1½ sticks of softened butter into pieces and cut into the dry ingredients. Add the cheese and mix thoroughly.
4. In a medium bowl, combine the eggs and buttermilk, then add to the dry ingredients, stirring until well blended.
5. Coat three 12-cup mini muffin pans with cooking spray and spoon ¼ cup of batter into each cup.
6. Transfer the pans to the grill, close the lid, and smoke, monitoring closely, for 12 to 15 minutes, or until the muffins are lightly browned.
7. While the muffins are cooking, make the topping: In a small bowl, stir together the remaining 1 stick of melted butter and the brown sugar until well combined.
8. Remove the muffins from the grill. Brush the tops with the sweet butter and serve warm.

Cornbread Chicken Stuffing

Servings: 6 - 8
Cooking Time: 95 Minutes

Ingredients:

- 2 Tbsp Butter
- 1 Cup Chicken Stock
- 6 Cups Cornbread, Cubed
- ½ Cup Dried Cranberries
- 1 Egg
- ½ Cup Heavy Whipping Cream
- 1 Lb. Italian Sausage
- 1 Diced Onion
- 1 ½ Tsp Pulled Pork Rub
- 2 Tbsp Sage, Fresh
- ½ Tsp Fresh Thyme

Directions:

1. Supply your smoker with wood pellets and follow the start-up procedure. Preheat the grill, with the lid

closed, to 250° F. If using a gas or charcoal grill, set the temp to low heat.

2. Portion sausage into quarter-size pieces and place on mesh grate. Place grate on the grill and cook for 1 hour. Sausage pieces will have a smoky deep brown color. Move the mesh tray of sausage to the side of the grill with indirect heat.

3. Open the Flame Broiler Plate and increase the temperature to 350°F. Place a large cast iron skillet on the grill, over direct flame. Add butter and onions and cook until the onions caramelize lightly, stirring often. Add the sage and thyme and stir to combine.

4. Gently fold in the dried cranberries and cubed cornbread, then add sausage directly from mesh grate.

5. In a small mixing bowl, whisk together the heavy cream, chicken stock, egg, and Pulled Pork Rub. Pour mixture over the cornbread stuffing mix.

6. Cover grill and cook 30 minutes or until heated through and crispy on top.

Smoky Pimento Cheese Cornbread

Servings: 4
Cooking Time: 30 Minutes

Ingredients:
- 2 Tsp Baking Powder
- 2 Cups Buttermilk, Low Fat
- 1/2 Cup Cornmeal, Yellow
- 2 Egg
- 1 1/2 Cups Flour, All-Purpose
- 16 Oz Pimento Cheese Spread
- 2 Tbsp Bacon Cheddar Seasoning
- 1/4 Cup Sugar

Directions:
1. Supply your smoker with wood pellets and follow the start-up procedure. Preheat the grill, with the lid closed, to 350° F. Place a cast iron skillet in the grill to preheat.

2. In a bowl, mix together the eggs, buttermilk, Bacon Cheddar Seasoning, and pimento cheese spread. Add in the sugar, baking powder, cornmeal and flour. Mix until well combined.

3. With cooking gloves, carefully remove the cast iron skillet from the grill, grease it, and add the cornbread batter.

4. Grill for 25-30 minutes, or until the cornbread is golden and pulling away from the edges of the skillet.

Butternut Squash Macaroni And Cheese

Servings: 2
Cooking Time: 50 Minutes

Ingredients:
- 1 Medium butternut squash
- 2 Cup macaroni, uncooked
- 1 Small yellow onion
- 1/2 Cup chicken broth
- 1 Cup milk
- salt
- pepper
- 1 Cup cheese, grated

Directions:
1. Supply your smoker with wood pellets and follow the start-up procedure. Preheat the grill, with the lid closed, to 225° F.

2. Puncture butternut squash with a fork several times and place on grill grate. Cook until tender, about 40 minutes to an hour. When cooked, scoop out meat and discard seeds. Grill: 225 ˚F

3. Cook elbow macaroni according to package instructions. Drain and set aside.

4. In a medium skillet, sauté chopped onion until fragrant and golden. Add broth, milk, salt, onions and butternut squash to a food processor. Puree until smooth and creamy. Add salt and pepper to taste.

5. Pour pureed sauce over cooked noodles and add the shredded cheese. Stir to melt the cheese and add milk to reach desired consistency. Serve warm. Enjoy!

Old Fashioned Cornbread

Servings: 4
Cooking Time: 25 Minutes

Ingredients:

- 1 Cup all-purpose flour
- 1 Cup Cornmeal
- 1 Tablespoon sugar
- 2 Teaspoon baking powder
- 1/2 Teaspoon salt
- 3 Tablespoon butter
- 1 Cup milk
- 1 Whole egg, lightly beaten

Directions:

1. In a mixing bowl, combine the flour, cornmeal, sugar, baking powder, and salt.

2. Melt the butter in a small saucepan. Remove from the heat, and stir in the milk and the egg. (Make sure the mixture isn't hot or the egg will curdle.)

3. Add the milk-egg mixture to the dry ingredients and stir to combine. Do not overmix.

4. Spread the batter evenly in a greased 8 or 9-inch square baking pan or pie plate.

5. Supply your smoker with wood pellets and follow the start-up procedure. Preheat the grill, with the lid closed, to 375° F.

6. Bake the cornbread until it begins to pull away from the sides of the pan and the top is beginning to brown, 25 to 35 minutes. Cut into squares (or wedges, if you used a pie plate) for serving. Grill: 375 ˚F

Green Bean Casserole Circa 1955

Servings: 6
Cooking Time: 30 Minutes

Ingredients:

- 1 1/2 Pound Green Beans, fresh
- 1 Can cream of mushroom soup
- 1/2 Cup milk
- 2 Teaspoon soy sauce
- 1/2 Teaspoon Worcestershire sauce
- 1/2 Teaspoon black pepper
- 1.334 Cup French's Original Crispy Fried Onions
- 1/4 Cup red bell pepper, diced

Directions:

1. In a mixing bowl, combine the beans (trimmed and cooked until tender, or may use 2 16 oz. cans), soup, milk, soy sauce, Worcestershire sauce, black pepper, 2/3 cup of the onion rings, and red pepper, if using. Transfer to a 1-1/2 quart casserole dish.

2. Supply your smoker with wood pellets and follow the start-up procedure. Preheat the grill, with the lid closed, to 375° F.

3. Cook the casserole until the filling is hot and bubbling, 25 to 30 minutes. Top with the remaining onions and cook for 5 to 10 minutes more, or until the onions are crisp and beginning to brown. Grill: 375 ˚F

Baked Bourbon Maple Pumpkin Pie

Servings: 6-8
Cooking Time: 60 Minutes

Ingredients:

- 1/4 Cup Cocoa Powder, Unsweetened
- 1 Tablespoon Cocoa Powder, Unsweetened
- 3 1/2 Tablespoon sugar
- 1 Teaspoon salt
- 1 1/4 Cup all-purpose flour
- 1 Tablespoon all-purpose flour
- 6 Tablespoon butter
- 2 Tablespoon vegetable oil
- 1 Large Egg Yolk
- 1/2 Teaspoon apple cider vinegar
- 1/4 Cup ice water
- 1 Large egg, beaten
- 15 Ounce Pumpkin, canned
- 1/4 Cup sour cream
- 2 Tablespoon bourbon
- 1 Teaspoon ground cinnamon
- 1/2 Teaspoon salt
- 1/4 Teaspoon ground ginger
- 1/4 Teaspoon ground nutmeg
- 1/8 Teaspoon Allspice, ground
- 1/8 Teaspoon Mace, ground
- 3 Large eggs
- 3/4 Cup maple syrup
- 2 Tablespoon sugar

- 1/2 Vanilla Bean, halved
- 1 Cup heavy cream

Directions:

1. For the Chocolate Pie Dough: Pulse cocoa powder, granulated sugar, salt, and 1-1/4 cups plus 1 Tbsp flour in a food processor to combine. Add butter and shortening and pulse until mixture resembles coarse meal with a few pea-sized pieces of butter remaining. Transfer to a large bowl.

2. Whisk together the egg yolk, vinegar, and 1/4 cup ice water in a small bowl. Drizzle half of the egg mixture over flour mixture and, using a fork, mix gently just until combined. Add remaining egg mixture and mix until the dough just comes together (you will have some unincorporated pieces).

3. Turn out dough onto a lightly floured surface, flatten slightly, and cut into quarters. Stack pieces on top of one another. Placing unincorporated dry pieces of dough between layers, and press down to combine. Repeat process twice more (all pieces of dough should be incorporated at this point). Form dough into a 1" thick disk. Wrap in plastic; chill at least 1 hour.

4. Roll out a disk of dough on a lightly floured surface into a 14" round. Transfer to a 9" pie dish. Lift up the edge and allow the dough to slump down into the dish. Trim. Leaving about 1" overhang. Fold overhang under and crimp edge. Chill in freezer 15 minutes.

5. When ready to cook, set the smoker to 350°F and preheat, lid closed for 15 minutes.

6. Line pie with parchment paper or heavy-duty foil, leaving a 1-1/2" overhang. Fill with pie weights or dried beans. Bake until crust is dry around the edge, about 20 minutes.

7. Remove paper and weights and bake until surface of the crust looks dry, 5-10 minutes.

8. Brush bottom and sides of crust with 1 beaten egg. Return to grill and bake until dry and set, about 3 minutes longer.

9. For the Pumpkin Maple Filling: Whisk together pumpkin puree, sour cream, bourbon, cinnamon, salt, ginger, nutmeg, allspice, mace (optional) and remaining 3 eggs in a large bowl; set aside.

10. Pour maple syrup and 2 tbsp sugar in a small saucepan. Scrape in the seeds from vanilla bean (reserve pod for another use) or add vanilla extract and bring syrup to a boil. Reduce heat to medium-high and simmer, stirring occasionally, until mixture is thickened and small puffs of steam start to release about 3 minutes.

11. Remove from heat and add cream in 3 additions, stirring with a wooden spoon after each addition until smooth. Gradually whisk hot maple cream into pumpkin mixture.

12. Place pie dish on a rimmed baking sheet and pour in pumpkin filling. Bake pie, rotating halfway through, until set around edge but center barely jiggles 50-60 minutes.

13. Transfer pie dish to a wire rack and let the pie cool. Slice and serve. Enjoy!

Bananas Rum Foster

Servings: 4

Cooking Time: 10 Minutes

Ingredients:

- 1/3 Cup Banana Nectar
- 4 Bananas, Quartered
- 3/4 Cup Brown Sugar
- 1/4 Cup Butter
- 1/2 Tsp Cinnamon, Ground
- 1/3 Cup Dark Rum
- Vanilla Ice Cream

Directions:

1. Supply your smoker with wood pellets and follow the start-up procedure. Preheat the grill, with the lid closed, to medium heat. If using a gas or charcoal grill, preheat a cast iron skillet.

2. Place a large skillet on the griddle, then melt butter in the skillet. Whisk in brown sugar and cinnamon, stirring until sugar dissolves.

3. Add the banana nectar and bananas. Stir to coat

4. Once the bananas begin to soften and turn brown, add the rum. Stir, then ignite the sauce with a stick lighter. After the flames subside, simmer the sauce for 2 minutes.

5. Divide the bananas among 4 scoops/bowls of vanilla ice cream, then spoon the warm sauce over the top of the ice cream. Serve immediately.

Smoker Wheat Bread

Servings: 6

Cooking Time: 60 Minutes

Ingredients:

- As Needed extra-virgin olive oil
- 2 Cup all-purpose flour
- 1 Cup whole wheat flour
- 1 1/4 Ounce Packet, Active Dry Yeast
- 1 1/4 Teaspoon salt
- 1 1/2 Cup water
- As Needed Cornmeal

Directions:

1. Oil a large mixing bowl and set aside. In a second mixing bowl, combine the flours, yeast, and salt.
2. Push your sleeve up to your elbow and form your fingers into a claw. Mix the dry ingredients until well-combined.
3. Add the water and mix until blended. The dough will be wet, shaggy, and somewhat stringy.
4. Tip the dough into the oiled mixing bowl and cover with plastic wrap.
5. Allow the dough to rise at room temperature-- about 70 degrees-- for 2 hours, or until the surface is bubbled.
6. Turn the dough out onto a lightly floured work surface and lightly flour the top. With floured hands, fold the dough over on itself twice. Cover loosely with plastic wrap and allow the dough to rest for 15 minutes.
7. Dust a clean lint-free cotton towel with cornmeal, wheat bran, or flour. With floured hands, gently form the dough into a ball and place it, seam side down, on the towel.
8. Dust the top of the ball with cornmeal, wheat bran, or flour, and cover the dough with a second towel. Let the dough rise until doubled in size; the dough will not spring back when poked with a finger.
9. In the meantime, start the smoker grill and set temperature to 450 F. Preheat, lid closed, for 10-15 minutes.
10. Put a lidded 6- to 8-quart cast iron Dutch oven - preferably one coated with enamel, on the grill grate.
11. When the dough has risen, remove the top towel, slide your hand under the bottom towel to support the dough, then carefully tip the dough, seam side up, into the preheated pot.
12. Remove the towel. Shake the pot a couple of times if the dough looks lopsided: It will straighten out as it bakes.
13. Cover the pot with the lid and bake the bread for 30 minutes. Remove the lid and continue to bake the bread for 15 to 30 minutes more, or until it is nicely browned and sounds hollow when rapped with your knuckles.
14. Turn onto a wire rack to cool. Slice with a serrated knife. Enjoy!

Basil Margherita Pizza

Servings: 6

Cooking Time: 25 Minutes

Ingredients:

- Basil, Chopped
- 2 Cups Flour, All-Purpose
- Mozzarella Cheese, Sliced Rounds
- 1 Cup Pizza Sauce
- 1 Teaspoon Salt
- 1 Teaspoon Sugar
- 1 Tomato, Sliced
- 1 Cup Water, Warm
- 1 Teaspoon Yeast, Instant

Directions:

1. Combine the water, yeast, and sugar in a small bowl and let sit for about 5 minutes.
2. In a large bowl, stir together the flour and salt. Pour in the yeast mixture and mix until a soft dough forms. Knead for about 2 minutes. Place in an oiled bowl and cover with a cloth. Let the dough sit and rise for about 45 minutes or until the dough has doubled in size.
3. Roll out on a flat, floured surface (or on a pizza stone) until you"ve reached your desired shape and thickness.
4. Supply your smoker with wood pellets and follow the start-up procedure. Preheat the grill, with the lid closed, to 350° F.

5. On the rolled out dough, pour on the pizza sauce, cheese, and then tomatoes and basil. Place in your Grill and bake for about 25 minutes, or until the cheese is melted and slightly golden brown.

Pineapple Cake

Servings: 4
Cooking Time: 30 Minutes

Ingredients:

- 2/3 cup of vegetable oil (olive oil works great, not virgin)
- 3 eggs
- 1/3 cup brown sugar (not too sweet)
- 3/4 cup self raising plain flour
- 1/4 cup wholemeal self raising flour
- 1/3 cup saltanas
- 1/3 cup diced canned pineapple (drained)
- 1/3 cup diced raw walnuts
- 2 large carrots grated
- Icing Ingredients
- 250 grams cream cheese
- 35 grams icing sugar (not too sweet)
- Whole lemon or orange zest

Directions:

1. Mix all ingredients in a large bowl.
2. Place into 6″ greased baking tray or un-greased silicone tray.
3. Supply your smoker with wood pellets and follow the start-up procedure. Preheat the grill, with the lid closed, to 190 °F. Cook for 25-30min until golden brown and no dough when probed.
4. Let cool on rack (not directly on plate or board) then apply icing.
5. Whip icing ingredients and place in fridge until ready to coat the cake.

Double Chocolate Chip Brownie Pie

Servings: 8-12
Cooking Time: 45 Minutes

Ingredients:

- 1/2 Cup Semisweet Chocolate Chips
- 1 Cup butter
- 1 Cup brown sugar
- 1 Cup sugar
- 4 Whole eggs
- 2 Teaspoon vanilla extract
- 2 Cup all-purpose flour
- 333/500 Cup Cocoa Powder, Unsweetened
- 1 Teaspoon baking soda
- 1 Teaspoon salt
- 1 Cup Semisweet Chocolate Chips
- 3/4 Cup White Chocolate Chips
- 3/4 Cup Nuts (optional)
- 1 Whole Hot Fudge Sauce, 8oz
- 2 Tablespoon Guinness Beer

Directions:

1. Coat the inside of a 10-inch (25 cm) pie plate with non-stick cooking spray.
2. When ready to cook, set the grill temperature to 350°F (180 C)and preheat, lid closed for 15 minutes.
3. Melt 1/2 cup (100 g) of the semi sweet chocolate chips in the microwave. Cream together butter, brown sugar and granulated sugar. Beat in the eggs, adding one at a time and mixing after each egg, and the vanilla. Add in the melted chocolate chips.
4. On a large piece of wax paper, sift together the cocoa powder, flour, baking soda and salt. Lift up the corners of the paper and pour slowly into the butter mixture.
5. Beat until the dry ingredients are just incorporated. Stir in the remaining semi sweet chocolate chips, white chocolate chips, and the nuts. Press the dough into the prepared pie pan.
6. Place the brownie pie on the grill and bake for 45-50 minutes or until the pie is set in the middle. Rotate the pan halfway through cooking. If the top or edges begin to brown, cover the top with a piece of aluminum foil.
7. In a microwave-safe measuring cup, heat the fudge sauce in the microwave. Stir in the Guinness.
8. Once the brownie pie is done, allow to sit for 20 minutes. Slice into wedges and top with the fudge sauce. Enjoy.

Quick Baked Dinner Rolls

Servings: 8
Cooking Time: 30 Minutes

Ingredients:

- 2 Tablespoon quick-rise yeast
- 1 Teaspoon salt
- 1/4 Cup sugar
- 3 1/3 Cup flour
- 1/4 Cup unsalted butter, softened
- 1 egg
- cooking spray
- 1 egg, for egg wash

Directions:

1. Combine yeast and warm water in a small bowl to activate the yeast. Let sit until foamy, about 5-10 minutes.
2. Combine salt, sugar, and flour in the bowl of a stand mixer fitted with the dough hook. Pour water and yeast into the dry ingredients with the machine running on low.
3. Add butter and egg and mix for 10 minutes gradually increasing the speed from low to high.
4. Form the dough into a ball and place in a buttered bowl. Cover with a cloth and let the dough rise for approximately 40 minutes.
5. Transfer the risen dough to a lightly floured surface and divide into 8 pieces forming a ball with each.
6. Lightly spray a cast iron pan with cooking spray and arrange balls in the pan. Cover with a cloth and let rise 20 minutes.
7. Supply your smoker with wood pellets and follow the start-up procedure. Preheat the grill, with the lid closed, to 375° F.
8. Brush rolls with egg wash and then bake for 30 minutes until lightly browned. Serve hot. Enjoy! Grill: 375 °F

Sopapilla Cheesecake By Doug Scheiding

Servings: 8
Cooking Time: 45 Minutes

Ingredients:

- 2 Tablespoon softened butter
- 24 Ounce cream cheese
- 2 Cup granulated sugar, divided
- 2 Teaspoon vanilla
- 2 Can Pillsbury Butter Flake Crescent Rolls
- 1/2 Cup butter, melted
- cinnamon

Directions:

1. Coat a 9x13 inch baking dish with 2 tablespoons softened butter and set aside.
2. Supply your smoker with wood pellets and follow the start-up procedure. Preheat the grill, with the lid closed, to 350° F.
3. In a mixer, combine cream cheese, 1 to 1-1/2 cups of sugar and vanilla. Mix for 60 to 90 seconds on high with paddle attachment.
4. Take crescents out of the refrigerator. Open one can and place into the buttered 9x13 inch rectangular metal pan or glass dish. Make sure to fill in the gaps in this bottom layer of crescents.
5. Put the cream cheese mixture on the top of the crescent layer using a spatula to make it level.
6. Open the second can of crescents and put on top of the cream cheese layer, again filling in the gaps in the crescents to cover middle.
7. Pour 1/2 cup of melted butter on the top of the last layer of crescent. Start on sides first then middle.
8. Then sprinkle 1/4 cup to 1/2 cup of sugar over the entire pan followed by a light, even dusting of cinnamon.
9. Place pan directly on the grill grate and bake for 40 to 50 minutes until top is brown and starting to get crusty. Grill: 350 °F
10. Remove from grill and let cool 5 to 10 minutes. This allows the cheesecake to set which makes portioning easier. This dessert can be served warm or cold. Enjoy!

Anzac Coconut Biscuits

Servings: 4
Cooking Time: 30 Minutes

Ingredients:

- This recipe makes a dozen biscuits.
- 1 cup rolled oats
- 3/4 cup raw sugar
- 3/4 cup desiccated coconut
- 1 cup plain flour, sifted
- 125 g butter, melted
- 2 tablespoons Golden Syrup
- 1/2 tsp bicarb soda
- 3 tablespoons boiling water

Directions:

1. Combine and mix thoroughly sifted flour, oats, sugar and coconut in a large bowl.
2. Melt the butter and Golden Syrup over low heat.
3. Add boiling water to the bicarb soda, once dissolved add into the butter/syrup mix, it will bubble/fizz up a bit.
4. Add the liquid into the dry ingredients and mix throughly.
5. Rolls the mix into golf ball size balls and layout on grease proof paper on baking tray and flatten the tops just slightly.
6. Space the balls with about 3 fingers between each ball as they will flatten to about triple the diameter as they cook.
7. Supply your smoker with wood pellets and follow the start-up procedure. Preheat the grill, with the lid closed, to 350° F. Cook for 25-30 minutes until golden brown.
8. Rest on cooling rack until at room temperature then store in air-tight container.

Pull-apart Dinner Rolls

Servings: 8
Cooking Time: 10 Minutes

Ingredients:

- 1/4 Cup warm water (110°F to 115°F)
- 1/3 Cup vegetable oil
- 2 Tablespoon active dry yeast
- 1/4 Cup sugar
- 1/2 Teaspoon salt
- 1 egg
- 3 1/2 Cup all-purpose flour
- cooking spray

Directions:

1. Supply your smoker with wood pellets and follow the start-up procedure. Preheat the grill, with the lid closed, to 400° F.
2. In the bowl of a stand mixer, combine warm water, oil, yeast and sugar. Let mixture rest for 5 to 10 minutes, or until frothy and bubbly.
3. With a dough hook, mix in salt, egg and 2 cups of flour until combined. Add remaining flour 1/2 cup at a time (dough will be sticky).
4. Prepare a cast iron pan with cooking spray and set aside.
5. Spray your hands with cooking spray and shape the dough into 12 balls.
6. After shaped, place in the prepared cast iron pan and let rest for 10 minutes. Bake in Traeger for about 10 to 12 minutes, or until tops are lightly golden. Enjoy! Grill: 400 °F

Baked Green Chile Mac & Cheese By Doug Scheiding

Servings: 8
Cooking Time: 120 Minutes

Ingredients:

- 24 Ounce shredded cheddar cheese, divided
- 8 Ounce mozzarella cheese, shredded
- 6 Tablespoon unsalted butter
- 16 Ounce large dry elbow macaroni noodles
- 2 1/2 Cup half-and-half
- 2 Cup heavy whipping cream
- 8 Ounce cream cheese
- 16 Ounce 505 Southwestern Hatch Valley Flame Roasted Green Chile
- 2 Tablespoon Prime Rib Rub

Directions:

1. Supply your smoker with wood pellets and follow the start-up procedure. Preheat the grill, with the lid closed, to 165° F.

2. Place 16 ounces of the shredded cheddar and the 8 ounces of shredded mozzarella cheese into a shallow pan or cookie sheet and place the pan directly on the grill grate. Smoke for 30 to 40 minutes. Remove from grill and set aside. Grill: 165 ˚F

3. Increase the grill temperature to 300˚F and place a large disposable aluminum half pan in the Traeger with the butter. Remove the pan from the grill after the butter has fully melted. Grill: 300 ˚F

4. Add the noodles to the pan, along with half-and-half, heavy whipping cream, 16 ounces of the cold smoked cheddar, all of the smoked mozzarella cheese and cream cheese broken into small pieces. Add the green chiles to taste (12 ounces for mild and 16 ounces for spicy) and stir to combine.

5. Place the pan in the grill and bake for 2 hours, stirring every 20 minutes. If macaroni and cheese looks like it is getting dry, add a little more half-and-half and stir to combine. Grill: 300 ˚F

6. During the last 20 minutes of cooking, sprinkle the remaining (unsmoked) cheddar cheese on top and add a light dusting of Traeger Prime Rib Rub. Serve hot. Enjoy!

Smoked Lemon Tea

Servings: 6 - 8
Cooking Time: 60 Minutes

Ingredients:
- 8 Black Tea Bags
- 4 Cups Boiling Water
- 2 Cups Ice
- 8 Lemons
- 2 Cups Sugar
- 2 Cups Water

Directions:
1. Place the tea bags in a heat-safe pitcher. Bring 4 Cups of water to a boil and pour over tea bags. Let steep for 5-10 minutes. Remove tea bags and set pitcher aside to cool.

2. Turn on your grill and set to smoke mode. Combine 2 cups of sugar and 2 cups water in a small aluminum pan. Smoke for about 45 minutes, stirring occasionally,

or until the mixture reduces to a thick, simple syrup. Remove from the grill and let it cool.

3. Supply your smoker with wood pellets and follow the start-up procedure. Preheat the grill, with the lid closed, to 450° F. If using a charcoal or gas grill, set heat to high.

4. Cut the lemons in half and sear over the flame broiler until charred, about 7 minutes. Remove from grill and set aside to cool.

5. Juice the lemons into a medium bowl. Pour lemon juice through a metal strainer into the tea pitcher to remove seeds and pulp.

6. Pour the cooled simple syrup into pitcher and stir until fully incorporated with tea and lemons. Add 2 cups of ice and refrigerate until serving.

Pumpkin Bread

Servings: 6
Cooking Time: 60 Minutes

Ingredients:
- 1 Cup Pumpkin, canned
- 2 eggs
- 2/3 Cup vegetable oil
- 1/2 Cup sour cream
- 1 Teaspoon vanilla extract
- 2 1/2 Cup flour
- 1 1/2 Teaspoon baking soda
- 1 Teaspoon salt
- 1/2 Teaspoon ground cinnamon
- 1/4 Teaspoon ground nutmeg
- 1/4 Teaspoon ground cloves
- 1/4 Teaspoon ground ginger
- As Needed butter

Directions:
1. In a large mixing bowl, combine the pumpkin, eggs, vegetable oil, sour cream, and vanilla and whisk to blend.

2. In a separate bowl, combine the flour, baking soda, salt, cinnamon, nutmeg, cloves, and ginger. Add the dry ingredients to the wet ingredients and stir to combine. Do not overmix.

3. If desired, stir in one or more of the optional ingredients (walnuts, dried cranberries, raisins, or chocolate chips). Butter the interiors of two loaf pans.

4. Sprinkle with flour to coat the buttered surfaces, and tap out any excess. Divide the batter evenly between the two pans.

5. When ready to cook, set the smoker to 350°F and preheat, lid closed for 15 minutes.

6. Arrange the loaf pans directly on the grill grate. Bake for 45 to 50 minutes, or until a skewer or toothpick inserted in the center comes out clean. Also, the top of the loaf should spring back when pressed gently with a finger.

7. Transfer the loaf pans to a cooling rack and let cool for 10 minutes before carefully turning out the pumpkin bread. Let the loaves cool thoroughly before slicing. Wrap in aluminum foil or plastic wrap if not eating right away. Serve and enjoy!

Smoky Apple Crepes

Servings: 6
Cooking Time: 60 Minutes

Ingredients:
- 1/2 Cup Apple Juice
- 2 Lbs Apples
- 2 Tbsp Brown Sugar
- 5 Tbsp Butter
- 3 Tbsp Butter, Melted
- Tt Caramel
- 3/4 Tsp Cinnamon, Ground
- Tt Cinnamon-Sugar
- 3/4 Tsp Cornstarch
- 2 Eggs
- 1 Cup Flour
- 2 Tsp Lemon Juice
- Tennessee Apple Butter Seasoning
- 1/2 Cup Water
- 3/4 Cup Milk

Directions:
1. Supply your smoker with wood pellets and follow the start-up procedure. Preheat the grill, with the lid closed, to 225° F. If using a gas or charcoal grill, set it up for low, indirect heat.

2. Peel, halve, and core apples.

3. Season apples with Tennessee Apple Butter then place directly on the grill grate, and smoke for 1 hour.

4. Meanwhile, prepare crêpe batter: combine eggs, milk, water, flour, and 3 tbsp of melted butter in a blender, and blend until smooth.

5. Refrigerate for 30 minutes.

6. Remove apples from grill, cool slightly, then slice thin.

7. Place a cast iron skillet on the grill and melt 3 tbsp butter with brown sugar, cinnamon, cornstarch, apple and lemon juices. Cook for 5 minutes until thick.

8. Add apples and cook for another 3 to 5 minutes, stirring to coat apples in sauce.

9. Remove from grill and set aside.

10. Preheat griddle to medium-low. If using a standard grill, preheat a cast iron skillet on medium-low heat.

11. Melt 1 teaspoon of butter on the griddle.

12. Then add ½ cup of batter, and spread with the bottom of a metal spatula, working quickly, as the batter cooks fast.

13. Cook one minute per side, until edges begin to brown. Remove from griddle, set aside, and repeat with remaining batter.

14. Spoon ¼ cup of apple filling into the center of each crêpe, then quarter-fold into a triangle.

15. Serve warm with additional apple filling, drizzle of warm caramel, and a dusting of cinnamon-sugar.

Double Vanilla Chocolate Cake

Servings: 12
Cooking Time: 40 Minutes

Ingredients:
- 1 1/2 Tsp Baking Soda
- 1/2 Cup Butter, Melted
- 1 Cup Buttermilk, Low Fat
- 1 Jar Chocolate Icing, Prepared
- 3/4 Cup Cocoa, Powder
- 1 Cup Coffee, Hot
- 2 Large Egg

- 1 3/4 Cups Flour, All-Purpose
- 3/4 Tsp Salt
- 2 Cups Sugar
- 1 Tbsp Vanilla

Directions:

1. Supply your smoker with wood pellets and follow the start-up procedure. Preheat the grill, with the lid closed, to 350° F.

2. Stir together flour, sugar, cocoa, baking soda and salt in a large bowl. Combine eggs, buttermilk, butter and coffee and mix until smooth. Add in hot coffee and stir until combined and the dough is runny.

3. Pour the batter into two prepared baking pans and bake on the top rack of your for 40 minutes, turning the pans 180 degrees halfway through.

4. Allow to cool and then frost with chocolate icing.

Grilled Apple Pie

Servings: 4
Cooking Time: 40 Minutes

Ingredients:

- 5 Whole Apples
- 1/4 Cup sugar
- 1 Tablespoon cornstarch
- 1 Whole refrigerated pie crust
- 1/4 Cup Peach, preserves

Directions:

1. Supply your smoker with wood pellets and follow the start-up procedure. Preheat the grill, with the lid closed, to 375° F.In a medium bowl, mix the apples, sugar, and cornstarch; set aside.

2. Unroll pie crust. Place in ungreased pie pan. With the back of a spoon, spread preserves evenly on crust. Arrange the apple slices in an even layer in the pie pan. Slightly fold crust over filling.

3. Place a baking sheet upside down on the grill grate to make an elevated surface. Put the pan with pie on top so it is elevated off grill. (This will help prevent the bottom from overcooking.) Cook the pie for 30 to 40 minutes or until crust is golden brown, the filling is bubbly. Grill: 375 °F

4. Remove from grill; cool 10 minutes before serving. Enjoy! *Cook times will vary depending on set and ambient temperatures.

Zucchini Bread

Servings: 6
Cooking Time: 50 Minutes

Ingredients:

- 1 Cup Walnuts, Chopped
- 2 Large zucchini
- 1 Teaspoon salt
- 1 Teaspoon ground cinnamon
- 1/4 Teaspoon ground cloves
- 1/4 Teaspoon baking powder
- 3 Cup all-purpose flour
- 1 eggs
- 2 Cup sugar
- 1/2 Cup vegetable oil
- 1/2 Cup Yogurt
- 1 1/2 Teaspoon vanilla extract

Directions:

1. Grease and flour two 9- by 5-inch bread pans, preferably nonstick.

2. When ready to cook, set the temperature to 350°F and preheat, lid closed for 15 minutes.

3. Spread the walnuts on a pie plate and toast for 10 minutes, stirring once. Let cool, then coarsely chop. Set aside.

4. Trim the ends off the zucchini, then coarsely grate into a colander set over the sink on a box grater (or use the shredding disk on a food processor). You'll need 2 cups.

5. Sprinkle with the salt and let drain for 30 minutes. Press on the zucchini with paper towels to expel excess water.

6. Sift the flour, baking powder, cinnamon, and cloves in a mixing bowl or on a large sheet of parchment or wax paper.

7. Combine the eggs, sugar, oil, yogurt, and vanilla in a large mixing bowl and mix on medium speed. (You can mix the batter by hand, if desired.) Add half the dry

ingredients and mix on low speed; add the remaining dry ingredients and mix until just combined.

8.   Stir in the walnuts and zucchini by hand.

9.   Divide the batter between the prepared baking pans.

10. Arrange the pans directly on the grill grate and bake for 50 minutes, or until a bamboo skewer inserted in the center of the breads comes out clean.

11. Transfer to a wire rack and let cool for 10 minutes, then remove the breads from the pans. For best results, let the breads cool completely before slicing.

Garlic Cheese Pull Apart Bread

Servings: 2
Cooking Time: 20 Minutes

Ingredients:
- 1 Loaf Bread, Sourdough Round
- 2 1/2 Tbsp Butter, Salted
- 8 Oz Fontina Cheese
- 1 Grated Garlic, Roasted
- 1/4 Cup Parsley, Minced Fresh
- 1 Tsp Red Flakes Pepper
- 1 Pinch Salt

Directions:
1.   Start your Grill on "smoke" with the lid open until a fire is established in the burn pot (3-7 minutes). Supply your smoker with wood pellets and follow the start-up procedure. Preheat the grill, with the lid closed, to 300° F.

2.   In a small bowl, add the soft butter, grated garlic, red pepper flakes, sea salt, and ¼ cup of the chopped parsley, and whisk together. With a bread serrated knife, cut 1-inch slices into the bread, not cutting all the way through the bottom of the load. With a butter knife, spread a thin layer of the butter mixture on each slice of the bread. Take the serrated knife again, and cut across the loaf to form 1 inch squares. Next, slice the cheese into small thin slices, then stuff one slice into each bread opening. Place the bread on a baking sheet, and cover tightly with aluminum foil. Place on the grill for about 10 minutes, remove the foil, and grill for a few more minutes until the top is nicely golden and the cheese is

oozing. Remove from the grill, sprinkle with fresh parsley leaves, then serve.

Garlic Lemon Pepper Chicken Wings

Servings: 4
Cooking Time: 30 Minutes

Ingredients:
- 1/4 Cup Black Peppercorns, Ground
- 4 Pounds Chicken, Wing
- 2 Tsp Coriander, Ground
- 2 Tsp Garlic Powder
- 2-3 Tbsp Lemon, Zest
- 1 Tsp Salt, Kosher
- 3 Tsp Dried Thyme, Fresh Sprigs

Directions:
1.   Supply your smoker with wood pellets and follow the start-up procedure. Preheat the grill, with the lid closed, to 400° F.

2.   In a bowl, begin to mix the ground pepper and zest of the lemon together, then add the rest of the ingredients.

3.   Place the wings in a bowl and toss with a little olive oil, add a few tablespoons of the seasoning, toss with your hands, then repeat until the wings are well seasoned to your liking.

4.   Place the wings on the grill, and cook them for about 15 minutes, then flip and grill for another 15 minutes.

5.   Continue to flip the wings, until they are done and crispy. Remove the wings from the grill, and serve.

Eyeball Cookies

Servings: 20
Cooking Time: 35 Minutes

Ingredients:
- 2 Packages Candy Eyeballs
- Green, Blue And Purple Food Coloring
- 1 Box Of Yellow Gluten Free Cake Mix
- 1/2 Cup (Optional) Granulated Sugar
- 2 Large Eggs
- 1/3 Cup Powdered Sugar
- 1 Teaspoon Pure Vanilla Extract

- 6 Tablespoon Melted Vegan Butter (Unsalted)

Directions:

1. Supply your smoker with wood pellets and follow the start-up procedure. Preheat the grill, with the lid closed, to 350° F.

2. Line two large baking sheets with parchment paper. In a large bowl, combine cake mix, melted butter, eggs (or egg substitute), powdered sugar, sugar (optional), and vanilla and stir until combined. (substitute 2 flax eggs for Vegan – 1 tbsp flax seed meal and 5 tbsp water per egg).

3. Divide dough between 3 bowls and dye each bowl a different color.(We used green, blue and purple).

4. Roll dough into tablespoon-sized balls.

5. Place about 2" apart on the baking sheet and grill until tops have cracked and the tops look set, 8 to 10 minutes. – Turn half way through baking, after 4-5 minutes.

6. Immediately, while the cookies are still warm, stick candy eyeballs all over the cookies.

7. Let cool completely before serving.

Baked Bourbon Monkey Bread

Servings: 6

Cooking Time: 40 Minutes

Ingredients:

- 3 Can Pillsbury Grands Buttermilk Biscuits
- 1 Cup sugar
- 3 Teaspoon ground cinnamon
- 1 Cup Butter, unsalted
- 1 Cup dark brown sugar
- Tablespoon bourbon

Directions:

1. Supply your smoker with wood pellets and follow the start-up procedure. Preheat the grill, with the lid closed, to 350° F.

2. Cut each biscuit into quarters. In a Ziploc bag, combine sugar and cinnamon and add quartered biscuits. Toss to coat in cinnamon sugar.

3. Dump coated biscuit dough into a bundt pan coated with non-stick spray.

4. In a small saucepan, combine the brown sugar, butter, and bourbon. Cook over medium heat until the sugar has dissolved.

5. Pour the butter mixture over the biscuits in the bundt pan.

6. Place in the center of the grill and cook for 40 minutes or until dark golden brown.

7. Let cool on the counter for 5-10 minutes, then flip out onto a serving plate. Enjoy!

Delicious Pellet Grill Cornbread

Servings: 6

Cooking Time: 35 Minutes

Ingredients:

- 1 cup flour
- 1 cup cornmeal
- 2 teaspoons baking powder
- 2 teaspoons salt
- 3/4 cup sugar
- 2 tablespoons honey
- 1/2 cup butter
- 1 cup sour cream
- 3 eggs
- 1 cup milk

Directions:

1. Supply your smoker with wood pellets and follow the start-up procedure. Preheat the grill, with the lid closed, to 350° F.

2. Grease a 12-inch cast iron skillet or an equivalent baking pan.

3. Add flour, cornmeal, baking powder, salt, sugar, honey, butter, sour cream, eggs, and milk into a mixing bowl.

4. Mix well then pour into pan and bake on the grill for 30-35 minutes or until the cornbread is baked through in the center.

Easy Smoked Cornbread

Servings: 4
Cooking Time: 75 Minutes

Ingredients:

- 2 cups self rising flour
- 1 1/2 cups white corn meal
- 2 cups sharp cheddar cheese
- 1/2 cup sour cream
- 1/2 cup sugar
- 1 Tbsp baking powder
- 1 teaspoon sea salt
- 1 12 oz can of evaporated milk
- 1/2 cup vegetable oil
- 2 large eggs beaten

Directions:

1. Mix all ingredients together well and fold into a greased baking pan (such as a round cake Pan).
2. Supply your smoker with wood pellets and follow the start-up procedure. Preheat the grill, with the lid closed, to 375° F. Smoke on 375 °F for 1 hour and 15 minutes or until toothpick comes clean and edges look brown.
3. Rub some butter on top and sprinkle a little Fred's Butt Rub on top before serving.
4. Enjoy!

Blueberry Pancakes

Servings: 4
Cooking Time: 10 Minutes

Ingredients:

- 2 Cups Blueberries, Fresh
- 1 Cup Pancake Mix
- 1/2 Cup Sugar
- 3/4 Cup Water, Warm

Directions:

1. Supply your smoker with wood pellets and follow the start-up procedure. Preheat the grill, with the lid closed, to 350° F.
2. Place the cast iron griddle on the grates of your grill.
3. In a large bowl, pour water, pancake mix and 1/2 cup of the blueberries and mix until combined.
4. Pour the batter onto the griddle in 4 equal parts. Cook with the lid closed for about 6 minutes, or until the edges of the pancakes are slightly cooked. Flip each pancake and continue cooking for another 4 minutes.
5. Pour the hot blueberry sauce over your freshly cooked pancakes and enjoy!

Rosemary Cranberry Apple Sage Stuffing

Servings: 7
Cooking Time: 45 Minutes

Ingredients:

- 10 Cups Day Old Diced Bread, Sliced Loaf
- 2 1/2 Cups Broth, Chicken
- 1 Cup Butter, Unsalted
- 1 Cup Diced Celery, Cut
- 1 1/2 Cups Fresh Cranberries
- 1 Beaten Egg
- 1 Medium Granny Smith Apple, Peel, Core And Dice
- 2 Tbsp Minced Parsley, Fresh
- 1 Tbsp Minced Rosemary, Fresh
- 2 Tbsp Roughly Chopped Sage
- Salt And Pepper
- 1 Tbsp Minced Thyme
- 2 Cups Diced Yellow Onion, Sliced

Directions:

1. Supply your smoker with wood pellets and follow the start-up procedure. Preheat the grill, with the lid closed, to 350° F.
2. Melt butter over medium heat. Add onions then celery and cook until onions start to become translucent.
3. In a large bowl, mix together bread, apples, cranberries, cooked onion and celery mixture, and fresh herbs.
4. Add half of the chicken broth to the mixture and stir.
5. Beat together eggs and the rest of the chicken broth in a small bowl. Pour into the bread mixture and stir until completely combined.
6. Add salt and pepper to taste.

7. Pour stuffing into a cast iron pan or baking dish. Cover with foil and bake on the grill for 30 minutes. Remove the foil and cook for an additional 15 minutes.

8. Serve immediately and enjoy!

Vanilla Chocolate Chip Cookies

Servings: 12
Cooking Time: 20 Minutes

Ingredients:

- 3/4 cup brown sugar
- 3/4 cup white sugar
- 1 stick butter, room temp
- 2 eggs
- 1 tsp vanilla
- 2 1/2 cups flour
- 1/2 tsp salt
- 1 tsp baking soda
- 1 cup Chocolate Chips

Directions:

1. Cream your butter and sugar together in a mixing bowl using a hand mixer or stand mixer on medium speed for about 4-5 minutes.

2. Once the butter is creamed, add the eggs and vanilla. Continue mixing for an additional minute.

3. Put flour, salt, and baking soda in a sifter. Sift it into your creamed butter mixture.

4. Scrape the sides of your mixing bowl with a rubber spatula, and then turn your mixer on to low speed.

5. Let it mix a little, and then scrape the sides again. Stop mixing when there are one or two streaks of flour left in the cookie dough.

6. Scrape the sides of your bowl and pour in a cup of chocolate chips, and turn the mixer to low again to mix the chocolate. It should take just a few turns for the chocolate pieces to be well incorporated.

7. Line a large baking sheet with parchment paper. Using a medium cookie scoop (about 1.5 tbsp), drop evenly spaced dollops of cookie dough onto the cookie sheet.

8. Supply your smoker with wood pellets and follow the start-up procedure. Preheat the grill, with the lid closed, to 350° F. Place the cookie sheet in your smoker, and let them cook for about 12 minutes.

9. Let them sit on a cooling rack while you continue to cook the additional cookies.

10. Cool for a few minutes to let cookies set.

11. Enjoy!

Onion Cheese Nachos

Servings: 6
Cooking Time: 10 Minutes

Ingredients:

- 1 Pound Beef, Ground
- 3 Cups Cheddar Cheese, Shredded
- 1 Green Bell Pepper, Diced
- 1/2 Cup Green Onion
- 1/2 Cup Red Onion, Diced
- 1 Large Bag Tortilla Chip

Directions:

1. Supply your smoker with wood pellets and follow the start-up procedure. Preheat the grill, with the lid closed, to 350° F.

2. While you're waiting, empty a large bag of nacho chips evenly onto a cast iron pan. Start loading up with toppings - cooked ground beef, red onion, red pepper, cheese, green onions. These are just the toppings we had on hand, so feel free to add anything you like! Make sure you do a couple layers of chips so everyone gets a good serving of nachos. And don't be skimpy with the cheese - lay it on heavy!

3. Place your loaded nachos on the grill and let the hot smoke melt your toppings into one cheesy creation. Heat at 350°F for 10 minutes or until the cheese has fully melted. Remove and serve with sour-cream and salsa.

Crème Brûlée

Servings: 2
Cooking Time: 45minutes

Ingredients:

- 1 Quart heavy whipping cream
- 1 Pieces Vanilla Bean, split and scraped
- 6 Large egg yolk
- 1 Cup sugar

Directions:

1. Supply your smoker with wood pellets and follow the start-up procedure. Preheat the grill, with the lid closed, to 325° F.

2. Pour the cream into a saucepan over medium-high heat, add the vanilla bean and the scraped seeds. Bring to a boil. Remove from the heat and allow to steep (about 15 minutes). Remove the vanilla bean from saucepan and discard.

3. In a bowl, whisk together egg yolks and 1/2 cup (100 g) of the sugar until the mix starts to lighten in color. Add the cream a little at a time, stirring continually.

4. Pour the mixture into 6 (8 oz) ramekins and place the ramekins into a large roasting pan. Pour hot water into the pan so that it comes halfway up the sides of the ramekins.

5. Place water bath pan on the grill and bake until the Crème Brûlées still jiggle in the center, about 40 to 45 minutes. Grill: 325 °F

6. Remove the ramekins from the roasting pan and refrigerate for at least 2 hours and up to 2 days.

7. To serve, let the Crème Brûlée come to temperature (about 20 minutes) before torching the tops.

8. Sprinkle the remaining 1/2 cup (100 g) sugar equally on top of each ramekin. Using a torch in a circular motion, melt the sugar until it caramelizes and forms a crispy top.

9. Allow the Crème Brûlée to sit for a few minutes before serving. Enjoy!

Traeger Baked Focaccia

Servings: 4
Cooking Time: 40 Minutes

Ingredients:
*   2 1/2 Cup all-purpose flour
*   1 Cup warm water (110°F to 115°F)
*   1 Tablespoon instant yeast
*   1 Teaspoon sugar
*   1 Teaspoon salt
*   3 Tablespoon olive oil, plus more as needed

*   1 Tablespoon fresh herbs such as thyme, rosemary and sage
*   2 Tablespoon freshly grated Parmesan, optional
*   flaky sea salt

Directions:

1. Place the flour, water, yeast, sugar, salt and oil in the bowl of a stand mixer and mix for 60 seconds. You may also use a food processor by adding the flour, sugar, salt and yeast to the bowl and process while streaming in the warm water followed by the olive oil. Process until combined and a ball forms.

2. Gently form the sticky dough into a ball, if needed, and place in a well-oiled 12 inch cast iron skillet. Drizzle the top of the dough with more olive oil. Cover with plastic wrap and a kitchen towel and let rise in a warm spot for 45 to 60 minutes.

3. After the dough has risen, press the dough to the edges of the pan and cover it again. Let rise for 15 minutes.

4. Supply your smoker with wood pellets and follow the start-up procedure. Preheat the grill, with the lid closed, to 375° F.

5. Uncover the dough and press it again to the edges of the pan using your fingertips to create divots.

6. Drizzle with olive oil, then sprinkle with herbs, Parmesan and flaky salt.

7. Bake it on the Traeger for 30 to 40 minutes, or until golden brown and cooked through. Allow it to cool slightly before removing from cast iron and slicing. Enjoy! Grill: 375 °F

Baked Pear Tarte Tatin

Servings: 6
Cooking Time: 45 Minutes

Ingredients:
*   2 1/2 Cup all-purpose flour
*   2 Tablespoon sugar
*   butter chilled
*   8 Tablespoon cold water
*   1/4 Cup granulated sugar
*   1/4 Cup butter
*   8 Whole Bartlett Pear

Directions:

1. Supply your smoker with wood pellets and follow the start-up procedure. Preheat the grill, with the lid closed, to 350° F.

2. For the crust: Place flour and sugar in a food processor and pulse to mix. Add butter a little at a time while pulsing. Once it starts to looks like cornmeal, add the water until dough start to come together.

3. Form a round with the dough, wrap in plastic and let it cool in the refrigerator.

4. While dough cools, make the caramel sauce. In a sauce pan, add 1/4 cup granulated sugar and 1/4 cup butter. Cook butter and sugar until it becomes a dark caramel, a couple minutes.

5. Pour caramel in the bottom of 10 inch deep cake pan. While the caramel is still hot, arrange pear wedges in a fan formation covering the caramel.

6. Roll the chilled pie dough into a circle big enough to cover the pan. Prick the pie dough with a fork and cover the pan with the pie dough. Trim the crust leaving room for shrinkage.

7. Place on the grill and bake for 45 minutes or until pears are soft. The pears will be soft and most of the juice will evaporate and thicken.

8. Let sit for 3 minutes. While pan is still hot, place a plate over pie and flip over. Slowly lift the plate.

9. Serve warm, topped with vanilla ice cream or whipped cream. Enjoy!

Pizza Bites

Servings: 6
Cooking Time: 20 Minutes

Ingredients:

- 4 1/2 Cup Bread Flour
- 1 1/2 Tablespoon sugar
- 2 Teaspoon Instant Yeast
- 2 Teaspoon kosher salt
- 3 Tablespoon extra-virgin olive oil
- 15 Fluid Ounce Water, Lukewarm
- 8 Ounce Pepperoni, sliced
- 1 Cup pizza sauce
- 1 Cup mozzarella cheese
- 1 Whole egg, for egg wash
- 1 As Needed salt

Directions:

1. For the Pizza Dough: Combine flour, sugar, salt, and yeast in food processor. Pulse 3 to 4 times until incorporated evenly. Add olive oil and water. Run food processor until mixture forms ball that rides around the bowl above the blade, about 15 seconds. Continue processing 15 seconds longer.

2. Transfer dough ball to lightly floured surface and knead once or twice by hand until smooth ball is formed. Divide dough into three even parts and place each into a 1 gallon zip top bag. Place in refrigerator and allow to rise at least one day.

3. At least two hours before baking, remove dough from refrigerator and shape into balls by gathering dough towards bottom and pinching shut. Flour well and place each one in a separate medium mixing bowl. Cover tightly with plastic wrap and allow to rise at warm room temperature until roughly doubled in volume.

4. When ready to cook, set the grill temperature to 350°F and preheat, lid closed for 15 minutes.

5. After the first rise remove the dough from the fridge and let come to room temperature. Roll dough on a flat surface. Cut dough into long strips 3" wide by 18" long.

6. Slice pepperoni into strips.

7. In a medium bowl combine the pizza sauce, mozzarella and pepperoni.

8. Spoon 1 TBSP of the pizza filling onto the pizza dough every two inches, about halfway down the length of the dough. Dip a pastry brush into the egg wash and brush around pizza filling. Fold the half side of the dough (without the pizza filling) over the other the half that contains the pizza filling.

9. Press down between each pizza bite slightly with your fingers. With a ravioli or pizza cutter, cut around each filling- creating a rectangle shape and sealing the crust in.

10. Transfer each pizza bite onto a parchment lined cookie sheet. Cover with a kitchen towel and let them rise for 30 minutes.

11. When ready to cook, preheat the grill to 350 ℉ with the lid closed for 10-15 minutes.

12. Brush the bites with remaining egg wash, sprinkle with salt and place directly on the sheet tray. Bake 10-15 minutes until the exterior is golden brown.

13. Remove from grill and transfer to a serving dish. Serve with extra pizza sauce for dipping and enjoy!

Strawberry Basil Daiquiri

Servings: 2
Cooking Time: 20 Minutes

Ingredients:
- 4 strawberries, stemmed
- 6 Tablespoon granulated sugar, divided
- 6 basil leaves
- 3 Ounce white rum
- 2 Ounce lime juice
- 1 Ounce Smoked Simple Syrup
- 2 fresh basil leaves, for garnish
- 2 lime slice, for garnish

Directions:
1. Supply your smoker with wood pellets and follow the start-up procedure. Preheat the grill, with the lid closed, to 375° F.
2. Cut strawberries in half and coat in 2 tablespoons granulated sugar. Place directly on grill grate and cook for 15 to 20 minutes. Remove from heat and cool. Grill: 375 °F
3. Add 1 tablespoon granulated sugar and basil leaves to shaking tin and lightly muddle. Add strawberries and muddle again.
4. Pour in white rum, lime juice and Smoked Simple Syrup. Shake with ice.
5. Strain contents into a chilled glass and garnish with large fresh basil leaf and sliced lime. Enjoy!

Cast Iron Pineapple Upside Down Cake

Servings: 6
Cooking Time: 40 Minutes

Ingredients:
- 1/4 Cup butter, melted
- 1 Cup brown sugar
- 20 Ounce Pineapple, sliced
- 6 Ounce maraschino cherries
- 1 Whole Yellow Cake Mix, Boxed
- vegetable oil
- eggs

Directions:
1. Supply your smoker with wood pellets and follow the start-up procedure. Preheat the grill, with the lid closed, to 350° F.
2. Pour melted butter into a 12-inch cast iron pan. Sprinkle brown sugar on top of the butter. Arrange pineapple slices on brown sugar, squeezing in as many slices as possible. Place a cherry in center of each pineapple slice; press gently into brown sugar.
3. Make cake batter as directed on box, substituting pineapple juice mixture for as much of the water as possible, and adding in required oil and eggs. Pour batter into cast iron dish, over pineapple and cherries.
4. Place the cast iron pan on the grill grate and cook for 20 minutes. Rotate the pan a half turn to ensure it cooks evenly. Cook for an additional 20 minutes, or until toothpick inserted in center comes out clean.
5. Immediately run knife around side of pan to loosen cake. Place heatproof serving plate upside down onto pan; turn plate and pan over.
6. Leave pan over cake 5 minutes so brown sugar topping can drizzle over cake. Cool 30 minutes. Enjoy!

Grilled Bourbon Pecan Pie

Servings: 6
Cooking Time: 45 Minutes

Ingredients:
- 2 Tbsp Bourbon
- 1/2 Cup Brown Sugar
- 1/3 Cup Unsalted Butter, Melted
- 1/2 Cup Light, 1/2 Cup Dark Corn Syrup
- 3 Egg
- 1/4 Tsp Hickory Honey Smoked Salt
- Decoration Pecan
- 1 1/4 Cup Chopped Pecans, Coarsely Broken
- 1 Prepared Or Homemade Pie Shell, Deep
- 1/2 Cup Sugar

- 1 Tsp Vanilla Extract

Directions:

1. Supply your smoker with wood pellets and follow the start-up procedure. Preheat the grill, with the lid closed, to 375° F. Meanwhile, prepare your pie crust in a 9 cast iron skillet or heat proof pie plate.

2. In a large bowl, beat the eggs until smooth. Add the brown sugar and white sugar and mix until smooth. Add the light corn syrup, dark corn syrup, vanilla, bourbon, melted butter, and Hickory Honey Salt. Mix until smooth. Stir in your chopped pecans and pour into the pie crust. Top with the whole pecans, if desired.

3. Grill covered for 35-45 minutes, until the pie is just set around the edges but still has a slight jiggle in the center.

4. Allow the pie to cool completely before slicing. Enjoy!

Smoked Lemon Cheesecake

Servings: 16

Cooking Time: 130 Minutes

Ingredients:

- For the crust
- Vegetable oil, for oiling the pan
- 12 ounces gingersnaps (about 36) or chocolate icebox cookies (about 36)
- 3 tablespoons light brown sugar
- 8 tablespoons (1 stick) unsalted butter, melted
- For the filling
- 4 packages (8 ounces each) cream cheese, at room temperature
- 1 cup firmly packed light brown sugar
- 2 teaspoons pure vanilla extract
- 2 teaspoons finely grated lemon zest
- 1 tablespoon fresh lemon juice
- 2 tablespoons (1/4 stick) unsalted butter, melted
- 5 large eggs
- Burnt Sugar Sauce (recipes follows, optional)

Directions:

1. Supply your smoker with wood pellets and follow the start-up procedure. Preheat the grill, with the lid closed, to 400° F. Lightly oil the springform pan with vegetable oil and wrap a sheet of aluminum foil around the outside.

2. Make the crust: Break the cookies into pieces and grind with the brown sugar to a fine powder in a food processor. You'll want about 1 3/4 cups of crumbs. Add the melted butter and run the processor in short bursts to obtain a crumbly dough. Press the mixture evenly across the bottom and halfway up the sides of the springform pan. Indirect-grill or bake the crust until lightly browned, 5 to 8 minutes. Transfer the pan to a wire rack and let cool.

3. Make the filling: Wipe out the food processor bowl. Add the cream cheese, brown sugar, vanilla, lemon zest, lemon juice, and butter, and process until smooth. Work in the eggs one by one, processing until smooth after each addition. (You can also use a stand mixer, beating the cream cheese mixture until smooth and beating in the eggs one at a time.) Pour the filling into the crust. Gently tap the pan on the countertop a few times to knock out any air bubbles.

4. Supply your smoker with wood pellets and follow the start-up procedure. Preheat the grill, with the lid closed, to 225 °F-250 °F.

5. Place the cheesecake in the smoker. Smoke until the top is bronzed with smoke and the filling is set, 1 1/2 to 2 hours. To test for doneness, gently poke the side of the pan—the filling will jiggle, not ripple. Alternatively, insert a slender metal skewer in the center of the cake; it should come out clean.

6. Transfer the cheesecake in its pan to a wire rack to cool to room temperature. Refrigerate until serving; the cheesecake can be made up to 8 hours ahead. Run a slender knife around the inside of the springform pan. Unclasp and remove the ring. (You'll serve the cheesecake off the bottom of the pan.) Let the cheesecake warm slightly at room temperature before serving.

7. If serving with the sauce, pour some of it over the cheesecake and the rest into a pitcher. Cut into wedges and pass the remaining sauce.

Baked Irish Creme Cake

Servings: 4
Cooking Time: 60 Minutes

Ingredients:

- 1 Cup Pecans, pieces
- 1 Yellow Cake Mix, Boxed
- 1 Vanilla Pudding Mix, Instant Package (3.4oz)
- 4 Large eggs
- 1/2 Cup water
- 1/2 Cup vegetable oil
- 1 Cup Irish Cream Liquor
- 1/2 Cup butter
- 1 Cup sugar

Directions:

1. Grease and flour a 10" (25 cm) Bundt pan. Sprinkle pecans along the bottom.
2. In a large bowl, with a mixer, combine yellow cake mix, pudding mix, eggs, water, oil, and Irish Cream liquor. Pour batter over nuts in the pan.
3. Supply your smoker with wood pellets and follow the start-up procedure. Preheat the grill, with the lid closed, to 325° F.
4. Place Bundt pan on the Traeger and bake for 1 hour, or until a toothpick comes out clean. Remove from heat, cool for 10 minutes. Grill: 325 °F
5. While the cake is cooling, combine the butter, water and sugar and bring to a boil. Boil for 5 minutes, stirring constantly. Remove from heat and add Irish cream liquor.
6. Use a bamboo skewer to poke holes in the cooled cake. Spoon glaze over the cake. Allow cake to absorb the glaze. Enjoy!

Cinnamon Pull-aparts

Servings: 6
Cooking Time: 20 Minutes

Ingredients:

- 16.3 Ounce Biscuits, Homestyle, Canned
- 1 Cup packed brown sugar
- 1/2 Cup butter
- 1/4 Cup water
- 1 Teaspoon ground cinnamon
- 1/2 Cup Nuts (optional)

Directions:

1. Cut each biscuit into 4 pieces and peel each piece in half; set aside.
2. Combine brown sugar, butter and water in a large saucepan and bring to a boil; reduce heat and simmer for 1 minute. Stir in cinnamon and nuts; add biscuit quarters and mix to coat. Pour into greased 13 by 9 inch casserole dish and spread evenly in the dish.
3. Supply your smoker with wood pellets and follow the start-up procedure. Preheat the grill, with the lid closed, to 350° F.
4. Place the casserole dish on the grill; close lid and cook for 20 to 25 minutes or until the biscuits are done. Grill: 350 °F
5. Remove from the grill and transfer to a serving platter making sure to get all the gooey syrup onto the biscuits. Serve warm. Enjoy!

Dark Chocolate Brownies With Bacon-salted Caramel

Servings: 8
Cooking Time: 40 Minutes

Ingredients:

- 8 Strips bacon
- 1/2 Cup kosher salt
- 1 Whole Brownie Mix
- 1 Jar caramel sauce

Directions:

1. For the bacon salt: Cook a few strips of bacon (6 to 8) until very crisp: 350 degrees for about 25 minutes should do it. Let cool, then pulse in a food processor until finely chopped. Mix with 1/2 cup kosher salt. Store in the refrigerator until ready to use.
2. Supply your smoker with wood pellets and follow the start-up procedure. Preheat the grill, with the lid closed, to 350° F.
3. Mix the brownies according to package directions and pour into a greased pan. Drizzle approximately 2 tablespoons of the caramel sauce over the brownie batter. Sprinkle with approximately 1 teaspoon of the bacon salt. Place directly on the grill grate of your preheated Traeger.

4. Bake the brownies for 20-25 minutes, until the batter has started to set up. Remove from the grill and drizzle with 2 more tablespoons of caramel sauce and sprinkle with more bacon salt. Return to the grill for 20-25 more minutes, or until a toothpick inserted in the middle of the brownies comes out clean.

5. If you like extra caramel, drizzle another layer of caramel on the hot brownies and sprinkle with a final bit of bacon salt. Allow the brownies to cool completely before cutting them into squares. Clean your knife in between each slice to prevent the brownies from sticking to the knife. Enjoy!

Mint Butter Chocolate Chip Cookies

Servings: 24
Cooking Time: 12 Minutes

Ingredients:
- 1/2 Cup Butter, Melted
- 1 Package Chocolate Chip Cookie Mix
- 8-10 Drop Food Coloring
- 1/2 Tsp Mint, Extract

Directions:
1. Supply your smoker with wood pellets and follow the start-up procedure. Preheat the grill, with the lid closed, to 350° F.
2. Follow the directions on the back of the Chocolate Chip Cookie mix and also add the mint extract and green food coloring. Mix until combined.
3. On a baking sheet lined with parchment paper, drop balls of dough about 2 tbsp in size onto the pan.
4. Place in your Grill and bake for 10-12 minutes. Let cool for a couple minutes before removing from the pan. Enjoy!

Savory Beaver Tails

Servings: 8
Cooking Time: 2 Minutes

Ingredients:
- 2 Tbsp Butter, Melted
- 1 Tbsp Cinnamon, Ground
- 1 Egg
- 2 1/2 Cups Flour, All-Purpose
- 1/2 Cup Milk, Warm
- 1/2 Tsp Salt
- 1 Tsp Sugar
- 1/2 Tsp Vanilla
- 1 L Vegetable Oil
- 1/4 Cup Water, Warm
- 2 1/2 Tsp Active Yeast, Instant

Directions:
1. In a small bowl, combine water, milk, yeast, and sugar. Let it sit for about 10 minutes or until frothy.
2. In another bowl, pour in the flour and make a well in the middle. Pour in butter, sugar, salt, vanilla and egg. Mix everything together until the dough is smooth. Knead for about 5 minutes and set the dough in a greased bowl. Cover with a towel and set aside for about an hour, or until the dough has doubled in size.
3. After one hour, supply your smoker with wood pellets and follow the start-up procedure. Preheat the grill, with the lid open, to 450° F.Pour 1L of vegetable oil into a cast iron pan and place on the grates of your Grill. Keep your flame broiler closed so as to prevent grease flareups. Preheat the oil so that it is 350 degrees F.
4. While you"re waiting for the oil to heat up, punch down the dough and separate into 8 small balls. Shape each piece of dough into a flat circle. Fry the dough in the preheated oil for about 1 minute per side, or until the dough is golden brown.
5. Sprinkle with cinnamon sugar immediately, or top with your desired toppings. Enjoy!

Baked Molten Chocolate Cake

Servings: 4
Cooking Time: 20 Minutes

Ingredients:
- all-purpose flour
- butter
- 4 Ounce butter
- 6 Ounce Chocolate, Bittersweet
- 2 eggs
- 2 egg yolk
- 1/2 Cup sugar
- 1 Pinch salt

Directions:

1. Supply your smoker with wood pellets and follow the start-up procedure. Preheat the grill, with the lid closed, to 450° F.

2. Butter and flour four (6oz) ramekins. Tap out excess flour. Place ramekins on a baking sheet and reserve.

3. Melt butter and chocolate in a double boiler over simmering water. In a medium bowl, beat eggs and yolks with sugar and salt on high until thick and pale.

4. Whisk in chocolate until smooth and quickly fold into the egg mixture along with flour.

5. Spoon the batter into prepared ramekins and bake for 20 minutes or until sides are firm but centers are soft. Grill: 450 °F

6. Let cool for 1 minute, then cover each with an inverted dessert plate. Carefully turn each over, let stand 10 seconds, then unmold.

7. Serve immediately with Maple Ice Cream with Candied Bacon. Enjoy!

Beer Bread

Servings: 4
Cooking Time: 60 Minutes

Ingredients:

- 400 g all-purpose flour
- 2 Tablespoon sugar
- 1 Tablespoon baking powder
- 1 Teaspoon salt
- 12 Ounce beer
- 2 Tablespoon honey
- 6 Tablespoon butter, melted

Directions:

1. Supply your smoker with wood pellets and follow the start-up procedure. Preheat the grill, with the lid closed, to 350° F.

2. Spray a loaf pan (9x5x3 inches) (55x12x20 cm) with nonstick cooking spray and set aside.

3. Put the flour, sugar, baking powder, and salt in a large mixing bowl. Whisk with a wire whisk to combine and aerate. Add the beer and honey and stir with a wooden spoon until the batter is just mixed. (Do not overmix.) If desired, gently stir in one or more of the optional add-ins.

4. Pour half of the melted butter in the prepared loaf pan and spoon in the batter. Pour the remainder of the butter over the top of the loaf.

5. Put the loaf pan directly on the grill grate and bake until a wooden skewer or toothpick inserted in the center of the loaf comes out clean, 50 to 60 minutes, and the bread is golden-brown. (Note: If using a glass loaf pan, the baking time might be shorter.)

6. Let the loaf cool slightly in the pan before removing from the pan. Leftovers make great toast.

7. Optional Add-ins: Bacon, cooked and crumbled, 1 cup (100 g) Grated Cheese, Red Bell Pepper and Onion, diced and sauted in Butter (1/4 cup each), Green Onions, minced, Dried Herbs such as Dill, Rosemary, Mixed Italian Herbs, etc,.Cracked Black Pepper, Your favorite Barbecue Rub, such as Traeger's Pork and Poultry Shake, Ground Cinnamon, Dry Ranch Dressing Mix, Coarse-grained Mustard.

Baked Peach Cobbler Cupcakes

Servings: 8
Cooking Time: 30 Minutes

Ingredients:

- 2 Large Peaches, fresh
- 3/4 Cup sugar
- 2 Teaspoon lemon juice
- 1/2 Teaspoon ground cinnamon
- Yellow Cake Mix, Boxed
- 1 Can vanilla icing

Directions:

1. Bring a pot of water to a boil. Turn peaches upside down and cut a small shallow X across the bottom. Put peaches in boiling water and boil for 1 minute to help loosen the skin.

2. Drain the peaches into a colander and rinse off with cold water. Peel skin off peaches.

3. Filling: Dice peaches and place into a large pan. Cook peaches over medium heat. As it starts to sizzle, add sugar, lemon and cinnamon. Cook mixture on

medium heat for 10-15 minutes until a majority of the juice from the peaches evaporates leaving a thick syrup.

4. Transfer to a bowl to cool.

5. Supply your smoker with wood pellets and follow the start-up procedure. Preheat the grill, with the lid closed, to 350° F.

6. Cupcakes: Follow the directions on box cake mix and put the mixture into cupcake pan with liners.

7. When grill has preheated, bake cupcakes for 13-16 minutes, until a light golden brown. Grill: 350 °F

8. When cupcakes have cooled, use a piping bag to pipe the peach cobbler mixture into the middle of the cupcake.

9. Ice with your favorite vanilla icing. Enjoy!

Chocolate Peanut Cookies

Servings: 4

Cooking Time: 12 Minutes

Ingredients:

- 1/2 Tsp Baking Soda
- 1/2 Cup Brown Sugar
- 1/2 Cup + 1 Tbsp Butter, Unsalted
- 1/3 Cup Cocoa Powder, Dark And Unsweetened
- 2 Eggs, Beaten
- 1 1/2 Cups Flour, All-Purpose
- 1/3 Cup Miniature Chocolate Chips
- 2 Cups Peanut Butter Chips, Divided
- 1/4 Tsp Sea Salt
- 1/2 Cup Sugar, Granulated
- 1 Tsp Vanilla Extract

Directions:

1. Supply your smoker with wood pellets and follow the start-up procedure. Preheat the grill, with the lid closed, to medium-low heat. If using a gas or charcoal grill, preheat a cast iron skillet.

2. In a mixing bowl, whisk together the flour, cocoa powder, baking soda, and salt. Set aside.

3. Set a metal saucepan on the griddle, then add ½ cup of butter to melt. Whisk in the sugars and vanilla extract and cook for 2 minutes. Remove the pan from the griddle, and transfer contents to a large mixing bowl.

4. Slowly pour the beaten eggs into the sugar mixture, whisking constantly to temper the eggs.

5. Add the dry mixture to the wet ingredients until just combined. Fold in 1 cup of peanut butter chips and chocolate chips. Refrigerate mixture for 15 to 30 minutes.

6. Remove the dough from the refrigerator, then add an additional cup of peanut butter chips.

7. Portion dough into 16 to 18 cookie balls.

8. Melt 1 tablespoon of butter on the griddle, then transfer the cookie balls to the griddle. Press down gently on the cookies, then cook for 10 to 12 minutes, flipping halfway.

9. Transfer cookies to a cooling rack for 5 minutes before enjoying.

Sweet And Spicy Baked Pork Beans

Servings: 20

Cooking Time: 120 Minutes

Ingredients:

- 1 - 21 Oz Apple Pie Filling, Can
- 1 Gallon Baked Beans
- 1 Tbs Chilli, Powder
- 1 Green Bell Pepper, Diced
- 1 10 Oz Drained Jalapeno, Can Diced
- 1 Cup Maple Syrup
- 1 Onion, Diced
- 1 Lb Pork, Pulled

Directions:

1. Supply your smoker with wood pellets and follow the start-up procedure. Preheat the grill, with the lid closed, to 350° F.

2. Place all ingredients in mixing bowl and mix well.

3. Pour bean mixture into foil pans.

4. Bake in grill till bubbling throughout – about 2 hours.

5. Rest at least 15 minutes before serving.

Grilled Beer Cheese Dip

Servings: 6

Cooking Time: 20 Minutes

Ingredients:

- 6 Oz Beer, Can
- 8 Oz Cream Cheese
- 1 Tsp Onion Powder
- ½ Tsp Pepper
- ½ Tsp Salt
- 2 Cups Shredded Cheese

Directions:

1. Supply your smoker with wood pellets and follow the start-up procedure. Preheat the grill, with the lid closed, to 350° F. If you're using a gas or charcoal grill, set it up for medium high heat. Preheat with lid closed for 10-15 minutes.

2. In the cast iron pan add cream cheese, shredded cheese, beer, onion powder, salt and pepper. Once grill is at 350°F place cast iron skillet onto the grill and cook for about 10 minutes, stir and cook for another 5-10 minutes.

3. Top with more shredded cheese and fresh parsley. Serve with fresh baked pretzels as well.

Baked Parker House Rolls

Servings: 8

Cooking Time: 15 Minutes

Ingredients:

- 1/2 Ounce (2 packets) active dry yeast
- 6 Tablespoon plus 1 teaspoon cane sugar
- 1 Cup warm water (110°F to 115°F)
- 5 Cup all-purpose flour, plus more as needed
- 2 Teaspoon salt
- 1 Cup warm milk (110°-115°F)
- 1 Large eggs
- oil
- 4 Tablespoon melted butter, divided
- 1 Tablespoon Maldon Sea Salt Flakes
- 2 Tablespoon poppy seeds
- 2 Tablespoon white sesame seeds
- 1 Tablespoon garlic flakes

Directions:

1. Place the yeast, 1 teaspoon of cane sugar and warm water in a mixing bowl or the base of a stand mixer. Stir to combine. Allow the yeast to proof for 5 minutes- it should start to bubble a bit, showing that the yeast is alive.

2. Sprinkle the flour, salt and remaining 6 tablespoons of sugar over the yeast mixture. Using a dough hook or a wooden spoon, stir for 30 seconds. Pour in the warm milk and egg.

3. Knead again on the medium-low setting, or on a floured work surface by hand until the dough is very soft, adding up to one more cup of flour so the dough is soft and smooth and has lost its sticky quality.

4. Coat the bowl with a small film of oil and place the dough in the bowl, turning to coat dough evenly with the oil. Cover the bowl with a clean cloth, place in a warm spot in the kitchen and allow to proof about 45 minutes. The dough will almost double in size.

5. Punch down the dough and place on a floured work surface. Divide the dough in half, then divide each half into 12 equal pieces.

6. Using your hands, tuck in the seams of each piece of dough then place the dough on a lightly floured surface.

7. Place your fingers around the piece of dough, and roll it in a circular motion to create a smooth, even ball. Alternately, roll the dough between your two hands to create a round ball shape. Repeat with the remaining 23 pieces.

8. Butter a 9x13 inch baking pan with a tablespoon of the melted butter. Place the dough balls evenly in the pan, creating rows of 4 pieces of dough across and 6 down. Cover again with a clean towel and allow the dough to rise in a warm spot, about 30 minutes longer.

9. While the dough is proofing, supply your smoker with wood pellets and follow the start-up procedure. Preheat the grill, with the lid closed, to 325° F. Brush the remaining 3 tablespoons of butter on the bread and sprinkle with the flake salt, seeds and garlic flakes.

10. Place the pan on the grill, cover and bake about 15 to 20 minutes, or until rolls are lightly browned on top and cooked through. When done, you should be able to pull apart two pieces and see that the dough is cooked and the bottoms are lightly browned. Grill: 325 °F

Bacon Chocolate Chip Cookies

Servings: 2
Cooking Time: 10-12 Minutes

Ingredients:

- 2¾ cups all-purpose flour
- 1½ teaspoons baking soda
- ½ teaspoon salt
- 12 tablespoons (1½ sticks) unsalted butter, softened
- 1 cup light brown sugar
- 1 cup granulated sugar
- 2 eggs, at room temperature
- 2½ teaspoons apple cider vinegar
- 1 teaspoon vanilla extract
- 2 cups semisweet chocolate chips
- 8 slices bacon, cooked and crumbled

Directions:

1. In a large bowl, combine the flour, baking soda, and salt, and mix well.
2. In a separate large bowl, using an electric mixer on medium speed, cream the butter and sugars. Reduce the speed to low and mix in the eggs, vinegar, and vanilla.
3. With the mixer speed still on low, slowly incorporate the dry ingredients, chocolate chips, and bacon pieces.
4. Supply your smoker with wood pellets and follow the start-up procedure. Preheat, with the lid closed, to 375°F.
5. Line a large baking sheet with parchment paper.
6. Drop rounded teaspoonfuls of cookie batter onto the prepared baking sheet and place on the grill grate. Close the lid and smoke for 10 to 12 minutes, or until the cookies are browned around the edges.

Delicious Smoked Candied Pecan Pie

Servings: 4
Cooking Time: 55 Minutes

Ingredients:

- 1 cup brown sugar
- 1/4 cup granulated sugar
- 1 1/2 teaspoon vanilla
- 1/2 teaspoon corn starch
- 1/2 teaspoon orange zest
- 1/2 teaspoon salt
- 3/4 cup light corn syrup
- 1/2 cup butter (aka- 1 stick), melted
- 3 eggs, beaten
- 1 1/2 cups smoked candied pecans
- 1 pie crust

Directions:

1. Supply your smoker with wood pellets and follow the start-up procedure. Preheat the grill, with the lid closed, to 350° F.
2. Put brown sugar, granulated sugar, vanilla, corn starch, orange zest, salt, light corn syrup, melted butter, and three eggs in a medium mixing bowl. Stir ingredients together.
3. Lightly grease a pie pan and put your rolled out pie crust in. Make sure pie crust conforms to the pie tin. Sprinkle half of your pecans onto pie crust in pie pan. Pour ingredients from mixing bowl into pie pan, then evenly top with the remaining pecans.
4. Cover pie in foil and put on the grill. After 30 minutes, remove foil and cook for another 25 minutes.
5. Remove the pecan pie from grill and let it cool to room temperature before serving.

Blueberry Bread Pudding

Servings: 4
Cooking Time: 60 Minutes

Ingredients:

- 5 eggs
- 3 Cup sugar
- 2 1/2 Cup milk
- 1 1/2 Teaspoon vanilla
- 1 Teaspoon cinnamon
- 1 Pinch salt
- 5 Cup Bread
- 3 Cup blueberries

Directions:

1. Beat the eggs in a large mixing bowl. Whisk in the sugar, milk, vanilla, cinnamon, and salt.
2. In another large bowl, combine the bread and 2 cups (200 g) of the blueberries.

3. Pour the egg mixture over the bread-blueberry mixture and let sit for 30 minutes. Meanwhile, place muffin liners in a muffin tin.

4. Supply your smoker with wood pellets and follow the start-up procedure. Preheat the grill, with the lid open.

5. Spoon the bread-blueberry mixture into the prepared cups; evenly top each with the remaining cup of blueberries, pressing them gently into the pudding with the back of a spoon.

6. Dust the top with sugar.

7. Arrange the pan directly on the grill grate and smoke for 30 minutes. Grill:180°F

8. Increase the temperature to 350F (180 C), and bake until the pudding is set and golden brown on top, about 25 minutes. Grill:350°F

9. Let cool slightly, then sift powdered sugar on top. Serve warm with sweetened whipped cream or vanilla ice cream, if desired.

Eggs Ham Benedict

Servings: 6
Cooking Time: 15 Minutes

Ingredients:
- 1 Biscuit Dough, Tube
- 6 Egg
- 16 Ham, Sliced
- 1 Packet Hollandaise Sauce, Package

Directions:
1. Supply your smoker with wood pellets and follow the start-up procedure. Preheat the grill, with the lid closed, to 350° F.

2. Grease a muffin tin and crack an egg in each cup. Place on the grate of the for about 10 minutes or until the whites are fully cooked.

3. At the same time, place your biscuit dough on a greased pan. Follow the directions on the packaging but bake on the . Place 2 slices of ham per biscuit on the pan as well.

4. While the ham, eggs, and biscuits are cooking, prepare the Hollandaise Sauce according to the directions on the packet.

5. When everything is fully cooked, cut a biscuit in half, and stack one or two slices of ham, 1 egg and a dollop of Hollandaise sauce. Repeat for each half biscuit. Serve with fresh fruit.

Chili Cheese Fries

Servings: 6
Cooking Time: 10 Minutes

Ingredients:
- 1 Cup Cheddar Cheese, Shredded
- 1 Cup Chili Con Carne, Prepared
- 1 Bag French Fries
- 1 Tablespoon Olive Oil
- 1 Tablespoon Sweet Heat Rub

Directions:
1. Supply your smoker with wood pellets and follow the start-up procedure. Preheat the grill, with the lid closed, to 350° F. If you're using charcoal or gas, set it up for medium high heat.

2. Bake the fries according to manufacturer's instructions. Once the fries are done, place them in a large bowl and add the olive oil and Sweet Heat Rub. Toss the fries to coat. Once everything is well coated with the oil and seasoning, spread the fries on a baking sheet.

3. Top the fries with the chili and the shredded cheddar cheese. Place the baking sheet on the grill and grill for 7-10 minutes, or until the cheese is melted and bubbly, and the chili is warm all the way through.

4. Remove the baking sheet from the grill and serve the fries immediately.

Baked Cheesy Parmesan Grits

Servings: 4
Cooking Time: 60 Minutes

Ingredients:
- 4 Cup chicken stock
- 3 Tablespoon butter
- 3/4 Teaspoon salt
- 1 Cup quick grits
- 1 Cup shredded cheddar cheese
- pepper

- 1/2 Cup Monterey Jack cheese, shredded
- 1/2 Cup whole milk
- 2 Large eggs

Directions:

1. Supply your smoker with wood pellets and follow the start-up procedure. Preheat the grill, with the lid closed, to 350° F.

2. Butter an 8" baking dish or a 10" cast iron pan.

3. Bring the chicken stock, butter, and salt to boil in medium saucepan. Gradually whisk in grits.

4. Reduce heat to medium and cook until mixture thickens slightly, stirring often about 8 minutes. Remove from heat.

5. Add cheeses and stir until melted. Season with pepper and salt to taste.

6. Whisk together milk and eggs in small bowl. Gradually whisk mixture into grits.

7. Pour the cheese grits into the buttered cast iron pan. Bake until grits feel firm to touch, about 1 hour. Grill: 350 °F

8. Remove from grill and let stand 10 minutes before serving. Enjoy!

SEAFOOD RECIPES

Barbecued Scallops

Servings: 4

Cooking Time: 10 Minutes

Ingredients:

- 1 pound large scallops
- 2 tablespoons olive oil
- 1 batch Dill Seafood Rub

Directions:

1. Supply your smoker with wood pellets and follow the start-up procedure. Preheat the grill, with the lid closed, to 375°F.

2. Coat the scallops all over with olive oil and season all sides with the rub.

3. Place the scallops directly on the grill grate and grill for 5 minutes per side. Remove the scallops from the grill and serve immediately.

Grilled Trout With Citrus & Basil

Servings: 4

Cooking Time: 10 Minutes

Ingredients:

- 6 Whole Trout
- 2 Teaspoon Blackened Saskatchewan Rub
- 10 Sprig fresh basil
- 2 Lemons, cut in half
- extra-virgin olive oil

Directions:

1. Supply your smoker with wood pellets and follow the start-up procedure. Preheat the grill, with the lid closed, to 450° F.

2. Season the center cavity of the trout with the Traeger Blackened Saskatchewan. Place two sprigs of Basil in each cavity, then add 4 lemon halves.

3. Next tie the fish closed using the Butchers twine, and then rub with olive oil.

4. Place the trout on the hot grill and cook 5 minutes on each side. Enjoy! Grill: 450 °F

Grilled Crab Legs With Herb Butter

Servings: 2

Cooking Time: 15 Minutes

Ingredients:

- 12 Tablespoon butter
- 3 Tablespoon Fresh Herbs (Parsley, Chives, Tarragon), finely chopped
- 4 Pound King Crab Legs or Dungeness Crab Leg Clusters
- 3 Whole Lemons, cut into wedges

Directions:

1. Supply your smoker with wood pellets and follow the start-up procedure. Preheat the grill, with the lid closed, to 375° F.

2. Place the butter, garlic, herbs, and a pinch of salt into a small cast iron sauce pan. Place on grill for 5 minutes to melt. Remove from grill and stir. Grill: 375 °F

3. If using king crab legs, split down the center and pour herb butter over meat reserving a quarter for serving. If using crab clusters, toss clusters with herb butter in a large mixing bowl reserving a quarter for serving.

4. Place crab legs directly on the grill grate, meat side up. Grill for 5 to 10 minutes or until hot and beginning to develop a little char on the shell. Grill: 375 °F

5. Serve crab legs with lemon wedges and reserved herb butter. Enjoy!

Seared Ahi Tuna Steak With Soy Sauce

Servings: 2

Cooking Time: 60 Minutes

Ingredients:

- 1/2 Cup Gluten Free Soy Sauce
- 1 Large Sushi Grade Ahi Tuna Steak, Patted Dry
- 1/4 Cup Lime Juice
- 2 Tablespoons Rice Wine Vinegar
- 2 Tablespoons Sesame Oil, Divided
- 2 Tablespoons Sriracha Sauce
- 4 Tablespoons Sweet Heat Rub

- 2 Cups Water

Directions:

1. Supply your smoker with wood pellets and follow the start-up procedure. Preheat the grill, with the lid closed, to 400° F. If using gas or charcoal, set it up for high heat over direct heat.

2. In the glass baking dish, pour in the water, soy sauce, lime juice, rice wine vinegar, 1 tablespoon sesame oil, sriracha sauce, and mirin. Whisk the marinade together with the whisk until everything is well combine. Place the ahi steak into the marinade and place the glass baking dish with the ahi steak in the refrigerator for 30 minutes. After 30 minutes, flip the ahi steak over so that the ahi has the chance to fully marinate on all sides, and allow to marinate for 30 more minutes.

3. After the tuna steak has finished marinating, drain off the marinade and pat the steak dry with paper towels on all sides. Pour the Sweet Heat Rub onto the plate and rub the remaining tablespoon of sesame oil generously on all sides of the tuna steak, and then gently place the tuna steak into the seasoning on the plate, turning on all sides to coat evenly.

4. Insert a temperature probe into the thickest part of the ahi steak and place the steak on the hottest part of the grill. Grill the ahi tuna steak for 45 seconds on each side, or just until the outside is opaque and has grill marks. Flip the steak and allow it to grill for another 45 seconds until the outside is just cooked through. The ahi tuna steak's internal temperature should be just at 115°F.

5. Remove the steak from the grill once it reaches 115°F, and immediately slice and serve. The inside of the steak should still be cool and ruby pink.

Spiced Smoked Swordfish

Servings: 4
Cooking Time: 60 Minutes

Ingredients:

- 4 swordfish fillets (about 4 ounces each)
- For the brine:
- 1 gallon water
- ½ cup kosher salt
- ½ cup brown sugar

- For the rub:
- 1 tablespoon olive oil
- 1 tablespoon kosher salt
- 1 tablespoon coarse ground black pepper
- 1 tablespoon garlic powder
- 1 tablespoon onion powder

Directions:

1. Make the brine by mixing the water, salt,and sugar in a large pot and stir. Add swordfish fillets to the bowl and refrigerate overnight in the mixture.

2. Supply your smoker with wood pellets and follow the start-up procedure. Preheat the grill, with the lid closed, to 225° F.

3. Remove the fillets from the brine, rinse,and blot dry.

4. Brush a coat of olive oil on each fillet and mix salt, pepper, garlic powder,and onion powder in a small bowl for the rub. Apply the rub liberally to each fillet.

5. Put the fillets skin-side down on the smoker and cook for about 1 hour or until the internal temperature in the thickest part of the fillets reaches 145 °F.

6. Enjoy.

Sweet Mandarin Salmon

Servings: 2
Cooking Time: 10 Minutes

Ingredients:

- 1 Whole lime juice
- 1 Teaspoon sesame oil
- 1 1/2 Cup Mandarin Orange Sauce
- 1 1/2 Tablespoon soy sauce
- 2 Tablespoon cilantro, finely chopped
- Freshly cracked black pepper
- 1 Whole (4 oz) wild salmon fillets

Directions:

1. Supply your smoker with wood pellets and follow the start-up procedure. Preheat the grill, with the lid closed, to 375° F.

2. For the glaze, combine Mandarin orange sauce, lime juice, sesame oil, soy sauce, cilantro and fresh cracked black pepper. Mix together.

3. Cut the salmon into 4 fillets. Brush with glaze and place directly on the grill grate, skin side down.

4. Cook until salmon reaches an internal temperature of 155 degrees F (about 15-20 minutes). Half way through cook time, brush salmon again with the glaze.

5. Remove the salmon from the grill and serve with remaining glaze if desired. Enjoy!

Barbecued Shrimp

Servings: 4

Cooking Time: 10 Minutes

Ingredients:

- 1 pound peeled and deveined shrimp, with tails on
- 2 tablespoons olive oil
- 1 batch Dill Seafood Rub

Directions:

1. Soak wooden skewers in water for 30 minutes.

2. Supply your smoker with wood pellets and follow the start-up procedure. Preheat the grill, with the lid closed, to 375°F.

3. Thread 4 or 5 shrimp per skewer.

4. Coat the shrimp all over with olive oil and season each side of the skewers with the rub.

5. Place the skewers directly on the grill grate and grill the shrimp for 5 minutes per side. Remove the skewers from the grill and serve immediately.

Citrus-smoked Trout

Servings: 6

Cooking Time: 120 Minutes

Ingredients:

- 6 to 8 skin-on rainbow trout, cleaned and scaled
- 1 gallon orange juice
- ½ cup packed light brown sugar
- ¼ cup salt
- 1 tablespoon freshly ground black pepper
- Nonstick spray, oil, or butter, for greasing
- 1 tablespoon chopped fresh parsley
- 1 lemon, sliced

Directions:

1. Fillet the fish and pat dry with paper towels.

2. Pour the orange juice into a large container with a lid and stir in the brown sugar, salt, and pepper.

3. Place the trout in the brine, cover, and refrigerate for 1 hour.

4. Cover the grill grate with heavy-duty aluminum foil. Poke holes in the foil and spray with cooking spray (see Tip).

5. Supply your smoker with wood pellets and follow the start-up procedure. Preheat, with the lid closed, to 225°F.

6. Remove the trout from the brine and pat dry. Arrange the fish on the foil-covered grill grate, close the lid, and smoke for 1 hour 30 minutes to 2 hours, or until flaky.

7. Remove the fish from the heat. Serve garnished with the fresh parsley and lemon slices.

Grilled Artichoke Cheese Salmon

Servings: 12

Cooking Time: 270 Minutes

Ingredients:

- 28 Oz Artichoke Hearts, Whole, Canned
- 1/2 Cup Breadcrumbs
- 1/2 Cup Brown Sugar
- 8 Oz Cream Cheese
- 1 Tbsp Garlic Powder
- 1 Cup Italian Cheese Blend, Shredded
- 1/4 Cup Kosher Salt
- 1 Cup Mayonnaise
- 2 Tsp Olive Oil
- 1 Tbsp Onion Powder
- 1/2 Cup Parmesan Cheese
- 2 Tbsp Parsley, Chopped
- Blackened Sriracha Rub
- 1 1/4 Lbs Salmon, Fillet, Scaled And Deboned
- Sour Cream
- 1/2 Tsp White Pepper, Ground

Directions:

1. In a small mixing bowl, whisk together the brown sugar, salt, garlic powder, onion powder, and white pepper. This will make twice the cure needed, so be sure and place the remaining half in a resealable plastic bag and save for smoking fish at a later date.

2.   Lay a sheet of plastic wrap on a sheet tray and sprinkle a thin layer of the cure on it. Place the salmon skin-side down on top of the cure, then sprinkle a couple tablespoons of cure on top. Gently press the cure on top of the salmon flesh, then wrap in plastic wrap.

3.   Refrigerate for 8 hours, or overnight.

4.   Remove salmon from the refrigerator and wash off the cure in the sink, under cold water.

5.   Blot salmon with a paper towel, then set salmon skin side on a wire rack. Dry at room temperature for two hours, or until a yellowish shimmer appears on the salmon.

6.   Supply your smoker with wood pellets and follow the start-up procedure. Preheat the grill, with the lid closed, to 250° F. If using a gas, charcoal or other grill, set it to low, indirect heat.

7.   Place the salmon in the upper cabinet. Smoke for 2 hours, then increase the grill temperature to 350° F to maintain a cabinet temperature of 225°F and smoke another 1 to 2 hours, until salmon reaches an internal temperature of 145° F.

8.   Remove salmon from the cabinet and set aside to rest for 15 minutes, then flake apart. Reserve ½ cup to top dip after grilling.

9.   While the salmon is resting, drain the artichokes, then skewer onto metal skewers (if using wooden skewers, make sure to soak in water for 1 hour prior to grilling, or you can use a grill basket as well).

10.   Season with Blackened Sriracha, then set on the grill. Grill for 2 to 3 minutes, until lightly browned.

11.   Remove from the grill, cool slightly, then roughly chop. Set aside.

12.   In a mixing bowl, combine shredded Italian cheese, grated parmesan, breadcrumbs and parsley. Set aside.

13.   Place cream cheese, mayonnaise, and sour cream in a cast iron skillet. Stir frequently, with a wooden spoon, for about 5 minutes, until the mixture is smooth.

14.   Carefully fold in flaked salmon and grilled artichoke hearts, then spread breadcrumb mixture over dip.

15.   Drizzle with olive oil, then close the grill lid and bake for 25 to 30 minutes, until dip begins to bubble around the edges, and cheese begins to caramelize on top.

16.   Remove dip from the grill, top with reserved salmon and a pinch of parsley. Serve warm with bagel chips, crackers, or crusty bread.

Oysters In The Shell

Servings: 4
Cooking Time: 20 Minutes

Ingredients:
*   8 medium oysters, unopened, in the shell, rinsed and scrubbed
*   1 batch Lemon Butter Mop for Seafood

Directions:
1.   Supply your smoker with wood pellets and follow the start-up procedure. Preheat the grill, with the lid closed, to 375°F.

2.   Place the unopened oysters directly on the grill grate and grill for about 20 minutes, or until the oysters are done and their shells open.

3.   Discard any oysters that do not open. Shuck the remaining oysters, transfer them to a bowl, and add the mop. Serve immediately.

Cured Cold-smoked Lox

Servings: 6
Cooking Time: 360 Minutes

Ingredients:
*   ¼ cup salt
*   ¼ cup sugar
*   1 tablespoon freshly ground black pepper
*   1 bunch dill, chopped
*   1 pound sashimi-grade salmon, skin removed
*   1 avocado, sliced
*   8 bagels
*   4 ounces cream cheese
*   1 bunch alfalfa sprouts
*   1 (3.5-ounce) jar capers

Directions:
1.   In a small bowl, combine the salt, sugar, pepper, and fresh dill to make the curing mixture. Set aside.

2.   On a smooth surface, lay out a large piece of plastic wrap and spread half of the curing salt mixture in the middle, spreading it out to about the size of the salmon.

3. Place the salmon on top of the curing salt.

4. Top the fish with the remaining curing salt, covering it completely. Wrap the salmon, leaving the ends open to drain.

5. Place the wrapped fish in a rimmed baking pan or dish lined with paper towels to soak up liquid.

6. Place a weight on the salmon evenly, such as a pan with a couple of heavy jars of pickles on top.

7. Put the salmon pan with weights in the refrigerator. Place something (a dishtowel, for example) under the back of the pan in order to slightly tip it down so the liquid drains away from the fish.

8. Leave the salmon to cure in the refrigerator for 24 hours.

9. Place the wood pellets in the smoker, but do not follow the start-up procedure and do not preheat.

10. Remove the salmon from the refrigerator, unwrap it, rinse it off, and pat dry.

11. Put the salmon in the smoker while still cold from the refrigerator to slow down the cooking process. You'll need to use a cold-smoker attachment or enlist the help of a smoker tube to hold the temperature at 80°F and maintain that for 6 hours to absorb smoke and complete the cold-smoking process.

12. Remove the salmon from the smoker, place it in a sealed plastic bag, and refrigerate for 24 hours. The salmon will be translucent all the way through.

13. Thinly slice the lox and serve with sliced avocado, bagels, cream cheese, alfalfa sprouts, and capers.

Cider Hot-smoked Salmon

Servings: 4

Cooking Time: 60 Minutes

Ingredients:
- 1 1/2 Pound Wild Caught Salmon Fillet, skinned, pin bones removed
- 12 Ounce apple juice or cider
- 4 Pieces juniper berries
- 1 Pieces Star Anise, Broken
- 1 Pieces bay leaf, coarsely crumbled
- 1/2 Cup kosher salt
- 1/4 Cup brown sugar
- 2 Teaspoon Blackened Saskatchewan Rub
- 1 Teaspoon coarse ground black pepper, divided

Directions:

1. Rinse the salmon fillet under cold running water and check for pin bones by running a finger over the fleshy part of the fillet. If you feel a bone, remove it with kitchen tweezers or a needle-nose pliers.

2. In a sturdy resealable plastic bag, combine the cider, crushed juniper berries, star anise, and bay leaf. Add the salmon fillet and put the bag in a bowl or pan in the refrigerator. Let sit for at least 8 hours, or overnight.

3. Remove the salmon from the bag and discard the cider mixture. Dry the salmon well on paper towels. Make the cure: In a small mixing bowl, combine the kosher salt, brown sugar, and Traeger rub.

4. Pour half into a shallow plate, or baking dish. Put the salmon fillet, skin-side down, on top of the cure. Generously sprinkle the top with the remaining cure, cover with plastic wrap, and refrigerate for 1 to 1-1/2 hours. Any longer, and the fish will get too salty.

5. Remove the salmon from the cure and pat dry with paper towels. Sprinkle the black pepper on top of the fillet.

6. Supply your smoker with wood pellets and follow the start-up procedure. Preheat the grill, with the lid closed, to 200° F.

7. Lay the salmon skin-side down on the grill grate. Cook for 1 hour, or until the internal temperature in the thickest part of the fish reaches 150 or the fish flakes easily when pressed with a finger or fork. Grill: 200 °F Probe: 150 °F

8. Let cool slightly. Turn the fillet over and remove the skin; it should come off in one piece.

9. If not serving immediately, let the salmon cool completely, then wrap in plastic wrap and refrigerate for up to 2 days. Transfer to a platter and serve with some or all of the suggested accompaniments. Enjoy!

Grilled Lobster Tails With Smoked Paprika Butter

Servings: 4

Cooking Time: 10-12 Minutes

Ingredients:

- 4 lobster tails, each about 8 to 10oz (225 to 285g), thawed if frozen
- 3 lemons, 1 quartered lengthwise, 2 halved through their equators
- for the butter
- 1¼ cup unsalted butter, at room temperature
- 2 garlic cloves, peeled and finely minced
- 3 tbsp chopped fresh parsley
- 2 tbsp chopped fresh chives
- 1 tbsp freshly squeezed lemon juice
- 2 tsp finely chopped lemon zest
- 2 tsp smoked paprika
- 1 tsp coarse salt

Directions:

1. Supply your smoker with wood pellets and follow the start-up procedure. Preheat the grill, with the lid closed, to 450° F.

2. In a medium bowl, make the paprika butter by combining the ingredients. Beat with a wooden spoon until well blended.

3. Use a sharp, heavy knife or sturdy kitchen shears to cut lengthwise through the top shell of each lobster tail in a straight line toward the tail fin. Gently loosen the meat from the bottom shell and sides. Lift the meat through the slit you just made so the meat sits on top of the shell. Slip a lemon quarter underneath the meat (between the meat and the bottom shell) to keep it elevated. Spread 1 tablespoon of paprika butter on top of each lobster. Melt the remaining butter and keep it warm.

4. Place the lobster tails flesh side up and lemon halves cut sides down on the grate. Grill the lobsters until the flesh is white and opaque and the internal temperature of the lobster meat reaches 135 to 140°F (57 to 60°C), about 10 to 12 minutes, basting at least once with some of the melted butter. (Don't overcook or the lobster will become unpleasantly rubbery.)

5. Transfer the lobsters and the lemon halves to a platter. Divide the remaining melted butter between 4 ramekins before serving.

Smoked Mango Shrimp

Servings: 4

Cooking Time: 5 Minutes

Ingredients:

- 2 Tablespoon Olive Oil
- 1 Pound Raw Tail-On, Thawed And Deveined Shrimp, Uncooked

Directions:

1. Supply your smoker with wood pellets and follow the start-up procedure. Preheat the grill, with the lid closed, to 425° F. Rinse shrimp off in sink with cold water. Place in bowl and season generously with Mango Magic seasoning and olive oil. Toss well in bowl.

2. Thread several shrimp onto a skewer, so that they are all just touching each other. Repeat with other skewers and remaining shrimp.

3. Grill shrimp for 2 - 3 minutes on each side, or until pink and opaque all the way through. Remove from grill and serve immediately.

Cold-smoked Salmon Gravlax

Servings: 6

Cooking Time: 30 Minutes

Ingredients:

- 1 Cup kosher salt
- 1 Cup sugar
- 1 Tablespoon freshly ground black pepper
- 2 Pound Sushi-Grad Salmon Fillet, Skin-on, Pin Bones Removed
- 2 Bunch Dill Weed, fresh
- capers, drained
- red onion, sliced
- cream cheese
- lemons

Directions:

1. In a bowl stir together the salt, sugar and black pepper until thoroughly combined. On a work surface,

turn salmon skin side up and sprinkle about half of salt mixture all over and rub in.

2.   Arrange half the dill on the bottom of a baking dish large enough to hold the salmon. Set salmon skin side down on bed of dill.

3.   Rub remaining salt mixture all over top and sides of salmon, then top with remaining dill. Cover with plastic, then top with a weight on a smaller baking dish or a plate with cans of beans on top, then place in refrigerator and allow to cure for 2 days.

4.   Remove salmon from refrigerator, rinse under cold water and pat dry with paper towels. Allow to sit at room temperature on the counter for 1 hour

5.   Supply your smoker with wood pellets and follow the start-up procedure. Preheat the grill, with the lid closed, to 180° F. Place salmon onto a baking pan. Fill another baking pan with ice and place baking pan with salmon over ice. Place onto grill and smoke for 30 minutes.

6.   Remove from grill and slice thin. Serve with capers, red onion, dill, cream cheese, and lemon. Enjoy!

Grilled Tilapia With Blistered Cherry Tomatoes

Servings: 4
Cooking Time: 15 Minutes

Ingredients:

- 1½lb (680g) tilapia fillets or other mild white fish fillets
- chopped fresh curly or flat-leaf parsley
- for the marinade
- ½ cup extra virgin olive oil
- 1 garlic clove, peeled and smashed with a chef's knife
- 3 tbsp freshly squeezed lemon juice
- 1 tsp smoked paprika
- ½ tsp coarse salt
- ¼ tsp freshly ground black pepper
- for the tomatoes
- 2 tbsp extra virgin olive oil
- 2 pints (1 liter) cherry tomatoes (red, yellow, or heirloom varieties)
- coarse salt
- freshly ground black pepper

Directions:

1.   Place a cast iron skillet on the grate. Supply your smoker with wood pellets and follow the start-up procedure. Preheat the grill, with the lid closed, to 400° F.

2.   In a jar with a tight-fitting lid, make the marinade by combining the ingredients. Shake the jar vigorously to emulsify the ingredients.

3.   Place the fillets in a single layer in a nonreactive baking dish. Pour half the marinade over them and turn the fillets to thoroughly coat. Cover with plastic wrap and refrigerate for 15 minutes. (Refrigerate no more than 30 minutes or the acid in the marinade will begin to cook the fish.)

4.   Place the olive oil in the skillet. Add the tomatoes and season with salt and pepper. Stir to coat. Cook the tomatoes until they begin to blister and collapse, about 5 minutes, stirring once or twice. Remove the skillet from the grill and transfer the tomatoes to a bowl.

5.   Carefully lift each fish fillet from the marinade and let the excess drip off. Place the fillets on the grate at a slight angle to the bars. Lightly season with salt and pepper. Grill until the fish flakes easily when pressed with a fork, about 4 to 5 minutes per side, turning carefully with a thin-bladed spatula.

6.   Transfer the fillets to a warmed platter. Top with some of the tomatoes. (Place the remaining tomatoes in a serving bowl.) Scatter the parsley around the platter. Drizzle some of the remaining marinade over the top. Serve immediately.

Grilled Salmon Steaks With Dill Sauce

Servings: 4
Cooking Time: 8 Minutes

Ingredients:

- 4 salmon steaks, each about 6 to 8oz (170 to 225g) and 1 inch (2.5cm) thick
- extra virgin olive oil
- coarse salt
- freshly ground rainbow peppercorns or freshly ground black pepper

* lemon wedges
* for the sauce
* 1 cup reduced-fat mayo
* ⅓ cup light sour cream
* ¼ cup chopped fresh dill
* 2 tbsp freshly squeezed lemon juice
* coarse salt
* freshly ground black pepper
* sprigs of fresh dill

Directions:

1. Supply your smoker with wood pellets and follow the start-up procedure. Preheat the grill, with the lid closed, to 450° F.

2. In a small bowl, make the dill sauce by combining the mayo, sour cream, dill, and lemon juice. Mix until smooth. Season with salt and pepper to taste. Transfer to a serving bowl. Scatter the dill sprigs over the top. Cover and refrigerate until ready to serve.

3. Brush the salmon with olive oil and season with salt and pepper. Place the salmon on the grate at an angle to the bars. Grill until grill marks begin to appear, about 4 minutes. Use a thin-bladed spatula to turn the salmon. Grill until the internal temperature reaches 140°F (60°C), about 4 minutes more.

4. Transfer the salmon to a platter. Serve immediately with the lemon wedges and dill sauce.

Traeger Baked Rainbow Trout

Servings: 2
Cooking Time: 20 Minutes

Ingredients:

* 2 Tablespoon olive oil, divided
* 2 Whole rainbow trout, gutted and cleaned, heads and tails still on
* 1/2 Teaspoon fresh dill
* 1/2 Teaspoon fresh thyme
* 1 Teaspoon Jacobsen Salt Co. Pure Kosher Sea Salt
* 1/2 Large onion, sliced
* 1 Large lemon, thinly sliced
* 1 Teaspoon freshly ground black pepper

Directions:

1. Supply your smoker with wood pellets and follow the start-up procedure. Preheat the grill, with the lid closed, to 400° F.

2. Grease a 9x13 inch baking dish with 1 tablespoon olive oil.

3. Place trout in the prepared baking dish and coat fish with remaining olive oil. Season the inside and outside of fish with dill, thyme and salt. Stuff each fish with onion and lemon slices then grind pepper over the top. Place 1 lemon slice on each fish.

4. Bake in the Traeger for 10 minutes. Add 2 tablespoons hot water to the baking dish. Continue baking until fish flakes easily with a fork, about 10 more minutes. Enjoy! Grill: 400 °F

Smoked Cedar Plank Salmon

Servings: 4
Cooking Time: 20 Minutes

Ingredients:

* 1/4 Cup Brown Sugar
* 1/2 Tablespoon Olive Oil
* Competition Smoked Seasoning
* 4 Salmon Fillets, Skin Off

Directions:

1. Soak the untreated cedar plank in water for 24 hours before grilling. When ready to grill, remove and wipe down.

2. Supply your smoker with wood pellets and follow the start-up procedure. Preheat the grill, with the lid closed, to 350° F.

3. In a small bowl, mix the brown sugar, oil, and Lemon Pepper, Garlic, and Herb seasoning. Rub generously over the salmon fillets.

4. Place the plank over indirect heat, then lay the salmon on the plank and grill for 15-20 minutes, or until the salmon is cooked through and flakes easily with a fork. Remove from the heat and serve immediately.

Grilled Fresh Fish

Servings: 2
Cooking Time: 15 Minutes

Ingredients:

- 1 Whole fillet of firm white fish: sea bass, halibut or cod
- Fin & Feather Rub
- 2 Whole lemons

Directions:

1. Supply your smoker with wood pellets and follow the start-up procedure. Preheat the grill, with the lid closed, to 325° F.
2. Season fish with Traeger Fin & Feather Rub and let sit for 30 minutes. Slice lemons in half.
3. Place the fish and the lemons (cut side down) directly on the grill grates. Cook for 10 to 15 minutes until the fish is flaky and is at least 145°F in the thickest part of fish. Be careful not to over cook.
4. Serve with the grilled lemons. Enjoy!

Oysters Margarita

Servings: 4
Cooking Time: 10minutes

Ingredients:

- 24 fresh oysters in the shell
- 4oz (120ml) freshly squeezed lime juice
- 2oz (60ml) tequila
- 2oz (60ml) orange liqueur, such as triple sec
- 6 tbsp cold butter, cut into 24 cubes
- crunchy salt, such as margarita rimming salt
- lime wedges
- hot sauce (optional)

Directions:

1. Supply your smoker with wood pellets and follow the start-up procedure. Preheat the grill, with the lid closed, to 450° F.
2. Carefully shuck each oyster to remove the top shell. Run your shucking knife under the oyster to release it from the bottom shell, but don't spill the juices. Discard the top shells, but keep the oysters in the bottom shells. Balance each oyster on a wire rack placed on a rimmed sheet pan.
3. Place 1 teaspoon of lime juice, ½ teaspoon of tequila, ½ teaspoon of orange liqueur, and 1 cube of butter on each oyster.
4. Place the pan on the grate and smoke until the butter has melted and the juices are bubbling, about 8 to 10 minutes. (The oysters should be just barely cooked.)
5. Remove the pan from the grill. Sprinkle a pinch of salt on each oyster. Serve immediately with lime wedges and hot sauce (if using).

Grilled Salmon

Servings: 4
Cooking Time: 25 Minutes

Ingredients:

- 1 (2-pound) half salmon fillet
- 3 tablespoons mayonnaise
- 1 batch Dill Seafood Rub

Directions:

1. Supply your smoker with wood pellets and follow the start-up procedure. Preheat the grill, with the lid closed, to 325°F.
2. Using your hands, rub the salmon fillet all over with the mayonnaise and sprinkle it with the rub.
3. Place the salmon directly on the grill grate, skin-side down, and grill until its internal temperature reaches 145°F. Remove the salmon from the grill and serve immediately.

Garlic Pepper Shrimp Pesto Bruschetta

Servings: 12
Cooking Time: 15 Minutes

Ingredients:

- 12 Slices Bread, Baguette
- 1/2 Tsp Chili Pepper Flakes
- 1/2 Tsp Garlic Powder
- 4 Cloves Garlic, Minced
- 2 Tbsp Olive Oil
- 1/2 Tsp Paprika, Smoked

- 1/4 Tsp Parsley, Leaves
- Pepper
- Pesto
- Salt
- 12 Shrimp, Jumbo

Directions:

1. Supply your smoker with wood pellets and follow the start-up procedure. Preheat the grill, with the lid closed, to 350° F. Place the baguette slices on a baking sheet lined with foil. Stir together the olive oil, and minced garlic, then brush both sides of the baguette slices with the mix. Place the pan inside the grill, and bake for about 10-15 minutes.

2. In a skillet, add a splash of olive oil, shrimp, chili powder, garlic powder, smoked paprika, salt pepper, and grill on medium-high heat for about 5 minutes (until the shrimp is pink). Be sure to stir often. Once pink, remove pan from heat. Once the baguettes are toasted, let them cool for 5 minutes, then spread a layer of pesto onto each one, then top with a shrimp, and serve.

Grilled Mussels With Lemon Butter

Servings: 4
Cooking Time: 15 Minutes

Ingredients:

- 2 Pound Mussels, debearded, washed
- 5 Quart water
- 1/3 Cup salt
- 2 Clove garlic, minced
- 1/3 Cup white wine
- 1 Whole lemon juice
- 3 Tablespoon parsley, chopped
- 1 loaf French country bread

Directions:

1. Supply your smoker with wood pellets and follow the start-up procedure. Preheat the grill, with the lid closed, to 375° F.

2. Scrub mussels well in running water making sure to remove all dirt and barnacles.

3. Place clean mussels in a large bowl with 5 quarts (5 L) water and 1/3 cup (91 g) of salt for about 15 minutes.

4. Drain, rinse and repeat soaking method two more times to purge and remove all sand.

5. Melt butter in a saute pan over medium high heat. Add garlic and cook for 1 minute until fragrant. Add wine and bring to a simmer. Add mussels and lemon juice to the pan and toss to coat.

6. Cover with a tight fitting lid and transfer to the grill. Let the mussels steam 8-10 minutes. Remove from the grill and discard any unopened mussels.

7. Sprinkle with chopped parsley and transfer to a serving dish. Serve with sliced bread. Enjoy!

Grilled Maple Syrup Salmon

Servings: 6
Cooking Time: 30 Minutes

Ingredients:

- 1 large salmon fillet (around 3 pounds)
- 1/2 cup salted butter (melted)
- 2 tablespoons soy sauce
- Salt and pepper
- 1/4 cup maple syrup

Directions:

1. Supply your smoker with wood pellets and follow the start-up procedure. Preheat the grill, with the lid closed, to 400° F.

2. Place the salmon fillet in a baking pan lined with parchment paper.

3. Sprinkle the fish with salt and pepper.

4. Add half of the melted butter to the salmon and place the baking pan on the grill.

5. Grill for 15-20 minutes or until fish is roughly 70% cooked. It will feel still gelatinous in the thickest parts of the salmon.

6. Combine the remaining melted butter, soy sauce, and maple syrup and pour over the salmon.It will run off the sides so use a spoon to pour it back over the fish. It's also perfectly fine that some will be left on the sides of the pan.

7. Cook for 5 to 10 additional minutes or until the fish is cooked through. The fish should be firm to the touch but still moist and soft when pressed on,and the ridges will flake or pull apart if pressed on.

Spicy Crab Poppers

Servings: 8
Cooking Time: 30 Minutes

Ingredients:
- 18 Whole jalapeño
- 8 Ounce cream cheese, softened
- 1 Cup Canned Corn, drained
- 1/2 Cup Crab meat, lump
- 1 1/4 Teaspoon Old Bay Seasoning
- 2 Scallions, minced

Directions:
1. Cut each jalapeño in half lengthwise through the stem and remove the ribs and seeds.
2. Filling: In a mixing bowl, combine the cream cheese, corn, crab meat, scallions, and Old Bay Seasoning and stir until blended. Stir in the scallions. Spoon the filling into the jalapeño halves, mounding it slightly.
3. Arrange the poppers on a baking sheet covered with foil or parchment paper.
4. Supply your smoker with wood pellets and follow the start-up procedure. Preheat the grill, with the lid closed, to 350° F.
5. Roast the jalapeños for 25 to 30 minutes, or until the peppers have softened and the filling is hot and bubbling.
6. Let cool slightly before serving. Enjoy!

Grilled Garlic Lobster Tails

Servings: 2
Cooking Time: 11 Minutes

Ingredients:
- 4 Lobster Tails (8 oz Each)
- 3 Sticks Unsalted Butter
- 4 Cloves Garlic Minced
- ½ Cup Fresh Parsley Chopped
- Juice of 1 Lemon
- 2 Tablespoons Fresh Lemon Zest
- 2 Teaspoons Crushed Red Pepper
- ¼ Cup Olive Oil
- 1 TBS Kosher Salt
- 1 TBS Cracked Black Pepper

Directions:

1. Supply your smoker with wood pellets and follow the start-up procedure. Preheat the grill, with the lid closed, to 375° F.
2. Split lobster tails in half lengthwise and season with salt, pepper, and olive oil.
3. Place butter in an aluminum pan and put the pan on the hot side of the grill to melt the butter.
4. Add garlic, parsley, lemon zest, lemon juice, and red pepper to butter and simmer for 5 minutes.
5. Place lobster tails meat side down on the grill and cook for 6 minutes. Baste the shell side with the butter mixture.
6. Dunk each tail in the butter mixture and then transfer to the grill, shell side down. Baste meat again with butter mixture.
7. Cook for an additional 5 minutes or until the lobster meat turns opaque and shells are bright pink.
8. Serve with remaining butter mixture, fresh parsley, and lemon wedges.

Smoked Sugar Halibut

Servings: 8
Cooking Time: 120 Minutes

Ingredients:
- 1/4 cup granulated sugar
- 1/4 cup brown sugar
- 1/2 cup kosher salt
- 1 tsp ground coriander
- 2 lbs fresh halibut

Directions:
1. In a small bowl, mix the sugars, salt, and coriander together. Season the halibut on all sides.
2. Wrap the halibut in plastic wrap, place on a rimmed sheet pan, and brine in the fridge for 3 hours.
3. Remove the plastic wrap and rinse the fish. Pat it dry. Set it on a drying rack over a sheet pan for 1-2 hours in the fridge.
4. Supply your smoker with wood pellets and follow the start-up procedure. Preheat the grill, with the lid closed, to 200° F. Smoke the fish for 2 hours or until its internal temperature reaches 140 °F.
5. Serve your preferred sauce with the fish.

Grilled Oysters With Mignonette

Servings: 2

Cooking Time: 15 Minutes

Ingredients:

- 4 Cup rock salt
- 18 Large oysters
- 4 Tablespoon unsalted butter
- 2 Clove garlic, minced
- kosher salt
- 12 Medium lemon wedges, for serving
- 2 Tablespoon minced shallot
- 1/4 Cup red wine vinegar
- 1/2 Teaspoon freshly ground black pepper

Directions:

1. Choose a shallow serving platter that will hold all of the oysters. Pour the rock salt onto the platter to create a 1/2 inch base. This will steady the oysters for serving.

2. To prepare the oysters, check to ensure they are completely closed. Discard oysters that are not. Wash and lightly scrub the oysters to ensure there is no grit on the surface. This will prevent the grit from entering the oyster once shucked.

3. Using a thick glove or kitchen towel, sturdy the oyster in the hand opposite of the one holding the knife. Using an oyster knife or very sturdy paring knife, locate the "hinge" on each oyster. Place the point of the knife in the hinge, and wiggle the tip of the knife into the oyster until it feels sturdy. Firmly turn the knife to apply a torquing pressure to gently open the oyster.

4. Remove the top shell of the oyster. Using the tip of the knife, loosen the oyster from its shell, leaving the juices intact. Place each loosened oyster on its half shell on a baking sheet.

5. Supply your smoker with wood pellets and follow the start-up procedure. Preheat the grill, with the lid closed, to 450° F.

6. In a small saucepan, melt the butter over medium-low heat. Add the garlic and a generous pinch of salt, and cook until fragrant but not burned, about 1 minute. Remove from the heat. Grill: 450 °F

7. For the Mignonette: Combine the minced shallot, red wine vinegar and 1/2 teaspoon freshly ground black pepper. Set aside.

8. Spoon 1 teaspoon of the garlic butter sauce onto each oyster in its half shell. Carefully place each oyster directly on the grill grates, ensuring they don't slip. Close the lid and allow them to cook for 3 to 4 minutes, until the edges of the oysters have pulled away from the shell. Remove carefully with tongs to keep the juices and butter in the shells. Place directly on the rock salt to balance them. Serve immediately with the mignonette and lemon wedges to squeeze onto the oysters. Enjoy!

Bacon Wrapped Scallops

Servings: 8

Cooking Time: 20 Minutes

Ingredients:

- 24 jumbo deep sea diver scallops, dry-packed
- 1/2 Cup butter
- salt
- freshly ground black pepper
- 1 Clove garlic, minced
- 12 Slices thin-cut bacon, cut in half crosswise
- lemon wedges, for serving

Directions:

1. Remove the small, crescent-shaped muscle from the side of each scallop, if still attached. Dry the scallops thoroughly on paper towels, then transfer to a medium bowl.

2. Melt butter in a small saucepan, add garlic and cook for 1 minute. Let cool slightly then pour over the scallops. Season with salt and pepper and gently toss to coat.

3. Wrap a piece of bacon around each scallop and secure with a toothpick.

4. Supply your smoker with wood pellets and follow the start-up procedure. Preheat the grill, with the lid closed, to 400° F.

5. Arrange the scallops directly on the grill grate. Grill for 15 to 20 minutes, or until the scallop is opaque and the bacon has begun to crisp. If desired, you can turn the scallops on their side, bacon-side down, turning occasionally to crisp the bacon. Do not overcook. Grill: 400 °F

6. Transfer the scallops to a platter and serve with lemon wedges.

Smoked Salmon Candy

Servings: 4
Cooking Time: 180 Minutes

Ingredients:

- 2 Cup gin
- 1 Cup dark brown sugar
- 1/2 Cup kosher salt
- 1 Cup maple syrup
- 1 Tablespoon black pepper
- 3 Pound salmon
- vegetable oil
- dark brown sugar

Directions:

1. In a large bowl, combine all ingredients for the cure.
2. Cut the salmon into 2 ounce pieces and place in the cure.
3. Cover and refrigerate overnight.
4. Supply your smoker with wood pellets and follow the start-up procedure. Preheat the grill, with the lid closed, to 180° F.
5. Spray foil with vegetable oil. Place salmon on foil and sprinkle with additional brown sugar.
6. Place foil directly on the grill grate. Close the lid and smoke the salmon for 3 to 4 hours or until fully cooked. Grill: 180 °F
7. Serve hot or chilled. Enjoy!

Lemon Shrimp Scampi

Servings: 3
Cooking Time: 10 Minutes

Ingredients:

- 2 Tsp Blackened Sriracha Rub Seasoning
- 1/2 Cup Butter, Cubed, Divided
- 1/2 Tsp Chili Pepper Flakes
- 3 Garlic Cloves, Minced
- To Taste, Lemon Wedges, For Serving
- 1 Lemon, Juice & Zest
- Linguine, Cooked
- 3 Tbsp Parsley, Chopped
- 1 1/2 Lbs Shrimp, Peeled & Deveined
- Toasted Baguette, For Serving

Directions:

1. Supply your smoker with wood pellets and follow the start-up procedure. Preheat the grill, with the lid closed, to medium-high heat. If using a gas or charcoal grill, set it up for medium-high heat.
2. Add half of the butter to the griddle, then sauté the garlic, Blackened Sriracha, and chili flakes for 1 minute, until fragrant.
3. Add the shrimp, turning occasionally for 2 minutes, until opaque.
4. Add the remaining butter, parsley, lemon zest and juice. Toss the shrimp to coat in lemon butter, then remove from the griddle, and transfer to a serving bowl.
5. Serve immediately, with fresh lemon wedges, and toasted baguette. Serve over linguine, spaghetti or zucchini noodles, if desired.

Spicy Lime Shrimp

Servings: 4
Cooking Time: 10 Minutes

Ingredients:

- 2 Tsp Chili Paste
- 1/2 Tsp Cumin
- 2 Cloves Garlic, Minced
- 1 Large Lime, Juiced
- 1/4 Tsp Paprika, Powder
- 1/4 Tsp Red Flakes Pepper
- 1/2 Tsp Salt

Directions:

1. In a bowl, whisk together the lime juice, olive oil, garlic, chili powder, cumin, paprika, salt, pepper, and red pepper flakes.
2. Then pour it into a resealable bag, add the shrimp, toss the coat, let it marinate for 30 minutes.
3. Supply your smoker with wood pellets and follow the start-up procedure. Preheat the grill, with the lid closed, to 400° F.
4. Next place the shrimp on skewers, place on the grill, and grill each side for about two minutes until it's done. One finished, remove the shrimp from the grill and enjoy!

Garlic Bacon Wrapped Shrimp

Servings: 4

Cooking Time: 11 Minutes

Ingredients:

- 8 Bacon, Strip
- 1/4 Cup Butter Style Shortening (Melted)
- 1 Clove Garlic, Minced
- 1 Tsp Lemon, Juice
- Pepper
- Salt
- 16 (Peeled And Veined) Shrimp, Jumbo

Directions:

1. Supply your smoker with wood pellets and follow the start-up procedure. Preheat the grill, with the lid closed, to 450° F.

2. Take one slice of bacon, and wrap it around each piece of shrimp, and lock it in place with a wooden toothpick.

3. Place the shortening into a mixing bowl and whisk in the garlic and lemon juice. Brush each shrimp with the sauce on both sides.

4. Place on the grill, and barbecue for 11 minutes.

5. Turn the grill off, remove the shrimp, serve and enjoy!

Lemon Lobster Rolls

Servings: 4

Cooking Time: 35 Minutes

Ingredients:

- 1/2 Cup Butter
- 4 Hot Dog Bun(S)
- 1 Lemon, Whole
- 4 Lobster, Tail
- 1/4 Cup Mayo
- Pepper

Directions:

1. Supply your smoker with wood pellets and follow the start-up procedure. Preheat the grill, with the lid closed, to 300° F.

2. Using kitchen shears, cut the shell of the tail and crack in half so that the meat is exposed. Pour in butter and season with pepper. Place the tails meat side up on the grill and cook until the shell has turned red and the meat is white, about 35 minutes.

3. Remove from the grill and separate the shell from the meat. Place the meat in a bowl with mayo, lemon juice and rind and season with pepper. Stir to combine and evenly distribute into the hot dog buns.

Bbq Oysters

Servings: 4

Cooking Time: 6 Minutes

Ingredients:

- 1 Pound unsalted butter, softened
- 1 Tablespoon Meat Church Holy Gospel BBQ Rub
- 1 Bunch green onions, chopped
- 2 Clove garlic, minced
- 12 oysters
- 1/4 Cup seasoned breadcrumbs
- 8 Ounce shredded pepper jack cheese
- Sweet & Heat BBQ Sauce
- 1/2 Bunch green onions, minced

Directions:

1. Supply your smoker with wood pellets and follow the start-up procedure. Preheat the grill, with the lid closed, to 375° F.

2. For the compound butter: Combine butter, garlic, onion and Meat Church Rub thoroughly.

3. Lay the butter on parchment paper or plastic wrap. Roll it up to form a log and tie each end with butcher's twine. Place in the freezer for an hour to solidify. You can use this butter on any grilled meat to enhance the flavor. You can also use a high-quality butter to replace the compound butter.

4. Shuck the oysters, keeping all of the juice in the shell. Sprinkle the oysters with breadcrumbs and place directly on the Traeger. Cook them for 5 minutes. You will be looking for the edge of the oyster to start to curl slightly.

5. After 5 minutes, place a spoonful of compound butter in the oysters. After the butter melts, add a pinch of pepper jack cheese.

6. Remove the oysters after 6 minutes on the grill total. Top oysters with a squirt of Traeger Sweet & Heat BBQ Sauce and a few chopped onions. Allow to cool for 5 minutes, then enjoy!

Mexican Mahi Mahi With Baja Cabbage Slaw

Servings: 4
Cooking Time: 10 Minutes

Ingredients:

- 1½lb (680g) skinless mahi mahi, cod, or other firm white fish fillets
- coarse salt
- freshly ground black pepper
- chili powder
- lime wedges
- for the slaw
- 2 cups finely shredded green cabbage
- 2 cups finely shredded purple cabbage
- 4 tbsp reduced-fat mayo
- 2 tsp hot sauce, plus more
- 2 tsp freshly squeezed lime juice
- ½ tsp coarse salt
- for the marinade
- ¼ cup freshly squeezed orange juice
- ¼ cup freshly squeezed lime juice
- 2 tbsp extra virgin olive oil

Directions:

1. In a medium bowl, make the slaw by combining the ingredients. Stir well. Transfer to a serving bowl. Cover and refrigerate until ready to serve.
2. Place the fish fillets in a baking dish and pour the orange and lime juices and olive oil over them. Turn the fillets to coat thoroughly. Cover and refrigerate for 15 to 20 minutes.
3. Supply your smoker with wood pellets and follow the start-up procedure. Preheat the grill, with the lid closed, to 450° F.
4. Drain the fish and pat dry with paper towels. (Discard the marinade.) Season the fillets on both sides with salt and pepper and chili powder. Place the fillets on the grate and grill until golden brown, about 4 to 5 minutes per side, turning with a thin-bladed spatula.
5. Transfer the fish to a platter. Serve with the slaw and lime wedges.

Baked Whole Fish In Sea Salt

Servings: 4
Cooking Time: 30 Minutes

Ingredients:

- 3 Pound Whole Branzino, (1.5 each)
- 10 Sprig thyme sprigs
- 1 Medium lemon, thinly sliced
- 5 Cup sea salt
- 10 Whole egg white
- olive oil
- 1 Whole lemon juice

Directions:

1. Supply your smoker with wood pellets and follow the start-up procedure. Preheat the grill, with the lid closed, to High heat.
2. Clip the fins and remove the gills from the fish. Stuff cavity with thyme and lemon slices. Whip the egg whites to soft peaks and fold in the sea salt.
3. Place directly on the grill grate and bake for 30 minutes or until a thermometer poked through the salt crust and into the flesh of the fish registers an internal temperature of 135-140 degrees F. Remove fish from the grill and let stand 10 minutes.
4. Using a wooden spoon, strike the crust to crack it open and brush remaining salt from the surface of the fish.
5. Remove the skin and drizzle fish with good olive oil and a squeeze of lemon. Enjoy!

Kimi's Simple Grilled Fresh Fish

Servings: 2
Cooking Time: 45 Minutes

Ingredients:

- 1 Cup soy sauce
- 1/3 Cup extra-virgin olive oil
- 1 Tablespoon garlic, minced
- 2 lemons, juiced
- fresh basil
- 4 Pound Fresh Fish, cut into portion-sized pieces

Directions:

1.   Mix all ingredients to create sauce and cover fish in marinade for 45 minutes.

2.   Supply your smoker with wood pellets and follow the start-up procedure. Preheat the grill, with the lid closed, to 140° F. Grill the marinated fish on the grill until it reaches an internal temperature of 140-145°F. Serve immediately, enjoy! Grill: 350 °F Probe: 145 °F

Peper Fish Tacos

Servings: 12
Cooking Time: 10 Minutes

Ingredients:

- 1 Tsp Black Pepper
- 1/4 Tsp Cayenne Pepper
- 1 1/2 Lbs Cod Fish
- 1/2 Tsp Cumin
- 1 Tsp Garlic Powder
- 1 Tsp Oregano
- 1 1/2 Tsp Paprika, Smoked
- 1/2 Tsp Salt

Directions:

1.   Supply your smoker with wood pellets and follow the start-up procedure. Preheat the grill, with the lid closed, to 350° F.

2.   Mix together paprika, garlic powder, oregano, cumin, cayenne, salt and pepper. Sprinkle over cod.

3.   Place the cod on your preheated for about 5 minutes per side. Toast tortillas over heat, if desired.

4.   Break the cod into pieces, smash the avocado, slice the tomatoes in half and place evenly among the tortillas. Top with red onion, lettuce, jalapenos, sour cream, and cilantro. Spritz with lime juice and enjoy!

Wood-fired Halibut

Servings: 4
Cooking Time: 20 Minutes

Ingredients:

- 1 pound halibut fillet
- 1 batch Dill Seafood Rub

Directions:

1.   Supply your smoker with wood pellets and follow the start-up procedure. Preheat the grill, with the lid closed, to 325°F.

2.   Sprinkle the halibut fillet on all sides with the rub. Using your hands, work the rub into the meat.

3.   Place the halibut directly on the grill grate and grill until its internal temperature reaches 145°F. Remove the halibut from the grill and serve immediately.

Mango Rice Wine Thai Shrimp

Servings: 4
Cooking Time: 15 Minutes

Ingredients:

- 2 Tablespoons Brown Sugar
- 2 Tablespoons Mango Magic Seasoning
- 1 Pinch (Optional) Red Pepper Flakes
- 1/2 Tablespoons Rice Wine Vinegar
- 1 Pound Raw Tail-On, Thaw And Deveined Shrimp, Uncooked
- 2 Tablespoons Soy Sauce
- 1 Teaspoon Sriracha Hot Sauce
- 1/2 Cup Sweet Chili Sauce

Directions:

1.   Supply your smoker with wood pellets and follow the start-up procedure. Preheat the grill, with the lid closed, to 425° F. Rinse shrimp off in sink with cold water. Place in bowl and put in all of the ingredients listed above. Let marinade for 2 - 4 hours.

2.   Thread several shrimp onto a skewer, so that they are all just touching each other. Repeat with other skewers and remaining shrimp.

3.   Grill shrimp for 2 - 3 minutes on each side, or until pink and opaque all the way through. Remove from grill and serve immediately.

Teriyaki Smoked Honey Tilapia

Servings: 4
Cooking Time: 120 Minutes

Ingredients:

- 4 tilapia fillets
- 1 cup teriyaki sauce
- 2/3 cup honey

- 1 tbsp sriracha sauce
- Green onions (optional)

Directions:

1. In a large bowl, make the marinade by mixing together the teriyaki sauce, honey,and sriracha. Make sure honey is dissolved and well blended.

2. Place the tilapia fillets in the marinade. Turn the fillets so they are completely coated. Cover with a plastic wrap and marinate in the fridge for about 2 hours.

3. Supply your smoker with wood pellets and follow the start-up procedure. Preheat the grill, with the lid closed, to 275° F.

4. Remove the tilapia fillets from the marinade and transfer them to the grill. Smoke the fillets until they reach an internal temperature of 145°F, about 2 hours.

5. Sprinkle with green onions if desired.

Cajun-blackened Shrimp

Servings: 4
Cooking Time: 20 Minutes

Ingredients:

- 1 pound peeled and deveined shrimp, with tails on
- 1 batch Cajun Rub
- 8 tablespoons (1 stick) butter
- ¼ cup Worcestershire sauce

Directions:

1. Supply your smoker with wood pellets and follow the start-up procedure. Preheat the grill, with the lid closed, to 450°F and place a cast-iron skillet on the grill grate. Wait about 10 minutes after your grill has reached temperature, allowing the skillet to get hot.

2. Meanwhile, season the shrimp all over with the rub.

3. When the skillet is hot, place the butter in it to melt. Once the butter melts, stir in the Worcestershire sauce.

4. Add the shrimp and gently stir to coat. Smoke-braise the shrimp for about 10 minutes per side, until opaque and cooked through. Remove the shrimp from the grill and serve immediately.

Grilled Lemon Shrimp Scampi

Servings: 4
Cooking Time: 6 Minutes

Ingredients:

- 1 ½ pounds medium shrimp, peeled and deveined
- ¼ cup olive oil
- ¼ cup lemon juice
- 3 tablespoons chopped fresh parsley
- 1 tablespoon minced garlic
- ground black pepper to taste
- ¼ teaspoon crushed red pepper flakes to taste

Directions:

1. In a large, non-reactive bowl, stir together the olive oil, lemon juice, parsley, garlic, and black pepper. Season with crushed red pepper, if desired. Add shrimp, and toss to coat. Marinate in the refrigerator for 30 minutes.

2. Supply your smoker with wood pellets and follow the start-up procedure. Preheat the grill, with the lid closed, to high heat.

3. Thread shrimp onto skewers, piercing once near the tail and once near the head. Discard any remaining marinade.

4. Lightly oil grill grate. Place the shrimp skewers on the grill grates.

5. Grill for 2 to 3 minutes per side, or until opaque.

Planked Trout With Fennel, Bacon & Orange

Servings: 4
Cooking Time: 40minutes

Ingredients:

- 4 whole trout, each about 14 to 16oz (400 to 450g), cleaned and gutted, fins removed
- coarse salt
- freshly ground black pepper
- for the filling
- 1 large navel orange
- 4 slices of thick-cut bacon, diced
- 1 large fennel bulb, trimmed, halved, decored, and diced, green fronds reserved
- 4oz (110g) baby spinach, about 6 cups
- coarse salt
- freshly ground black pepper

Directions:

1. Supply your smoker with wood pellets and follow the start-up procedure. Preheat the grill, with the lid closed, to 450° F. Place 4 cedar planks on the grate and allow them to singe slightly on both sides. Remove them from the grill and place them on a heatproof surface to cool.

2. Lower the temperature to 300°F (149°C).

3. Slice 4 thin rounds from the center of the orange and then slice each in half for 8 pieces total. Zest the remainder of the orange and set aside.

4. In a cold skillet on the stovetop over medium heat, sauté the bacon, until the fat has rendered and the bacon is golden brown, about 6 to 8 minutes, stirring frequently. Use a slotted spoon to transfer the bacon to paper towels to drain. Add the fennel to the fat in the skillet and cook until tender crisp, about 5 minutes. Add the spinach and stir until it wilts, about 1 to 2 minutes. Squeeze the juice of one of the reserved orange ends over the mixture. Add the drained bacon. Season with salt and pepper and then stir. Remove the skillet from the stovetop and set aside.

5. Rinse each trout inside and out under cold running water and pat dry with paper towels. Place three 12-inch (30.5cm) pieces of butcher's twine on each plank and place a trout on top. Season the inside of each fish with salt and pepper. Place two half-rounds of orange in each belly, rind side facing out. Top with some of the filling. Tie the trout with the butcher's twine and trim any ends. Repeat with the remaining trout.

6. Place the planks on the grate and cook the trout until they're cooked through, about 30 to 40 minutes.

7. Remove the planks from the grill and remove the twine. Top each trout with a few curls of orange zest and some reserved fennel fronds. Serve the trout on the planks.

Tequila & Lime Shrimp With Smoked Tomato Sauce

Servings: 4
Cooking Time: 6 Minutes

Ingredients:
- 24 to 28 jumbo shrimp, about 2lb (1kg) total, peeled and deveined
- 1 lime, quartered
- Smoked Tomato Sauce
- for the marinade
- ½ cup tequila or mezcal
- juice and zest of 1 lime
- 2 garlic cloves, peeled and roughly chopped
- ½ cup freshly squeezed orange juice
- ¼ cup extra virgin olive oil
- 2 tsp agave, light brown sugar, or low-carb substitute
- 2 tsp Mexican hot sauce, plus more
- 1½ tsp coarse salt
- 1 tsp baking soda
- 1 tsp chili powder
- ½ tsp ground cumin

Directions:

1. In a medium bowl, make the marinade by whisking together the ingredients. Whisk until the salt dissolves. Taste for seasoning, adding more hot sauce if desired.

2. Place the shrimp in a resealable plastic bag and pour the marinade over them, turning the bag several times to coat thoroughly. Refrigerate for 30 minutes.

3. Supply your smoker with wood pellets and follow the start-up procedure. Preheat the grill, with the lid closed, to 450° F.

4. Drain the shrimp and discard the marinade. Pat the shrimp dry with paper towels. Thread the shrimp on 4 bamboo skewers (preferably flat ones). Make sure all the shrimp face the same direction. Finish each skewer with a lime wedge.

5. Place the skewers on the grate and grill until the shrimp are white and opaque, about 2 to 3 minutes per side, turning once. (Don't overcook.)

6. Remove the shrimp from the grill. Serve immediately with the warm tomato sauce.

Smoked Lobster Scampi

Servings: 2
Cooking Time: 30 Minutes

Ingredients:
- 1 Lobster Tail
- 1 Handful Pasta, Angel Hair
- 2 Tablespoon butter

- 1 Teaspoon garlic, minced
- 1/2 Teaspoon lemon juice
- 2 Teaspoon Parmesan cheese, grated
- 2 Tablespoon Sun Dried Tomato Pesto
- fresh parsley

Directions:

1. Supply your smoker with wood pellets and follow the start-up procedure. Preheat the grill, with the lid closed, to 180° F.

2. Use kitchen shears to cut along the top of the lobster on both sides to expose the meat. Place the lobster directly on the grill for 20-25 minutes, depending on the size of the lobster. Grill: 180 °F

3. While lobster smokes, cook pasta according to packaged directions.

4. After 20-25 minutes, take lobster off the grill and remove the meat from the tail. Cut meat into chunks.

5. While the pasta is boiling, melt butter over medium high heat. Once butter starts to brown, add the garlic and lobster chunks. Toss in pan a few times then add lemon and parmesan. Set aside.

6. When pasta has finished, place 1 tbsp of the sun dried tomato pesto on the bottom of a bowl or plate. Top with pasta, then finish with the lobster scampi. Garnish with parsley. Enjoy!

Grilled Blackened Saskatchewan Salmon

Servings: 4
Cooking Time: 30 Minutes

Ingredients:
- 1 salmon fillets
- zesty Italian dressing
- Blackened Saskatchewan Rub
- lemon wedges

Directions:

1. Brush salmon with Italian dressing and season with Traeger Blackened Saskatchewan Rub.

2. Supply your smoker with wood pellets and follow the start-up procedure. Preheat the grill, with the lid closed, to 325° F.

3. Place salmon on the grill and cook for 20 to 30 minutes, until it reaches an internal temperature of 145°F and flakes easily. Remove salmon from grill. Serve with lemon wedges. Enjoy! Grill: 325 °F Probe: 145 °F

Sweet Smoked Salmon Jerky

Servings: 6
Cooking Time: 300 Minutes

Ingredients:
- 2 Quart water
- 3/4 Cup kosher salt
- 1 Cup Morton Tender Quick Home Meat Cure, optional
- 4 Cup dark brown sugar
- 2 Cup maple syrup, divided
- 1 (2-3 lb) wild caught salmon fillet, skinned and pin bones removed

Directions:

1. In a large nonreactive bowl, combine 2 quarts water, salt, curing salt (if using), brown sugar and 1 cup of the maple syrup. Stir with a long-handled spoon to dissolve the salts and sugar.

2. With a sharp, serrated knife, slice the salmon into 1/2 inch thick slices with the short side parallel to you on the cutting board. In other words, make your cuts from the head end to the tail end. (This is considerably easier if the fish is frozen.) Cut each strip crosswise into 4 or 5 inch lengths.

3. Immerse the strips in the brine, weighing down with a plate or a bag of ice. Cover with plastic wrap and refrigerate for 12 hours.

4. Supply your smoker with wood pellets and follow the start-up procedure. Preheat the grill, with the lid closed, to 180° F.

5. Drain the salmon strips and discard the brine. Arrange the salmon strips in a single layer directly on the grill grate. Smoke for several hours (5 to 6), or until the jerky is dry but not rock-hard. You want it to yield when you bite into it. Halfway through the smoking time, mix the remaining cup of maple syrup with 1/4 cup of warm water and brush the salmon strips on all sides with the mixture. Grill: 180 °F

6. Transfer to a resealable bag while the jerky is still warm. Let the jerky rest for an hour at room temperature. Squeeze any air from the bag, and refrigerate the jerky. Enjoy!

Grilled Lemon Lobster Tails

Servings: 3

Cooking Time: 7 Minutes

Ingredients:

- 6 lobster tails
- 1/4 cup melted butter
- 1/4 cup fresh lemon juice
- 1 tablespoon fresh dill
- 1 teaspoon salt
- 6 lime wedges

Directions:

1. Supply your smoker with wood pellets and follow the start-up procedure. Preheat the grill, with the lid closed, to 375° F.

2. Split the lobster tails in half place then back side down.

3. Cut down through the center to the shell the whole length of each tail.

4. Pull the shell back, exposing the meat.

5. Pat the lobster tails with paper towel to dry.

6. Combine in a small mixing bowl the butter, lemon juice, dill, and salt until the salt has dissolved.

7. Brush the mixture onto the flesh side of each lobster tail.

8. Place the lobster tails onto the grill and cook for 5 to 7 minutes, turning them once during the cooking process. (The shells should turn a bright pink).

9. Remove the heat.

10. Serve with lime wedges!

Garlic Grilled Shrimp Skewers

Servings: 3

Cooking Time: 6 Minutes

Ingredients:

- 1 pound large shrimp
- 1/4 cup olive oil
- 1/4 cup fresh cilantro, finely chopped
- 1/4 cup fresh parsley, finely chopped
- 4 cloves garlic, minced
- 1 tablespoon lemon juice
- 1/2 teaspoon salt
- 1/4 teaspoon black pepper
- Pinch cayenne pepper, adjust to spice preference

Directions:

1. Add the olive oil, herbs, and spices to a small mixing bowl and whisk together.

2. Place the shrimp in a bowl and pour 3/4 of the marinade on top of the shrimp. Mix together gently to coat the shrimp evenly.

3. Cover the bowl and marinate the shrimp for 30 minutes to an hour.

4. Thread the shrimp on the skewers and make sure to get all the good garlic and herbs from the bowl and spread on to the shrimp.

5. Supply your smoker with wood pellets and follow the start-up procedure. Preheat the grill, with the lid closed, to medium high heat.

6. Once the grill is hot, arrange the shrimp skewers on the grill and cook for 2-3 minutes per side, or until they turn pink and opaque.

7. Remove the shrimp skewers to a plate and spoon the remaining marinade on top before serving.

Roasted Halibut With Spring Vegetables

Servings: 4

Cooking Time: 20 Minutes

Ingredients:

- 4 thick-cut halibut fillets
- 2 Tablespoon Fin & Feather Rub
- Butcher Paper
- 1 Pound Carrots, Peeled and Cut into 3/4" Inch Slices
- 1 Pound asparagus, ends trimmed
- 1/2 Pound Oyster Mushrooms
- 2 Tablespoon butter
- salt and pepper
- 1/2 Cup white wine

Directions:

1. Season the halibut fillets with Traeger Fin and Feather Rub.

2. To build the packets: Start with four sheets of parchment paper about twenty inches long. Fold in half, then open it back up.

3.   Divide the carrots, asparagus, and mushrooms between the four pieces of parchment and top each with a little bit of butter. Season with salt and pepper. Place a halibut fillet on top of the vegetables in each packet.

4.   Next, fold the paper over so the two ends meet, enclosing the food. Beginning at either end of the center crease, make small, overlapping diagonal folds around the filling, sealing the packet tight. Before finishing the final fold, pour a little bit of wine in each packet then seal completely.

5.   Supply your smoker with wood pellets and follow the start-up procedure. Preheat the grill, with the lid closed, to 500° F.

6.   Place all four packets on a sheet tray and place in the grill. Cook for 7-10 minutes or until the internal temperature of the fish reaches 145°F. Remove from the grill and place packet on a serving dish. Grill: 500 °F Probe: 145 °F

7.   Using a knife or scissors, cut open each packet and fold the edges back. Finish with a little bit of lemon juice if desired. Enjoy!

Dijon-smoked Halibut

Servings: 6
Cooking Time: 120 Minutes

Ingredients:
- 4 (6-ounce) halibut steaks
- ¼ cup extra-virgin olive oil
- 2 teaspoons kosher salt
- 1 teaspoon freshly ground black pepper
- ½ cup mayonnaise
- ½ cup sweet pickle relish
- ¼ cup finely chopped sweet onion
- ¼ cup chopped roasted red pepper
- ¼ cup finely chopped tomato
- ¼ cup finely chopped cucumber
- 2 tablespoons Dijon mustard
- 1 teaspoon minced garlic

Directions:
1.   Rub the halibut steaks with the olive oil and season on both sides with the salt and pepper. Transfer to a plate, cover with plastic wrap, and refrigerate for 4 hours.

2.   Supply your smoker with wood pellets and follow the start-up procedure. Preheat, with the lid closed, to 200°F.

3.   Remove the halibut from the refrigerator and rub with the mayonnaise.

4.   Put the fish directly on the grill grate, close the lid, and smoke for 2 hours, or until opaque and an instant-read thermometer inserted in the fish reads 140°F.

5.   While the fish is smoking, combine the pickle relish, onion, roasted red pepper, tomato, cucumber, Dijon mustard, and garlic in a medium bowl. Refrigerate the mustard relish until ready to serve.

6.   Serve the halibut steaks hot with the mustard relish.

Smoked Salt Cured Lox

Servings: 8
Cooking Time: 30 Minutes

Ingredients:
- 1 Cup kosher salt
- 1 Cup sugar
- 1 Tablespoon cracked black pepper
- 1 Whole lemon zest
- 1 Whole orange zest
- 1 Whole Packaged Dill, roughly chopped including stems
- 2 Pound salmon fillet, skin on

Directions:
1.   Mix together salt, sugar, black pepper, lemon zest, orange zest, and dill.

2.   Slice salmon in half. Coat all flesh of salmon completely with salt sugar mixture. Sandwich the 2 pieces together, flesh to flesh and completely cover with salt sugar mixture.

3.   Wrap tightly with plastic wrap and place into a gallon zip top bag. Squeeze out as much air as possible. Place wrapped salmon into a baking dish and place something heavy on top like a pot filled with water or a brick wrapped in foil. Place into the refrigerator for 10 hours. After 10 hours, flip over and put the weight back on top. Refrigerate for another 10 hours.

4. Remove from refrigerator, unwrap and rinse of remaining salt with cold water. Pat dry and leave on counter for 1 hour.

5. Supply your smoker with wood pellets and follow the start-up procedure. Preheat the grill, with the lid closed, to 180° F.

6. Place salmon onto a baking pan. Fill another baking pan with ice and place baking pan with salmon over ice.

7. Place onto grill and smoke for 30 minutes. Remove from grill and slice thin. Grill: 180 ˚F

8. Serve with bagels, cream cheese, capers, dill, lemon wedges, sliced tomatoes, and red onion. Enjoy!

Coconut Shrimp Jalapeño Poppers

Servings: 6
Cooking Time: 55 Minutes

Ingredients:
- 8 Whole shrimp, peeled and deveined
- 1/2 Teaspoon Chicken Rub, plus more as needed
- olive oil
- 6 Whole jalapeños
- 8 Ounce cream cheese, softened
- 2 Tablespoon fresh chopped cilantro
- 1/2 Cup unsweetened coconut flakes
- 12 Slices bacon

Directions:
1. Supply your smoker with wood pellets and follow the start-up procedure. Preheat the grill, with the lid closed, to 425° F.

2. Rinse and season the shrimp with the Traeger Chicken Rub.

3. Drizzle the shrimp with olive oil and cook on the Traeger for about 5 minutes per side, or until the shrimp is opaque. Grill: 425 ˚F

4. Remove the shrimp and let cool.

5. Reduce Traeger temperature to 350°F. Grill: 350 ˚F

6. Meanwhile, get those poppers going. Cut the jalapeños in half then remove the stems and seeds.

7. Chop the shrimp. Mix together the softened cream cheese, chopped shrimp, 1/2 teaspoon Traeger Chicken Rub and 2 tablespoons chopped cilantro.

8. Load a generous amount of the filling in each pepper half. Top with a sprinkle of coconut.

9. Wrap each stuffed pepper with a slice of bacon and place on a foil-lined baking sheet.

10. Cook the peppers on the Traeger for about 45 minutes, or until the bacon fat has rendered and the cream cheese is golden. Enjoy! Grill: 350 ˚F

Traeger Jerk Shrimp

Servings: 8
Cooking Time: 10 Minutes

Ingredients:
- 1 Tablespoon brown sugar
- 1 Tablespoon smoked paprika
- 1 Teaspoon garlic powder
- 1/4 Teaspoon Thyme, ground
- 1/4 Teaspoon ground cayenne pepper
- 1 Teaspoon sea salt
- 1 lime zest
- 2 Pound shrimp in shell
- 3 Tablespoon olive oil

Directions:
1. Combine spices, salt, and lime zest in a small bowl and mix. Place shrimp into a large bowl, then drizzle in the olive oil, Add the spice mixture and toss to combine, making sure every shrimp is kissed with deliciousness.

2. Supply your smoker with wood pellets and follow the start-up procedure. Preheat the grill, with the lid closed, to 450° F.

3. Arrange the shrimp on the grill and cook for 2 – 3 minutes per side, until firm, opaque, and cooked through. Grill: 450 ˚F

4. Serve with lime wedges, fresh cilantro, mint, and Caribbean Hot Pepper Sauce. Enjoy!

Seared Bluefin Tuna Steaks

Servings: 2
Cooking Time: 5 Minutes

Ingredients:
- 3 Whole Tuna, steak
- olive oil
- salt and pepper

- soy sauce
- Sriracha

Directions:

1. Lightly baste both sides of tuna steaks in olive oil; sprinkle sea salt and ground pepper on each side.
2. Supply your smoker with wood pellets and follow the start-up procedure. Preheat the grill, with the lid closed, to High heat.
3. Grill tuna steaks on each side for 2 to 2-1/2 minutes.
4. Remove tuna from grill and allow to cool slightly.
5. Cut into 1/2 - 3/4" pieces. Serve with a mixture of Soy Sauce and Sriracha. Enjoy!"

Honey Balsamic Salmon

Servings: 2
Cooking Time: 25 Minutes

Ingredients:
- 1 Medium salmon fillet
- Fin & Feather Rub
- 1/2 Cup balsamic vinegar
- 1 Tablespoon minced garlic
- 2 Tablespoon honey

Directions:

1. Season the fillet with the Traeger Fin & Feather Rub.
2. Make the glaze: Combine the vinegar, garlic and honey in a small saucepan. Simmer over medium heat until reduced by half. Usually 10 to 15 minutes. The glaze will be properly reduced when it coats the back of a spoon. Using a basting brush, coat the fillet with the glaze.
3. Supply your smoker with wood pellets and follow the start-up procedure. Preheat the grill, with the lid closed, to 350° F.
4. Arrange the salmon fillet on the grill grate. Grill for 25 to 30 minutes, or until the salmon is opaque and flakes easily with a fork. Grill: 350 °F
5. Transfer to a platter or plates and serve immediately. If desired, heat any remaining glaze to a boil and drizzle over top of the salmon. Enjoy!

Whole Vermillion Red Snapper

Servings: 6
Cooking Time: 20 Minutes

Ingredients:
- 1 Whole Vermillion Red Snapper, scaled & gutted
- 4 Clove garlic, chopped
- 1 Whole lemon, thinly sliced
- 2 Sprig rosemary sprigs
- sea salt and freshly ground black pepper

Directions:

1. Supply your smoker with wood pellets and follow the start-up procedure. Preheat the grill, with the lid closed, to High heat.
2. Stuff the cavity of the fish with chopped garlic. Sprinkle the fish with sea salt, pepper, rosemary, and lemon.
3. Grill fish directly on the grill grate. Cook for 20-25 minutes. Serve. Enjoy!

Lime Mahi Mahi Fillets

Servings: 4
Cooking Time: 8 Minutes

Ingredients:
- 3/4 cup extra-virgin olive oil
- 1 clove garlic, minced
- 1/8 teaspoon ground black pepper
- 1/2 teaspoon cayenne pepper
- 2 tablespoons dill weed.
- 1 pinch salt
- 2 tablespoons lime juice
- 1/8 teaspoon grated lime peel
- 2 (4 ounce) mahi mahi fillets

Directions:

1. Supply your smoker with wood pellets and follow the start-up procedure. Preheat the grill, with the lid closed, to 325° F.
2. Lightly oil the grate.
3. Combine in a bowl the extra-virgin olive oil, minced garlic, black pepper, cayenne pepper, salt, lime juice, and grated lime zest.
4. Wisk to prepare the marinade.

5. Place the mahi mahi fillets in the marinade and turn to coat.

6. Allow to marinate at least 15 minutes.

7. Cook on preheated grill until fish flakes easily with a fork and is lightly browned (Typically 3 to 4 minutes per side).

8. Garnish with the twists of lime zest to serve.

Traeger Smoked Salmon

Servings: 6
Cooking Time: 240 Minutes

Ingredients:
- 1 (2-1/2 to 3 lb) salmon fillet
- 1/2 Cup kosher salt
- 1 Cup brown sugar, firmly packed
- 1 Tablespoon ground black pepper

Directions:
1. Remove all pin bones from salmon.

2. In a small bowl, combine salt, sugar and black pepper. Lay a large piece of plastic wrap on a flat surface that is at least 6 inches longer than the fillet. Spread 1/2 of the mixture on top of the plastic and lay the fillet skin side down on top of the cure. Top with the other 1/2 of the cure spreading it evenly over the top of the fillet. Fold up the edges of the plastic and wrap tightly.

3. Place the wrapped salmon fillet in the bottom of a flat, rectangle baking dish or hotel pan. Place another identical pan on top of the fillet. Place a couple of cans or something heavy inside the top pan to weigh it down making sure the weight is distributed evenly.

4. Transfer the weighted salmon to the refrigerator and cure for 4 to 6 hours.

5. Remove the salmon from the plastic wrap and rinse the cure thoroughly (not rinsing thoroughly will result in a salty finished product). Place skin side down on a wire rack atop a sheet tray and pat dry. Place the sheet tray in the refrigerator and allow the salmon to dry overnight. This allows a tacky film called a pellicle to form on the surface of the salmon. The pellicle helps smoke adhere to the fish.

6. Supply your smoker with wood pellets and follow the start-up procedure. Preheat the grill, with the lid closed, to 180° F.

7. Place the salmon skin side down directly on the grill grate and smoke for 3 to 4 hours or until the internal temperature of the fish registers 140°F. Enjoy warm or chilled. Grill: 180 °F Probe: 140 °F

Charleston Crab Cakes With Remoulade

Servings: 4
Cooking Time: 45 Minutes

Ingredients:
- 1¼ cups mayonnaise
- ¼ cup yellow mustard
- 2 tablespoons sweet pickle relish, with its juices
- 1 tablespoon smoked paprika
- 2 teaspoons Cajun seasoning
- 2 teaspoons prepared horseradish
- 1 teaspoon hot sauce
- 1 garlic clove, finely minced
- 2 pounds fresh lump crabmeat, picked clean
- 20 butter crackers (such as Ritz brand), crushed
- 2 tablespoons Dijon mustard
- 1 cup mayonnaise
- 2 tablespoons freshly squeezed lemon juice
- 1 tablespoon salted butter, melted
- 1 tablespoon Worcestershire sauce
- 1 tablespoon Old Bay seasoning
- 2 teaspoons chopped fresh parsley
- 1 teaspoon ground mustard
- 2 eggs, beaten
- ¼ cup extra-virgin olive oil, divided

Directions:
1. For the remoulade:

2. In a small bowl, combine the mayonnaise, mustard, pickle relish, paprika, Cajun seasoning, horseradish, hot sauce, and garlic.

3. Refrigerate until ready to serve.

4. For the crab cakes:

5. Supply your smoker with wood pellets and follow the start-up procedure. Preheat, with the lid closed, to 375°F.

6. Spread the crabmeat on a foil-lined baking sheet and place over indirect heat on the grill, with the lid closed, for 30 minutes.

7. Remove from the heat and let cool for 15 minutes.

8. While the crab cools, combine the crushed crackers, Dijon mustard, mayonnaise, lemon juice, melted butter, Worcestershire sauce, Old Bay, parsley, ground mustard, and eggs until well incorporated.

9. Fold in the smoked crabmeat, then shape the mixture into 8 (1-inch-thick) crab cakes.

10. In a large skillet or cast-iron pan on the grill, heat 2 tablespoons of olive oil. Add half of the crab cakes, close the lid, and smoke for 4 to 5 minutes on each side, or until crispy and golden brown.

11. Remove the crab cakes from the pan and transfer to a wire rack to drain. Pat them to remove any excess oil.

12. Repeat steps 6 and 7 with the remaining oil and crab cakes.

13. Serve the crab cakes with the remoulade.

Smoky Crab Dip

Servings: 6
Cooking Time: 20 Minutes

Ingredients:
- 1/3 Cup mayonnaise
- 3 Ounce sour cream
- 1 Teaspoon smoked paprika
- 1/4 Teaspoon cayenne pepper
- 1 1/2 Pound Crab meat, lump
- salt and pepper
- scallions, chopped
- butter crackers

Directions:

1. Supply your smoker with wood pellets and follow the start-up procedure. Preheat the grill, with the lid closed, to 350° F.

2. Meanwhile, in a large bowl gently stir together all of the ingredients except the crackers, garnish scallions and the crab meat until thoroughly combined. Gently fold in the crab meat, being careful not to break it up too much.

3. Season to taste and transfer to an oven-safe serving dish.

4. Bake for 20 to 25 minutes, until bubbly and golden on top. Grill: 350 °F

5. Garnish with the additional chopped scallions and serve warm with butter crackers. Enjoy!

Moules Marinières With Garlic Butter Sauce

Servings: 4
Cooking Time: 12 Minutes

Ingredients:
- 3lb (1.4kg) fresh mussels, scrubbed under cold running water and debearded
- lemon wedges
- crusty bread (optional)
- for the sauce
- 6 tbsp unsalted butter
- 3 garlic cloves, peeled and minced
- 1 cup dry white wine or hard cider
- 1 tbsp freshly squeezed lemon juice
- 2 tsp hot sauce, plus more
- coarse salt
- freshly ground black pepper
- 2 tbsp chopped fresh curly parsley or tarragon

Directions:

1. Supply your smoker with wood pellets and follow the start-up procedure. Preheat the grill, with the lid closed, to 450° F.

2. In a small saucepan on the stovetop over medium-low heat, make the sauce by melting the butter. Add the garlic and sauté for 1 to 2 minutes. Add the wine, lemon juice, and hot sauce. Season with salt and pepper to taste. Simmer for 5 minutes. Remove the saucepan from the heat and stir in the parsley. Keep warm.

3. Discard any mussels that are cracked or don't snap shut when tapped. Place the mussels in a large aluminum foil roasting pan and cover tightly with heavy-duty aluminum foil.

4. Place the pan on the grate and steam the mussels until the shells open, about 10 to 12 minutes. Remove the pan from the grill and use long-handled tongs to remove the foil from the pan. (Be careful of escaping steam.) Use the tongs to discard any mussels that don't open.

5. Pour the reserved garlic butter sauce over the mussels. Serve from the pan or transfer the mussels to a shallow serving bowl. Serve immediately with lemon wedges, additional hot sauce, and crusty bread (if using) to sop up the juices.

Lobster Tail

Servings: 2
Cooking Time: 25 Minutes

Ingredients:
- 2 lobster tails
- Salt
- Freshly ground black pepper
- 1 batch Lemon Butter Mop for Seafood

Directions:
1. Supply your smoker with wood pellets and follow the start-up procedure. Preheat the grill, with the lid closed, to 375°F.
2. Using kitchen shears, slit the top of the lobster shells, through the center, nearly to the tail. Once cut, expose as much meat as you can through the cut shell.
3. Season the lobster tails all over with salt and pepper.
4. Place the tails directly on the grill grate and grill until their internal temperature reaches 145°F. Remove the lobster from the grill and serve with the mop on the side for dipping.

Garlic Blackened Catfish

Servings: 4
Cooking Time: 10 Minutes

Ingredients:
- ½ Cup Cajun Seasoning
- ¼ Tsp Cayenne Pepper
- 1 Tsp Granulated Garlic
- 1 Tsp Ground Thyme
- 1 Tsp Onion Powder
- 1 Tsp Ground Oregano
- 1 Tsp Pepper
- 4 (5-Oz.) Skinless Catfish Fillets
- 1 Tbsp Smoked Paprika
- 1 Stick Unsalted Butter

Directions:
1. In a small bowl, combine the Cajun seasoning, smoked paprika, onion powder, granulated garlic, ground oregano, ground thyme, pepper and cayenne pepper.
2. Sprinkle fish with salt and let rest for 20 minutes.
3. Supply your smoker with wood pellets and follow the start-up procedure. Preheat the grill, with the lid closed, to 450° F. If you're using a gas or charcoal grill, set it up for medium-high heat. Place cast iron skillet on the grill and let it preheat.
4. While grill is preheating, sprinkle catfish fillets with seasoning mixture, pressing gently to adhere. Add half the butter to preheated cast iron skillet and swirl to coat, add more butter if needed. Place fillets in hot skillet and cook 3-5 minutes or until a dark crust has been formed. Flip and cook an additional 3-5 minutes or until the fish flakes apart when pressed gently with your finger.
5. Remove fish from grill and sprinkle evenly with fresh parsley. Serve with lemon wedges and enjoy!

Mezcal Shrimp With Salsa De Molcajete

Servings: 4
Cooking Time: 14 Minutes

Ingredients:
- 18 to 24 jumbo shrimp, about 1½lb (680g) total, peeled and deveined
- ⅓ cup mezcal
- juice of ½ lime
- 2 tbsp extra virgin olive oil
- 2 tsp coarse salt
- 1 tsp ground cumin
- lime wedges
- for the salsa
- 2 Roma tomatoes
- 2 tomatillos, husked and washed

- 2 garlic cloves, peeled and impaled on a toothpick
- 1 jalapeño or serrano pepper
- 1 small white onion, halved
- ½ tsp coarse salt, plus more
- juice of ½ lime
- ¼ cup loosely packed fresh cilantro leaves

Directions:

1. Supply your smoker with wood pellets and follow the start-up procedure. Preheat the grill, with the lid closed, to 450° F.

2. In a large bowl, combine the shrimp, mezcal, lime juice, olive oil, salt, and ground cumin. Toss with your hands to mix thoroughly. Set aside for 15 minutes and then toss once more.

3. Begin to make the salsa by placing the tomatoes, tomatillos, garlic, jalapeño, and onion on the grate. Grill until they begin to char, about 3 minutes for the garlic and about 6 to 8 minutes for the other vegetables, turning as needed. Transfer the vegetables to a rimmed sheet pan. Remove the skewers from the garlic. Let everything cool. Coarsely chop the vegetables and leave them in separate piles.

4. Place the garlic in the molcajete and add the salt. Mash the garlic to a purée using the temolote. Add the onion and grind it into the garlic paste. Stir in the jalapeño (deseeded for a milder salsa), tomatoes, and tomatillos. Stir in the lime juice and cilantro leaves. Taste, adding salt. (If you don't own a molcajete or temolote, prepare the salsa using a small food processor.)

5. Drain the shrimp and discard the marinade. Thread the shrimp on wood or bamboo skewers. Place the shrimp on the grate and grill until they're white and opaque, about 4 to 6 minutes, tossing with tongs.

6. Transfer the shrimp to a platter. Serve with the salsa and lime wedges.

Grilled Salmon Gravlax

Servings: 4
Cooking Time: 10 Minutes

Ingredients:

- 1 center-cut salmon fillet, about 2lb (1kg), preferably wild caught, skin on
- ½ cup aquavit or vodka
- 4 whole juniper berries
- ¼ cup finely chopped fresh dill, plus more
- lemon wedges
- for the rub
- 3 tbsp granulated light brown sugar or low-carb substitute
- 2 tbsp coarse salt
- 2 tsp freshly ground black pepper
- 1 tsp freshly ground white pepper
- 1 tsp ground coriander

Directions:

1. Run your fingers over the fillet, feeling for bones. Remove them with kitchen tweezers or needle-nosed pliers. Rinse the salmon under cold running water and pat dry with paper towels.

2. Place the salmon skin side down in a nonreactive baking dish and pour the aquavit over it. Crush the berries with the flat of a chef's knife and add them to the dish. Cover and refrigerate for 1 hour.

3. In a small bowl, make the rub by combining the ingredients.

4. Remove the salmon from the aquavit and pat dry with paper towels. Discard the soaking liquid and juniper berries. Rinse out the baking dish and place the salmon in the dish. Lightly but evenly sprinkle the rub on the flesh side of the fillet and gently distribute it with your fingertips. Scatter the dill over the top. Cover the dish and refrigerate for 4 hours.

5. Supply your smoker with wood pellets and follow the start-up procedure. Preheat the grill, with the lid closed, to 400° F.

6. With a sharp knife, slice the fillet into 4 equal portions. Place the fillets on the grate and grill until the fish is somewhat opaque but still translucent in the center and the internal temperature reaches 125°F (52°C), about 3 to 5 minutes per side.

7. Transfer the fillets to a platter. Scatter more dill over the top. Serve with lemon wedges.

Bbq Roasted Salmon

Servings: 4
Cooking Time: 15 Minutes

Ingredients:
- 1/3 Cup honey
- 3 Tablespoon Mustard, whole-grain
- 1 Cup ketchup
- 1/2 Cup dark brown sugar
- 1 Teaspoon Cider Vinegar
- 1/2 Teaspoon Thyme Leaves, finely chopped
- 1/8 Teaspoon Jacobsen Salt Co. Pure Kosher Sea Salt
- 1/8 Teaspoon freshly ground black pepper
- 4 Whole Salmon Fillets, 6oz each, skin-on

Directions:
1. Combine all sauce ingredients in a large bowl, preferably one day prior to making the salmon.
2. Rub salmon fillets on both sides with sauce. Reserve any extra, unused sauce.
3. Supply your smoker with wood pellets and follow the start-up procedure. Preheat the grill, with the lid closed, to 350° F.
4. Place fillets on grill, skin-side down, and cook for 15 minutes. Grill: 350 °F
5. Let the fish rest for about 3-5 minutes. Serve with extra sauce. Enjoy!

Delicious Smoked Trout

Servings: 8
Cooking Time: 120 Minutes

Ingredients:
- 6 rainbow trout fillets
- Brine:
- 2 Tablespoons kosher salt
- 2 Tablespoons brown sugar
- 4 cups cool water

Directions:
1. For the brine, dissolve the kosher salt and brown sugar in water.
2. Place the trout fillets in the brine, skin side up, and brine the fillets for 15 minutes.
3. Supply your smoker with wood pellets and follow the start-up procedure. Preheat the grill, with the lid closed, to 180° F.
4. Remove the trout from the brine and transfer it to the grill grates.
5. Smoke the trout for 1.5 to 2 hours with the lid closed, depending on the thickness of your fillets.
6. Smoke until the trout reaches an internal temperature of 145 °F, or until the trout flakes easily.
7. Remove the trout from the smoker and serve warm, or let it cool completely and serve chilled with your favorite accouterments.

Smoked Honey Salmon

Servings: 2
Cooking Time: 25 Minutes

Ingredients:
- 1 lb. salmon fillets
- 1/2 tsp. pepper
- 1/4 tsp. salt
- 2 tbsp. sriracha
- 2 tsp. honey
- 2 tsp. chili sauce
- 1 tsp. lime juice
- 1/2 tsp. fish sauce

Directions:
1. Supply your smoker with wood pellets and follow the start-up procedure. Preheat the grill, with the lid closed, to 350° F.
2. Sprinkle the salmon with salt and pepper.
3. In a bowl, whisk together the sriracha, honey, chili sauce, lime juice, and fish sauce.
4. Once the grill is hot, place the salmon on the grill and leave for 15 minutes.
5. After 15 minutes, brush the salmon with the sriracha chili sauce and keep cooking for 5-10minutes. The salmon should be firm to the touch and crispy on the edges.
6. Serve hot!

Traeger Crab Legs

Servings: 4

Cooking Time: 30 Minutes

Ingredients:

- 3 Pound crab legs, thawed and halved
- 1 Cup butter, melted
- 2 Tablespoon fresh lemon juice
- 2 Clove garlic, minced
- 1 Tablespoon Fin & Feather Rub or Old Bay Seasoning, plus more to taste
- lemon wedges
- Italian Parsley, chopped

Directions:

1.   If the crab legs are too long to fit in the roasting pan, break them down at the joints by twisting, or use a heavy knife or cleaver. Split the shells open lengthwise. Transfer to the roasting pan.

2.   Combine the butter, lemon juice and garlic; whisk to mix. Pour mixture over the crab legs, turning the legs to coat. Sprinkle the Traeger Fin & Feather Rub or Old Bay Seasoning over the legs.

3.   Supply your smoker with wood pellets and follow the start-up procedure. Preheat the grill, with the lid closed, to 350° F.

4.   Cook the crab legs, basting once or twice with the butter sauce from the bottom of the pan, for 20 to 30 minutes (depending on the size of the crab legs) or until warmed through. Grill: 350 °F

5.   Transfer the crab legs to a large platter and divide the sauce and accumulated juices between 4 dipping bowls. Enjoy!

Grilled Shrimp Brochette

Servings: 6

Cooking Time: 20 Minutes

Ingredients:

- 1 Pound extra-large shrimp, peeled and deveined
- 6 Whole fresh jalapeños
- 8 Ounce block Monterey Jack cheese
- 1 Pound bacon
- 2 Tablespoon Meat Church The Gospel All-Purpose Rub

- oil

Directions:

1.   Fillet shrimp open slightly and set aside. Core the jalapeños and cut them into small slivers. Slice the cheese into similar-sized slivers as the peppers. Cut the bacon slices in half.

2.   Place one slice of jalapeño and one slice of cheese inside each shrimp. Wrap stuffed shrimp in a half piece of bacon and secure with a toothpick.

3.   After you have constructed all of the shrimp, season lightly with Meat Church The Gospel All-Purpose Rub.

4.   Supply your smoker with wood pellets and follow the start-up procedure. Preheat the grill, with the lid closed, to 425° F.

5.   Lightly oil the grill grate then place shrimp directly on the grate. Cook for about 20 minutes, turning at least once halfway through. Shrimp should turn pink and bacon will begin to crisp up. Grill: 425 °F

6.   Remove from the grill and let rest for at least 10 minutes. Enjoy!

Cedar Smoked Garlic Salmon

Servings: 6

Cooking Time: 60 Minutes

Ingredients:

- 1 Tsp Black Pepper
- 3 Cedar Plank, Untreated
- 1 Tsp Garlic, Minced
- 1/3 Cup Olive Oil
- 1 Tsp Onion, Salt
- 1 Tsp Parsley, Minced Fresh
- 1 1/2 Tbsp Rice Vinegar
- 2 Salmon, Fillets (Skin Removed)
- 1 Tsp Sesame Oil
- 1/3 Cup Soy Sauce

Directions:

1.   Soak the cedar planks in warm water for an hour or more.

2.   In a bowl, mix together the olive oil, rice vinegar, sesame oil, soy sauce, and minced garlic.

3.   Add in the salmon and let it marinate for about 30 minutes.

4. Start your grill on smoke with the lid open until a fire is established in the burn pot (3-7 minutes).

5. Supply your smoker with wood pellets and follow the start-up procedure. Preheat the grill, with the lid closed, to 225° F.

6. Place the planks on the grate. Once the boards start to smoke and crackle a little, it's ready for the fish.

7. Remove the fish from the marinade, season it with the onion powder, parsley and black pepper, then discard the marinade.

8. Place the salmon on the planks and grill until it reaches 140°F internal temperature (start checking temp after the salmon has been on the grill for 30 minutes).

9. Remove from the grill, let it rest for 10 minutes, then serve.

Salmon Cakes With Homemade Tartar Sauce

Servings: 4
Cooking Time: 15 Minutes

Ingredients:
- 1 1/2 Cups Breadcrumb, Dry
- 1/2 Tablespoon Capers, Diced
- 1/4 Cup Dill Pickle Relish
- 2 Eggs
- 1 1/4 Cup Mayonnaise, Divided
- 1 Tablespoon Mustard, Grainy
- 1/2 Tablespoon Olive Oil
- 1/2 Red Pepper, Diced Finely
- 1/2 Tablespoon Sweet Rib Rub
- 1 Cup Cooked Salmon, Flaked

Directions:
1. In a large bowl, mix together the salmon, eggs, ¼ cup mayonnaise, breadcrumbs, red bell pepper, Sweet Rib Rub, and mustard. Allow the mixture to sit for 15 minutes to hydrate the breadcrumbs.

2. Supply your smoker with wood pellets and follow the start-up procedure. Preheat the grill, with the lid closed, to 350° F.

3. In a small bowl, mix together the remaining mayonnaise, dill pickle relish, and diced capers. Set aside.

4. Place the baking sheet on the grill to preheat. Once the baking sheet is hot, drizzle the olive oil over the pan and drop rounded tablespoons of the salmon mixture onto the sheet pan. Press the mixture down into a flat patty with a spatula. Allow to grill for 3 to 5 minutes, then flip and grill for 1 to 2 more minutes. Remove from the grill and serve with the reserved tartar sauce.

Simple Glazed Salmon Fillets

Servings: 2
Cooking Time: 25 Minutes

Ingredients:
- 4 (6-8 oz) center-cut salmon fillets, skin on
- Fin & Feather Rub
- 1/2 Cup mayonnaise
- 2 Tablespoon Dijon mustard
- 1 Tablespoon fresh lemon juice
- 1 Tablespoon fresh chopped tarragon or dill
- lemon wedges

Directions:
1. Season the fillets with the Traeger Fin & Feather Rub.

2. Make the Glaze: Combine the mayonnaise and mustard in a small bowl. Stir in the lemon juice and dill or tarragon.

3. Spread the flesh-side of the fillets with the glaze.

4. Supply your smoker with wood pellets and follow the start-up procedure. Preheat the grill, with the lid closed, to 350° F.

5. Arrange the salmon fillets on the grill grate, skin-side down. Grill for 25 to 30 minutes, or until the salmon is opaque and flakes easily with a fork. Grill: 350 °F

6. Transfer to a platter or plates, garnish with sliced lemons and chopped dill and serve immediately. Enjoy!

Grilled Whole Steelhead Fillet

Servings: 6
Cooking Time: 30 Minutes

Ingredients:
- (2-1/2 to 3 lb) steelhead or salmon fillet, skin-on
- 2 Tablespoon Montana Mex Sweet Seasoning

- 1 Teaspoon Montana Mex Jalapeño Seasoning Blend
- 1 Teaspoon Montana Mex Mild Chile Seasoning Blend
- 2 Tablespoon Montana Mex Avocado Oil
- 2 Tablespoon freshly grated ginger
- 1 lemon, thinly sliced

Directions:

1. Coat fillet evenly with all three dry seasonings, avocado oil, grated ginger and thinly sliced lemon.

2. Supply your smoker with wood pellets and follow the start-up procedure. Preheat the grill, with the lid closed, to 380° F.

3. Place the fish skin-side down on the grill grate and cook for 20 minutes. Grill: 380 °F

4. Remove fillet from grill and let rest for 5 minutes. Enjoy!

Prosciutto-wrapped Scallops

Servings: 4
Cooking Time: 10 Minutes

Ingredients:

- 1½lb (680g) jumbo sea or diver scallops (size U-10)
- 8 to 10 thin slices of prosciutto, each halved lengthwise
- coarse salt
- freshly ground black pepper
- for the butter
- 8oz (225g) unsalted butter
- 2 tsp minced fresh curly or flat-leaf parsley
- 1½ tsp finely grated orange zest
- 1 tbsp freshly squeezed orange juice
- 1 tsp finely grated lemon zest
- 1 tsp finely grated lime zest
- ½ tsp coarse salt

Directions:

1. Supply your smoker with wood pellets and follow the start-up procedure. Preheat the grill, with the lid closed, to 450° F.

2. In a small saucepan on the stovetop over medium-low heat, make the citrus butter by melting the butter.

Add the remaining ingredients and simmer for 3 to 5 minutes to blend the flavors. Keep warm.

3. Rinse the scallops under cold running water and dry with paper towels. Place each scallop on its side at the end of a piece of prosciutto and wrap the prosciutto around the scallop. Secure with a toothpick. Season the exposed sides of the scallop with salt and pepper.

4. Place the scallops exposed sides down on the grate and grill until the edges of the prosciutto begin to frizzle and the scallop is warm inside, about 3 to 5 minutes per side.

5. Transfer the scallops to a platter. Brush with some of the warm citrus butter before serving. Serve the remaining butter on the side.

Smoked Fish Chowder

Servings: 4
Cooking Time: 60 Minutes

Ingredients:

- 12 Ounce (1-1/2 to 2 lb) skin-on salmon fillet, preferably wild-caught
- Fin & Feather Rub
- 2 Corn Husks
- 3 Slices Bacon, sliced
- 4 Can Cream of Potato Soup, Condensed
- 3 Cup whole milk
- 8 Ounce cream cheese
- 3 green onions, thinly sliced
- 2 Teaspoon hot sauce

Directions:

1. Supply your smoker with wood pellets and follow the start-up procedure. Preheat the grill, with the lid closed, to 180° F.

2. Sprinkle Traeger Fin & Feather rub as needed on salmon. Arrange the salmon skin-side down on the grill grate. Smoke for 30 minutes. Grill: 180 °F

3. Increase the grill temperature to 350°F. Grill: 350 °F

4. Cook the salmon for 30 minutes, or until the fish flakes easily with a fork. (The exact time will depend on the thickness of the fillet.) There is no need to turn the fish. Using a large thin spatula, transfer the salmon to a wire rack to cool. Remove the skin. (The salmon can be

made a day ahead, wrapped in plastic wrap and refrigerated.) Break into flakes and set aside.

5.   Arrange the corn and bacon strips on the grill grate. (The salmon will be roasting while you do this.) Roast the corn and the bacon until the corn is cooked through and browned in spots, turning as needed, and the bacon is crisp, about 15 minutes.

6.   In the meantime, bring the cream of potato soup and the milk to a simmer over medium heat in a large saucepan or Dutch oven on the stovetop. Gradually stir in the cream cheese and whisk to blend. Chop the bacon into bits and slice the corn off the cobs using long strokes of a chef's knife.

7.   Add to the soup along with the green onions. Stir in the salmon. Heat gently for 5 to 10 minutes. Add the hot sauce to taste. If the chowder is too thick, add more milk. Serve at once. Enjoy!

PORK RECIPES

Baked Beans

Servings: 12
Cooking Time: 180 Minutes

Ingredients:

- 1 Pack Bacon
- 1/2 Cup Brown Sugar
- 1 Coca Cola, Can
- 2 Cans Mixed Beans
- 1/3 Cup Molasses
- 4 Cans Pork And Beans
- 1 Red Onion, Chopped
- 1/3 Cup Yellow Mustard

Directions:

1. Supply your smoker with wood pellets and follow the start-up procedure. Preheat the grill, with the lid closed, to 275° F.
2. Combine all the ingredients and stir until combined.
3. Smoked for 2.5 hours covered. For the last 30 minutes, smoke uncovered.
4. Serve hot. Enjoy!

Bbq Bacon-wrapped Water Chestnuts

Servings: 6
Cooking Time: 35 Minutes

Ingredients:

- 1 Pound bacon
- 2 Can Water Chestnuts
- 1/3 Cup brown sugar
- 1/3 Cup mayonnaise
- 1/3 Cup Texas Spicy BBQ Sauce

Directions:

1. Supply your smoker with wood pellets and follow the start-up procedure. Preheat the grill, with the lid closed, to 350° F.
2. Line a rimmed baking sheet with aluminum foil. Cut each piece of bacon into thirds or halves. Wrap each water chestnut with a piece of bacon large enough to encircle it and secure the bacon with a toothpick.
3. Arrange the bacon-wrapped chestnuts in a single layer on the prepared baking sheet. Bake for 20 minutes. Leave the grill on. Grill: 350 °F
4. Meanwhile, whisk the mayonnaise, brown sugar, and Traeger Spicy Barbecue Sauce in a mixing bowl. Pour the sauce over the chestnuts and return to the grill to bake for 10 to 15 minutes more. Transfer to a platter for serving. Enjoy!

Grilled German Sausage With A Smoky Traeger Twist

Servings: 8
Cooking Time: 120 Minutes

Ingredients:

- 2 Tablespoon Jacobsen Salt Co. Pure Kosher Sea Salt
- 1 Teaspoon The Sausage Maker Instacure #1
- 1 Tablespoon ground nutmeg
- 2 Teaspoon ground mace
- 1 Teaspoon ground ginger
- 4 Pound ground pork, 80% lean
- 1 Pound ground veal or ground beef
- 2 Large eggs
- 1 Cup nonfat dry milk powder

Directions:

1. Combine salt, Instacure #1, nutmeg, mace and ginger in a large pitcher or small bowl. Add the milk and eggs. Beat until well combined. Pour the egg mixture over the ground meat and mix gently. Using your hands, mix in the milk powder until evenly distributed.
2. Form the meat into sausage links, roughly 4 to 6 inches in length.
3. Supply your smoker with wood pellets and follow the start-up procedure. Preheat the grill, with the lid closed, to 225° F.
4. Smoke for approximately 2 hours, or until the internal temperature reaches 175°F. Serve immediately or refrigerate until ready to serve. Enjoy! Grill: 225 °F Probe: 175 °F

Pork Belly Burnt Ends

Servings: 8-10

Cooking Time: 360 Minutes

Ingredients:

- 1 (3-pound) skinless pork belly (if not already skinned, use a sharp boning knife to remove the skin from the belly), cut into 1½- to 2-inch cubes
- 1 batch Sweet Brown Sugar Rub
- ½ cup honey
- 1 cup The Ultimate BBQ Sauce
- 2 tablespoons light brown sugar

Directions:

1. Supply your smoker with wood pellets and follow the start-up procedure. Preheat the grill, with the lid closed, to 250°F.

2. Generously season the pork belly cubes with the rub. Using your hands, work the rub into the meat.

3. Place the pork cubes directly on the grill grate and smoke until their internal temperature reaches 195°F.

4. Transfer the cubes from the grill to an aluminum pan. Add the honey, barbecue sauce, and brown sugar. Stir to combine and coat the pork.

5. Place the pan in the grill and smoke the pork for 1 hour, uncovered. Remove the pork from the grill and serve immediately.

Bbq Brown Sugar Pork Belly

Servings: 8

Cooking Time: 180 Minutes

Ingredients:

- 1 (3-4 lb) pork belly
- 4 Tablespoon brown sugar
- 4 Tablespoon salt

Directions:

1. The night before you plan to cook, take your pork belly out of the fridge and pat dry with paper towels. Score fat with a very sharp knife in a diamond pattern making sure not to cut into the meat.

2. Combine salt and brown sugar and rub pork belly on all sides. Place on a drying rack on a pan and refrigerate uncovered overnight.

3. Thirty minutes before cooking, remove pork belly from fridge. Rinse under cold water and pat very dry with paper towels.

4. Supply your smoker with wood pellets and follow the start-up procedure. Preheat the grill, with the lid closed, to 450° F.

5. Place the pork belly directly on grill grate, fat side up, for 30 minutes. Grill: 500 °F

6. After 30 minutes, reduce the grill temperature to 325°F and cook for 3 hours or until pork is tender and fat is crisp. Grill: 325 °F

7. Remove from grill and allow to rest for 30 minutes before slicing.

8. Serve with baked beans, potato salad, coleslaw, white bread, BBQ sauce, or your favorite BBQ sides. Enjoy!

Apricot Glazed Breakfast Sausage

Servings: 6

Cooking Time: 20 Minutes

Ingredients:

- 1/2 Cup Apricot BBQ Sauce or Apricot Jam
- 1 Tablespoon Dijon mustard
- 1 Pound Breakfast Sausage Links

Directions:

1. In a small saucepan, combine the Traeger Barbecue sauce and mustard and warm over low heat. Keep warm.

2. Supply your smoker with wood pellets and follow the start-up procedure. Preheat the grill, with the lid closed, to 350° F.

3. Arrange the sausage links on the grill grate, turning once or twice with tongs, until cooked through, 10 to 15 minutes. Using tongs, roll several sausages at a time in the barbecue sauce and mustard mixture, and return to the grill for 2 to 3 minutes to set the glaze. Grill: 350 °F

4. Serve with the remaining glaze. Enjoy!

Cider Glazed Baked Holiday Ham

Servings: 6

Cooking Time: 120 Minutes

Ingredients:

- 3 apples, cored and cut into thick slices
- 1 Large ham

- 4 Cup apple cider, divided
- 1/4 Cup bourbon
- 1/4 Cup Dijon mustard
- 1/4 Cup honey or maple syrup
- 1/2 Teaspoon ground cinnamon
- 1/4 Teaspoon ground cloves
- 1 Pinch ground nutmeg or allspice

Directions:

1. Supply your smoker with wood pellets and follow the start-up procedure. Preheat the grill, with the lid closed, to 325° F.

2. Line a roasting pan with heavy-duty foil for easier clean-up.

3. Arrange the apple slices in the bottom of the roasting pan for a natural roasting rack. Place ham on top of the apple slices and pour remaining 1 cup of apple cider around the ham.

4. Place roasting pan directly on grill grate and bake for 1-1/2 hours. Grill: 325 °F

5. For the glaze, combine remaining 3 cups of apple cider and bourbon in a small saucepan and bring to a boil over medium-high heat. Simmer until reduced by one-third. Whisk in the mustard, honey, cinnamon, cloves and nutmeg.

6. Glaze ham with apple cider mixture as needed (use any left over for serving) and continue cooking for another 30 minutes or until a thermometer inserted into the thickest part of the meat reaches an internal temperatures of 140°F. Grill: 325 °F Probe: 140 °F

7. Remove ham from grill and allow to rest for 20 minutes before serving.

8. Warm remaining sauce and serve with ham if desired. Enjoy!

Bbq Pork Chops

Servings: 4
Cooking Time: 30 Minutes

Ingredients:

- 4 8-To-10-Ounce Bone-In Pork Loin Chops, Trimmed Of Excess Fat
- 1/2 Cup Brown Sugar
- 2 Garlic Clove, Minced

- 2 Tbsp Honey
- 1 Cup Ketchup
- 1/4 Cup Molasses
- Sweet Rib Rub Seasoning
- 2 Tbsp Worcestershire Sauce

Directions:

1. First, place pork chops onto sheet pan lined with butcher paper. Season generously with Sweet Rib Rub, making sure to coat all sides of the chops. Set aside while you make the glaze.

2. In a medium sized mixing bowl, combine the ketchup, brown sugar, molasses, honey, garlic, Worcestershire, and 1 tbsp Sweet Rib Rub. Mix well, add 1 shot of bourbon, mix again until sauce becomes smooth. Transfer sauce into an oven proof sauce pan.

3. Supply your smoker with wood pellets and follow the start-up procedure. Preheat the grill, with the lid open, to 375° F. If you're using a gas or charcoal grill, set it up for medium direct heat.

4. Grill the pork chops for 10-15 minutes per side. Place the saucepan on the grill and allow the sauce to come to a boil. Glaze the chops on both sides and let the glaze caramelize onto the chops.

5. Grill the pork chops until they are lightly charred and reach an internal temperature of 145°F - 165°F. Remove the pork chops from the grill and allow them to rest for 5 minutes.

6. Once the pork chops have finished resting, glaze them again if you choose to. Serve immediately.

Bbq Pork Belly Burnt Ends

Servings: 8
Cooking Time: 240 Minutes

Ingredients:

- 1 (5-7 lb) skinless pork belly, cut into 1 inch cubes
- Meat Church Honey Hog, Honey Hog Hot or The Gospel Rub
- 1 Cup apple juice, for spritzing
- 1 1/2 Cup Apricot BBQ Sauce
- 1/2 Cup clover honey

Directions:

1. Supply your smoker with wood pellets and follow the start-up procedure. Preheat the grill, with the lid closed, to 275° F.

2. Thoroughly coat all sides of the pork belly cubes with your choice of Meat Church Honey Hog, Honey Hog Hot or The Gospel Rub. I prefer a spicier rub because I finish these with a sweet sauce.

3. Allow the rub to adhere on all sides for at least 15 minutes. Place the pork belly in the Traeger fat-side down. I prefer to do this on a wire rack.

4. Cook the pork belly for 3 hours, spritzing with apple juice every 45 minutes or whenever it starts to look dry. Grill: 275 °F

5. Pull the belly when the meat reaches an internal temperature of 190°F to 195°F. Some people pull the belly a lot earlier, but I want it really tender. Grill: 275 °F Probe: 190 °F

6. Place the cubes in the half-size aluminum pan. Season and toss the cubes with more Meat Church rub.

7. Cover the cubes with Traeger Apricot BBQ Sauce. Drizzle clover honey across the top. Finally, toss the cubes thoroughly to ensure they are completely covered.

8. Return the pan (uncovered) to the Traeger and cook for another hour or until all liquid has reduced and caramelized. Grill: 275 °F

9. Allow them to cool for 15 minutes before serving. Enjoy!

Whiskey- & Cider-brined Pork Shoulder

Servings: 8

Cooking Time: 540 Minutes

Ingredients:

- 1 bone-in pork shoulder, about 5 to 7lb (2.3 to 3.2kg)
- fresh coarsely ground black pepper
- granulated garlic
- 1 cup apple juice or apple cider
- low-carb barbecue sauce, warmed
- hamburger buns (optional)
- for the brine
- 1 gallon (3.8 liters) cold distilled water
- 1 cup coarse salt
- 1¼ cup whiskey, divided
- ½ cup light brown sugar or low-carb substitute

Directions:

1. In a large saucepot on the stovetop over medium-high heat, make the brine by bringing the water, salt, 1 cup of whiskey, and brown sugar to a boil. Stir with a long-handled wooden spoon until the salt and sugar dissolve. Let the brine cool to room temperature. Cover and cool completely in the refrigerator.

2. Submerge the pork in the brine. If it floats, place a resealable bag of ice on top. Refrigerate for 24 hours.

3. Supply your smoker with wood pellets and follow the start-up procedure. Preheat the grill, with the lid closed, to 250° F.

4. Remove the pork shoulder from the brine and pat dry with paper towels. (Discard the brine.) Season the pork with pepper and granulated garlic. Place the pork on the grate and smoke until the internal temperature reaches 165°F (74°C), about 5 hours.

5. Transfer the pork to an aluminum foil roasting pan and add the apple juice and the remaining ¼ cup of whiskey. Cover tightly with aluminum foil. Place the pan on the grate and cook the pork until the bone releases easily from the meat and the internal temperature reaches 200°F (93°C), about 3 hours more. (Be careful when lifting a corner of the foil to check on the roast because steam will escape.)

6. Remove the pan from the grill and let the pork rest for 20 minutes. Reserve the juices.

7. Wearing heatproof gloves, pull the pork into chunks. Discard the bone or any large lumps of fat. Pull the meat into shreds and transfer to a clean aluminum foil roasting pan. Moisten with the barbecue sauce or serve the sauce on the side. Stir in some of the drippings—not too much because you don't want the pork to be swimming in its juices. Serve on buns (if using).

Smoked Pork Loin

Servings: 6
Cooking Time: 180 Minutes

Ingredients:

- 1 Pork, Loins
- Rub

Directions:

1. Season pork loin with Traeger Rub.
2. Supply your smoker with wood pellets and follow the start-up procedure. Preheat the grill, with the lid closed, to 180° F.
3. Place pork loin on the grill grates, on a diagonal, and smoke for 3 to 4 hours. Grill: 180 °F
4. Increase grill temperature to 350°F and cook for 20 to 30 minutes. Grill: 350 °F
5. Remove from grill, cut into 1-1/2" steaks. Serve. Enjoy!

Honey Glazed Pork Chops

Servings: 6
Cooking Time: 16 Minutes

Ingredients:

- 4-6 Pork Chop
- 1/2 Cup of Honey
- 4 Tablespoons Soy Sauce
- 2 Tablespoons Olive Oil
- 2 Garlic Cloves, pressed
- Salt & Pepper

Directions:

1. Supply your smoker with wood pellets and follow the start-up procedure. Preheat the grill, with the lid closed, to 350° F.
2. Mix together the honey, soy sauce, and garlic in a small dish.
3. Brush the olive oil over the pork chops and sprinkle with salt and pepper.
4. Place the pork chops on the grill and brush the honey mixture over the top side.
5. When you flip the pork chops over, brush the second side with the honey mixture.
6. Grill for about 8 minutes on each side or until a thermometer inserted reads 170 degrees. Brush a final layer of the honey glaze over the pork chops before serving. Enjoy!

Smoked Chorizo & Arugula Pesto

Servings: 4
Cooking Time: 20 Minutes

Ingredients:

- 4 Cup Arugula, fresh
- 1 Clove garlic
- 1/2 Cup Parmesan cheese, grated
- 1/2 Cup pine nuts
- 1/4 Cup extra-virgin olive oil
- 1/4 Cup grapeseed oil
- sea salt
- freshly ground black pepper
- water

Directions:

1. To make the pesto, add arugula, garlic, cheese, and nuts to the bowl of a food processor or blender, and puree. As the processor is running, drizzle in the oil. Season the mixture with salt and pepper, to taste. If the pesto is too thick, thin it out with water.
2. Supply your smoker with wood pellets and follow the start-up procedure. Preheat the grill, with the lid closed, to 375° F.
3. Smoke the sausages whole for 20 minutes, or until it reaches an internal temperature of 170°F. Grill: 375 °F Probe: 170 °F
4. Let rest for 10 minutes, then cut the sausage links into large 1-1/2" chunks. Transfer the sausage to a platter and serve with dollops of the arugula pesto. Enjoy!

Teriyaki Pork Tenderloin

Servings: 12-15
Cooking Time: 120 Minutes

Ingredients:

- 2 (1-pound) pork tenderloins
- 1 batch Quick and Easy Teriyaki Marinade
- Smoked salt

Directions:

1. In a large zip-top bag, combine the tenderloins and marinade. Seal the bag, turn to coat, and refrigerate the pork for at least 30 minutes—I recommend up to overnight.

2. Supply your smoker with wood pellets and follow the start-up procedure. Preheat the grill, with the lid closed, to 180°F.

3. Remove the tenderloins from the marinade and season them with smoked salt.

4. Place the tenderloins directly on the grill grate and smoke for 1 hour.

5. Increase the grill's temperature to 300°F and continue to cook until the pork's internal temperature reaches 145°F.

6. Remove the tenderloins from the grill and let them rest for 5 to 10 minutes, before thinly slicing and serving.

Smoked Pork Spare Ribs

Servings: 8
Cooking Time: 240 Minutes

Ingredients:
- 2 Rack (6 lb) pork spare ribs, trimmed
- 3 Tablespoon Pork & Poultry Rub
- 1 Cup apple juice, cider or beer
- 9 Ounce BBQ Sauce

Directions:

1. Supply your smoker with wood pellets and follow the start-up procedure. Preheat the grill, with the lid closed, to 250° F.

2. If your butcher hasn't done so already, remove the silver-skin on the back of the ribs and trim off any excess fat.

3. Season the ribs on all sides with Traeger Pork & Poultry rub.

4. Arrange the racks of spare ribs on the grill grate, bone-side down and cook for 3 to 4 hours. After the first hour, spray the ribs with apple juice. Continue spraying every hour after that with apple juice. Grill: 250 ˚F

5. Start checking the temp after 2 hours. The finished internal temperature should be 203°F, about 3 to 4 hours. Grill: 250 ˚F Probe: 203 ˚F

6. When the internal temperature registers 203°F, brush the ribs on all sides with Traeger BBQ sauce of your choice. Return ribs to the grill and cook for an additional 30 to 60 minutes to tighten the sauce.

7. To serve, cut each slab in half or into individual ribs and serve with additional BBQ sauce on the side. Enjoy!

Brats In Beer

Servings: 4
Cooking Time: 60 Minutes

Ingredients:
- 4 Can (12 oz) cans beer
- 2 Large onions, peeled and sliced into rings
- 2 Tablespoon butter
- 10 uncooked bratwurst
- 10 hot dog buns
- mustard, for serving

Directions:

1. Pour beer into a large saucepan. Add onions and butter. Bring to a simmer on the stovetop.

2. Supply your smoker with wood pellets and follow the start-up procedure. Preheat the grill, with the lid closed, to 350° F.

3. Put a deep disposable aluminum foil pan on one side of the Traeger. Carefully pour the beer and onions from the saucepan into the pan on the grill.

4. Arrange the brats on the other side of the grill grate. Grill the brats until cooked through, turning frequently with tongs, about 20 to 25 minutes. Grill: 350 ˚F

5. Transfer the brats to the beer mixture and cover the pan tightly with aluminum foil.

6. Let the brats simmer until the onions are tender, 45 minutes to an hour. Grill: 350 ˚F

7. Butter the cut sides of the buns and toast on the grill.

8. To serve, lift a brat out of the mixture and put it on a bun. Top it with onions and mustard. Enjoy!

Spiced Smoked Pork Carnitas

Servings: 12
Cooking Time: 360 Minutes

Ingredients:

- 1 Pork Butt/Shoulder Roast (3-5 lb)
- 1 Tablespoon Ground Cumin
- 1 1/2 Teaspoons Chili Powder
- 1 1/2 Teaspoon Salt
- 1 Teaspoon Cayenne Pepper
- 1 Teaspoon Garlic Powder
- 1/2 Teaspoon Ground Cloves
- 1/2 Cup Vegetable Oil

Directions:

1. Supply your smoker with wood pellets and follow the start-up procedure. Preheat the grill, with the lid closed, to 225° F.
2. Cut pork into 1 inch-thick strips and place into a disposable aluminum foil pan.
3. Sprinkle cumin, chili powder, salt, cayenne pepper, garlic powder, and cloves on the pork stripes. Drizzle on the vegetable oil. Using tongs, toss until pork strips are well coated.
4. Cover the pan with a piece of aluminum foil and place it on the grill grate. Smoke it at 225 °F for 4 hours.
5. After 4 hours, take the pan out and remove the aluminum foil. Then return to the smoker and cook approximately 2 more hours until pork is tender and easily shreds with a fork.

Grilled Prosciutto Wrapped Asparagus

Servings: 6
Cooking Time: 15 Minutes

Ingredients:

- 2 Bunch asparagus
- 4 Ounce prosciutto
- olive oil
- salt and pepper
- 1 Medium lemon, zested
- 2 Tablespoon balsamic vinegar, divided
- 3 Tablespoon toasted pine nuts, for serving

Directions:

1. Supply your smoker with wood pellets and follow the start-up procedure. Preheat the grill, with the lid closed, to 400° F.
2. Rinse the asparagus and pat dry with a paper towel. Cut the bottom third off of the asparagus stalks and discard.
3. Wrap a piece of prosciutto around 4 to 5 stalks, and place on a baking sheet. Drizzle the asparagus with olive oil, then sprinkle with salt, pepper and lemon zest.
4. Place the baking sheet on the grill and cook. After 5 minutes, shake the pan to turn the asparagus once, then drizzle with 1 tablespoon balsamic vinegar. Grill: 400 °F
5. Place back on the grill and cook until the prosciutto is crispy and the asparagus is cooked through, about 5 to 8 minutes. Grill: 400 °F
6. Place the asparagus on the serving tray and sprinkle with the pine nuts and drizzle with remaining balsamic. Enjoy!

Pulled Pork Taquitos With Sour Cream

Servings: 4
Cooking Time: 300 Minutes

Ingredients:

- ⅓ Cup Apple Cider Vinegar
- ½ Cup, Plus Extra For Dipping Bbq Sauce
- 4 Cups Chicken Broth
- 1 Teaspoon Chili Powder
- ⅓ Cup Mustard
- 2 Tbsp Olive Oil
- 6 Tbsp Pulled Pork Rub
- 4 Lb. Pork Shoulder, Bone In
- 1 ½ Cup Sharp Cheddar Cheese, Shredded
- ¼ Cup Sour Cream
- 10 Flour Tortillas

Directions:

1. Supply your smoker with wood pellets and follow the start-up procedure. Preheat the grill, with the lid open, to 400° F. If using a gas or charcoal grill, set the temp to medium heat. In a bowl, combine the chicken broth, mustard, apple cider vinegar, and 1 tablespoon of

Pulled Pork Seasoning. Whisk well to combine and set aside.

2. Generously season the pork shoulder with the remaining 3 tablespoons of Pulled Pork Seasoning on all sides of the pork shoulder, then place on the grill and sear on all sides until golden brown, about 10 minutes.

3. Remove the pork shoulder from the grill and place in the disposable aluminum pan. Pour the chicken broth mixture over the pork shoulder. It should come about 1/3 to ½ way up the side of the pork shoulder. Cover the top of the pan tightly with aluminum foil.

4. Reduce the temperature of your grill to 250°F. Place the foil pan on the grill and grill for four to five hours, or until the pork is tender and falling off the bone.

5. Remove the pork from the grill and allow to cool slightly. Place on a cutting board and shred with meat claws, reserving about 2.5 cups. Fire up grill to 425°F.

6. In a mixing bowl, combine sour cream, BBQ sauce, and chili powder. Stir in cheddar cheese and pork until well combined.

7. Lay each tortilla flat on your work surface and scoop about ¼ cup of pork mixture in the center, lengthwise. Roll up tightly and place seam side down on baking sheet. Repeat with all tortillas, then brush tops lightly with olive oil.

8. Transfer baking sheet to grill and cook for 15-20 minutes at 400°F , or until cheese has melted and tortilla edges have turned a golden brown. Serve with extra BBQ sauce for dipping and enjoy!

Baked Eggs In Bacon Nest

Servings: 4
Cooking Time: 30 Minutes

Ingredients:
- 6 Strips bacon
- 6 Whole eggs
- 1/4 Teaspoon salt
- 1/4 Teaspoon pepper

Directions:
1. Supply your smoker with wood pellets and follow the start-up procedure. Preheat the grill, with the lid closed, to 375° F.

2. Place bacon strips directly on the grill grate and cook about 15 minutes. Transfer to a paper towel and pat dry.

3. Spray a muffin tin liberally with cooking spray. Line each muffin cup with one slice of bacon then crack one egg into each cup. Season each cup with salt and pepper.

4. Transfer muffin tin to the grill and cook for 15-20 minutes until the bacon is crisp, whites are just set, and yolk is still runny. Enjoy!

The Dan Patrick Show Chorizo Armadillo Eggs

Servings: 8
Cooking Time: 45 Minutes

Ingredients:
- 2 Pound Ground Pork
- 1/4 Cup Chili Powder
- 4 Tablespoon Paprika
- 3 Tablespoon Oregano
- 2 Teaspoon Ground Cumin
- 2 Teaspoon Salt
- 3 Clove Garlic, Minced
- 4 Ounce Cream Cheese, Softened
- 1/2 Cup Shredded Cheddar Cheese
- 1 Tablespoon Chopped Cilantro
- 6 Large Jalapeños, Halved And Seeded
- 2 Tablespoon Pork & Poultry Rub

Directions:
1. To mix the chorizo, place ground pork, chili powder, paprika, oregano, ground cumin, salt and minced garlic in a small bowl and mix just until combined being careful not to overwork. Set aside.

2. In the bowl of a stand mixer, combine cream cheese, cheddar cheese and cilantro. Mix with the paddle attachment until well combined.

3. Spoon cheese mixture into each jalapeño half then cut in half again. Take 1/4 cup of chorizo and flatten it into a 1/4 inch thick disk. Place the cheese-stuffed jalapeño in the center and wrap the sausage around the jalapeño forming it into an egg shape. Repeat with remaining jalapeños. Season chorizo balls with Traeger Pork & Poultry Rub.

4.   Supply your smoker with wood pellets and follow the start-up procedure. Preheat the grill, with the lid closed, to 300° F.

5.   Place the chorizo balls directly on the grill grate and cook for 30 minutes until lightly browned and cooked through, turning once.

6.   Let cool 5 to 10 minutes before serving. Enjoy!

St. Louis–style Pork Steaks

Servings: 4
Cooking Time: 120 Minutes

Ingredients:
- 1 cup low-carb barbecue sauce
- ¼ cup low-carb beer or sugar-free dark-colored soda or sugar-free root beer
- 4 bone-in pork shoulder steaks, each about 1lb (450g) and at least 1 inch (2.5cm) thick
- for the rub
- 1 tbsp coarse salt
- 1 tbsp freshly ground black pepper
- 1 tbsp granulated light brown sugar or low-carb substitute
- 1 tbsp sweet or smoked paprika
- 1 tsp granulated garlic or garlic powder
- 1 tsp celery salt

Directions:
1.   Supply your smoker with wood pellets and follow the start-up procedure. Preheat the grill, with the lid closed, to 250° F.

2.   In a small bowl, combine the barbecue sauce and beer. Set aside.

3.   In a small bowl, make the rub by combining the ingredients. Mix well. Season the steaks on both sides with some of the rub.

4.   Place the steaks on the grate at an angle to the bars and smoke for 30 minutes. Transfer the steaks to an aluminum foil roasting pan. Pour the barbecue mixture over them. Use tongs to turn the steaks, making sure each is coated well with the sauce.

5.   Tightly wrap aluminum foil over the top of the pan and place it on the grate. Braise the steaks until they're fork tender, about 1½ hours. (Protect your hands when lifting a corner of the foil because steam will escape.)

6.   Remove the pan from the grill and serve the steaks immediately.

Baby Back Ribs With Mustard Slather

Servings: 4
Cooking Time: 120 Minutes

Ingredients:
- 2 racks of baby back ribs, each about 2lb (1kg)
- all-purpose barbecue rub
- low-carb barbecue sauce (optional)
- for the mustard
- ½ cup yellow or brown mustard
- 2 tbsp dill pickle juice or apple cider vinegar

Directions:
1.   Supply your smoker with wood pellets and follow the start-up procedure. Preheat the grill, with the lid closed, to 325° F.

2.   Remove the thick membrane on the bone side of the ribs. Don't remove the thin membrane on top of the bones because it holds them together. Trim off any odd bits of meat or excess fat. Place the ribs on a rimmed sheet pan.

3.   In a small bowl, make the mustard slather by combining the mustard and pickle juice. Brush the ribs on both sides with the mixture and then season with the barbecue rub.

4.   Place the ribs on the grate and smoke until the ribs are tender, about 1½ to 2 hours. (A toothpick inserted between bones should go in with little resistance. The meat will also have pulled back from the bone about ½ inch [1.25cm].) Brush the ribs with barbecue sauce (if using) during the last 10 minutes of smoking. Place the ribs meat side down on the grate for 5 minutes. Turn and grill for 5 minutes more. This sets the sauce.

5.   Transfer the ribs to a cutting board. Use a sharp knife to cut the slabs in half or into individual ribs. Serve immediately with more barbecue sauce.

Beer Braised Pork Belly And Beef

Servings: 4
Cooking Time: 90 Minutes

Ingredients:

- 1, Dark Beer, Any Brand
- 3 Cups Broth, Beef
- 1 Tablespoon Chinese Cooking Wine (Such As Shaoxing) Or Dry Sherry Wine
- 1 Teaspoon Chinese Five Spice Powder
- 2, Smashed Garlic, Cloves
- 1 Inch Knob Ginger, Peeled And Thinly Sliced
- 1 Onion, Sliced
- 2 Pounds Pork Belly, Cut Into 1 Inch Chunks
- 2 Tablespoons Rice Wine Vinegar
- 2 Tablespoons, Dark Soy Sauce, Low Sodium
- 3 Tablespoons Sugar

Directions:

1. Place a heavy dutch oven on a stovetop over medium high heat. Add the pork belly and brown on all sides, about 5 minutes. Once the pork belly has browned, add in the onion, ginger, and garlic, and stir well.
2. Pour the beer, beef broth, soy sauce, dark soy sauce, sugar, Chinese cooking wine, rice wine vinegar, and Chinese five spice powder into the pan. Place a lid on the pan and bring it to a boil. Once it boils, remove it from the heat.
3. Supply your smoker with wood pellets and follow the start-up procedure. Preheat the grill, with the lid open, to 325° F. Place the pan of pork belly on the grill and braise for 1 ½ hours, or until the pork belly is falling apart tender and glazed.
4. Remove the pork belly from the grill and serve immediately.

Pretzel Bun With Pulled Pork

Servings: 4
Cooking Time: 300 Minutes

Ingredients:

- ⅓ Cup Apple Cider Vinegar
- 1 ½ Cups Bbq Sauce, Divided
- 1 Qt. Chicken Stock
- ⅓ Cup Ketchup
- 3 Tbsp Pulled Pork Rub, Divided
- 1, 4 Lb. Pork Shoulder, Bone In
- 4 Pretzel Buns

Directions:

1. Supply your smoker with wood pellets and follow the start-up procedure. Preheat the grill, with the lid open, to 400° F. If using a gas or charcoal grill, set it up for medium-high heat. In a bowl, combine the apple cider vinegar, chicken stock, ketchup, and 1 tablespoon of Pulled Pork Rub. Whisk well to combine and set aside.
2. Season the pork shoulder with the remaining 2 tablespoons of Pulled Pork Seasoning on all sides of the pork shoulder, then place on the grill and sear on all sides until golden brown, about 10 minutes.
3. Remove the pork shoulder from the grill and place in the disposable aluminum pan. Pour the sauce over the pork shoulder. It should come about 1/3 to ½ way up the side of the pork shoulder. Cover the top of the pan tightly with aluminum foil.
4. Reduce the temperature of your grill to 250°F. Place the foil pan on the grill and cook for 4 to 5 hours, or until the pork is tender and falling off the bone.
5. Remove the pork from the grill and allow to rest for 15 minutes. Drain the liquid from the pan, reserving about a cup, then shred the pork and cover with the reserved liquid. Set 3 ½ to 4 cups of pulled pork aside for sandwiches, and save the remaining for future use.
6. While pork is resting, place 1 cup of BBQ sauce in a skillet and heat to simmer. Toss in reserved shredded pork. Divide pork among 4 pretzel buns, spoon additional BBQ sauce over the top and dig in!

Cajun Double-smoked Ham

Servings: 12-15
Cooking Time: 300 Minutes

Ingredients:

- 1 (5- or 6-pound) bone-in smoked ham
- 1 batch Cajun Rub
- 3 tablespoons honey

Directions:

1. Supply your smoker with wood pellets and follow the start-up procedure. Preheat the grill, with the lid closed, to 225°F.

2. Generously season the ham with the rub and place it either in a pan or directly on the grill grate. Smoke it for 1 hour.

3. Drizzle the honey over the ham and continue to smoke it until the ham's internal temperature reaches 145°F.

4. Remove the ham from the grill and let it rest for 5 to 10 minutes, before thinly slicing and serving.

Spicy Ribs

Servings: 4
Cooking Time: 300 Minutes

Ingredients:
- 2 Finely Minced Chipotle In Adobo
- 1 Cup (Any Kind) Barbecue Sauce
- 1/2 Cup Brown Sugar
- 1/4 Cup Honey
- 1/4 Cup Olive Oil
- 1 Rack St. Louis-Style Rib(S)
- 3 Tablespoons Sweet Heat Rub

Directions:
1. Remove the ribs from their packaging, drain, and pat dry. Using a paper towel, grip the membrane on the back of the ribs and pull off. Discard the membrane and paper towel.

2. In a small mixing bowl, combine the brown sugar, olive oil, honey, BBQ sauce, and chiles in adobo. Using a basting brush, brush the front and back of the ribs generously with the BBQ mixture. Save the basting brush for later along with half of the sauce.

3. Generously season the ribs with Sweet Heat rub, making sure to focus especially on the front of the ribs.

4. Supply your smoker with wood pellets and follow the start-up procedure. Preheat the grill, with the lid open, to 225° F. If you're using a gas or charcoal grill, set it up for low heat. Place the ribs on the grill and smoke at 225°F for 4-6 hours making sure to baste in the sauce every 2 hours.

5. Remove from the grill and serve with additional barbecue sauce.

Cheese Potato Stuffed Pork Chops

Servings: 4
Cooking Time: 45 Minutes

Ingredients:
- 4 Bone-In Pork Chops
- 1 Package Frozen Shredded Hash Browns, Thawed
- 1 Tbsp Parsley, Minced Fresh
- Pulled Pork Seasoning
- 1 Cup Shredded Cheddar Cheese
- ¼ Cup Sour Cream
- White Onion, Diced

Directions:
1. Place the pork chops on a flat work surface. Using a sharp knife, cut a pocket into the side of each pork chop, being careful not to cut all the way through the sides of the chop. Season the pork chops generously on both sides with Pulled Pork Seasoning.

2. In a large mixing bowl, mix together the hash browns, shredded cheddar, sour cream, diced onion, parsley, and 1 tablespoon of Pulled Pork seasoning. Stuff each pork chop with about ¼ cup of the potato filling. Use a toothpick to securely close the chop if needed.

3. Supply your smoker with wood pellets and follow the start-up procedure. Preheat the grill, with the lid open, to 350° F. If you're using a gas or charcoal grill, set it up for medium heat. Insert a temperature probe into the thickest part of one of the chops and place the meat on the grill. Grill the chops on one side for 10-15 minutes, then flip and grill for another 10-15, or until the internal temperature of the chops reach 145°F.

4. Remove the chops from the grill, take the toothpicks out of the meat, and serve immediately.

Bbq Rib Sandwich

Servings: 2

Cooking Time: 180 Minutes

Ingredients:

- 3 Rack baby back pork ribs
- cracked black pepper
- kosher salt
- 1 Cup 'Que BBQ Sauce
- 4 hoagie rolls
- 1 Jar Pickles
- 1 yellow onion, thinly sliced

Directions:

1. Peel membrane from back side of the ribs. Lightly season with cracked black pepper and salt.

2. Supply your smoker with wood pellets and follow the start-up procedure. Preheat the grill, with the lid closed, to 225° F.

3. Cook meaty side up for two hours, then flip the ribs to meaty side down and cook for one more hour. Grill: 225 °F

4. Remove ribs from grill and flip over so they are laying bone side up on a cutting board. Using a sharp knife, cut down the center of each bone and remove bones using your fingers.

5. Flip ribs back over and brush with half of the Traeger 'Que BBQ Sauce. Place back on the grill for 5-10 minutes to set the sauce. Remove from the grill and set aside.

6. Cut rib racks to match the length of the hoagie rolls. Split the hoagie rolls in half and place ribs on the bottom bun.

7. Top with pickles, onions, more BBQ sauce and top bun. Enjoy!

Barbecued Tenderloin

Servings: 4-6

Cooking Time: 30 Minutes

Ingredients:

- 2 (1-pound) pork tenderloins
- 1 batch Sweet and Spicy Cinnamon Rub

Directions:

1. Supply your smoker with wood pellets and follow the start-up procedure. Preheat the grill, with the lid closed, to 350°F.

2. Generously season the tenderloins with the rub. Using your hands, work the rub into the meat.

3. Place the tenderloins directly on the grill grate and smoke until their internal temperature reaches 145°F.

4. Remove the tenderloins from the grill and let them rest for 5 to 10 minutes, before thinly slicing and serving.

Big Game Day Bbq Ribs

Servings: 6

Cooking Time: 180 Minutes

Ingredients:

- 2 Rack St. Louis-style ribs
- 1/4 Cup Big Game Rub
- 1 Cup peach nectar
- 1 Cup Apricot BBQ Sauce

Directions:

1. Wash ribs and pat dry. Pull membrane off the back of ribs.

2. Supply your smoker with wood pellets and follow the start-up procedure. Preheat the grill, with the lid closed, to 275° F.

3. Apply a thin coat of rub to the back of the ribs and all sides. Let rest 5 minutes. Turn ribs over, apply a heavy coat of rub to the top and let rest or "sweat" for 15 minutes.

4. Place ribs bone side down directly on the grill grate and cook for 2 to 2-1/2 hours. Check for doneness, the internal temperature should be 160°F and the meat should be pulling away from the bones. Grill: 275 °F Probe: 160 °F

5. Remove ribs from the grill placing them meat side down on top of a piece of foil. Pour 1/2 cup peach nectar over ribs and wrap foil tightly around the ribs creating a packet. Grill: 275 °F

6. Put ribs back on the grill, bone side up and cook for another 30 to 45 minutes or until tender, but not fall-off-the-bone. Grill: 275 °F

7. Remove from the grill and sauce the front and back of the ribs. Place the ribs back on the Traeger for 15 minutes to set the sauce.

8. Remove, let rest for 15 minutes, slice and serve. Enjoy!

Bbq Pork Shoulder Roast With Sugar Lips Glaze

Servings: 8
Cooking Time: 540 Minutes

Ingredients:
- 1 (8-10 lb) bone-in pork butt
- 1/4 Cup Pork & Poultry Rub, divided
- 1 1/2 Cup apple juice, divided
- 4 Tablespoon brown sugar
- 1 Tablespoon salt
- 1/2 Cup apple juice
- Sugar Lips Glaze

Directions:
1. Trim pork butt of all excess fat leaving 1/4 inch of the fat cap attached.

2. Combine 2 tablespoons Traeger Pork & Poultry Rub, 1 cup apple juice, brown sugar and salt in a small bowl stirring until most of the sugar and salt are dissolved. Inject the pork butt every square inch or so with the apple juice mixture.

3. Season the exterior of the pork butt with remaining Traeger Pork & Poultry Rub.

4. Supply your smoker with wood pellets and follow the start-up procedure. Preheat the grill, with the lid closed, to 250° F.

5. Place pork butt directly on the grill grate and cook for about 6 hours or until the internal temperature reaches 160°F. Grill: 250 °F Probe: 160 °F

6. Wrap the pork butt in two layers of foil and pour in 1/2 cup of apple juice. Secure tin foil tightly to contain the apple juice.

7. Increase Traeger temperature to 275°F and return wrapped pork butt to grill in a pan large enough to hold the pork butt in case it leaks. Cook an additional 3 hours or until internal temperature reaches 195°F. Grill: 275 °F Probe: 195 °F

8. Remove from the grill and allow to rest 10 to 15 minutes. Slice the pork butt around the bone and top with Traeger Sugar Lips BBQ Sauce. Serve with your favorite sides. Enjoy!

Home-cured Hickory-smoked Bacon

Servings: 4
Cooking Time: 180 Minutes

Ingredients:
- 1 pork belly, about 5lb (2.3kg) and 1½ inches (3.75cm) thick, rind removed
- for the cure
- ⅓ cup kosher salt
- ⅓ light brown sugar, turbinado sugar, or maple sugar or low-carb substitute
- 3 tbsp freshly ground black pepper
- 3 bay leaves, crumbled
- 2 tsp pink curing salt #1
- 2 tsp granulated garlic

Directions:
1. Rinse the pork belly under cold running water and pat dry with paper towels. Place in a resealable plastic bag.

2. In a small bowl, make the cure by combining the ingredients, ensuring to especially distribute the pink curing salt. Sprinkle the rub as evenly as possible on the pork belly and use your hands to thoroughly distribute it. (You might want to wear disposable gloves.) Close the bag and refrigerate for 7 days, turning once a day and occasionally massaging the spices into the meat. Some liquid will appear in the bag and the pork belly will start firming up.

3. Rinse the pork under cold running water and pat dry with paper towels. Place the pork belly on a wire rack placed on a rimmed sheet pan. Refrigerate uncovered for 48 hours so it has an opportunity to develop a pellicle—a surface that's very amenable to receiving smoke.

4. Supply your smoker with wood pellets and follow the start-up procedure. Preheat the grill, with the lid closed, to 200° F.

5. Place the sheet pan on the grate and smoke the pork until the internal temperature reaches 150°F (66°C), about 2 to 3 hours.

6. Remove the pan from the grill and let the bacon cool. Cover and refrigerate until it's firmed up again. Slice while cold and either grill or fry the first slices of the batch. Wrap the bacon in plastic wrap. Refrigerate for up to 1 week or freeze for up to 3 months.

Jamaican Jerk Pork Chops

Servings: 4
Cooking Time: 720 Minutes

Ingredients:

* 4 thick pork rib or loin chops, each about 12oz (340g) and 1 inch (2.5cm) thick
* for the marinade
* ½ to 1 Scotch bonnet or habanero pepper, destemmed, deseeded, and coarsely chopped, plus more
* 2 scallions, trimmed, white and green parts coarsely chopped
* 1 garlic clove, peeled and coarsely chopped
* juice of 1 lime
* 2 tbsp vegetable oil
* 2 tbsp distilled water
* 1 tbsp light soy sauce
* 2 tsp coarsely chopped fresh thyme leaves
* 2 tsp peeled and minced fresh ginger
* 2 tsp dark brown sugar or low-carb substitute, plus more
* 1 tsp coarse salt, plus more
* ½ tsp freshly ground black pepper
* ½ tsp ground allspice
* ½ tsp ground nutmeg
* ½ tsp ground cinnamon

Directions:

1. In a blender, make the jerk marinade by combining the ingredients. Blend until fairly smooth. Taste for seasoning, adding more Scotch bonnet, brown sugar, or salt. Place the pork chops in a resealable plastic bag and pour the marinade over them, turning and massaging the bag to thoroughly coat the meat. Refrigerate for 2 to 4 hours.

2. Supply your smoker with wood pellets and follow the start-up procedure. Preheat the grill, with the lid closed, to 425° F.

3. Remove the pork from the marinade and scrape off the excess. (Discard the marinade.) Grill the chops until the internal temperature reaches 145°F (63°C), about 6 to 8 minutes per side.

4. Transfer the chops to a platter. Let rest for 2 minutes before serving.

Bacon Onion Ring

Servings: 6
Cooking Time: 60 Minutes

Ingredients:

* 16 Slices bacon
* 2 Whole Vidalia onion, sliced
* 1 Tablespoon Chili Garlic Sauce
* 1 Tablespoon yellow mustard
* 1 Teaspoon honey

Directions:

1. Wrap a piece of bacon around an individual onion ring; continue until bacon is gone. Some onion slices may be larger and require 2 pieces of bacon to complete a ring.

2. Place a skewer through the bacon-wrapped onion slice, to keep bacon from unraveling while cooking.

3. Supply your smoker with wood pellets and follow the start-up procedure. Preheat the grill, with the lid closed, to 400° F.

4. Meanwhile, mix chili garlic sauce and yellow mustard in a small bowl until incorporated; add honey.

5. Place skewers on the grill grate and cook for approximately 90 minutes, flipping after 45 minutes. Enjoy! Grill: 400 °F

Smoked Porchetta With Italian Salsa Verde

Servings: 8-12
Cooking Time: 180 Minutes

Ingredients:

* 3 Tablespoon dried fennel seed

- 2 Tablespoon red pepper flakes
- 2 Tablespoon sage, minced
- 1 Tablespoon rosemary, minced
- 3 Clove garlic, minced
- As Needed lemon zest
- As Needed orange zest
- To Taste salt and pepper
- 6 Pound Pork Belly, skin on
- As Needed salt and pepper
- 1 Whole shallot, thinly sliced
- 6 Tablespoon parsley, minced
- 2 Tablespoon freshly minced chives
- 1 Tablespoon Oregano, fresh
- 3 Tablespoon white wine vinegar
- 1/2 Teaspoon kosher salt
- 3/4 Cup olive oil
- 1/2 Teaspoon Dijon mustard
- As Needed fresh lemon juice

Directions:

1. Prepare herb mixture: In a medium bowl, mix together fennel seeds, red pepper flakes, sage, rosemary, garlic, citrus zest, salt and pepper.

2. Place pork belly skin side up on a clean work surface and score in a crosshatch pattern. Flip the pork belly over and season flesh side with salt, pepper and half of the herb mixture.

3. Place trimmed pork loin in the center of the belly and rub with remaining herb mixture. Season with salt and pepper.

4. Roll the pork belly around the loin to form a cylindrical shape and tie tightly with kitchen twine at 1" intervals.

5. Season the outside with salt and pepper and transfer to refrigerator, uncovered and let air dry overnight.

6. When ready to cook, start the smoker grill and set to Smoke.

7. Fit a rimmed baking sheet with a rack and place the pork on the rack seam side down.

8. Place the pan directly on the grill grate and smoke for 1 hour.

9. Increase the grill temperature to 325 degrees F and roast until the internal temperature of the meat reaches 135 degrees, about 2 1/2 hours. If the exterior begins to burn before the desired internal temperature is reached, tent with foil.

10. Remove from grill and let stand 30 minutes before slicing.

11. To make the Italian salsa verde: Combine shallot, parsley, chives, vinegar, oregano and salt in a medium bowl. Whisk in olive oil then stir in mustard and lemon juice.

12. Drizzle slices with Italian salsa verde and enjoy!

Bbq Pork Belly

Servings: 6
Cooking Time: 180 Minutes

Ingredients:

- 1 (3 lb) pork belly, skin removed
- 4 Tablespoon salt
- 1/2 Teaspoon black pepper
- Pork & Poultry Rub

Directions:

1. Supply your smoker with wood pellets and follow the start-up procedure. Preheat the grill, with the lid closed, to 275° F.

2. Meanwhile, season pork belly on both sides with salt, pepper and Traeger Pork & Poultry Rub. Place pork belly directly on the grill grate and cook for 3 to 3-1/2 hours or until the internal temperature reaches 200°F. Grill: 275 °F Probe: 200 °F

3. Remove from grill and let rest 10 to 15 minutes before slicing.

4. Serve in tacos, mac and cheese, nachos or your favorite dish. Enjoy!

Leftover Pulled Pork With Eggs

Servings: 4
Cooking Time: 20 Minutes

Ingredients:

- 1 Teaspoon Coarse Black Pepper
- 4 Eggs
- 1 Green Bell Pepper, Diced
- 1 Teaspoon Kosher Salt
- 3 Tablespoons Olive Oil
- 1 Small Onion, Diced

- 1 Tablespoon Hickory Bacon Seasoning
- 2 Cups Of Leftover Pulled Pork
- 1 Red Bell Peppers, Diced
- 1 ½ Pounds Red Potatoes, Diced

Directions:

1. Supply your smoker with wood pellets and follow the start-up procedure. Preheat the grill, with the lid open, to 350° F.

2. In a large bowl, toss the potatoes with 2 tablespoons of olive oil and Hickory Bacon seasoning. You want to get the potatoes coated well and evenly with the oil and seasoning.

3. Add the potatoes to the skillet and cook on the grill for 12-15 minutes or until they're cooked all the way through and browned. Remove from the pan and set aside.

4. Add 1 more tablespoon of olive to the pan and cook the peppers and onion for 2-3 minutes or until soft. Remove from the pan and set aside.

5. Add the pork to the pan and cook until warmed through. Because the pork is already cooked this should only be 1-2 minutes so the meat stays moist.

6. Add the potatoes, peppers and onions back to the pan, then give everything in the skillet a quick mix, so the hash is evenly blended.

7. Crack the 4 eggs on top of the hash. Try to space them evenly around. Sprinkle the teaspoons of salt and pepper on top of the eggs, then place the lid on top of the pan and allow the eggs to cook for 5-6 minutes, or until the whites are firm and the yolks are still runny.

8. Remove from the grill and serve immediately.

Stuffed Pork Crown Roast

Servings: 2-4
Cooking Time: 180 Minutes

Ingredients:

- 10 Pound Crown Roast of Pork, 12-14 ribs
- 1 Cup apple juice or cider
- 2 Tablespoon apple cider vinegar
- 2 Tablespoon Dijon mustard
- 1 Tablespoon brown sugar
- 2 Clove garlic, minced
- 2 Tablespoon Thyme or Rosemary, fresh
- 1 Teaspoon salt
- 1 Teaspoon coarse ground black pepper, divided
- 1/2 Cup olive oil
- 8 Cup Your Favorite Stuffing, Prepared According to the Package Directions, or Homemade

Directions:

1. Set the pork on a flat rack in a shallow roasting pan. Cover the end of each bone with a small piece of foil.

2. Make the marinade: Bring the apple cider to a boil over high heat and reduce by half. Remove from the heat, and whisk in the vinegar, mustard, brown sugar, garlic, thyme, and salt and pepper. Slowly whisk in the oil.

3. Using a pastry brush, apply the marinade to the roast, coating all surfaces. Cover it with plastic wrap and allow it to sit until the meat comes to room temperature, about 1 hour.

4. When ready to cook, set grill temperature to High and preheat, lid closed for 15 minutes.

5. Arrange the roasting pan with the pork on the grill grate. Roast for 30 minutes.

6. Reduce the heat to 325°F. Loosely fill the crown with the stuffing, mounding it at the top. Cover the stuffing with foil. (Alternatively, you can bake the stuffing in a separate pan alongside the roast.)

7. Roast the pork for another 1-1/2 hours. Remove the foil from the stuffing and continue to roast until the internal temperature of the meat is 150°F, about 30 minutes to an hour. Make sure the temperature probe doesn't touch bone or you will get a false reading.

8. Remove roast from grill and allow to rest for 15 minutes. Remove the foil covering the bones, but leave the butcher's string on the roast until ready to carve. Transfer to a warm platter.

9. To serve, carve between the bones. Enjoy!

Apple-smoked Pork Tenderloin

Servings: 4-6

Cooking Time: 300 Minutes

Ingredients:

- 2 (1-pound) pork tenderloins
- 1 batch Pork Rub

Directions:

1. Supply your smoker with wood pellets and follow the start-up procedure. Preheat the grill, with the lid closed, to 180°F.

2. Generously season the tenderloins with the rub. Using your hands, work the rub into the meat.

3. Place the tenderloins directly on the grill grate and smoke for 4 or 5 hours, until their internal temperature reaches 145°F.

4. Remove the tenderloins from the grill and let them rest for 5 to 10 minutes before thinly slicing and serving.

Double Smoked Apple Spiral Ham

Servings: 12

Cooking Time: 150 Minutes

Ingredients:

- 1 10 lb ham spiral cut
- 1 cup apple jelly
- 1 cup raspberry chipotle BBQ sauce

Directions:

1. Supply your smoker with wood pellets and follow the start-up procedure. Preheat the grill, with the lid closed, to 275° F.

2. Remove ham from all packaging and transfer to a chicken tray, cut-side-down. Then place on a cooking tray and transfer to the smoker. Close the lid and cook for 2 hours.

3. Heat up saucepan over medium heat. Add apple jelly and stir well, until it reaches a liquid consistency.

4. Add raspberry chipotle. Stir in and bring glaze to a simmer. Leave saucepan on warm heat until ham is ready.

5. After two hours, transfer ham to a shallow aluminum pan. Apply the glaze to ham generously using a basting brush. Make sure all cracks on ham surfaceare glazed.

6. Still in a shallow pan, put ham back in smoker. Close the lid and leave to smoke for over 30 minutes.

7. Remove ham from smoker and transfer to a cutting board. Leave to rest for 10 minutes.

8. Cut along the outer seam of the ham, allowing the slices to fall away.

St Louis Style Bbq Ribs With Texas Spicy Bbq Sauce

Servings: 8

Cooking Time: 300 Minutes

Ingredients:

- 3 Rack St. Louis-style ribs, membrane removed
- 4 Tablespoon Rub
- 6 Tablespoon butter
- 1 1/2 Cup brown sugar
- 1 1/2 Cup agave
- 1 1/2 Cup Texas Spicy BBQ Sauce

Directions:

1. Supply your smoker with wood pellets and follow the start-up procedure. Preheat the grill, with the lid closed, to 250° F.

2. Season ribs with Traeger rub and place directly on grill grate rib side down or in a Traeger rib rack with the bone resting on the rack. Cook for 3 hours. Grill: 250 °F

3. Stack 2 pieces of tin foil on the table large enough to cover one rack of ribs. In the center of the foil place 3 tablespoons butter, 1/2 cup brown sugar, and 1/2 cup agave. Place the rib rack meat side down on top of the brown sugar mixture and wrap tightly. Repeat with remaining 2 racks.

4. Place all ribs directly on the grill grate meat side down and cook an additional 1-1/2 to 2 hours or until internal temperature reaches 203°F. Grill: 250 °F Probe: 203 °F

5. Remove ribs from the grill and cover each rack with 1/2 cup Texas Spicy BBQ sauce.

6. Rewrap and return to grill an additional 10 minutes allowing sauce to thicken. Grill: 250 °F

7. Remove ribs from the grill, slice and enjoy!

Smoked Traeger Pulled Pork

Servings: 8

Cooking Time: 540 Minutes

Ingredients:

- 1 (6-9 lb) bone-in pork shoulder
- Pork & Poultry Rub
- 2 Cup apple cider
- 'Que BBQ Sauce

Directions:

1. Supply your smoker with wood pellets and follow the start-up procedure. Preheat the grill, with the lid closed, to 250° F.

2. While the Traeger comes to temperature, trim excess fat off pork butt.

3. Generously season with Traeger Pork & Poultry Rub on all sides and let sit for 20 minutes.

4. Place the pork butt fat side up directly on the grill grate and cook until the internal temperature reaches 160°F, about 3 to 5 hours. Grill: 250 °F Probe: 160 °F

5. Remove the pork butt from the grill.

6. On a large baking sheet, stack 4 large pieces of aluminum foil on top of each other, ensuring they are wide enough to wrap the pork butt entirely on all sides. If not, overlap the foil pieces to create a wider base. Place the pork butt in the center on the foil, then bring up the sides of the foil a little bit before pouring the apple cider on top of the pork butt. Wrap the foil tightly around the pork, ensuring the cider does not escape.

7. Place the foil-wrapped pork butt back on the grill fat side up and cook until the internal temperature reaches 204°F, in the thickest part of the meat, about 3 to 4 hours longer depending on the size of the pork butt. Grill: 250 °F Probe: 204 °F

8. Remove from the grill. Allow the pork to rest for 45 minutes in the foil packet.

9. Remove the pork from the foil and pour off any excess liquid into a fat separator.

10. Place the pork in a large dish and shred the meat, removing and discarding the bone and any excess fat. Add separated liquid back into pork and season to taste with additional Traeger Big Game Rub. Optionally, add Traeger 'Que BBQ Sauce or your favorite BBQ sauce to taste.

Grilled Lasagna With Cold-smoked Mozzarella

Servings: 8-12

Cooking Time: 70 Minutes

Ingredients:

- 15 Oz. Ricotta Cheese
- 3 Cups Cold-Smoked Mozzarella, Grated Divided
- 2 Eggs
- 6 Garlic Cloves, Chopped
- 1 Tsp Garlic Powder
- 1 Cup Grated Parmesan Cheese, Divided
- 1 Lb. Italian Sausage
- 1 Tbsp Italian Seasoning
- 1 Pkg. "No-Bake" Lasagna Noodles
- 48 Oz. Marinara Sauce
- 1 Lb. Mozzarella Block
- 1 Tbsp Olive Oil
- 1 Tbsp Chopped Oregano
- ¼ Cup Italian Parsley, Chopped
- 1 Yellow Onion, Chopped

Directions:

1. In a glass bowl, mix together the eggs, Italian seasoning, garlic powder, ricotta cheese, ½ cup parmesan cheese, and 1 cup of smoked mozzarella, and 2 tablespoons of parsley. Cover and refrigerate for 1 hour.

2. Supply your smoker with wood pellets and follow the start-up procedure. Preheat the grill, with the lid open, to 400° F. If using a gas or charcoal grill, set it up for medium-high heat. Place a cast iron skillet on the grill grates and allow to preheat.

3. Heat olive oil in skillet, then add Italian sausage and cook for 5 minutes, then add in onion and garlic, and cook an additional 3 minutes. Remove from heat and stir in 1 tablespoon of parsley and dried oregano. Set aside and reduce grill temperature to 350° F.

4. To assemble, begin by covering the bottom of a 9x13 pan with 1 cup of sauce. For the first layer, place a single layer of uncooked noodles over the sauce, followed by ⅓ of the ricotta cheese mixture, half of the Italian sausage,

1 cup of mozzarella cheese, and 1 cup of sauce. Repeat for layer two with a single layer of uncooked lasagna noodles, ⅓ of the ricotta cheese mixture, and 1 ½ cups of sauce. Repeat for layer three with a layer of uncooked lasagna noodles, remaining ricotta mixture, remaining Italian sausage, 1 cup of sauce. For the final layer, add a layer of uncooked lasagna noodles, remaining sauce, and remaining 1 cup mozzarella plus ½ cup parmesan.

5.   Transfer lasagna to grill and cook, covered with foil, for 35 minutes. Remove foil and continue cooking for 10 minutes, sprinkle with additional parmesan and parsley, if desired. Remove from grill and let stand 15 minutes before serving.

Pulled Pork Shoulder And Chicken

Servings: 6 - 8
Cooking Time: 300 Minutes

Ingredients:
- 1/3 Cup Apple Cider Vinegar
- 4 Cups Chicken Broth
- 1/3 Cup Ketchup
- 2 Tbsp Pulled Pork Seasoning
- 4 Lbs. Pork Shoulder, Bone In

Directions:
1.   Supply your smoker with wood pellets and follow the start-up procedure. Preheat the grill, with the lid open, to 350° F. In a bowl, combine the chicken broth, ketchup, apple cider vinegar, and 1 tablespoon of Pulled Pork Seasoning. Whisk well to combine and set aside.
2.   Generously season the pork shoulder with the remaining 3 tablespoons of Pulled Pork Seasoning on all sides of the pork shoulder, then place on the grill and sear on all sides until golden brown, about 10 minutes.
3.   Remove the pork shoulder from the grill and place in the disposable aluminum pan. Pour the chicken broth mixture over the pork shoulder. It should come about 1/3 to ½ way up the side of the pork shoulder. Cover the top of the pan tightly with aluminum foil.
4.   Reduce the temperature of your   grill to 250°F. Place the foil pan on the grill and grill for four to five hours, or until the pork is tender and falling off the bone.
5.   Remove the pork from the grill and allow to cool slightly. Drain the liquid from the pan, reserving about a cup, then shred the pork and cover with the reserved liquid. Serve and enjoy!

Bbq Breakfast Grits

Servings: 12-15
Cooking Time: 40 Minutes

Ingredients:
- 2 cups chicken stock
- 1 cup water
- 1 cup quick-cooking grits
- 3 tablespoons unsalted butter
- 2 tablespoons minced garlic
- 1 medium onion, chopped
- 1 jalapeño pepper, stemmed, seeded, and chopped
- 1 teaspoon cayenne pepper
- 2 teaspoons red pepper flakes
- 1 tablespoon hot sauce
- 1 cup shredded Monterey Jack cheese
- 1 cup sour cream
- Salt
- Freshly ground black pepper
- 2 eggs, beaten
- ⅓ cup half-and-half
- 3 cups leftover pulled pork (preferably smoked)

Directions:
1.   Supply your smoker with wood pellets and follow the start-up procedure. Preheat, with the lid closed, to 350°F.
2.   On your kitchen stove top, in a large saucepan over high heat, bring the chicken stock and water to a boil.
3.   Add the grits and reduce the heat to low, then stir in the butter, garlic, onion, jalapeño, cayenne, red pepper flakes, hot sauce, cheese, and sour cream. Season with salt and pepper, then cook for about 5 minutes.
4.   Temper the beaten eggs (see Tip below) and incorporate into the grits. Remove the saucepan from the heat and stir in the half-and-half and pulled pork.
5.   Pour the grits into a greased grill-safe 9-by-13-inch casserole dish or aluminum pan.
6.   Transfer to the grill, close the lid, and bake for 30 to 40 minutes, covering with aluminum foil toward the end of cooking if the grits start to get too brown on top.

Bacon Stuffed Smoked Pork Loin

Servings: 4-6
Cooking Time: 60 Minutes

Ingredients:

- 3 Pound Pork Loin, Butterflied
- As Needed Pork Rub
- 1/4 Cup Walnuts, Chopped
- 1/3 Cup Craisins
- 1 Tablespoon Oregano, fresh
- 1 Tablespoon fresh thyme
- 6 Pieces Asparagus, fresh
- 6 Slices Bacon, sliced
- 1/3 Cup Parmesan cheese, grated
- As Needed Bacon Grease

Directions:

1. Lay down 2 large pieces of butcher's twine on your work surface. Place butterflied pork loin perpendicular to twine.
2. Season the inside of the pork loin with the pork rub.
3. On one end of the loin, layer in a line all of the ingredients, beginning with the chopped walnuts, craisins, oregano, thyme, and asparagus.
4. Add bacon and top with the parmesan cheese.
5. Starting at the end with all of the fillings, carefully roll up the pork loin and secure on both ends with butcher's twine.
6. Roll the pork loin in the reserved bacon grease and season the outside with more Pork Rub.
7. When ready to cook, set temperature to 180°F and preheat, lid closed for 15 minutes. Place stuffed pork loin directly on the grill grate and smoke for 1 hour.
8. Remove the pork loin; increase the temperature to 350°F and allow to preheat.
9. Place the loin back on the smoker and grill for approximately 30 to 45 minutes or until the temperature reads 135°F on an instant-read thermometer.
10. Move the pork loin to a plate and tent it with aluminum foil. Let it rest for 15 minutes before slicing and serving. Enjoy!

Roasted Bacon Weave Holiday Ham

Servings: 6
Cooking Time: 180 Minutes

Ingredients:

- 1 1/2 Pound Bacon, sliced
- 1 Large Ham, Bone-In
- whole cloves
- 1 1/2 Cup pineapple juice
- 2 Cup ginger beer
- 1/4 Cup brown sugar
- 2 Tablespoon mustard

Directions:

1. Create a bacon weave on parchment paper.
2. Put the ham in a disposable roasting pan. Gently transfer the bacon weave to the top of the ham and stud the bacon with the cloves (if desired).
3. Pour 1 cup of pineapple juice and 1 cup of ginger beer/ale into the bottom of the roasting pan.
4. Supply your smoker with wood pellets and follow the start-up procedure. Preheat the grill, with the lid closed, to 300° F.
5. Cover the roasting pan with foil and put on the Traeger. Cook the ham until it reaches 145°F (somewhere between 2 to 3 hours). Grill: 300 °F Probe: 145 °F
6. Meanwhile mix together the glaze. Combine the remaining 1/2 cup of pineapple juice, 1 cup ginger beer/ale, brown sugar and mustard in a saucepan on the stovetop. Cook until it thickens slightly, then brush on the ham.
7. Put the uncovered ham back on Traeger and cook until the temperature reaches 160°F. Grill: 300 °F Probe: 160 °F
8. Let the ham rest 5 minutes before slicing and serving. Reserve the juices to pour over the ham. Enjoy!

Raspberry Spiral Ham With Glaze

Servings: 12
Cooking Time: 120 Minutes

Ingredients:

- 1 Ham, Spiral (Precooked)
- Raspberry Chipotle Spice Rub
- 1/2 Jar Raspberry Jam
- 1 Quart Raspberry, Fresh

- 1/4 Cup Sugar
- 1/3 Cup Water, Warm

Directions:

1. Supply your smoker with wood pellets and follow the start-up procedure. Preheat the grill, with the lid open, to 225° F.

2. Season the ham with Raspberry Chipotle Spice, taking care to season in between each slice. Place in your Grill and smoke for about 2 hours.

3. Just before you pull the ham, combine glaze ingredients in a saucepan over medium heat until raspberries are no longer whole and the glaze is runny. If you want a smoother glaze, remove the raspberry seeds by draining the glaze through cheesecloth.

4. Pour glaze over the ham just before serving. Slice and serve hot. Enjoy!

Bacon Grilled Cheese Sandwich

Servings: 4

Cooking Time: 10 Minutes

Ingredients:

- mayonnaise
- 8 Slices Texas toast
- 16 Slices cheddar cheese
- 1 Pound applewood smoked bacon slices, cooked
- butter, softened

Directions:

1. Supply your smoker with wood pellets and follow the start-up procedure. Preheat the grill, with the lid closed, to 350° F.

2. Spread a little bit of mayonnaise on each piece of bread.

3. Place 1 piece of cheddar cheese on bread slice then top with a couple slices of bacon. Add another slice of cheese then top with the other piece of bread. Spread softened butter on the exterior of the top piece of bread.

4. When the grill is hot, place the grilled cheese directly on a cleaned, oiled grill grate buttered side down. Spread softened butter on the exterior of the top slice. Grill: 350 °F

5. Cook the grilled cheese on the first side for 5 to 7 minutes until grill marks develop and the cheese has begun to melt. Flip the sandwich and repeat on the other side. Grill: 350 °F

6. Remove from the grill when the cheese is melted and the exterior is lightly toasted. Enjoy!

Rub-injected Pork Shoulder

Servings: 8-12

Cooking Time: 1200 Minutes

Ingredients:

- 1 (6- to 8-pound) bone-in pork shoulder
- 2 cups Tea Injectable made with Pork Rub
- 2 tablespoons yellow mustard
- 1 batch Pork Rub

Directions:

1. Supply your smoker with wood pellets and follow the start-up procedure. Preheat the grill, with the lid closed, to 225°F.

2. Inject the pork shoulder throughout with the tea injectable.

3. Coat the pork shoulder all over with mustard and season it with the rub. Using your hands, work the rub into the meat.

4. Place the shoulder directly on the grill grate and smoke until its internal temperature reaches 160°F and a dark bark has formed on the exterior.

5. Pull the shoulder from the grill and wrap it completely in aluminum foil or butcher paper.

6. Increase the grill's temperature to 350°F.

7. Return the pork shoulder to the grill and cook until its internal temperature reaches 195°F.

8. Pull the shoulder from the grill and place it in a cooler. Cover the cooler and let the pork rest for 1 or 2 hours.

9. Remove the pork shoulder from the cooler and unwrap it. Remove the shoulder bone and pull the pork apart using just your fingers. Serve immediately.

Simple Smoked Baby Backs

Servings: 4-8
Cooking Time: 360 Minutes

Ingredients:

- 2 (2- or 3-pound) racks baby back ribs
- 2 tablespoons yellow mustard
- 1 batch Pork Rub

Directions:

1. Supply your smoker with wood pellets and follow the start-up procedure. Preheat the grill, with the lid closed, to 225°F.
2. Remove the membrane from the backside of the ribs. This can be done by cutting just through the membrane in an X pattern and working a paper towel between the membrane and the ribs to pull it off.
3. Coat the ribs on both sides with mustard and season them with the rub. Using your hands, work the rub into the meat.
4. Place the ribs directly on the grill grate and smoke until their internal temperature reaches between 190°F and 200°F.
5. Remove the racks from the grill and cut into individual ribs. Serve immediately.

Maple Syrup Bacon Wrapped Tenderloin

Servings: 5
Cooking Time: 30 Minutes

Ingredients:

- 1 Package Bacon, Thick Cut
- 1/4 Cup Maple Syrup
- 2 Tbsp Olive Oil
- 3 Tbsp Competition Smoked Rub
- 1 Trimmed With Silver Skin Removed Pork, Tenderloin

Directions:

1. Lay the strips of bacon out flat, with each strip slightly overlapping the other.
2. Sprinkle the pork tenderloin with 1 tablespoon of the Competition Smoked Rub and lay in the center.
3. Wrap with bacon over the tenderloin and tuck in the ends.
4. In a small bowl, mix the olive oil, maple syrup and remaining seasoning together and brush onto the wrapped tenderloin.
5. Supply your smoker with wood pellets and follow the start-up procedure. Preheat the grill, with the lid open, to 350° F.
6. When the grill is ready, place your tenderloin on the grill and cook, turning, for 15 minutes.
7. Increase the grill temperature to 400°F and grill for another 15 minutes or until the internal temperature is 145°F. Serve and enjoy!

Home-cured Picnic Ham With Mustard Caviar

Servings: 8
Cooking Time: 420 Minutes

Ingredients:

- 1 pork shoulder roast, about 5lb (2.3kg) total
- 1 cup distilled water, apple cider, or apple juice, plus more
- Mustard Caviar
- for the brine
- 1 cup kosher salt
- 5 tsp pink curing salt #1
- 1 cup light brown sugar or turbinado sugar or low-carb substitute
- ¼ cup molasses or honey
- 1 gallon (3.8 liters) distilled water, divided, plus more

Directions:

1. Trim any excess fat from the pork shoulder, leaving at least ¼ inch. Use a sharp knife to score the skin of the ham in the classic diamond pattern, making the cuts about 1 inch (2.5cm) apart, but don't penetrate the meat. (If you purchased a shoulder without skin, skip this step.)
2. In a stockpot on the stovetop over medium-high heat, make the brine by combining the salts, brown sugar, molasses, and water. Bring the mixture to a boil. Whisk to dissolve the salts and sugar. Remove the stockpot

from the stovetop and let the brine cool to room temperature.

3. Submerge the pork shoulder in the brine. If it floats, place a resealable bag of ice on top. Refrigerate for 3 days.

4. Place the ham in a clean container and cover with cold water. Let the ham soak for 30 minutes. Drain and pat dry with paper towels.

5. Supply your smoker with wood pellets and follow the start-up procedure. Preheat the grill, with the lid closed, to 225° F.

6. Place the ham on the grate and grill until the internal temperature in the thickest part of the meat reaches 160°F (71°C), about 4 to 5 hours. Remove the ham from the grill. Let the ham come to room temperature. Cover and refrigerate for up to 3 days. This helps establish the ham's smokiness.

7. Preheat the grill to 325°F (163°C).

8. Transfer the ham to an aluminum foil roasting pan and add the water to the bottom of the pan. Place the pan on the grate and roast the ham until the skin is nicely browned and the internal temperature reaches 145°F (63°C), about 1½ to 2 hours.

9. Remove the ham from the grill and let rest for 10 minutes. Carve the ham and serve with the mustard caviar.

Traeger Roasted Easter Ham

Servings: 8
Cooking Time: 60 Minutes

Ingredients:
- 1 (6-7 lb) bone-in ham
- 1 Cup Sweet & Heat BBQ Sauce
- 2 Cup brown sugar
- 1/2 Cup pineapple juice

Directions:
1. Supply your smoker with wood pellets and follow the start-up procedure. Preheat the grill, with the lid closed, to 225° F.

2. Place ham in grill and cook for 60 minutes. Grill: 225 °F

3. While the ham is cooking, mix together the Traeger Sweet & Heat BBQ Sauce, brown sugar and pineapple juice.

4. Glaze ham with the sauce every 10 minutes during the last 30 minutes. Remove ham from grill and serve. Enjoy!

Honey Pork Belly Burnt Ends

Servings: 4
Cooking Time: 270 Minutes

Ingredients:
- 2/3 Cup Bbq Sauce
- 2 Tbsp Butter, Melted
- 2 Tbsp Honey
- 2 Tbsp Olive Oil
- Blackened Sriracha Rub
- 3 Lbs Pork Belly, Skin Removed

Directions:
1. Supply your smoker with wood pellets and follow the start-up procedure. Preheat the grill, with the lid open, to 225° F. If using a gas or charcoal grill, set it up for low, indirect heat.

2. Cut pork belly into 2-inch cubes and place into a large mixing bowl.

3. Drizzle olive oil over pork belly, then generously season with Blackened Sriracha.

4. Transfer seasoned pork belly to a wire rack and place on the grill grate. Cook for 3 hours.

5. Remove the pork belly from the wire rack and transfer into a foil-lined aluminum pan or disposable foil pan.

6. Whisk together BBQ sauce, melted butter, and honey, then pour mixture over pork.

7. Toss to coat, then cover the pan with aluminum foil and return to the grill rack.

8. Cook for another 1 to 1 ½ hours, until the internal temperature reaches 200° F.

9. Remove the foil, transfer pork belly to a cast iron skillet and place in the center of the grill.

10. Open the sear slide and continue cooking for another 5 to 7 minutes, turning halfway, to crisp up the pork.

11. Remove pork belly from the grill, and serve warm.

Southern Sugar-glazed Ham

Servings: 12-15

Cooking Time: 300 Minutes

Ingredients:

- 1 (12- to 15-pound) whole bone-in ham, fully cooked
- ¼ cup yellow mustard
- 1 cup pineapple juice
- ½ cup packed light brown sugar
- 1 teaspoon ground cinnamon
- ½ teaspoon ground cloves

Directions:

1. Supply your smoker with wood pellets and follow the start-up procedure. Preheat, with the lid closed, to 275°F.

2. Trim off the excess fat and skin from the ham, leaving a ¼-inch layer of fat. Put the ham in an aluminum foil–lined roasting pan.

3. On your kitchen stove top, in a medium saucepan over low heat, combine the mustard, pineapple juice, brown sugar, cinnamon, and cloves and simmer for 15 minutes, or until thick and reduced by about half.

4. Baste the ham with half of the pineapple–brown sugar syrup, reserving the rest for basting later in the cook.

5. Place the roasting pan on the grill, close the lid, and smoke for 4 hours.

6. Baste the ham with the remaining pineapple–brown sugar syrup and continue smoking with the lid closed for another hour, or until a meat thermometer inserted in the thickest part of the ham reads 140°F.

7. Remove the ham from the grill, tent with foil, and let rest for 20 minutes before carving.

Bbq Pork Short Ribs

Servings: 4

Cooking Time: 360 Minutes

Ingredients:

- 2 Pork Short Rib Racks With At Least 1 1/2-2" of Meat On Bone
- Pork & Poultry Rub

Directions:

1. Clean and trim short ribs. Season generously on all sides with Traeger Pork and Poultry rub.

2. Supply your smoker with wood pellets and follow the start-up procedure. Preheat the grill, with the lid closed, to 250° F.

3. Place ribs directly on the grill grate and cook for 4-6 hours or until the internal temperature reaches 202-204°F when an instant read thermometer is inserted in the thickest part of meat. Spritz with apple juice every hour if desired. Grill: 250 °F Probe: 202 °F

4. Remove from grill and allow to rest 10 minutes before slicing. Cut into individual ribs and serve with your favorite sides. Enjoy!

Maple-smoked Pork Chops

Servings: 4

Cooking Time: 55 Minutes

Ingredients:

- 1 (12-pound) full packer brisket
- 2 tablespoons yellow mustard
- 1 batch Espresso Brisket Rub
- Worcestershire Mop and Spritz, for spritzing

Directions:

1. Supply your smoker with wood pellets and follow the start-up procedure. Preheat the grill, with the lid closed, to 180°F.

2. Season the pork chops on both sides with salt and pepper.

3. Place the chops directly on the grill grate and smoke for 30 minutes.

4. Increase the grill's temperature to 350°F. Continue to cook the chops until their internal temperature reaches 145°F.

5. Remove the pork chops from the grill and let them rest for 5 minutes before serving.

Bbq Pulled Coleslaw Pork Sandwiches

Servings: 12
Cooking Time: 480 Minutes

Ingredients:

- 1 Bottle Bbq Sauce
- Coleslaw, Prepared
- 12 Kaiser Rolls
- 8-10Lbs Pork Butt Roast, Bone-In
- 5 Oz Sugar
- 1 Cup Yellow Mustard

Directions:

1. Supply your smoker with wood pellets and follow the start-up procedure. Preheat the grill, with the lid open, to 225° F. While your grill is heating, remove the pork roast from its packaging and place on a cookie sheet. Rub the pork roast down with yellow mustard.

2. Mix BBQ sauce and sugar in a bowl. Rub the roast down with entire mixture, allowing time for the rub to melt into the meat.

3. Place the roast in the smoker and cook for 6 hours.

4. After 6 hours, remove the roast and double wrap in tin foil. Turn the grill up to 250°F and cook the roast for another 2 hours or until the roast is probe tender (around an internal temperature of 204°F). Let the pork butt rest in the foil for up to an hour before pulling.

5. Cut each Kaiser roll in half, mix pulled pork with some more barbecue sauce and pile on each half of roll. Top with coleslaw and green onions. Don't mix all the pulled pork with barbecue sauce so that you can use the extra pulled pork for different recipes. Serve hot and enjoy!

Kodiak Cakes Candied Bacon Crumble Brownies

Servings: 6
Cooking Time: 45 Minutes

Ingredients:

- 1 Box Big Bear Brownie Mix, Kodiak Cakes
- 2 eggs
- 1 Stick butter, melted
- 2 Tablespoon coconut oil
- 2 Tablespoon water
- 2 Cup cooked bacon
- 1/2 Cup Almonds, chopped
- 1/2 Cup sugar

Directions:

1. Supply your smoker with wood pellets and follow the start-up procedure. Preheat the grill, with the lid closed, to 300° F.

2. Spray an 8" baking pan with non-stick spray.

3. Empty Kodiak Cake brownie mix into a medium-size mixing bowl. Add eggs, melted butter, coconut oil, and water. Gently mix, being careful not to overmix. Pour into prepared pan.

4. Place brownies in center of grill grate; bake for 45 minutes. Grill: 300 °F

5. While the brownies are baking, begin assembling bacon crumble. Add honey or sugar to a medium-size saucepan, over high heat. Add bacon and almonds. Stir for 2-3 minutes, or until sugar has dissolved. Remove from heat and let cool.

6. Remove brownies from grill and cool completely. Sprinkle candied bacon crumble over the top of brownies. Enjoy!

Hawaiian Pineapple Pork Butt

Servings: 8 - 10
Cooking Time: 720 Minutes

Ingredients:

- 6 - 8 Pineapple Rings
- 2 Cups Pineapple, Juice
- 1 8-10Lb Pork Butt Roast, Bone-In
- ¼ Cup Sweet Heat Rub

Directions:

1. Supply your smoker with wood pellets and follow the start-up procedure. Preheat the grill, with the lid open, to 225° F. If not using a pellet smoker, set up the smoker for indirect smoking.

2. Remove the pork butt from its packaging and drain any excess liquid from the pork butt. Pat the pork butt dry with paper towels and discard the paper towels.

3. Generously season the pork butt with the Sweet Heat seasoning, making sure that the roast is coated on all sides.

4. Place the pineapple rings evenly over the pork shoulder, fat side up, and pin with toothpicks. Place the pork butt into the 9x13 pan and pour the pineapple juice over the top.

5. Set the pan into the smoker. Make sure that the pork butt is placed as close to the center of the rack as possible for even cooking.

6. Place a temperature probe into the thickest part of the pork butt, and smoke the pork until it reaches an internal temperature of 201°F. The pork should be deeply browned and smell very porky.

7. Once the pork butt reaches its internal temperature, remove the pork butt from the grill and wrap it tightly in foil. Allow the roast to rest for at least 1 hour before shredding.

8. After the roast has rested for an hour, shred the pork with your meat claws, discarding any large chunks of fat. Serve immediately.

Chinese Alcoholic Bbq Pork Tenderloin

Servings: 4
Cooking Time: 30 Minutes

Ingredients:
- 14 Cup Bbq Sauce
- 2 Garlic Cloves, Minced
- 14 Cup Hoisin Sauce
- 2 Lbs Pork Tenderloin, Trimmed With Silver Skins Removed
- 1 Tbsp Sugar, Granulated
- 1 Tsp Sweet Rib Rub Seasoning
- 14 Cup Tamari
- 14 Cup White Wine

Directions:
1. In a glass measuring cup, whisk together the hoisin sauce, tamari, wine, garlic, sugar, and Sweet Rib Rub.

2. Place pork tenderloin in a resealable bag, then pour the marinade over the pork and allow to marinate in the refrigerator for 4 to 6 hours.

3. Supply your smoker with wood pellets and follow the start-up procedure. Preheat the grill, with the lid open, to 400° F. If using a gas or charcoal grill, preheat to medium-high heat.

4. Remove the pork from the marinade, then pour the marinade into a grill-safe pan.

5. Place the marinade on the grill and bring to a boil for 3 minutes. Add the BBQ sauce and simmer for 2 minutes. Remove from the grill, and set aside.

6. Place the pork on the grill and cook for 18 to 20 minutes, until an internal temperature of 145° F. Flip and baste the pork with the sauce every 3 to 5 minutes.

7. Remove the pork from the grill and allow it to rest on a cutting board for 10 minutes, prior to serving warm with additional sauce.

Pulled Pork Stew

Servings: 4
Cooking Time: 120 Minutes

Ingredients:
- 16 Ounce salsa verde
- 15 Ounce black beans, drained and rinsed
- 15 Ounce fire roasted red peppers, drained and rinsed
- 1 Pound pulled pork
- 1 Teaspoon ground cumin
- 2 Cup chicken stock
- salt and pepper
- Avocado, Sliced

Directions:
1. Supply your smoker with wood pellets and follow the start-up procedure. Preheat the grill, with the lid closed, to 375° F.

2. Stir in salsa verde, black beans, fire-roasted tomatoes, shredded pork, cumin and chicken broth. Season with salt and pepper to taste.

3. Cook on Traeger for 1 hour stirring every 20 minutes. After 1 hour, cover Dutch oven with lid and cook an additional hour.

4. Top stew with fresh herbs, avocado and sour cream. Serve hot, enjoy!

Bbq Baby Back Ribs With Bacon Pineapple Glaze By Scott Thomas

Servings: 4
Cooking Time: 180 Minutes

Ingredients:

- 2 Rack baby back ribs
- 1 As Needed salt and pepper
- 1 As Needed Your Favorite Spicy Rub
- 6 Slices bacon
- 6 Fluid Ounce pineapple juice
- 1 Teaspoon garlic, minced
- 2 Tablespoon honey

Directions:

1. Remove the membrane from the bone side of the ribs and apply the salt, pepper and rub to that side. Flip the ribs over and season the meat side.
2. Supply your smoker with wood pellets and follow the start-up procedure. Preheat the grill, with the lid closed, to 350° F.
3. While the grill heats up, cook the bacon in a frying pan. As the bacon is cooking, pour the pineapple juice, garlic and honey into an oven safe pot.
4. Remove the bacon from the grease and let the pan and bacon fat cool down. After the pan has cooled for a while, pour the bacon grease in with the pineapple juice, garlic and honey and stir to combine.
5. Place the ribs and the pot on the grill and close the lid. After an hour, the slurry will have reduced down a bit and can be applied to the ribs. Slather the ribs with the reduction every 15 minutes. When the bones peek out about a quarter to a third of an inch, the ribs are done which is about 2 hours and 15 minutes. Grill: 350 °F
6. For fall off the bone ribs, go another 30-45 minutes, continuing to glaze every 15 minutes. Grill: 350 °F
7. The sweet and savory of the reduction will temper the heat of the spicy rub forming an outstanding and complex blend of flavors. Enjoy!

Baked German Pork Schnitzel With Grilled Lemons

Servings: 2
Cooking Time: 20 Minutes

Ingredients:

- 16 Ounce pork chops
- salt
- black pepper
- 1 Teaspoon garlic powder
- 1 Teaspoon paprika
- 2 eggs
- 1 Cup panko breadcrumbs
- 1/2 Cup flour
- 2 Whole lemon, halved

Directions:

1. Supply your smoker with wood pellets and follow the start-up procedure. Preheat the grill, with the lid closed, to High heat.
2. Place pork chops individually between 2 pieces of plastic wrap. Pound with a meat mallet until they are around 1/4 to 1/8" thick. Season both sides generously with salt and black pepper.
3. Mix the garlic powder and paprika in a bowl. In another bowl whisk the eggs. In a third bowl add the breadcrumbs.
4. Dip pork cutlets one by one into flour shaking off any excess, then into eggs and then into the breadcrumbs. Place breaded pork cutlets onto a lightly oiled wire rack over a baking sheet.
5. Cook for 15 minutes then flip and bake for another 5 minutes. When you open the grill to flip pork, place sliced lemons directly on grill grate flesh side down. Grill: 500 °F
6. Remove from grill and serve immediately with grilled lemons. Enjoy!

Triple Threat Pork Fattywith Stuffed Jalapeños

Servings: 10

Cooking Time: 150 Minutes

Ingredients:

- 16 strips of bacon, about 1¼lb (565g) total, not thick cut
- 1½ tsp Tajin seasoning, plus more
- 8oz (225g) light cream cheese, at room temperature
- 3 large jalapeños, decored, destemmed, and deseeded
- 1lb (450g) seasoned breakfast sausage
- 1lb (450g) ground pork
- 6 to 8oz (170 to 225g) thinly sliced pepper Jack cheese

Directions:

1. Supply your smoker with wood pellets and follow the start-up procedure. Preheat the grill, with the lid closed, to 275° F.

2. Moisten a workspace with a damp towel. Place a 15-inch (38cm) rectangle of plastic wrap on the workspace. Place 8 strips of bacon, sides touching, parallel to the edge of the plastic. Fold back the even-numbered strips at the halfway point and place a 9th snugly against the folds (perpendicular to the first 8). Unfold.

3. Fold back the odd-numbered strips and place a 10th snugly against the folds. Unfold. Repeat until the weave is complete. Place another sheet of plastic over the weave. Use a rolling pin to thin and tighten the weave.

4. In a small bowl, combine the Tajin and cream cheese. Tightly stuff each jalapeño with the mixture. Reserve any extra filling.

5. Place the sausage and pork in a large bowl. Wet your hands with cold water and knead the meats to combine. Transfer to a resealable plastic bag. Use a rolling pin to create a rectangle that's smaller than the dimensions of your bacon weave. (For reference, place the weave alongside the bag.) Slit the sides of the bag to release the meat and then position the bag over the weave and remove the remaining plastic.

6. Cover the meat with the pepper Jack, leaving 1 inch (2.5cm) around the edges. Pipe the reserved cream cheese mixture randomly over the surface. Position the stuffed jalapeños end to end on the long side of the meat. Use the plastic under the weave to tightly roll up the fatty from the side with the jalapeños. Use bamboo skewers to secure the weave. Lightly season the outside with more Tajin seasoning.

7. Place the fatty seam side down on the grate and smoke until the internal temperature reaches 160°F (71°C), about 2 to 2½ hours.

8. Transfer the fatty to a cutting board and let rest for 10 minutes. Use an electric knife to slice the fatty into 1-inch (2.5cm) rounds before serving.

Grilled Pork Loin

Servings: 4

Cooking Time: 30 Minutes

Ingredients:

- 2 Tablespoons Balsamic Vinegar
- 2 Cups Fresh Washed And Dried Blackberries
- ¼ Cup Seedless Blackberry Preserve
- ½ Teaspoon Dijon Mustard
- Pinch Of Kosher Salt
- 1 Tablespoon Olive Oil
- 1 Pound Silver Skin And Extra Fat Removed Pork Loin
- 2 Tablespoons Sweet Rib Rub
- 1 Tablespoon Worcestershire Sauce

Directions:

1. Place your pork loin on a flat work surface. Trim the pork loin if necessary. Rub the tenderloin all over with olive oil until it is fully coated. Once the pork loin is completely coated, generously season all over with Sweet Rib Rub until every part of the pork loin is coated. Allow the pork tenderloin to rest at room temperature for 30 minutes.

2. While the pork loin rests, make the blackberry sauce. In a small bowl, place a metal strainer on top combine the fresh blackberries, seedless blackberry preserves, balsamic vinegar, Worcestershire sauce, Dijon mustard, and Sweet Rib Rub. Mix well and set aside.

3. Supply your smoker with wood pellets and follow the start-up procedure. Preheat the grill, with the lid open, to 350° F. If you're using a gas or charcoal grill, set

it up for medium heat. Insert a temperature probe into the thickest part of the pork loin and smoke at 225°F for 4-5 hours, flipping once, until the pork loin is golden brown and charred in some spots, and reaches an internal temperature of 145°-165°F. Remove the pork loin from the grill and allow it to rest for 5 minutes.

4. Slice the pork loin thinly and serve with the blackberry sauce.

Roasted Ham With Apricot Sauce

Servings: 8
Cooking Time: 120 Minutes

Ingredients:
- 1 (8-10 lb) Snake River Farms Kurobuta Whole Bone-In Ham
- 1 Bottle Apricot BBQ Sauce
- 1/4 Cup horseradish
- 2 Tablespoon Dijon mustard

Directions:
1. Supply your smoker with wood pellets and follow the start-up procedure. Preheat the grill, with the lid closed, to 325° F.
2. Place ham in a large roasting pan lined with aluminum foil. Place pan on grill and cook for 90 minutes. Grill: 325 °F
3. For the Glaze: In a saucepan over medium heat, combine the Traeger Apricot BBQ Sauce, horseradish and mustard. Set aside and keep warm.
4. After 90 minutes, brush the ham with the glaze. Continue to cook for another 30 minutes or until a thermometer inserted into the thickest part of the ham reaches an internal temperatures of 135°F. Grill: 325 °F Probe: 135 °F
5. Remove ham from grill and rest for 20 minutes before slicing.
6. Serve with remaining glaze if desired. Enjoy!

Hanging St. Louis-style Grilled Ribs

Servings: 4
Cooking Time: 270 Minutes

Ingredients:
- 1 1/3 Cup Apple Juice
- 1 2/3 Cup BBQ Sauce, Divided
- Pulled Pork Rub
- 4 Half Racks Spare Ribs, St. Louis Style

Directions:
1. Supply your smoker with wood pellets and follow the start-up procedure. Preheat the grill, with the lid open, to 250° F. If using a gas or charcoal grill, set it up for low, indirect heat.
2. Using a sharp knife, remove the back membrane from the rib racks and pat dry with paper towel. Cut rib racks in half, then season generously with Pulled Pork Rub.
3. Insert a hanging hook under the top rib, then transfer racks to the smoking cabinet. Smoke for 2 ½ hours.
4. Remove ribs from the smoking cabinet and set on heavy duty foil. Mix together ⅔ cup BBQ sauce and ⅓ cup apple juice, then brush thinned BBQ sauce on both sides of ribs. Pour ¼ cup of apple juice around each of the ribs. Fold over foil, then transfer to the grill, meat side down. Increase temperature to 300° F and continue cooking for an additional 2 hours.
5. Remove ribs from the grill, baste with BBQ, then return to the grill and cook for another 10 to 15 minutes. Allow to rest for 15 minutes, then slice and serve hot.

Grilled Raspberry Chipotle Pork Ribs

Servings: 4
Cooking Time: 180 Minutes

Ingredients:
- Baby Back Rib
- Original Bbq Sauce
- Raspberry Chipotle Spice Rub

Directions:
1. Begin by gently rinsing off your ribs in cool water. Pat dry and remove the flavor blocker (thin membrane on the underside of the ribs) to allow the seasoning to permeate right into the meat.
2. Generously season your ribs with Raspberry Chipotle seasoning and place in the refrigerator for an hour for flavor to set in.

3. Supply your smoker with wood pellets and follow the start-up procedure. Preheat the grill, with the lid open, to 250° F. Place your seasoned rack of ribs on the grill and let cook for 2 hours. Next, lather on a thick coating of Original BBQ Sauce, turn up the grill to 300°F and let your ribs roast for another hour. Remove, cut and serve for a meal that will surely make its way into the weekly rotation.

Grilled Pork Tacos Al Pastor

Servings: 8
Cooking Time: 15 Minutes

Ingredients:

- 2 Tsp Annatto Powder
- Cilantro, Chopped
- Corn Tortillas
- 2 Tsp Cumin
- 1 Tsp Granulated Garlic
- 2 Tbsp Guajillo Chili Powder
- Jalapeno Pepper, Minced
- Lime, Wedges
- 1 Tsp Oregano, Dried
- 1/2 Tsp Pepper
- 1/2 Cup Pineapple, Juice
- 1/2 Pineapple, Skinned & Cored
- 2 Lbs Pork Shoulder, Boneless, Sliced Thin
- 1 1/2 Tsp Salt
- 2 Tbsp Tomato Paste
- 2 Tbsp Vegetable Oil
- 1/4 Cup White Vinegar
- Yellow Onion, Chopped

Directions:

1. Prepare marinade: In a mixing bowl, whisk together pineapple juice, vinegar, oil, tomato paste, chili powder, annatto, cumin, granulated garlic, oregano, salt, and pepper. Set aside.
2. Slice pork shoulder into thin slices (around ¼" thick), then place in a resealable plastic bag. Pour marinade over pork, seal bag, and turn to coat. Refrigerate overnight.
3. Supply your smoker with wood pellets and follow the start-up procedure. Preheat the grill, with the lid open, to 450° F. If using a gas or charcoal grill, set it up for high heat.
4. Remove the pork from the marinade and set on the grill. Grill over high heat for 3 to 5 minutes, turning frequently. Transfer to a cutting board to rest for 10 minutes, then slice thin.
5. Grill pineapple for 3 minutes, turning once. Set aside on a cutting board, and chop once cooled.
6. Assemble tacos: tortillas, pork, pineapple, jalapeño, onion, and cilantro. Serve warm with fresh lime wedges.

Cheese Bacon

Servings: 6-8
Cooking Time: 30 Minutes

Ingredients:

- 2 Teaspoon Applewood Bacon Seasoning
- 1 Pack Cheddar Cheese, Shredded
- 1 Pack Cream Cheese, Softened
- Cut In Half Lengthwise, Destemmed, Deveined And Deseeded Jalapeno Peppers
- 8 Strips Smoked Applewood Bacon, Cut In Half

Directions:

1. In a large bowl, combine cream cheese, Applewood Bacon seasoning and cheddar cheese. Mix until completely combined.
2. Using a spoon, fill the peppers with the cream cheese mixture. Wrap each pepper with a half slice of bacon and secure with a toothpick. Repeat until all jalapeno poppers are finished.
3. Supply your smoker with wood pellets and follow the start-up procedure. Preheat the grill, with the lid open, to 400° F. Place your jalapeno poppers on the grill basket and grill for 15-20 minutes, or until the bacon is cooked and crispy.
4. Serve and enjoy!

Traeger Smoked Sausage

Servings: 4
Cooking Time: 120 Minutes

Ingredients:

- 3 Pound ground pork
- 1/2 Tablespoon ground mustard

- 1 Tablespoon onion powder
- 1 Tablespoon garlic powder
- 1/2 Teaspoon pink curing salt
- 1 Tablespoon salt
- 4 Teaspoon black pepper
- 1/2 Cup ice water
- Hog casings, soaked and rinsed in cold water

Directions:

1. In a medium bowl, combine the meat and seasonings, mix well.

2. Add ice water to meat and mix with hands working quickly until everything is incorporated.

3. Place mixture in a sausage stuffer and follow manufacturers Directions:for operating. Use caution not to overstuff or the casing might burst.

4. Once all the meat is stuffed, determine your desired link length and pinch and twist a couple of times or tie it off. Repeat for each link.

5. Supply your smoker with wood pellets and follow the start-up procedure. Preheat the grill, with the lid closed, to 225° F.

6. Place links directly on the grill grate and cook for 1 to 2 hours or until the internal temperature registers 155°F. Let sausage rest a few minutes before slicing. Enjoy! Grill: 225 °F Probe: 155 °F

Baked Sage & Sausage Stuffing

Servings: 4
Cooking Time: 45 Minutes

Ingredients:

- 1 Pound Sage-Flavored Sausage, Such as Bob Evans Or Jimmy Dean
- 1/2 Cup onion, diced
- 1/2 Cup celery, diced
- 14 Ounce (14 oz) package herb seasoned stuffing
- 1/2 Cup dried sweetened cranberries
- 2 Cup low sodium chicken broth
- 6 Tablespoon butter
- butter

Directions:

1. Brown the sausage in a large frying pan, breaking up the sausage with a wooden spoon.

2. Add the onion and celery and cook until softened. Drain any excess fat. Transfer to a large mixing bowl. Add the stuffing mix and cranberries, if using.

3. Warm the chicken broth over medium-low heat; add butter and cook until melted. Toss with the bread/sausage mixture and mix lightly.

4. Butter a 3-qt casserole or baking dish. Do not compress the mixture or it will be dense.

5. Supply your smoker with wood pellets and follow the start-up procedure. Preheat the grill, with the lid closed, to 350° F.

6. Bake the stuffing, covered, for 35 to 45 minutes; uncover during the last 20 minutes of cooking if you prefer a crunchier texture. Grill: 350 °F

7. Remove from grill and serve. Enjoy!

Smoked Pork Loin With Sauerkraut And Apples

Servings: 4
Cooking Time: 120 Minutes

Ingredients:

- 1 (2 to 2-1/2 lb) pork loin roast
- Pork & Poultry Rub
- 1 Pound sauerkraut
- 2 Large cooking apples, peeled, cored and sliced
- 1 Large sweet onion, thinly sliced
- 1/3 Cup brown sugar
- 1 Cup dark beer
- 2 Tablespoon butter
- 2 Whole bay leaves

Directions:

1. Supply your smoker with wood pellets and follow the start-up procedure. Preheat the grill, with the lid closed, to 180° F.

2. Season the pork loin on all sides with Traeger Pork & Poultry Rub or salt and pepper. Place the roast directly on the grill grate, close the lid, and smoke for 1 hour. Grill: 180 °F

3. In a large Dutch oven or glass baking dish, layer the sauerkraut, apples, onions, brown sugar, beer, butter and bay leaves. Lay the smoked pork loin directly on top of

the sauerkraut mixture. Top the pan with a lid or a layer of foil.

4. Increase Traeger temperature to 350°F, and return the pan to the grill. Close the lid and roast the pork for an additional hour, or until the internal temperature on an instant-read meat thermometer reads 160°F. Grill: 350 °F Probe: 160 °F

5. Transfer the roast to a cutting board and let it rest. Meanwhile, gently stir the sauerkraut mixture and arrange on a serving platter. Slice the pork roast and layer on the sauerkraut and apples. Enjoy!

Smoked Pork Tenderloin

Servings: 4
Cooking Time: 180 Minutes

Ingredients:
- 1/2 Cup apple juice
- 3 Tablespoon honey
- 3 Tablespoon Pork & Poultry Rub
- 1/4 Cup brown sugar
- 2 Tablespoon thyme leaves
- 1/2 Tablespoon black pepper
- 2 (1-1/2 lb) pork tenderloins, silverskin removed

Directions:
1. For the Marinade: In a large bowl, add the apple juice, honey (warmed), Traeger Pork & Poultry rub, brown sugar, thyme leaves and black pepper. Whisk to combine.

2. Add pork loins to the bowl with the marinade. Turn pork to coat and cover bowl with plastic wrap.

3. Transfer to the refrigerator and marinate for 2 to 3 hours.

4. Supply your smoker with wood pellets and follow the start-up procedure. Preheat the grill, with the lid closed, to 225° F.

5. Place the tenderloins directly on the grill grate and smoke until the internal temperature registers 145°F, about 2-1/2 to 3 hours. Grill: 225 °F Probe: 145 °F

6. Remove from grill and let rest 5 minutes before slicing. Enjoy!

Brown Sugar And Bacon Wrapped Lil Smokies

Servings: 6
Cooking Time: 30 Minutes

Ingredients:
- 1 Pound bacon
- 1 (14 oz) cocktail sausages
- 1/2 Cup brown sugar

Directions:
1. Lay strips of bacon out on a clean, flat surface. Roll out bacon strips using a rolling pin, so they are a bit longer with even thickness. Cut bacon strips in half.

2. Wrap each sausage in a 1/2 strip of bacon and secure with a toothpick. Place the bacon-wrapped sausages in a casserole dish in a single layer and cover with brown sugar.

3. Transfer to the fridge and let sit for 30 minutes.

4. Supply your smoker with wood pellets and follow the start-up procedure. Preheat the grill, with the lid closed, to 350° F.

5. Lay the sausages out on a parchment lined sheet tray and place the sheet directly on the grill grate.

6. Cook for 25 to 30 minutes until the bacon is crispy. Enjoy! Grill: 350 °F

Pineapple-pepper Pork Kebabs

Servings: 12-15
Cooking Time: 240 Minutes

Ingredients:
- 1 (20-ounce) bottle hoisin sauce
- ½ cup Sriracha
- ¼ cup honey
- ¼ cup apple cider vinegar
- 2 tablespoons canola oil
- 2 teaspoons minced garlic
- 2 teaspoons onion powder
- 1 teaspoon ground ginger
- 1 teaspoon salt
- 1 teaspoon freshly ground black pepper
- 2 pounds thick-cut pork chops or pork loin, cut into 2-inch cubes

- 10 ounces fresh pineapple, cut into chunks
- 1 red onion, cut into wedges
- 1 bag mini sweet peppers, tops removed and seeded
- 12 metal or wooden skewers (soaked in water for 30 minutes if wooden)

Directions:

1. In a small bowl, stir together the hoisin, Sriracha, honey, vinegar, oil, minced garlic, onion powder, ginger, salt, and black pepper to create the marinade. Reserve ¼ cup for basting.

2. Toss the pork cubes, pineapple chunks, onion wedges, and mini peppers in the remaining marinade. Cover and refrigerate for at least 1 hour or up to 4 hours.

3. Supply your smoker with wood pellets and follow the start-up procedure. Preheat, with the lid closed, to 450°F.

4. Remove the pork, pineapple, and veggies from the marinade; do not rinse. Discard the marinade.

5. Use the double-skewer technique to assemble the kebabs (see Tip below). Thread each of 6 skewers with a piece of pork, a piece of pineapple, a piece of onion, and a sweet mini pepper, making sure that the skewer goes through the left side of the ingredients. Repeat the threading on each skewer two more times. Double-skewer the kebabs by sticking another 6 skewers through the right side of the ingredients.

6. Place the kebabs directly on the grill, close the lid, and smoke for 10 to 12 minutes, turning once. They are done when a meat thermometer inserted in the pork reads 160°F.

Buffalo Pork Tenderloin

Servings: 4

Cooking Time: 20 Minutes

Ingredients:

- 2 Pork Tenderloins (about 12 to 15 oz. each)
- 6 Tablespoon butter, melted
- 6 Tablespoon Louisiana-style hot sauce
- Cajun Shake

Directions:

1. Trim any silverskin from the tenderloins with a sharp knife.

2. Combine the melted butter and the hot sauce and roll the tenderloins in the mixture.

3. Supply your smoker with wood pellets and follow the start-up procedure. Preheat the grill, with the lid closed, to 400° F.

4. Arrange the tenderloins on the grill grate and grill for 6 to 8 minutes per side, rolling with tongs, or until the internal temperature is 145F when read on an instant-read meat thermometer. (The pork will still be slightly pink in the center. If you prefer your pork well-done, cook it to 160F.) Grill: 400 °F Probe: 150 °F

5. Transfer the tenderloins to a cutting board. Let rest for several minutes before carving on a diagonal into 1/2-inch slices. Enjoy!

Classic Pulled Pork

Servings: 8-12

Cooking Time: 1200 Minutes

Ingredients:

- 1 (6- to 8-pound) bone-in pork shoulder
- 2 tablespoons yellow mustard
- 1 batch Pork Rub

Directions:

1. Supply your smoker with wood pellets and follow the start-up procedure. Preheat the grill, with the lid closed, to 225°F.

2. Coat the pork shoulder all over with mustard and season it with the rub. Using your hands, work the rub into the meat.

3. Place the shoulder on the grill grate and smoke until its internal temperature reaches 195°F.

4. Pull the shoulder from the grill and wrap it completely in aluminum foil or butcher paper. Place it in a cooler, cover the cooler, and let it rest for 1 or 2 hours.

5. Remove the pork shoulder from the cooler and unwrap it. Remove the shoulder bone and pull the pork apart using just your fingers. Serve immediately as desired. Leftovers are encouraged.

VEGETABLES RECIPES

Grilled Chili-lime Corn

Servings: 8
Cooking Time: 45 Minutes

Ingredients:

- 12 Corn, ears
- 1 Teaspoon chili powder
- 1/2 Teaspoon onion powder
- 1 Teaspoon Leinenkugel's Summer Shandy Rub
- 2 lime, juiced
- 1 Tablespoon lime zest

Directions:

1. Soak the ears of corn, still in their husk, in water for 4 to 8 hours.
2. Supply your smoker with wood pellets and follow the start-up procedure. Preheat the grill, with the lid closed, to 350° F.
3. Place corn directly on grill grates. Turn corn every 15 minutes for 45 minutes total cooking time. Grill: 350 °F
4. Combine chili powder, onion powder, Summer Shandy rub, lime juice, lime zest and butter in an oven safe dish and place in grill for 10 minutes. Remove corn and butter from the grill.
5. Pull corn husk back, but not off and remove corn silk. Using the corn husk as a handle, brush the corn with the melted chili-lime butter. Enjoy!

Roasted Asparagus

Servings: 4
Cooking Time: 30 Minutes

Ingredients:

- 1 Bunch asparagus
- 2 Tablespoon olive oil, plus more as needed
- Veggie Rub

Directions:

1. Coat asparagus with olive oil and Veggie Rub, stirring to coat all pieces.

2. Supply your smoker with wood pellets and follow the start-up procedure. Preheat the grill, with the lid closed, to 350° F.
3. Place asparagus directly on the grill grate for 15-20 minutes.
4. Remove from grill and enjoy!

Roasted Fall Vegetables

Servings: 6
Cooking Time: 30 Minutes

Ingredients:

- 1/2 Pound Potatoes, new
- 2 Tablespoon olive oil
- salt and pepper
- 1/2 Pound Butternut Squash, diced
- 1/2 Pound fresh Brussels sprouts
- 1 Pint mushrooms, sliced

Directions:

1. Supply your smoker with wood pellets and follow the start-up procedure. Preheat the grill, with the lid closed, to 200° F.
2. Toss potatoes and squash with olive oil, salt and pepper and spread out on a sheet tray.
3. Place directly on the grill grate and cook for 15 minutes. Add brussels sprouts and mushrooms and toss to coat.
4. Cook another 15-20 minutes until veggies are lightly browned and cooked through.
5. Adjust seasoning as needed. Enjoy!

Mashed Red Potatoes

Servings: 4
Cooking Time: 40 Minutes

Ingredients:

- 8 Large red potatoes
- salt
- black pepper
- 1/2 Cup heavy cream
- 1/4 Cup butter

Directions:

1. Supply your smoker with wood pellets and follow the start-up procedure. Preheat the grill, with the lid closed, to 180° F.

2. Slice red potatoes in half, lengthwise then cut in half again to make quarters. Season potatoes with salt and pepper.

3. Increase the heat to High and preheat. Once the grill is hot, set potatoes directly on the grill grate. Grill: 450 ˚F

4. Every 15 minutes flip potatoes to ensure all sides get color. Continue to do this until potatoes are fork tender.

5. When tender, mash potatoes with cream, butter, salt, and pepper to taste. Serve warm, enjoy!

Roasted Mashed Potatoes

Servings: 8
Cooking Time: 40 Minutes

Ingredients:
- 5 Pound Yukon Gold potatoes
- 1 1/2 Stick butter, softened
- 1 1/2 Cup heavy whipping cream, room temperature
- kosher salt
- white pepper

Directions:
1. Supply your smoker with wood pellets and follow the start-up procedure. Preheat the grill, with the lid closed, to 300° F.

2. Peel and cut potatoes into 1/2 inch cubes. Place the potatoes in a shallow baking dish with 1/2 cup water and cover. Bake until tender, about 40 minutes. Grill: 300 ˚F

3. In a medium saucepan, combine cream and butter. Cook over medium heat until butter is melted.

4. Remove potatoes from the grill and drain water.

5. Transfer potatoes to a bowl and mash using a potato masher. Gradually add in cream and butter mixture and mix using the masher. Be careful not to overwork or the potatoes will becomes gluey. Season with salt and pepper to taste. Enjoy!

Roasted Pickled Beets

Servings: 8
Cooking Time: 60 Minutes

Ingredients:
- 6 Medium Red Beets, scrubbed and trimmed
- 1 Cup red wine vinegar
- 1/2 Cup sugar
- 10 Whole peppercorns
- 1 Cup water
- 1 1/2 Teaspoon coarse salt
- 8 whole cloves
- 2 Pieces Star Anise, Broken
- 1 cinnamon stick, broken in half

Directions:
1. Make a foil pouch large enough to enclose the beets. Poke a few holes in the top to allow steam to escape.

2. Supply your smoker with wood pellets and follow the start-up procedure. Preheat the grill, with the lid closed, to 350° F.

3. Roast the beets until they are tender, 50 to 60 minutes. Carefully remove the foil and allow the beets to cool until they can be comfortably handled. Grill: 350 ˚F

4. Slip the skins off with your fingers. (You may wish to wear latex gloves to avoid staining your hands.) Cut the beets into quarters or slices. (Candy cane beets are especially pretty when sliced.)

5. In the meantime, make the brine: Bring the vinegar, sugar, salt, and water to a boil in a small saucepan over high heat.

6. Put the cloves, peppercorns, star anise, and cinnamon in a clean lidded jar, such as a canning jar

7. Add the beets to the jar. Pour the hot brine over the beets. Put the lid on the jar. Cool the beets to room temperature, then refrigerate for 3 to 5 days before serving. Enjoy!

Red Potato Grilled Lollipops

Servings: 4
Cooking Time: 25 Minutes

Ingredients:
- 8 Large red bliss potatoes, halved
- 2 Clove garlic, minced
- 2 Sprig rosemary, minced
- 2 Tablespoon olive oil
- 1 Teaspoon salt

- 1/2 Teaspoon black pepper
- 5 Wooden Skewers, soaked in water
- 1/4 Cup Parmesan cheese, grated

Directions:

1. Supply your smoker with wood pellets and follow the start-up procedure. Preheat the grill, with the lid closed, to 450° F.

2. Halve potatoes and poke each several times with a fork.

3. Put the potatoes in a large bowl and toss with the minced garlic, rosemary leaves, a few tablespoons of olive oil, kosher salt, and pepper. Microwave the potatoes for 4 minutes. Gently toss potatoes and microwave for another 3 minutes.

4. Skewer potato halves threading about 4 or 5 potato halves on each skewer. Brush potatoes with olive oil.

5. Place the potato skewers on the Traeger, cut side down, and grill until the sides begin to brown (4-7 minutes).

6. Flip and grill skin side down for another 7-10 minutes.

7. They are done when a sharp knife tip easily penetrates the sides. Remove potatoes from grill and top with grated parmesan cheese. Enjoy!

Roasted Hasselback Potatoes By Doug Scheiding

Servings: 6
Cooking Time: 120 Minutes

Ingredients:
- 6 Large russet potatoes
- 1 Pound bacon
- 1/2 Cup butter
- salt
- black pepper
- 1 Cup cheddar cheese
- 3 Whole scallions

Directions:

1. To cut potatoes, place two wooden spoons on either side of the potato (this prevents your knife from going all the way through). Slice potato into thin chips leaving about 1/4" attached on the bottom.

2. Freeze bacon slices for about 30 minutes then cut into small pieces about the size of a stamp. Place these in the cracks between every other slice.

3. Place the potato in a large cast iron skillet. Top the potato with slices of hard butter (you can also place thin slivers of cold butter between the potato slices with the bacon if desired). Season with salt and pepper.

4. Supply your smoker with wood pellets and follow the start-up procedure. Preheat the grill, with the lid closed, to 350° F.

5. Place the cast iron directly on the grill grate and cook for two hours. Top potatoes with more butter and baste with melted butter every 30 minutes.

6. In the last 10 minutes of cooking, sprinkle with cheddar and return to grill to melt.

7. To finish, top with chives or scallions. Enjoy!

Grilled Fingerling Potato Salad

Servings: 6
Cooking Time: 15 Minutes

Ingredients:
- 10 Whole scallions
- 2/3 Cup extra-virgin olive oil, divided
- 1 1/2 Pound fingerling potatoes, cut in half lengthwise
- pepper
- 2 Teaspoon kosher salt, divided, plus more as needed
- 2 Tablespoon rice vinegar
- 2 Teaspoon lemon juice
- 1 Small jalapeño, sliced

Directions:

1. Supply your smoker with wood pellets and follow the start-up procedure. Preheat the grill, with the lid closed, to 450° F.

2. Brush the scallions with oil and place on the grill.

3. Cook until lightly charred, about 2 to 3 minutes. Remove and let cool. Grill: 450 °F

4. Once the scallions have cooled, slice and set aside.

5. Brush the fingerling potatoes with oil (reserving 1/3 cup for later use), then salt and pepper. Place cut-side

down on the grill until cooked through, about 4 to 5 minutes. Grill: 450 °F

6.   In a bowl, whisk the remaining 1/3 cup olive oil, 1 teaspoon salt, rice vinegar and lemon juice. Next mix in the scallions, potatoes and sliced jalapeño.

7.   Season with salt and pepper, and serve. Enjoy!

Smoked Pickled Green Beans

Servings: 4
Cooking Time: 45 Minutes

Ingredients:
- 1 Pound Green Beans, blanched
- 1/2 Cup salt
- 1/2 Cup sugar
- 1 Tablespoon red pepper flakes
- 2 Cup white wine vinegar
- 2 Cup ice water

Directions:
1.   Supply your smoker with wood pellets and follow the start-up procedure. Preheat the grill, with the lid closed, to 180° F.

2.   Place the blanched green beans on a mesh grill mat and place mat directly on the grill grate. Smoke the green beans for 30-45 minutes until they've picked up the desired amount of smoke. Remove from grill and set aside until the brine is ready. Grill: 180 °F

3.   In a medium sized saucepan, bring all remaining ingredients, except ice water, to a boil over medium high heat on the stove. Simmer for 5-10 minutes then remove from heat and steep 20 minutes more. Pour brine over ice water to cool.

4.   Once brine has cooled, pour over the green beans and weigh them down with a few plates to ensure they are completely submerged. Let sit 24 hours before use. Enjoy!

Spicy Asian Brussels Sprouts

Servings: 4
Cooking Time: 10 Minutes

Ingredients:
- 2 Cup fresh Brussels sprouts
- 2 Tablespoon vegetable oil
- 1 Tablespoon Asian BBQ Rub
- 1/4 Cup Thai sweet chile sauce

Directions:
1.   Supply your smoker with wood pellets and follow the start-up procedure. Preheat the grill, with the lid closed, to 350° F.

2.   Spread the halved brussel sprouts in a single layer on a lined cookie sheet. Drizzle with the oil and toss to coat.

3.   Sprinkle the brussel sprouts evenly with an Asian BBQ rub and put the cookie sheet on the grill. Close the lid and cook for 7-8 minutes. Grill: 350 °F

4.   Toss the brussels sprouts in the Thai Chili Sauce and return to the grill for an additional 3-4 minutes, or until the sprouts are crisp-tender. Grill: 350 °F

5.   Serve immediately. Enjoy!

Smoked Parmesan Herb Popcorn

Servings: 2
Cooking Time: 15 Minutes

Ingredients:
- 4 Tablespoon butter
- 2 Teaspoon Italian Seasoning
- 1 Teaspoon garlic powder
- 1 Teaspoon salt
- 1/4 Cup popcorn kernels
- 1/2 Cup Parmesan cheese, grated

Directions:
1.   Supply your smoker with wood pellets and follow the start-up procedure. Preheat the grill, with the lid closed, to 250° F.

2.   In a small saucepan, melt the butter over medium heat. Add Italian seasoning, garlic powder, and salt and stir to combine. Remove from heat and set aside.

3.   Add 1/4 cup of popcorn to a brown paper lunch bag. Fold the top of the bag over twice to close. Place the bag in the microwave and microwave on high for 1 to 2 minutes, or until there are about 5 seconds between pops. Open the bag with care and dump into a large mixing bowl.

4.   Pour butter mixture of popcorn in a bowl and toss to combine. Dump popcorn onto a baking sheet and place in grill.

5.   Smoke for 10 minutes; remove from grill. Toss with parmesan cheese to serve. Enjoy! Grill: 250 °F

Roasted Vegetable Napoleon

Servings: 4

Cooking Time: 30 Minutes

Ingredients:

- 2 Whole sweet potatoes
- 2 Whole zucchini
- 2 Whole Squash
- 1 Whole red onion
- 2 Whole Bell Pepper, Red
- salt and pepper

Directions:

1. Supply your smoker with wood pellets and follow the start-up procedure. Preheat the grill, with the lid closed, to High heat.

2. Salt and pepper all vegetables and grill them on both sides. Begin with the peppers and onions as they will take a little longer to cook. Grill: 450 °F

Grilled Asparagus And Hollandaise Sauce

Servings: 4

Cooking Time: 10 Minutes

Ingredients:

- 1 Pound asparagus
- 2 Teaspoon red pepper flakes
- 2 Tablespoon olive oil
- salt and pepper
- 4 egg yolk
- 1 Tablespoon lemon juice
- 1/2 Cup butter, melted
- cayenne pepper
- salt

Directions:

1. Supply your smoker with wood pellets and follow the start-up procedure. Preheat the grill, with the lid closed, to 375° F.

2. In a large bowl, mix asparagus with olive oil, red pepper flakes and salt. Arrange asparagus on a cooking sheet and take to the grill. Cook for approximately 10 to 15 minutes. Grill: 375 °F

3. In an aluminum bowl, whisk the egg yolks well. Add the lemon juice and whisk until creamy.

4. Place bowl over a double boiler, over low heat, making sure that it does not touches the water.

5. While whisking, add the melted butter slowly. Whisk until it doubles the volume. Take off the heat, still whisking and add the cayenne pepper and salt.

6. Arrange asparagus over a serving plater. Pour hollandaise sauce over asparagus and serve. Enjoy!

Grilled Street Corn

Servings: 6

Cooking Time: 10 Minutes

Ingredients:

- 6 ears corn, husked
- 1 As Needed extra-virgin olive oil
- 1/4 Cup mayonnaise
- 1 Tablespoon ancho or guajillo chile powder
- 1/2 Cup chopped cilantro, plus more for serving
- 1 lime, zested and juiced
- salt
- 1/2 Cup Cotija cheese
- 1 As Needed cilantro, finely chopped

Directions:

1. Supply your smoker with wood pellets and follow the start-up procedure. Preheat the grill, with the lid closed, to 450° F.

2. Brush corn with oil and place on grill, turning occasionally.

3. While corn is on the grill, mix mayonnaise with chile powder, cilantro, lime juice and zest in a bowl. Season with salt.

4. After about 10 minutes corn should be cooked through and slightly charred on the outside. Remove from grill.

5. Top corn with chile mayonnaise then sprinkle on the Cotija cheese and chopped cilantro. Enjoy!

Roasted Potato Poutine

Servings: 6
Cooking Time: 40 Minutes

Ingredients:

- 4 Large russet potatoes
- Tablespoon olive oil or vegetable oil
- Prime Rib Rub
- Cup chicken or beef gravy (homemade or jarred)
- 1 1/2 Cup white or yellow cheddar cheese curds
- freshly ground black pepper
- 2 Tablespoon scallions

Directions:

1. Supply your smoker with wood pellets and follow the start-up procedure. Preheat the grill, with the lid closed, to 500° F.
2. Scrub the potatoes and slice into fries, wedges or preferred shape.
3. Put potatoes into a large mixing bowl and coat with oil. Season generously with Traeger Prime Rib rub.
4. Tip the potatoes onto a rimmed baking sheet and spread in a single layer, cut sides down.
5. Roast for 20 minutes, then using a spatula, turn the potatoes to the other cut side. Continue to roast until the potatoes are tender and golden brown, about 15 to 20 minutes more.
6. While potatoes cook, warm the gravy on the stovetop or in a heat-proof saucepan on your Traeger.
7. To assemble the poutine, arrange the potatoes in a large shallow bowl or on a serving platter. Distribute the cheese curds on top. Pour the hot gravy evenly over the potatoes and cheese curds.
8. Season with black pepper and garnish with thinly sliced scallions. Serve immediately. Enjoy!

Bacon Wrapped Corn On The Cob

Servings: 4
Cooking Time: 21 Minutes

Ingredients:

- 4 Whole Corn, ears
- 8 Slices bacon
- 1 Teaspoon freshly ground black pepper
- 1 Teaspoon chili powder
- 1 To Taste Parmesan cheese, grated

Directions:

1. Peel back the corn husks, remove silk strings and rinse corn under cold water.
2. Wrap 2 pieces of bacon around each ear of corn, securing with toothpicks.
3. Dust each ear of corn with some chili powder and cracked black pepper.
4. Supply your smoker with wood pellets and follow the start-up procedure. Preheat the grill, with the lid closed, to 375° F.
5. Place the ears of corn directly on the Traeger and grill for approximately 20 minutes or until the bacon is cooked crisp. Grill: 375 °F
6. Take the corn off the Traeger. Carefully remove the toothpicks and season with a little more chili powder and a grating of parmesan cheese, if desired. Serve & enjoy!

Grilled Zucchini Squash Spears

Servings: 4
Cooking Time: 10 Minutes

Ingredients:

- 4 Medium zucchini
- 2 Tablespoon olive oil
- 1 Tablespoon sherry vinegar
- 2 thyme, leaves pulled
- salt and pepper

Directions:

1. Clean the zucchini and cut the ends off. Cut each in half lengthwise, then each half into thirds.
2. Combine remaining ingredients in a medium Ziplock bag and add the spears. Toss and mix well to coat the zucchini.
3. Supply your smoker with wood pellets and follow the start-up procedure. Preheat the grill, with the lid closed, to 350° F.
4. Remove the spears from the bag and place directly on the grill grate cut side down.
5. Cook for 3-4 minutes per side, until grill marks appear and zucchini is tender. Grill: 350 °F
6. Remove from grill and finish with more thyme leaves if desired. Enjoy!

Roasted Tomatoes

Servings: 2

Cooking Time: 180 Minutes

Ingredients:

- 3 Large ripe tomatoes
- 1/2 Tablespoon kosher salt
- 1 Teaspoon coarse ground black pepper
- 1/4 Teaspoon sugar
- 1/4 Teaspoon thyme or basil
- olive oil

Directions:

1. Line a rimmed baking sheet with parchment paper.

2. Supply your smoker with wood pellets and follow the start-up procedure. Preheat the grill, with the lid closed, to 225° F.

3. Remove the stem end from each tomato and cut the tomatoes into 1/2 inch thick slices.

4. Combine the salt, pepper, sugar and thyme or basil in a small bowl and mix.

5. Pour olive oil into the well of a dinner plate.

6. Dip one side of each tomato slice in the olive oil and arrange on the baking sheet. Dust the tomato slices with the seasoning mixture.

7. Arrange the pan directly on the grill grate and roast the tomatoes until the juices stop running and the edges have contracted, about 3 hours. Remove from grill and enjoy!

Tater Tot Bake

Servings: 4

Cooking Time: 15 Minutes

Ingredients:

- 1 Whole frozen tater tots
- salt and pepper
- 1 Cup sour cream
- 1 Cup shredded cheddar cheese, divided
- 1/2 Cup bacon, chopped
- 1/4 Cup green onion, diced

Directions:

1. Supply your smoker with wood pellets and follow the start-up procedure. Preheat the grill, with the lid closed, to 375° F.

2. Line a baking sheet with aluminum foil for easy clean up and spread frozen tater tots onto sheet.

3. Sprinkle with Veggie Shake or salt and pepper to taste.

4. Place the baking sheet on the preheated grill grate and cook the tater tots for 10 minutes.

5. Drizzle sour cream over cooked tater tots.

6. Sprinkle the cheese, bacon bits and green onions on top of the tater tots.

7. Turn heat up to High heat and cook for 5 more minutes until the cheese melts and serve immediately. Enjoy!

Skillet Potato Cake

Servings: 4

Cooking Time: 40 Minutes

Ingredients:

- 8 Tablespoon butter, melted
- 2 Pound russet potatoes, peeled and thinly sliced
- 3 Tablespoon kosher salt
- 2 Tablespoon freshly ground black pepper
- thyme

Directions:

1. Supply your smoker with wood pellets and follow the start-up procedure. Preheat the grill, with the lid closed, to 375° F.

2. Brush the bottom of a cast iron skillet with part of the melted butter. Place potato slices vertically around the outer edges then fill in the middle in the same fashion.

3. Pour additional melted butter over the top of the layers and sprinkle with salt and pepper.

4. Place skillet in grill and cook for 35 to 40 minutes or until potatoes are fork tender and golden brown.

5. Garnish with a sprinkle of fresh thyme over the top of the potatoes. Enjoy!

Grilled Asparagus & Honey-glazed Carrots

Servings: 4
Cooking Time: 35 Minutes

Ingredients:

- 1 Bunch asparagus, woody ends removed
- 1 Pound Carrots, peeled
- 2 Tablespoon olive oil
- sea salt
- 2 Tablespoon honey
- lemon zest

Directions:

1. Rinse all vegetables under cold water. Drizzle asparagus with olive oil and a generous sprinkling of sea salt. Generously drizzle carrots with honey and lightly sprinkle with sea salt.

2. Supply your smoker with wood pellets and follow the start-up procedure. Preheat the grill, with the lid closed, to 350° F.

3. Place carrots on the grill first and cook for 10-15 minutes, then add asparagus and cook both for another 15 to 20 minutes, or until they're done to your liking. Grill: 350 °F

4. Top the asparagus with some fresh lemon zest. Enjoy!

Sweet Potato Marshmallow Casserole

Servings: 6
Cooking Time: 60 Minutes

Ingredients:

- 5 Yams
- 1 1/2 Stick butter
- 1/2 Cup brown sugar
- 1 Teaspoon vanilla
- 1 Teaspoon kosher salt
- 1 Teaspoon cracked black pepper
- 1 Marshmallows, miniature
- 1/4 Unsalted Butter, Softened

Directions:

1. Supply your smoker with wood pellets and follow the start-up procedure. Preheat the grill, with the lid closed, to 375° F.

2. Pierce the skin of the yams with a fork a few times. Place on a baking sheet or foil tin inside the grill and let roast for 50 minutes or until extremely softened. Grill: 375 °F

3. Remove yams from the grill and set aside until cool enough to handle. While the potatoes cool, with a stiff whisk, whip together 1/2 cup softened butter, the brown sugar, vanilla, salt and pepper.

4. Remove and discard skins from sweet potatoes and mash until smooth. Fold in the butter mixture and transfer to a cast iron pan.

5. Place cast iron on the grill and bake for 15-20 minutes. Remove from the grill, top with marshmallows and dot with remaining 1/4 cup butter.

6. Place back in the grill for 15 minutes until warm and the marshmallows are golden. Enjoy! Grill: 375 °F

Grilled Ratatouille Salad

Servings: 4
Cooking Time: 25 Minutes

Ingredients:

- 1 Whole sweet potatoes
- 1 Whole red onion, diced
- 1 Whole zucchini
- 1 Whole Squash
- 1 Large Tomato, diced
- vegetable oil
- salt and pepper

Directions:

1. Supply your smoker with wood pellets and follow the start-up procedure. Preheat the grill, with the lid closed, to High heat.

2. Slice all vegetables to a ¼ inch thickness.

3. Lightly brush each vegetable with oil and season with Traeger's Veggie Shake or salt and pepper.

4. Place sweet potato, onion, zucchini, and squash on grill grate and grill for 20 minutes or until tender, turn halfway through.

5. Add tomato slices to the grill during the last 5 minutes of cooking time.

6. For presentation, alternate vegetables while layering them vertically. Enjoy!

Roasted Artichokes With Garlic Butter

Servings: 2

Cooking Time: 60 Minutes

Ingredients:

- 2 Large artichokes
- 3 Tablespoon olive oil
- sea salt
- 1 Stick unsalted butter
- 2 Clove garlic, chopped
- 2 Tablespoon chives, parsley, tarragon or cilantro
- 1 lemon

Directions:

1. Supply your smoker with wood pellets and follow the start-up procedure. Preheat the grill, with the lid closed, to 375° F.

2. Meanwhile, break off and discard any small outer leaves on the artichokes. Use a knife to slice off the tops of the artichokes, then using scissors, cut off any thorns on the remaining artichoke leaves. Trim the very bottom of the stem, then peel the tough and fibrous outer layer of the stem. Finally, cut artichokes in half and rinse off.

3. Transfer artichokes to a large mixing bowl, drizzle with olive oil and generously sprinkle with sea salt. Toss to coat the artichokes thoroughly. Grill: 375 °F

4. Add the artichokes to the grill, cut side down, and roast at 375°F until the artichoke bottoms are tender when poked with a fork or knife, about 50 to 60 minutes. Grill: 375 °F

5. When artichokes are almost done, add butter, chopped garlic and a pinch of sea salt to a small sauce pan and melt slowly over medium-low heat. Once the butter melts all the way and starts to bubble slightly, add the herbs.

6. When the artichokes are done, transfer to a butcher paper lined tray with the cut sides up. Drizzle half the garlic butter and squeeze half of the lemon over the artichokes. Add a small sprinkle of sea salt over the artichokes.

7. Serve with a ramekin of the remaining butter for dipping and extra wedges of lemon. Enjoy! Chef Tip: You can also serve with a ramekin of good mayonnaise mixed with a bit of hot sauce.

Smoked Mashed Potatoes

Servings: 6

Cooking Time: 45 Minutes

Ingredients:

- 2 Pound red bliss potatoes, washed and diced medium
- chicken stock or water
- 1/2 Stick salted butter
- 1 Cup whole milk
- 1/2 Cup sour cream
- 1/2 Cup shredded or grated Parmesan cheese
- kosher salt
- freshly ground black pepper
- 1/2 Cup fresh sliced green onions

Directions:

1. Place the diced red potatoes into a small saucepan or stockpot and cover with chicken stock or water.

2. Bring to a boil and cook on a simmer until fork tender, then cook 4 to 5 minutes past that until soft.

3. Supply your smoker with wood pellets and follow the start-up procedure. Preheat the grill, with the lid closed, to 400° F.

4. In a separate ovenproof pan, such as a cast iron skillet, add butter and milk and place in the Traeger during start up, until melted (approximately 7 to 10 minutes). Grill: 400 °F

5. Carefully remove the butter/milk mixture from the Traeger using heatproof gloves.

6. Drain the potatoes and place into a large bowl. Add the melted butter/milk mixture and slowly mash.

7. Add sour cream, cheese and green onions, then season to taste with salt and pepper.

8. Place into the cast iron skillet, then place the skillet back into the Traeger and cook until the potatoes have a slight crust and are bubbling, about 15 minutes. Grill: 400 °F

9. Carefully remove the mashed potatoes from the Traeger using heatproof gloves. Allow to cool for 5 minutes. Scoop and enjoy!

Chef Curtis' Famous Chimichurri Sauce

Servings: 4
Cooking Time: 5 Minutes

Ingredients:

- 2 Whole lemon, halved
- 2 Medium flat-leaf Italian parsley, washed and chopped with the majority of stems cut off
- 4 Clove garlic, diced
- 1/4 Cup red wine vinegar
- 1/2 Teaspoon black pepper
- 1/4 Cup extra-virgin olive oil
- 1 Teaspoon salt

Directions:

1. Supply your smoker with wood pellets and follow the start-up procedure. Preheat the grill, with the lid closed, to 450° F.
2. Place lemon halves directly on the grill grate and cook for 5 minutes or until grill marks appear. Grill: 450 °F
3. Take lemons off grill and juice. Combine all of the ingredients in a food processor or blender and purée until smooth, or leave slightly chunky for some texture.
4. Add additional olive oil to taste for a milder flavor if preferred. Serve on protein or as a dip. Enjoy!

Double-smoked Cheese Potatoes

Servings: 12
Cooking Time: 35 Minutes

Ingredients:

- 4 large baking potatoes (12 to 14 ounces each—preferably organic)
- 1 1/2 tablespoons bacon fat or butter, melted, or extra virgin olive oil
- Coarse salt (sea or kosher) and freshly ground black pepper
- 4 strips artisanal bacon (like Nueske's), cut crosswise into 1/4-inch slivers
- 6 tablespoons (3/4 stick) cold unsalted butter, thinly sliced
- 2 scallions, trimmed, white and green parts finely chopped (about 4 tablespoons)
- 2 cups coarsely grated smoked or regular white cheddar cheese (about 8 ounces)
- 1/2 cup sour cream
- Spanish smoked paprika (pimentón) or sweet paprika, for sprinkling

Directions:

1. Supply your smoker with wood pellets and follow the start-up procedure. Preheat the grill, with the lid closed, to 400° F.Add enough wood for 1 hour of smoking as specified by the manufacturer.
2. Scrub the potatoes on all sides with a vegetable brush. Rinse well under cold running water and blot dry with paper towels. Prick each potato several times with a fork (this keeps the spud from exploding and facilitates the smoke absorption). Brush or rub the potato on all sides with the bacon fat and season generously with salt and pepper.
3. Place the potatoes on the smoker rack. Smoke until the skins are crisp and the potatoes are tender in the center (they'll be easy to pierce with a slender metal skewer), about 1 hour.
4. Meanwhile, place the bacon in a cold skillet and fry over medium heat until browned and crisp, 3 to 4 minutes. Drain off the bacon fat (save the fat for future potatoes).
5. Transfer the potatoes to a cutting board and let cool slightly. Cut each potato in half lengthwise. Using a spoon, scrape out most of the potato flesh, leaving a 1/4-inch-thick shell. (It's easier to scoop the potatoes when warm.) Cut the potato flesh into 1/2-inch dice and place in a bowl.
6. Add the bacon, 4 tablespoons of the butter, the scallions, and cheese to the potato flesh and gently stir to mix. Stir in the sour cream and salt and pepper to taste; the mixture should be highly seasoned. Stir as little and as gently as possible so as to leave some texture to the potatoes.
7. Spoon the potato mixture back into the potato shells, mounding it in the center. Top each potato half with a thin slice of the remaining butter and sprinkle with

paprika. The potatoes can be prepared up to 24 hours ahead to this stage, covered, and refrigerated.

8.   Just before serving, preheat your smoker to 400 °F. Add enough wood for 30 minutes of smoking. Place the potatoes in a shallow aluminum foil pan and re-smoke them until browned and bubbling, 15 to 20 minutes.

Christmas Brussel Sprouts

Servings: 6
Cooking Time: 50 Minutes

Ingredients:
- 1/2 Pound thick-cut bacon
- 1 Medium onion, diced
- 2 Pound fresh Brussels sprouts
- 2 Tablespoon olive oil
- salt and pepper

Directions:
1.   Supply your smoker with wood pellets and follow the start-up procedure. Preheat the grill, with the lid closed, to 350° F.
2.   Place bacon directly on grill grate and cook for 15-20 minutes, or until lightly browned. Remove from grill and set aside on paper towel lined plate.
3.   Slice onion in half and then slice into 1⁄4 inch moons and add to large mixing bowl. Slice brussels sprouts in half lengthwise and add to bowl.
4.   Cut reserved bacon into 1⁄2 inch pieces and add to bowl. Drizzle with olive oil and sprinkle with salt and pepper. Toss to coat and pour into baking pan.
5.   Turn the temperature on grill to 375 and place baking pan on grill. Roast for 30 minutes mixing halfway through cooking. Grill: 375 °F

Cast Iron Potatoes

Servings: 4
Cooking Time: 60 Minutes

Ingredients:
- 4 Tablespoon butter, cut into cubes
- 2 1/2 Pound potatoes, peeled and cut into 1/8 inch slices
- 1/2 Large sweet onion, thinly sliced
- salt

- black pepper
- 1 1/2 Cup grated mild cheddar or jack cheese
- 2 Cup milk
- paprika

Directions:
1.   Butter the inside of a cast iron skillet and layer half the potato slices on the bottom. Top with half the onions. Season with salt and pepper.
2.   Sprinkle 1 cup of the cheese over the potatoes and onions and dot with half the butter. Layer the remaining potatoes and onions on top. Dot with remaining butter.
3.   Pour the milk into the skillet. Cover the skillet tightly with aluminum foil.
4.   Supply your smoker with wood pellets and follow the start-up procedure. Preheat the grill, with the lid closed, to 350° F.
5.   Bake for 1 hour, or until the potatoes are very tender. Grill: 350 °F
6.   Remove the foil and top with the remaining 1/2 cup of cheese. Bake for 30 minutes more (uncovered) until the cheese is lightly browned. Dust the top with paprika and serve immediately.

Salt Crusted Baked Potatoes

Servings: 4
Cooking Time: 60 Minutes

Ingredients:
- 6 russet potatoes, scrubbed and dried
- 3 Tablespoon canola oil
- 1 Tablespoon kosher salt
- butter
- sour cream
- Chives, fresh
- Bacon Bits
- cheddar cheese

Directions:
1.   In a large bowl, coat the potatoes in canola oil and sprinkle heavily with salt.
2.   Supply your smoker with wood pellets and follow the start-up procedure. Preheat the grill, with the lid closed, to 450° F.
3.   Place the potatoes directly on the grill grate and bake for 30-40 minutes, or until soft in the middle when pricked with a fork. Serve loaded with your favorite toppings. Enjoy! Grill: 450 °F

Roasted Beet & Bacon Salad

Servings: 4

Cooking Time: 45 Minutes

Ingredients:

- 2 Medium raw beets, peeled and thinly sliced
- 8 Slices bacon
- 1/4 Cup raw pecans or walnuts
- 2 Medium ripe pears, sliced
- 2 Large avocados, diced
- 1 Head red leaf lettuce or baby spinach, torn into bite-size pieces
- 1/4 Cup champagne vinaigrette

Directions:

1. Supply your smoker with wood pellets and follow the start-up procedure. Preheat the grill, with the lid closed, to 400° F.

2. Place beets on a foil-lined baking sheet and top with bacon. Place baking sheet directly on the grill grate (while preheating) and cook for 25 minutes. Grill: 400 °F

3. Toss to coat beets in rendered bacon fat.

4. Spread everything out in a single layer and continue to cook for another 15 minutes, or until beets are tender and bacon is crispy. Grill: 400 °F

5. Add pecans or walnuts and roast for 5 more minutes. Spoon out nuts and place on paper towels to drain and cool.

6. Once bacon is cool to the touch, roughly chop into medium pieces.

7. Place bacon, beets, nuts, pears, avocado and lettuce in a large salad bowl. Drizzle with champagne vinaigrette, toss to coat, and serve. Enjoy!

Whole Roasted Cauliflower With Garlic Parmesan Butter

Servings: 4

Cooking Time: 45 Minutes

Ingredients:

- 1 Whole head cauliflower
- 1/4 Cup olive oil
- salt and pepper
- 1/2 Cup butter, melted
- 1/4 Cup shredded Parmesan cheese
- 2 Clove garlic, minced
- 1/2 Tablespoon chopped parsley

Directions:

1. Supply your smoker with wood pellets and follow the start-up procedure. Preheat the grill, with the lid closed, to 450° F.

2. Brush the cauliflower with olive oil and season liberally with salt and pepper.

3. Put cauliflower in a cast iron skillet, place directly on the grill grate and cook for 45 minutes until golden brown and the center is tender.

4. While the cauliflower is cooking, combine the melted butter, parmesan, garlic and parsley in a small bowl.

5. During the last 20 minutes of cooking, baste the cauliflower with the melted butter mixture.

6. Remove the cauliflower from the grill and top with extra parmesan and parsley if desired. Enjoy!

Baked Sweet Potato Casserole With Marshmallow Fluff

Servings: 6

Cooking Time: 60 Minutes

Ingredients:

- 3 Pound sweet potatoes
- 1/2 Cup milk
- 1 Cup brown sugar
- 3 eggs
- 4 Tablespoon butter
- 1/2 Teaspoon salt
- 3 egg white
- 1 Pinch salt
- 1 Pinch ground cinnamon

Directions:

1. Supply your smoker with wood pellets and follow the start-up procedure. Preheat the grill, with the lid closed, to 375° F.

2. Rinse, dry and pierce the sweet potatoes and place in grill whole. Cook for 45 minutes or until fork tender. Remove from grill and peel. Grill: 375 °F

3. Once peeled, mash the sweet potatoes in a large bowl with the milk, brown sugar, eggs, butter and salt. Place mashed potatoes in a baking dish and cook for 35 minutes. Grill: 375 °F

4. While the potatoes bake, make the fluff. Make a double boiler by bringing a small pot of water to a simmer, then placing the bowl of your stand mixer or another large stainless steel bowl atop the water.

5. Add the 3 egg whites, 2/3 cup brown sugar, a pinch of salt and a pinch of cinnamon to the bowl and whisk continuously until the sugar dissolves and the liquid is warm to the touch.

6. Transfer the bowl from the stovetop to your stand mixer and use the whisk attachment to whip the whites on medium-high speed until it turns glossy with stiff peaks, about 5-8 minutes.

7. Once the casserole has finished baking, use a rubber spatula to cover the sweet potato mixture with the fluff. Use the back of the spatula to create dramatic peaks.

8. Return to the grill for 5-7 minutes, or until the fluff starts to turn golden and the peaks are just shy of burnt. Remove from grill and enjoy!

Smoked Jalapeño Poppers

Servings: 4
Cooking Time: 60 Minutes

Ingredients:
- 12 Medium jalapeño
- 6 Slices bacon, cut in half
- 8 Ounce cream cheese
- 2 Tablespoon Pork & Poultry Rub
- 1 Cup grated cheese

Directions:
1. Supply your smoker with wood pellets and follow the start-up procedure. Preheat the grill, with the lid closed, to 180° F. For optimal flavor, use Super Smoke if available.

2. Slice the jalapeños in half lengthwise. Scrape out any seeds and ribs with a small spoon or paring knife. Mix softened cream cheese with Traeger Pork & Poultry rub and grated cheese. Spoon mixture onto each jalapeño half. Wrap with bacon and secure with a toothpick.

3. Place the jalapeños on a rimmed baking sheet. Place on grill and smoke for 30 minutes. Grill: 180 °F

4. Increase the grill temperature to 375°F and cook an additional 30 minutes or until bacon is cooked to desired doneness. Serve warm, enjoy! Grill: 375 °F

Baked Winter Squash Au Gratin

Servings: 8
Cooking Time: 45 Minutes

Ingredients:
- 2 Cup heavy cream
- salt and pepper
- 3 Cup shredded Gruyere cheese
- 4 Clove garlic, diced
- 2 Tablespoon butter
- 3 yellow potatoes, peeled and cubed
- 1 butternut squash seeded, peeled and cubed
- 1 acorn squash seeded, peeled and cubed

Directions:
1. Supply your smoker with wood pellets and follow the start-up procedure. Preheat the grill, with the lid closed, to 375° F.

2. In a medium saucepan, cook the cream, stirring constantly, until it comes to a low boil. Add salt, pepper, garlic and shredded Gruyere cheese. Stir until cheese is melted.

3. Grease a 9x13 inch baking dish with 2 tablespoons of butter. In a large mixing bowl, combine potatoes, butternut and acorn squash. Stir in the cheese sauce. Place mixture in the prepared baking dish and place in grill.

4. Cook for 45 minutes or until potatoes and squash are fork tender. Remove from grill and let cool for 10 minutes before serving. Enjoy! Grill: 375 °F

Roasted Do-ahead Mashed Potatoes

Servings: 6
Cooking Time: 50 Minutes

Ingredients:
- 5 Pound Yukon Gold or russet potatoes
- 9 Tablespoon butter
- 8 Ounce cream cheese

- 1/2 Cup milk
- salt and pepper

Directions:

1. Peel the potatoes and cut into chunks that are roughly the same size. Cover with cold water and add a teaspoon of salt. Bring to a boil over high heat, then reduce the heat to medium and simmer the potatoes until they are tender.

2. Drain the potatoes and return them to the pot. Stir over low heat for 2 to 3 minutes to evaporate any excess moisture.

3. Mash the potatoes with a hand-held potato masher. (Alternative, rice the potatoes using a ricer.) Incorporate 8 tbsp butter and cream cheese. Add milk until the potatoes are of a good consistency. Stir in salt and pepper to taste.

4. Butter the inside of a casserole dish. Spread the potatoes out in an even layer in the casserole dish, smoothing the top with a spatula. Cool, cover, and refrigerate if not cooking right away. Before cooking, let the potatoes warm to room temperature (about an hour).

5. Supply your smoker with wood pellets and follow the start-up procedure. Preheat the grill, with the lid closed, to 350° F.

6. Bake the potatoes for 45 to 50 minutes, or until hot through. Grill: 350 °F

Baked Stuffed Avocados

Servings: 6
Cooking Time: 15 Minutes

Ingredients:

- 4 avocados, halved and pit removed
- 8 eggs
- 2 Cup shredded cheddar cheese
- 1/4 Cup cherry tomatoes, halved
- 4 Slices Bacon, cooked & chopped
- salt and pepper
- 1 scallion, thinly sliced

Directions:

1. Supply your smoker with wood pellets and follow the start-up procedure. Preheat the grill, with the lid closed, to 450° F.

2. After removing the pit from the avocado, scoop out a little of the flesh to make enough room to fit 1 egg per half.

3. Fill the bottom of a cast iron pan with kosher salt and nestle the avocado halves into the salt, cut side up. The salt helps to keep them in place while cooking, like ice with oysters.

4. Crack one egg into each half, top with shredded cheddar cheese, cherry tomatoes and bacon. Season with salt and pepper to taste.

5. Place the cast iron pan directly on the grill grate and bake the avocados for 12 to 15 minutes until the cheese is melted and the egg is just set. Grill: 450 °F

6. Remove from the grill and let rest 5 to 10 minutes. Top with sliced scallions and enjoy!

Grilled Asparagus And Spinach Salad

Servings: 8
Cooking Time: 10 Minutes

Ingredients:

- 4 Fluid Ounce apple cider vinegar
- 8 Fluid Ounce Honey Bourbon BBQ Sauce
- 2 Bunch asparagus, ends trimmed
- 3 Fluid Ounce extra-virgin olive oil
- 2 Ounce Beef Rub
- 24 Ounce Spinach, fresh
- 4 Ounce candied pecans
- 4 Ounce feta cheese

Directions:

1. Combine apple cider vinegar and Traeger Apricot BBQ Sauce to create salad dressing.

2. Supply your smoker with wood pellets and follow the start-up procedure. Preheat the grill, with the lid closed, to High heat.

3. Toss the asparagus with Olive Oil and the Beef Shake. Put asparagus in the Traeger Grilling Basket and move the basket to the grill grate.

4. Grill for about 10 minutes. Remove the asparagus once it is cooked. Grill: 350 °F

5. Place the hot asparagus right on top of the bowl of spinach.

6. Add candied pecans, feta cheese & salad dressing then toss and serve. Enjoy!

Roasted Sweet Potato Steak Fries

Servings: 4

Cooking Time: 40 Minutes

Ingredients:

- 3 Whole sweet potatoes
- 4 Tablespoon extra-virgin olive oil
- salt and pepper
- 2 Tablespoon fresh chopped rosemary

Directions:

1. Supply your smoker with wood pellets and follow the start-up procedure. Preheat the grill, with the lid closed, to 450° F.

2. Cut sweet potatoes into wedges and toss with olive oil, salt, pepper and rosemary. Spread on a parchment lined baking sheet and put in the grill. Cook for 15 minutes then flip and continue to cook until lightly browned and cooked through, about 40 to 45 minutes total. Grill: 450 °F

3. Serve with your favorite dipping sauce. Enjoy! Grill: 450 °F

Grilled Beer Cabbage

Servings: 4

Cooking Time: 50 Minutes

Ingredients:

- 2 Cabbage, head
- 1 Tablespoon extra-virgin olive oil
- 1 Teaspoon salt
- 1 Teaspoon freshly ground black pepper
- 14 Fluid Ounce Guinness Extra Stout

Directions:

1. Clean and core cabbages. Drizzle with olive oil and salt and pepper. Rub into the cabbage.

2. Supply your smoker with wood pellets and follow the start-up procedure. Preheat the grill, with the lid closed, to 180° F.

3. Place cabbages directly on grill grate; smoke for 15 to 20 minutes. Remove from grill and thickly slice cabbage. Grill: 180 °F

4. Place sliced cabbage in cast-iron skillet. Pour beer over cabbage and return to grill.

5. Increase temperature to 375°F and cook for 30 minutes, or until cabbage has reached desired softness. Grill: 375 °F

6. Serve with corned beef. Enjoy!

Roasted Garlic Herb Fries

Servings: 4

Cooking Time: 45 Minutes

Ingredients:

- 4 Whole russet potatoes
- 1 Teaspoon salt
- 2 Tablespoon avocado oil
- 1 Teaspoon fresh chopped rosemary
- 1 Teaspoon fresh chopped thyme
- 2 Clove garlic, minced
- 2 Teaspoon flake salt
- 1 Teaspoon chopped parsley, for garnish

Directions:

1. Supply your smoker with wood pellets and follow the start-up procedure. Preheat the grill, with the lid closed, to 425° F.

2. Chop potatoes into fries, (a mandolin works great for this) and place directly into an ice water bath with 1 teaspoon salt for 15 to 30 minutes.

3. Combine oil, rosemary, thyme and garlic in a big bowl. Remove potatoes from ice water and dry thoroughly with paper towels.

4. Toss potatoes in the oil mixture and place them on 2 to 3 parchment-lined baking sheets in a single layer. Sprinkle the flake salt over the fries.

5. Place baking sheets on the grill and roast for 30 minutes, flip the fries, then cook for an additional 15 minutes until golden and crispy. Dust with parsley. Grill: 425 °F

6. Serve with your favorite dipping sauce, side dish or as a nacho base.

Traeger Baked Potato Torte

Servings: 6
Cooking Time: 25 Minutes

Ingredients:

- 6 Yukon Gold potatoes, sliced 1/4 inch thick
- 2 Stick butter, melted
- 3 Clove garlic, crushed
- 2 Tablespoon rosemary, chopped
- 1 Cup Parmesan cheese, grated
- salt and pepper

Directions:

1. Supply your smoker with wood pellets and follow the start-up procedure. Preheat the grill, with the lid closed, to 375° F.
2. While the Traeger is heating up, peel and slice the potatoes (make sure to put them in water so they will not oxidize). Melt the butter and combine it with the crushed garlic.
3. Grease a 12" cast iron pan with butter and start to layer the torte. The layers should go as follows, potatoes, butter garlic mixture, rosemary, parmesan, continue layering to the top of the pan, about 4 to 5 layers.
4. Place the pan in the Traeger and bake for 20 to 25 minutes, or until the potatoes are fully cooked. If the top of the torte starts to darken before it is finished cooking, reduce the heat to 325°F. Serve hot and enjoy! Grill: 375 °F

Roasted Red Pepper White Bean Dip

Servings: 4
Cooking Time: 40 Minutes

Ingredients:

- 4 Whole garlic
- 4 Tablespoon extra-virgin olive oil
- 2 Bell Pepper, Red
- 3 Tablespoon Dill Weed, fresh
- 3 Tablespoon chopped flat-leaf parsley
- 2 Can cannellini beans, mashed
- 4 Teaspoon lemon juice
- 1 1/2 Teaspoon salt

Directions:

1. Roasting the garlic and red peppers:
2. Supply your smoker with wood pellets and follow the start-up procedure. Preheat the grill, with the lid closed, to 400° F.
3. Peel away the outside layers of the garlic husk. Cut off the top of the garlic bulb, exposing each of the individual cloves. Drizzle olive oil over the top of the head of garlic and rub it in. Wrap the garlic in foil, completely covering it. Put the head of garlic and the two red peppers (washed and dried) on the Traeger.
4. Roast the garlic for 25-30 minutes and the peppers for about 40 minutes. Rotate the peppers a quarter-turn every 10 minutes until the exterior is blistered and blackened. Grill: 400 °F
5. Pull the peppers off the grill and put them in a bowl. Cover the bowl with plastic wrap and leave them for 15 minutes. The steam will loosen the skins so that they slip off like a drumstick covered in barbecue sauce.
6. Peel off the pepper skin. Cut off the stems and scrape out the seeds and they're ready to use.
7. As for the garlic, let it cool and then pull out the individual cloves as needed.
8. The dip:
9. In a blender put the roasted red peppers, 4 cloves of roasted garlic, dill, parsley, drained and rinsed beans, olive oil, lemon juice and salt.
10. Blend until the dip is smooth and creamy. You may need to scrape down the sides of the blender a couple of times. If it's having difficulty blending or looks too thick add more olive oil or lemon juice. (Add more lemon juice if it tastes like it needs more acid or brightness.) Enjoy!

Parmesan Roasted Cauliflower

Servings: 4
Cooking Time: 40 Minutes

Ingredients:

- 1 Head cauliflower, cut into florets
- 1 Medium onion, sliced
- 4 Clove garlic, unpeeled
- 4 Tablespoon olive oil
- salt

- black pepper
- 1 Teaspoon fresh thyme
- 1/2 Cup Parmesan cheese, grated

Directions:

1. Supply your smoker with wood pellets and follow the start-up procedure. Preheat the grill, with the lid closed, to 400° F.

2. On a baking tray, mix together cauliflower, onion, thyme, garlic, olive oil, salt and pepper.

3. Place tray on preheated grill and cook until cauliflower is firm and almost tender (about 25 minutes). Grill: 400 °F

4. Sprinkle cauliflower with Parmesan cheese and continue to cook on the Traeger for another 10 to 15 minutes. Cauliflower should be tender and the Parmesan crisp. Serve immediately, enjoy!

Roasted Pumpkin Seeds

Servings: 8
Cooking Time: 40 Minutes

Ingredients:

- 1 Whole Pumpkin, seeds
- olive oil or vegetable oil
- Jacobsen Salt Co. Pure Kosher Sea Salt

Directions:

1. As soon as possible after removing the seeds from the pumpkin, rinse pumpkin seeds under cold water in a colander and pick out the pulp and strings.

2. Place the pumpkin seeds in a single layer on an oiled baking sheet, stirring to coat. Supply your smoker with wood pellets and follow the start-up procedure. Preheat the grill, with the lid closed, to 180° F.

3. Place the baking sheet with the seeds on the grill grate, close the lid, and smoke for 20 minutes. Grill: 180 °F

4. Sprinkle your seeds with salt and turn the temperature on your grill up to 325°F. Roast the seeds until toasted, about 20 minutes. Check and stir seeds after the first 10 minutes. Grill: 325 °F

5. Seeds will be brown because they were smoked before being roasted. Enjoy!

Twice-smoked Potatoes

Servings: 16
Cooking Time: 95 Minutes

Ingredients:

- 8 Idaho, Russet, or Yukon Gold potatoes
- 1 (12-ounce) can evaporated milk, heated
- 1 cup (2 sticks) butter, melted
- ½ cup sour cream, at room temperature
- 1 cup grated Parmesan cheese
- ½ pound bacon, cooked and crumbled
- ¼ cup chopped scallions
- Salt
- Freshly ground black pepper
- 1 cup shredded Cheddar cheese

Directions:

1. Supply your smoker with wood pellets and follow the start-up procedure. Preheat, with the lid closed, to 400°F.

2. Poke the potatoes all over with a fork. Arrange them directly on the grill grate, close the lid, and smoke for 1 hour and 15 minutes, or until cooked through and they have some give when pinched.

3. Let the potatoes cool for 10 minutes, then cut in half lengthwise.

4. Into a medium bowl, scoop out the potato flesh, leaving ¼ inch in the shells; place the shells on a baking sheet.

5. Using an electric mixer on medium speed, beat the potatoes, milk, butter, and sour cream until smooth.

6. Stir in the Parmesan cheese, bacon, and scallions, and season with salt and pepper.

7. Generously stuff each shell with the potato mixture and top with Cheddar cheese.

8. Place the baking sheet on the grill grate, close the lid, and smoke for 20 minutes, or until the cheese is melted.

Grilled Corn On The Cob With Parmesan And Garlic

Servings: 6
Cooking Time: 30 Minutes

Ingredients:

- 4 Tablespoon butter, melted
- 2 Clove garlic, minced
- salt and pepper
- 8 ears fresh corn
- 1/2 Cup shaved Parmesan
- 1 Tablespoon chopped parsley

Directions:

1. Supply your smoker with wood pellets and follow the start-up procedure. Preheat the grill, with the lid closed, to 450° F.
2. Place butter, garlic, salt and pepper in a medium bowl and mix well.
3. Peel back corn husks and remove the silk. Rub corn with half of the garlic butter mixture.
4. Close husks and place directly on the grill grate. Cook for 25 to 30 minutes, turning occasionally until corn is tender. Grill: 450 °F
5. Remove from grill, peel and discard husks. Place corn on serving tray, drizzle with remaining butter and top with Parmesan and parsley.

Smoked Macaroni Salad

Servings: 4
Cooking Time: 20 Minutes

Ingredients:

- 1 Pound macaroni, uncooked
- 1/2 Small red onion, diced
- 1 green bell pepper, diced
- 1/2 Cup shredded carrot
- 1 Cup mayonnaise
- 3 Tablespoon white wine vinegar
- 2 Tablespoon sugar
- salt
- black pepper

Directions:

1. Bring a large stock pot of salted water to a boil over medium heat and cook pasta according to package directions. Make sure to cook to al dente, strain, and rinse under cold water.
2. Supply your smoker with wood pellets and follow the start-up procedure. Preheat the grill, with the lid closed, to 225° F.
3. Spread cooked pasta out on a sheet tray and place sheet tray directly on the grill grate. Smoke for 20 minutes, remove from heat, and transfer directly to the refrigerator to cool. Grill: 225 °F
4. While the pasta is cooling mix the dressing. Place all ingredients in a medium bowl and whisk to combine.
5. When pasta is cool combine chopped veggies, smoked pasta and dressing in a large bowl.
6. Cover with plastic wrap and place in the fridge for 20 minutes before serving. Enjoy!

Potluck Salad With Smoked Cornbread

Servings: 6
Cooking Time: 45 Minutes

Ingredients:

- 1 cup all-purpose flour
- 1 cup yellow cornmeal
- 1 tablespoon sugar
- 2 teaspoons baking powder
- 1 teaspoon salt
- 1 cup milk
- 1 egg, beaten, at room temperature
- 4 tablespoons (½ stick) unsalted butter, melted and cooled
- Nonstick cooking spray or butter, for greasing
- ½ cup milk
- ½ cup sour cream
- 2 tablespoons dry ranch dressing mix
- 1 pound bacon, cooked and crumbled
- 3 tomatoes, chopped
- 1 bell pepper, chopped
- 1 cucumber, seeded and chopped
- 2 stalks celery, chopped (about 1 cup)
- ½ cup chopped scallions

Directions:

1. For the cornbread:
2. In a medium bowl, combine the flour, cornmeal, sugar, baking powder, and salt.
3. In a small bowl, whisk together the milk and egg. Pour in the butter, then slowly fold this mixture into the dry ingredients.
4. Supply your smoker with wood pellets and follow the start-up procedure. Preheat, with the lid closed, to 375°F.
5. Coat a cast iron skillet with cooking spray or butter.
6. Pour the batter into the skillet, place on the grill grate, close the lid, and smoke for 35 to 45 minutes, or until the cornbread is browned and pulls away from the side of the skillet.
7. Remove the cornbread from the grill and let cool, then coarsely crumble.
8. For the salad:
9. In a small bowl, whisk together the milk, sour cream, and ranch dressing mix.
10. In a medium bowl, combine the crumbled bacon, tomatoes, bell pepper, cucumber, celery, and scallions.
11. In a large serving bowl, layer half of the crumbled cornbread, half of the bacon-veggie mixture, and half of the dressing. Toss lightly.
12. Repeat the layering with the remaining cornbread, bacon-veggie mixture, and dressing. Toss again.
13. Refrigerate the salad for at least 1 hour. Serve cold.

Smoked Asparagus Soup

Servings: 4
Cooking Time: 40 Minutes

Ingredients:
- Pound Asparagus Spears
- 1 Tablespoon olive oil
- salt and pepper
- 1/2 yellow onion, diced
- 1 Tablespoon butter
- 2 Clove garlic, minced
- 1 1/2 Cup chicken stock
- 1 1/2 Cup cream
- 2 Stalk Raw Asparagus, Shaved

Directions:

1. Supply your smoker with wood pellets and follow the start-up procedure. Preheat the grill, with the lid closed, to 180° F.
2. Drizzle 1 pound of asparagus with olive oil and season with salt and pepper. Place directly on the grill grate and smoke for 20-30 minutes. Taste along the way to assess smoke level pulling earlier if needed. Grill: 180 °F
3. Place 1 Tbsp butter in a saucepan and melt over medium heat. Add onion and garlic and saute for 2-3 minutes or until onion is translucent.
4. Remove asparagus from the grill and cut into 1" pieces. Place asparagus in the pan with the onions and add stock and cream. Bring to a simmer.
5. Remove from heat and puree using a blender or immersion blender until smooth.
6. Season with salt and pepper and serve. Top with fresh shaved asparagus, sprinkle with salt, pepper, and smoked paprika if desired. Enjoy!

Braised Creamed Green Beans

Servings: 4
Cooking Time: 25 Minutes

Ingredients:
- 6 Tablespoon butter
- 2 Clove garlic, pressed or minced
- 1 shallot, thinly sliced
- 1 Cup heavy cream
- 1 Pinch ground nutmeg
- salt
- 3 Pound mixed greens such as kale, chard or collards; washed, stems removed and torn into bite sized pieces

Directions:

1. Supply your smoker with wood pellets and follow the start-up procedure. Preheat the grill, with the lid closed, to 325° F.
2. In a saucepan, heat 2 tablespoons of the butter over high heat until it foams. Add the garlic and shallot and cook over medium-low heat, stirring, until softened and golden, about 5 minutes.

3. Add the cream, bring to a simmer and cook until slightly thickened, about 10 minutes.

4. Add the nutmeg and salt to taste. Using a hand blender, purée until smooth.

5. In a cast iron pan, heat the remaining 4 tablespoons butter over high heat until it foams.

6. Add the greens and cook until tender but still bright green, about 5 minutes.

7. Sprinkle with salt and add the cream mixture. Cover and transfer to the grill.

8. Braise greens for 15-20 minutes until the cream is bubbling and greens are tender. Grill: 325 °F

9. Season to taste with nutmeg and salt. Serve hot. Enjoy!

Baked Sweet Potatoes

Servings: 8
Cooking Time: 60 Minutes

Ingredients:
- 1 Cup butter, softened
- 1/4 Cup pure maple syrup
- 1/2 Teaspoon ground cinnamon
- 8 Medium sweet potatoes

Directions:
1. Make the Maple-Cinnamon Butter: In a mixing bowl, combine the butter, maple syrup, and cinnamon and whip with a wooden spoon. (Alternatively, blend the ingredients using a hand-held mixer or a stand mixer.) Transfer to a small bowl, cover, and chill until serving time.

2. Supply your smoker with wood pellets and follow the start-up procedure. Preheat the grill, with the lid closed, to 375° F. Arrange the sweet potatoes on the grill grate and bake until soft, 1 to 1-1/2 hours, depending on the size of the potatoes. Make a slit in the side of each, and squeeze the ends gently to fluff.

3. Serve hot with the Maple-Cinnamon Butter. Enjoy!

Smoked & Loaded Baked Potato

Servings: 4
Cooking Time: 60 Minutes

Ingredients:

- 6 Yukon Gold or russet potatoes
- 8 Slices bacon
- 1/2 Cup butter, melted
- 1 Cup sour cream
- 1 1/2 Cup shredded cheddar cheese, divided
- salt and pepper
- 1 Bunch green onions, thinly sliced

Directions:
1. Supply your smoker with wood pellets and follow the start-up procedure. Preheat the grill, with the lid closed, to 375° F.

2. Poke potatoes with a fork, then place straight onto the grill. Cook for 1 hour. Grill: 375 °F

3. At the same time, cook bacon on a baking sheet on the grill for about 20 minutes; remove, cool and crumble. Grill: 375 °F

4. Once potatoes are done, remove and allow to cool for 15 minutes.

5. Cut each potato lengthwise, creating long halves. Use a small spoon to scoop out about 70% of the potato to make a boat, keeping a thick layer of potato near skin.

6. Place excess potato in a bowl and reserve. Lightly mash extra potato with a fork; add butter, sour cream, 1/2 cup cheese and season with salt and pepper.

7. Take the potato skins and fill with potato mixture, then sprinkle with extra cheese and bacon.

8. Place back on grill for about 10 minutes or until warm and cheese has melted. Garnish with green onions and extra sour cream. Enjoy! Grill: 375 °F

Portobello Marinated Mushroom

Servings: 2
Cooking Time: 15 Minutes

Ingredients:
- 1 Teaspoon chopped thyme
- 1 Teaspoon rosemary, chopped
- 1 Teaspoon Oregano, chopped
- 3 Tablespoon extra-virgin olive oil
- 1 To Taste Jacobsen Salt Co. Pure Kosher Sea Salt
- 1 To Taste pepper
- 6 Whole Portobello Mushroom
- 2 Whole russet potatoes

Directions:

1. Supply your smoker with wood pellets and follow the start-up procedure. Preheat the grill, with the lid closed, to 450° F.

2. Mix fresh herbs, olive oil, salt, and pepper together in a bowl. Rub over mushrooms. Grill both sides of mushrooms for approximately 2-3 minutes on each side. Grill: 450 °F

3. Clean the potatoes and slice into long strips.

4. Heat the oil on the Traeger in a sauce pan; drop the potatoes in the hot oil and fry for 7-8 minutes. Let the potatoes cool slightly on a sheet pan. Enjoy! Grill: 450 °F

Butternut Squash

Servings: 4

Cooking Time: 45 Minutes

Ingredients:

- 1 Whole butternut squash
- Veggie Rub
- Blackened Saskatchewan Rub
- olive oil

Directions:

1. Cut squash in half and lightly coat with mixture of olive oil, Traeger Veggie Shake, and Traeger Blackened Saskatchewan.

2. Wrap in foil with 1/2 cup (120mL) of water.

3. Supply your smoker with wood pellets and follow the start-up procedure. Preheat the grill, with the lid closed, to 450° F.

4. Place squash on grill for 45 minutes. Remove from grill and unwrap. Enjoy!

Roasted Jalapeno Cheddar Deviled Eggs

Servings: 6

Cooking Time: 30 Minutes

Ingredients:

- 7 Eggs, hard boiled
- 3 Tablespoon mayonnaise
- 1 Teaspoon brown mustard
- 1 Teaspoon apple cider vinegar
- 1 Dash hot sauce
- 1 jalapeño pepper, seeded and minced
- salt and pepper
- 1/2 Cup shredded cheddar cheese
- paprika

Directions:

1. Supply your smoker with wood pellets and follow the start-up procedure. Preheat the grill, with the lid closed, to 180° F.

2. Place your eggs directly on the grill grate and smoke for 30 minutes.

3. Remove from the grill and allow the eggs to cool. Smoking the eggs will give them a slightly yellowed color, but an intense smoky flavor. If a classic white egg is your preference, then skip this step.

4. Slice the eggs lengthwise and scoop the egg yolks directly into a gallon zip top bag.

5. Add the mayo, mustard, vinegar, hot sauce, roasted jalapeños and salt and pepper to the bag.

6. Zip the bag closed and, using your hands, knead all of the ingredients together in the bag until completely smooth.

7. Squeeze the yolk mixture into one corner of the bag and then cut the corner off. Pipe the yolk mixture into the whites.

8. Sprinkle with the finely shredded cheddar or paprika and chill until you are ready to serve. Enjoy!

Smoked Bbq Onion Brussels Sprout

Servings: 4

Cooking Time: 110 Minutes

Ingredients:

- 4 strip bacon
- 1 onion minced
- 2 cloves garlic minced
- 1 lb brussels sprouts stems trimmed and cut in half
- 1 tbsp BBQ Spice Blend
- 1/2 cup Apple Habanero Bar-B-Que Sauce (or other BBQ sauce)

Directions:

1. Supply your smoker with wood pellets and follow the start-up procedure. Preheat the grill, with the lid

closed, to High heat. Place a cast iron skillet over the highest heat spot and cook the bacon until crisp.

2. Remove the bacon from pan and drain, reserving the bacon fat in the pan.

3. Reduce the heat on your smoker to 250°F.

4. Add the onions, garlic, and brussels to the pan and toss to coat in the bacon drippings. Sprinkle the BBQ spice blend over top.

5. Cover the lid and allow to smoke for 1 to 1 1/2 hours, until the sprouts are fork tender.

6. For the last 20 minutes of smoking, toss the brussels sprouts in half of the barbecue sauce.

7. Remove the sprouts from the smoker.

8. Chop the bacon and add it and the remaining barbecue sauce to the pan of sprouts, tossing to coat.

9. Serve hot.

Traeger Grilled Whole Corn

Servings: 4
Cooking Time: 25 Minutes

Ingredients:
- 3 green onions
- 6 Tablespoon butter, softened
- 1 Teaspoon chile powder
- 1 Teaspoon toasted sesame seeds
- 4 ears corn, in husk

Directions:
1. Supply your smoker with wood pellets and follow the start-up procedure. Preheat the grill, with the lid closed, to 325° F.

2. Place green onions directly on the grill grate and cook 15 minutes until lightly charred. Remove from grill and set aside.

3. Sesame-Chile Butter: Take butter out of fridge and let soften. Chop up charred green onions and add to butter along with chile powder and sesame seeds. Mash all ingredients together.

4. Grill corn, rotating occasionally, until husks are blackened (some will flake and fall off) and kernels are tender with some browned and charred spots, about 25 to 35 minutes. Grill: 325 °F

5. Let corn cool slightly, then shuck. Serve with the Sesame-Chile Butter. Enjoy

Stuffed Jalapenos

Servings: 8
Cooking Time: 60 Minutes

Ingredients:
- 40 Whole jalapeño
- 8 Ounce cream cheese, room temperature
- 1 Cup Sharp Cheddar Grated
- 1 1/2 Teaspoon Pork & Poultry Rub
- 2 Tablespoon sour cream
- 1 Whole (14 oz) cocktail sausages
- 20 Whole Slices of Smoked Bacon, Cut in Half

Directions:
1. Wash and dry the peppers. Cut the stem ends off with a paring knife, and using the same knife or a small metal spoon, carefully scrape the seeds and ribs out of each pepper. Set aside.

2. In a small bowl, combine the cream cheese, grated cheese, Traeger Pork and Poultry Rub, and the sour cream.

3. Transfer the mixture to a sturdy resealable plastic bag and trim 1/2-inch off one of the lower corners with a scissors. Squeeze the cream cheese mixture into each pepper, filling each a little over the halfway point.

4. Stuff one sausage into each pepper. Wrap the outside of each with a piece of bacon, securing with 1 or 2 toothpicks.

5. Arrange the peppers on a foil-lined baking sheet. Supply your smoker with wood pellets and follow the start-up procedure. Preheat the grill, with the lid closed, to 180° F, and smoke the peppers for 1 to 1-1/2 hours.

6. Increase the heat to 350 degrees F and continue to cook for 20 to 30 minutes, or until the bacon begins to render its fat and crisp. Enjoy! Grill: 350 °F

Grilled Broccoli Rabe

Servings: 4
Cooking Time: 10 Minutes

Ingredients:

- 4 Tablespoon extra-virgin olive oil
- 4 Bunch broccoli rabe or broccolini
- kosher salt
- 1 lemon, halved

Directions:

1. Supply your smoker with wood pellets and follow the start-up procedure. Preheat the grill, with the lid closed, to 450° F.
2. On a platter or in a mixing bowl, drizzle the olive oil over the broccoli rabe. Use your hands to mix thoroughly, coating the vegetables evenly with the oil. Season with sea salt.
3. Place the broccoli rabe in one layer directly on the lowest grill grate. Close the lid and cook for 5 to 10 minutes. You want there to be some color and slight char on the first side. Flip and cook for a few more minutes. Grill: 450 °F
4. Transfer the broccoli rabe to a serving platter and squeeze the juice of half a lemon evenly over the top.
5. Serve with more lemon wedges on the side. Enjoy!

Broccoli-cauliflower Salad

Servings: 4
Cooking Time: 25 Minutes

Ingredients:

- 1½ cups mayonnaise
- ½ cup sour cream
- ¼ cup sugar
- 1 bunch broccoli, cut into small pieces
- 1 head cauliflower, cut into small pieces
- 1 small red onion, chopped
- 6 slices bacon, cooked and crumbled (precooked bacon works well)
- 1 cup shredded Cheddar cheese

Directions:

1. In a small bowl, whisk together the mayonnaise, sour cream, and sugar to make a dressing.
2. In a large bowl, combine the broccoli, cauliflower, onion, bacon, and Cheddar cheese.
3. Pour the dressing over the vegetable mixture and toss well to coat.
4. Serve the salad chilled.

Blt Pasta Salad

Servings: 6
Cooking Time: 45 Minutes

Ingredients:

- 1 pound thick-cut bacon
- 16 ounces bowtie pasta, cooked according to package directions and drained
- 2 tomatoes, chopped
- ½ cup chopped scallions
- ½ cup Italian dressing
- ½ cup ranch dressing
- 1 tablespoon chopped fresh basil
- 1 teaspoon salt
- 1 teaspoon freshly ground black pepper
- 1 teaspoon garlic powder
- 1 head lettuce, cored and torn

Directions:

1. Supply your smoker with wood pellets and follow the start-up procedure. Preheat, with the lid closed, to 225°F.
2. Arrange the bacon slices on the grill grate, close the lid, and cook for 30 to 45 minutes, flipping after 20 minutes, until crisp.
3. Remove the bacon from the grill and chop.
4. In a large bowl, combine the chopped bacon with the cooked pasta, tomatoes, scallions, Italian dressing, ranch dressing, basil, salt, pepper, and garlic powder. Refrigerate until ready to serve.
5. Toss in the lettuce just before serving to keep it from wilting.

Roasted Green Beans With Bacon

Servings: 4

Cooking Time: 20 Minutes

Ingredients:

- 1 1/2 Pound green beans, ends trimmed
- 4 Strips bacon, cut into small pieces
- 4 Tablespoon extra-virgin olive oil
- 2 Clove garlic, minced
- 1 Teaspoon kosher salt

Directions:

1. Supply your smoker with wood pellets and follow the start-up procedure. Preheat the grill, with the lid closed, to 350° F.

2. Toss all ingredients together and spread out evenly on a sheet tray.

3. Place the tray directly on the grill grate and roast until the bacon is crispy and beans are lightly browned, about 20 minutes. Enjoy! Grill: 450 °F

Green Bean Casserole

Servings: 6

Cooking Time: 25 Minutes

Ingredients:

- 1/2 Stick butter
- 1 Small onion
- 1/2 Cup sliced button mushrooms
- 4 Can green beans, drained
- 2 Can cream of mushroom soup
- 1 Teaspoon Lawry's Seasoned Salt
- pepper
- 1 Can French's Original Crispy Fried Onions
- 1 Cup grated sharp cheddar cheese

Directions:

1. Supply your smoker with wood pellets and follow the start-up procedure. Preheat the grill, with the lid closed, to 375° F.

2. Melt butter in a cast iron skillet and add onions and mushrooms, stirring occasionally until softened.

3. Add drained green beans and cream of mushroom soup and stir gently to combine.

4. Season with seasoned salt and pepper and sprinkle the top with grated cheddar cheese and fried onions.

5. Bake for 25 minutes. Serve warm, enjoy! Grill: 375 °F

Baked Garlic Duchess Potatoes

Servings: 8

Cooking Time: 60 Minutes

Ingredients:

- 12 Medium Potatoes, Yukon gold
- salt
- 5 Large Egg Yolk
- 2 Clove garlic, minced
- 1.24 Cup heavy cream
- 3/4 Cup sour cream
- 10 Tablespoon butter, melted
- black pepper

Directions:

1. Place potatoes in a large pot and fill with water. Season with salt. Bring to a boil over medium-high heat.

2. Reduce heat and simmer until a paring knife easily slides through potatoes, about 25 to 35 minutes. Drain and let cool slightly.

3. Supply your smoker with wood pellets and follow the start-up procedure. Preheat the grill, with the lid closed, to 450° F.

4. Whisk together egg yolks, garlic, cream, sour cream, butter, and pepper in a large bowl. Season with salt.

5. Peel potatoes and push flesh through a ricer or a food mill directly into bowl with egg mixture. Fold in the egg mixture being careful not to overmix.

6. Transfer to a 3-quart baking dish and bake until golden brown and slightly puffed, about 30–40 minutes. Enjoy! Grill: 450 °F

Roasted Olives

Servings: 4

Cooking Time: 45 Minutes

Ingredients:

- 2 Cup mixed olives
- 3 Sprig fresh rosemary
- 2 Clove garlic, minced

* 2 Tablespoon orange zest
* 1/3 Cup extra-virgin olive oil
* 2 Tablespoon orange juice
* 1/2 Teaspoon red pepper flakes

Directions:

1. Combine the olives, rosemary, garlic, orange zest, red pepper flakes, olive oil, and orange juice in a glass oven-safe pie plate or baking dish. Cover with foil.

2. Supply your smoker with wood pellets and follow the start-up procedure. Preheat the grill, with the lid closed, to 300° F.

3. Roast the olives for 45 minutes, stirring once or twice. Serve warm in an attractive bowl. Enjoy! Grill: 300 ˚F

Baked Bacon Green Bean Casserole

Servings: 6
Cooking Time: 50 Minutes

Ingredients:

* 1 1/2 Pound Green Beans, fresh
* 1 Can cream of mushroom soup
* 1/2 Cup milk
* 1/2 Teaspoon Worcestershire sauce
* 1/2 Teaspoon black pepper
* 2/3 Cup French's Original Crispy Fried Onions
* 8 Slices bacon
* 1/4 Cup red bell pepper, diced
* 2/3 French's Original Crispy Fried Onions

Directions:

1. In a mixing bowl, combine beans, soup, milk, Worcestershire sauce, black pepper, 2/3 cup of the onions, 6 of the slices of crumbled bacon, and red bell pepper. Transfer to a 1-1/2 quart casserole dish.

2. Supply your smoker with wood pellets and follow the start-up procedure. Preheat the grill, with the lid closed, to 350° F.

3. Cook casserole until the filling is hot and bubbling, 35 to 40 minutes. Grill: 350 ˚F

4. Top with remaining onions and the last 2 slices of crumbled bacon and cook for 5 to 10 minutes more, or until the onions are crisp and beginning to brown. Serve, enjoy! Grill: 350 ˚F

Grilled Cabbage Steaks With Warm Bacon Vinaigrette

Servings: 4
Cooking Time: 10 Minutes

Ingredients:

* 3 Strips thick-cut lean bacon, cut into 1/4 inch strips
* 1 Large shallot, minced
* 2 Tablespoon sherry vinegar
* 1 Tablespoon whole grain mustard
* 1 Teaspoon chopped thyme
* 2 Tablespoon olive oil, plus more as needed
* 1 Head green cabbage, cut into 3/4 inch thick slices (about 6 steaks)
* salt and pepper

Directions:

1. Supply your smoker with wood pellets and follow the start-up procedure. Preheat the grill, with the lid closed, to 450° F.

2. For the Vinaigrette: In a large skillet, cook the bacon in 2 tablespoons olive oil over medium-high heat until browned and crisp. Remove bacon from heat and stir in the shallot, vinegar, mustard and thyme then set aside.

3. Brush cabbage steaks with olive oil and season with salt and pepper. Place cabbage steaks directly on grill grate and grill for 5 minutes per side. Grill: 450 ˚F

4. Remove cabbage steaks from grill and drizzle with bacon vinaigrette. Enjoy!

Roasted Jalapeño Poppers

Servings: 2
Cooking Time: 30 Minutes

Ingredients:

* 8 Slices Bacon, Center Cut
* 2 Cup cream cheese
* 2 Ounce Cheese, sharp cheddar
* 1/2 Cup green onions, minced
* 2 Teaspoon fresh squeezed lime juice
* 4 Tablespoon Seeded Tomato, Chopped
* 4 Tablespoon cilantro, chopped
* 1/2 Teaspoon kosher salt
* 2 Small garlic clove, minced

- 12 Whole Jalapeños

Directions:

1. Supply your smoker with wood pellets and follow the start-up procedure. Preheat the grill, with the lid closed, to 350° F.

2. Place 2 bacon slices directly on the grill grate and cook 10-15 minutes until cooked through and crispy flipping halfway through. Remove from grill, but leave the grill on. When cool enough to handle, coarsely chop the bacon and reserve. Grill: 350 °F

3. In the bowl of a stand mixer, combine cream cheese, cheddar cheese, green onions, chopped bacon, lime juice, tomatoes, cilantro, salt and garlic. Mix on medium speed with a paddle until combined. Transfer mixture to a piping bag.

4. Cut the tops off the jalapeños and remove the seeds and ribs with a small paring knife.

5. Pipe the filling into each pepper so that the filling comes up a 1/4" over the top of the pepper. Place the tops back on each pepper.

6. With a rolling pin, flatten out the remaining six slices of bacon until they are 1/8" thick. Cut each slice in half. Wrap 1/2 a bacon slice around each pepper and secure with a toothpick.

7. Place the peppers in the Traeger Jalapeno Popper Tray. Place the tray directly on the grill grate and cook for 30-40 minutes until the peppers are tender, bacon is crispy, and cheese is melted. Enjoy! Grill: 350 °F

Roasted New Potatoes

Servings: 4
Cooking Time: 25 Minutes

Ingredients:

- 2 Pound small new potatoes
- 3 Tablespoon butter, melted
- 2 Tablespoon olive oil
- 2 Tablespoon whole mustard seeds
- salt and pepper
- 2 Tablespoon freshly minced chives
- 2 Tablespoon freshly minced parsley

Directions:

1. Place potatoes in a colander and rinse with cold water. Dry on paper towels and transfer to a rimmed baking sheet large enough to hold them in a single layer.

2. Drizzle the potatoes with butter and olive oil, then sprinkle them with the mustard seeds. Season with salt and pepper.

3. Supply your smoker with wood pellets and follow the start-up procedure. Preheat the grill, with the lid closed, to 400° F.

4. Place the baking sheet with the potatoes on the grill grate. Roast for about 25 minutes shaking the pan once or twice, until potatoes are tender and the skins are slightly wrinkled. Grill: 400 °F

5. Transfer potatoes to a bowl or platter. Top with fresh chives and parsley. Enjoy!

Roasted Sheet Pan Vegetables

Servings: 4
Cooking Time: 25 Minutes

Ingredients:

- 1 Small head purple cauliflower, stemmed and cut into 2 inch florets
- 1 Small head yellow cauliflower, stemmed and cut into 2 inch florets
- 4 Cup butternut squash
- 2 Cup oyster or shiitake mushrooms, rinsed and sliced
- 3 Tablespoon olive oil
- 2 Teaspoon kosher salt
- freshly ground black pepper
- 1/4 Cup chopped flat-leaf parsley

Directions:

1. Supply your smoker with wood pellets and follow the start-up procedure. Preheat the grill, with the lid closed, to 450° F.

2. In a large mixing bowl, combine all of the vegetables. Drizzle olive oil over the top, along with kosher salt and a generous grinding of black pepper.

3. Using your hands, toss the vegetables until they are evenly coated.

4. Spread out onto 1 or 2 half sheet pans or baking sheets, ensuring there is a little space between the veggies.

(If they are too crowded, the vegetables will steam instead of roast and you won't get that crispy texture.)

5. Place the sheet pans on the grill and cook for 15 minutes. Open and stir, then close the lid and continue to cook until the vegetables are brown around the edges, about 5 to 15 minutes longer. Grill: 450 °F

6. Toss with parsley and serve immediately. The vegetables are also delicious at room temperature. Enjoy!

Baked Breakfast Mini Quiches

Servings: 8
Cooking Time: 15 Minutes

Ingredients:
- cooking spray
- 1 Tablespoon extra-virgin olive oil
- 1/2 yellow onion, diced
- 3 Cup Spinach, fresh
- 10 eggs
- 4 Ounce shredded cheddar, mozzarella or Swiss cheese
- 1/4 Cup fresh basil
- 1 Teaspoon kosher salt
- 1/2 Teaspoon black pepper

Directions:
1. Spray a 12-cup muffin tin generously with cooking spray.

2. In a small skillet over medium heat, warm the oil. Add the onion and cook, stirring frequently, until softened, about 7 minutes. Add the spinach and cook until wilted, about 1 minute longer.

3. Transfer to a cutting board to cool, then chop the mixture so the spinach if broken up a little.

4. Supply your smoker with wood pellets and follow the start-up procedure. Preheat the grill, with the lid closed, to 350° F.

5. In a large bowl, whisk the eggs until frothy. Add the cooled onions and spinach, cheese, basil, 1 tsp salt and 1/2 tsp pepper. Stir to combine. Divide egg mixture evenly among the muffin cups.

6. Place tray on the grill and bake until the eggs have puffed up, are set, and are beginning to brown, about 18 to 20 minutes. Grill: 350 °F

7. Serve immediately, or allow to cool on a wire rack, then refrigerate in an air tight container for up to 4 days. Enjoy!

Smoked Beet-pickled Eggs

Servings: 4
Cooking Time: 30 Minutes

Ingredients:
- 6 Eggs, hard boiled
- 1 Red Beets, scrubbed and trimmed
- 1 Cup apple cider vinegar
- 1 Cup Beet, juice
- 1/4 Onion, Sliced
- 1/3 Cup granulated sugar
- 3 Cardamom
- 1 star anise

Directions:
1. Supply your smoker with wood pellets and follow the start-up procedure. Preheat the grill, with the lid closed, to 275° F.

2. Place the peeled hard boiled eggs directly on the grill and smoke for 30 minutes. Grill: 275 °F

3. Put the smoked eggs in a quart size glass jar with the cooked/chopped beets in the bottom.

4. In a medium sauce pan, add the vinegar, beet juice, onion, sugar, cardamom and anise.

5. Bring to a boil and cook, uncovered, until sugar has dissolved and the onions are translucent (about 5 minutes).

6. Remove from the heat and let cool for a few minutes.

7. Pour the vinegar and onions mixture over the eggs and beets in the jar, covering the eggs completely.

8. Securely close with the jar lid. Refrigerate up to a month. Enjoy!

Baked Heirloom Tomato Tart

Servings: 4
Cooking Time: 45 Minutes

Ingredients:
- 1 Whole Puff Pastry Sheet
- 2 Pound heirloom tomatoes, various shapes and sizes
- 1/2 Tablespoon kosher salt

- 1/2 Cup Ricotta Cheese
- 5 Whole eggs
- 1 To Taste salt and pepper
- 1/2 Teaspoon thyme leaves
- 1/2 Teaspoon red pepper flakes
- 4 Sprig thyme

Directions:

1. Supply your smoker with wood pellets and follow the start-up procedure. Preheat the grill, with the lid closed, to 350° F.

2. Place the puff pastry on a parchment lined sheet tray, and make a cut ¾ of the way through the pastry, ½" from the edge.

3. Slice the tomatoes and season with salt. Place on a sheet tray lined with paper towels.

4. In a small bowl combine the ricotta, 4 of the eggs, salt, thyme leaves, red pepper flakes and black pepper. Whisk together until combined. Spread the ricotta mixture over the puff pastry, staying within ½" from the edge.

5. In a small bowl whisk the last egg. Brush the egg wash onto the exposed edges of the pastry.

6. Place the sheet tray directly on the grill grate and bake for 45 minutes, rotating half-way through. Grill: 350 °F

7. When the edges are browned and the moisture from the tomatoes has evaporated, remove from the grill and let cool 5-7 minutes before serving. Enjoy!

Roasted New Potatoes With Compound Butter

Servings: 4
Cooking Time: 45 Minutes

Ingredients:

- 2 Pound Small Red, White or Purple Potatoes (or Combination of All Three)
- 3 Tablespoon olive oil
- salt and pepper
- 2 Stick Butter, unsalted
- 1 Tablespoon shallot, minced
- 3 Tablespoon Finely Chopped Herbs, Such As Tarragon, Parsley, Basil or Combination
- 2 Teaspoon kosher salt

Directions:

1. Supply your smoker with wood pellets and follow the start-up procedure. Preheat the grill, with the lid closed, to 400° F. Cut the potatoes in half and place in a large mixing bowl. Cover with the olive oil, a teaspoon of salt and generous grinding of pepper.

2. Place on a large baking sheet so there is space between the potatoes. Place on the grill and roast for 45 minutes to 1 hour, until crispy skinned. Toss once during cooking. Grill: 400 °F

3. To make the butter: Place it in a medium sized shallow mixing bowl. Use a wooden spoon or strong spatula to break it up and soften it even more. Sprinkle the shallot, herbs, and salt over the butter, then use the spoon to combine the ingredients. Taste, adding more salt or herbs if necessary. Reserve a few tablespoons of the butter to serve on the potatoes.

4. To freeze the butter for future use, place a foot long piece of plastic wrap on the counter. Spread the butter out into a 6" log across the long direction of the plastic wrap towards the bottom. Begin to roll the plastic wrap away from you to roll it into a log, twisting the sides of the plastic wrap like a candy wrapper to secure.

5. Using your hands, shape the log into an even cylinder. Once it's wrapped tightly, place in the freezer. Then when more is needed, simply slice off coins of it to serve over grilled steak, chicken, veggies, or roasted potatoes. The butter holds well in the freezer for up to one month. Enjoy! *Cook times will vary depending on set and ambient temperatures.

Traeger Smoked Coleslaw

Servings: 8
Cooking Time: 20 Minutes

Ingredients:

- 1 Head purple cabbage, shredded
- 1 Head green cabbage, shredded
- 1 Cup shredded carrots
- 2 scallions, thinly sliced
- 1 1/2 Cup mayonnaise
- 1/8 Cup white wine vinegar

- 1 Teaspoon celery seed
- 1 Teaspoon sugar
- salt and pepper

Directions:

1. Supply your smoker with wood pellets and follow the start-up procedure. Preheat the grill, with the lid closed, to 180° F.

2. Spread cabbage and carrots out on a sheet tray and place directly on the grill grates. Smoke for 20 to 25 minutes or until cabbage picks up desired amount of smoke. Grill: 180 °F

3. Remove from grill and transfer to the refrigerator immediately to cool. While cabbage is cooling, make the dressing.

4. For the dressing, combine all ingredients in a small bowl and mix well.

5. Place smoked cabbage and carrots in a large bowl and pour dressing over them. Stir to coat well.

6. Transfer to a serving dish and sprinkle with scallions. Enjoy!

Baked Kale Chips

Servings: 4

Cooking Time: 20 Minutes

Ingredients:

- 2 Bunch kale, leaves washed and stems removed
- 1 As Needed extra-virgin olive oil
- 1 To Taste sea salt

Directions:

1. Dry the kale leaves well and lay them out on a sheet tray. Drizzle lightly with olive oil and sprinkle with sea salt.

2. Supply your smoker with wood pellets and follow the start-up procedure. Preheat the grill, with the lid closed, to 250° F.

3. Place the sheet tray directly on the grill grate and cook until kale is lightly browned and crispy, about 20 minutes. Enjoy! Grill: 250 °F

Baked Artichoke Parmesan Mushrooms

Servings: 8

Cooking Time: 30 Minutes

Ingredients:

- 8 Cremini Mushroom Caps
- 6 1/2 Ounce artichoke hearts
- 1/3 Cup Parmesan cheese, grated
- 1/4 Cup mayonnaise
- 1/2 Teaspoon garlic salt
- your favorite hot sauce
- paprika

Directions:

1. Clean the mushrooms with a damp paper towel. Remove the stems and discard or save for another use.

2. Using a small spoon, scoop out the inside (gills, etc.). Combine the artichoke hearts, parmesan, mayonnaise, garlic salt, and hot sauce and mix well.

3. Mound the filling in the mushroom caps. Dust the tops with paprika.

4. Arrange the mushrooms in an oven-safe baking dish.

5. Supply your smoker with wood pellets and follow the start-up procedure. Preheat the grill, with the lid closed, to 350° F.

6. Bake the mushrooms (uncovered) until the filling is bubbling and just beginning to brown, about 25 to 30 minutes. Serve immediately. Grill: 350 °F

7. For a simple variation, stuff the mushrooms with your favorite bulk sausage and bake on your Traeger as directed above. Enjoy!

Sicilian Stuffed Mushrooms

Servings: 6

Cooking Time: 25 Minutes

Ingredients:

- 12 Medium Fresh Mushrooms, about 1-1/2 inches in diameter
- 4 Ounce cream cheese, room temperature
- 1/4 Cup Parmesan cheese, grated
- 1/4 Cup shredded mozzarella cheese
- 8 Whole Pimento Stuffed Green Olives, chopped

- 3 Tablespoon Pepperoni, finely diced
- 1 1/2 Tablespoon Sun Dried Tomatoes, drained & minced
- 1/4 Teaspoon freshly ground black pepper

Directions:

1. Dampen a paper towel and wipe the outside of the mushrooms clean. Remove the stem. Using a small spoon, scoop out the inside of the mushroom leaving a shell.
2. Filling: In a small mixing bowl, beat together the cream cheese, Parmesan, and mozzarella. Stir in olives, pepperoni, tomatoes, basil, and pepper.
3. Mound the filling in the mushroom caps. Set each filled cap into the well of a muffin tin.
4. Supply your smoker with wood pellets and follow the start-up procedure. Preheat the grill, with the lid closed, to 350° F.
5. Arrange the muffin tin on the grill grate and bake the mushrooms for 25 to 30 minutes, or until the mushrooms are tender and the filling is beginning to brown.
6. Transfer to a serving plate or platter. Enjoy!

Smoked Pico De Gallo

Servings: 4
Cooking Time: 30 Minutes

Ingredients:

- 3 Cup diced Roma tomatoes
- 1 jalapeño, diced
- 1/2 red onion, diced
- 1/2 Bunch cilantro, finely chopped
- 2 lime, juiced
- salt
- olive oil

Directions:

1. Supply your smoker with wood pellets and follow the start-up procedure. Preheat the grill, with the lid closed, to 180° F.
2. Place the diced tomatoes on a small sheet pan spreading them into a thin layer. Place the sheet pan directly on the grill and smoke for 30 minutes. Grill: 180 °F
3. When the tomatoes are finished, toss all ingredients in a medium bowl and finish with lime juice, salt and olive oil to taste. Serve and enjoy!

POULTRY RECIPES

Lollipop Drumsticks

Servings: 4-6
Cooking Time: 75 Minutes

Ingredients:
- 1 Cup Barbecue Sauce
- 10 Tablespoons Butter, Salted
- 12 Chicken Drumsticks
- 1 Cup Hot Sauce
- Champion Chicken Seasoning
- Blue Cheese Or Ranch Dressing

Directions:
1. Supply your smoker with wood pellets and follow the start-up procedure. Preheat the grill, with the lid open, to 300° F.
2. Rinse chicken and pat dry with a paper towel.
3. Chop the very top of the drumstick on the larger, meaty side so the lollipops sit flatly. On the small end of the drumstick, about an inch above the knuckle, use a sharp knife or kitchen shears to cut the skin and tendons all the way down to the bone and pull the skin and cartilage off the knuckle.
4. Remove the tiny, sharp bone that sits right against the exposed chicken leg. Then, push all the meat and skin down to form the lollipop ball. Use your knife or shears to remove any excess tendons.
5. Season each lollipop generously with Champion Chicken seasoning and place in the aluminum pan with the flat side done and bones standing straight up. Then, cut 10 tablespoons of butter into cubes of 1 tablespoon each and place evenly throughout the rows of lollipops.
6. Cook lollipop drumsticks on your   at 300°F for 1 hour; checking back every 20 minutes to baste the meat with the melted butter on the bottom of the pan.
7. For the Sauce: add your favorite bbq sauce into one aluminum loaf pan. Then, add 1 cup of hot sauce and 10 tablespoons of butter into the other aluminum loaf pan. Place them on the grill 5 minutes before your chicken is done. Stir well once it's warm and the butter has melted.

8. After 1 hour, use a thermometer to check the internal temperature of the lollipops. They will be ready to glaze when the temperature reaches 165°F.
9. Once ready, dip 6 lollipops in the bbq sauce and 6 in the buffalo sauce making sure to hold the leg and cover the meat entirely. Then, place the lollipops on the wing rack and put back on the grill for 15 more minutes or until the sauce is set.

Yucatán-spiced Chicken Thighs

Servings: 4
Cooking Time: 40 Minutes

Ingredients:
- 8 skin-on, bone-in chicken thighs, about 2½lb (1.2kg) total
- for the marinade
- 2oz (55g) achiote paste
- ¼ cup hot distilled water
- ¼ cup freshly squeezed orange juice
- 2 tbsp freshly squeezed lime juice
- 2 tbsp apple cider vinegar or distilled white vinegar
- 2 tbsp vegetable oil or extra virgin olive oil
- 2 garlic cloves, peeled and minced
- 1 tsp kosher salt, plus more
- 1 tsp dried Mexican oregano
- ½ tsp ground cumin
- ¼ tsp ground cinnamon

Directions:
1. In a small bowl, make the marinade by using a fork to crumble the achiote paste. Add the hot water and mash the paste with the fork until blended. Whisk in the orange juice, lime juice, vinegar, oil, garlic, salt, oregano, cumin, and cinnamon.
2. Place the chicken thighs in a resealable plastic bag. Pour the marinade over the chicken, turning and massaging the bag to thoroughly coat the chicken. Refrigerate for 2 hours.
3. Supply your smoker with wood pellets and follow the start-up procedure. Preheat the grill, with the lid closed, to 400° F.

4. Remove the chicken thighs from the marinade and let any excess drip off. (Discard the marinade.) Place the chicken thighs skin side down on the grate at an angle to the bars. Grill for 20 minutes and then turn. Continue to grill until the internal temperature in the thighs reaches 165°F (74°C), about 20 minutes more.

5. Transfer the thighs to a platter and serve immediately.

Smoked Quarters

Servings: 2-4
Cooking Time: 120 Minutes

Ingredients:
- 4 chicken quarters
- 2 tablespoons olive oil
- 1 batch Chicken Rub
- 2 tablespoons butter

Directions:
1. Supply your smoker with wood pellets and follow the start-up procedure. Preheat the grill, with the lid closed, to 180°F.
2. Coat the chicken quarters all over with olive oil and season them with the rub. Using your hands, work the rub into the meat.
3. Place the quarters directly on the grill grate and smoke for 1½ hours.
4. Baste the quarters with the butter and increase the grill's temperature to 375°F. Continue to cook until the chicken's internal temperature reaches 170°F.
5. Remove the quarters from the grill and let them rest for 10 minutes before serving.

Tandoori Chicken Leg Quarters

Servings: 4
Cooking Time: 40 Minutes

Ingredients:
- 4 skinless chicken leg quarters, about 2½lb (1.2kg) total
- juice of 2 lemons
- ¼ cup cold distilled water
- 1½ tsp coarse salt
- ½ tsp ground turmeric
- 3 tbsp vegetable oil, plus more
- 3 garlic cloves, peeled and minced
- 1½-inch (3.75cm) piece of fresh ginger, peeled and minced
- 2 tsp sweet paprika
- 1 tsp chili powder, preferably Kashmiri
- 1 tsp ground coriander
- 1 tsp ground cumin
- ½ tsp ground cayenne
- ¼ tsp ground nutmeg
- ½ cup plain Greek yogurt
- 4 tbsp unsalted butter, melted
- for serving
- 1 large red onion, peeled and thinly sliced crosswise
- ½ cup cilantro leaves
- lemon wedges

Directions:
1. Use a sharp, thin-bladed knife to cut several deep slashes in the fleshy side of each leg quarter to increase the surface area exposed to the marinade and to help the chicken cook faster. Place the chicken legs in a resealable plastic bag.
2. In a small bowl, combine the lemon juice, water, salt, and turmeric. Stir until the salt dissolves. Pour the mixture over the chicken legs and massage the bag to thoroughly coat the chicken, forcing the liquid into the slashes. Refrigerate for 15 minutes.
3. In a medium bowl, combine the vegetable oil, garlic, ginger, paprika, chili powder, coriander, cumin, cayenne, and nutmeg. Whisk in the yogurt. Add this mixture to the plastic bag and again massage the bag to thoroughly coat the chicken legs. Refrigerate for 4 to 8 hours.
4. Supply your smoker with wood pellets and follow the start-up procedure. Preheat the grill, with the lid closed, to 400° F.
5. Remove the chicken from the plastic bag and discard the marinade. Place the leg quarters fleshy side down on the grate and grill until the chicken is nicely browned and the temperature in the thickest part of the thigh reaches 170°F (77°C), about 35 to 40 minutes, turning once or twice.
6. Remove the chicken leg quarters from the grill and let rest for 2 minutes. Brush on both sides with butter. Place the legs on a platter. Scatter the red onion, cilantro leaves, and lemon wedges on the platter. Serve immediately.

Smoked Spatchcocked Cornish Game Hens

Servings: 2
Cooking Time: 45 Minutes

Ingredients:

- 4 Cornish game hens
- 2 Ounce Big Game Rub

Directions:

1.   Place the game hen breast side down on a cutting board. Using poultry shears, cut from the neck to the tailbone to remove the backbone.

2.   Once backbone is removed, you will be able to see the inside of the bird. Make a small slit in the cartilage at the base of the breastbone to reveal the keel bone. Grab the bird with both hands on the ribs and open like a book, facing down towards the cutting board. Remove the keel bone. Cut small slits in the skin of the bird behind the legs and tuck the drumsticks into them to hold them in place.

3.   Season on both sides with Traeger Big Game Rub.

4.   Supply your smoker with wood pellets and follow the start-up procedure. Preheat the grill, with the lid closed, to 275° F.

5.   Place the game hens on the Traeger skin side up and cook until internal temperature reaches 160°F (about 45 minutes). Grill: 275 °F Probe: 160 °F

6.   Remove from Traeger and place on a cutting board; tent with foil. Let stand 10 minutes, then serve. Enjoy!

Chicken Egg Rolls With Buffalo Sauce

Servings: 4
Cooking Time: 75 Minutes

Ingredients:

- 1/4 Cup Bleu Cheese, Crumbled
- 1/4 Cup Buffalo Sauce
- 1 Lb Chicken Breasts - Boneless, Skinless
- 4 Oz Cream Cheese, Softened
- 8 Egg Roll Wrappers
- 1/2 Jalapeno Pepper, Minced
- Pinch Sweet Heat Rub
- 1/4 Red Bell Pepper, Chopped
- 4 Scallion, Sliced Thin
- 1/4 Cup Sour Cream
- 2 Cups Vegetable Oil

Directions:

1.   Supply your smoker with wood pellets and follow the start-up procedure. Preheat the grill, with the lid open, to 200° F. If using a gas or charcoal grill, set it up for low, indirect heat.

2.   Season chicken breasts with Sweet Heat Rub, then place on the grill. Smoke for 1 hour, then remove from the grill, cool, shred, and set aside.

3.   Prepare the filling: In a mixing bowl, use a hand mixer to blend cream cheese, bleu cheese, Buffalo sauce and sour cream.

4.   Fold in scallions, jalapeño, red bell pepper, and shredded chicken.

5.   Prepare egg rolls: Lay an egg roll wrapper on a flat surface and add 3 tablespoons of filling to the middle.

6.   Fold the bottom of the wrapper over the top of the filling, then fold over each side. Brush the top point of the wrapper with warm water, then roll the wrapper tight. Transfer to a tray while filling the remaining wrappers.

7.   Increase the temperature of the grill to 425°F, then set a cast iron Dutch oven on the grill. Add vegetable oil and heat for 5 minutes.

8.   Place 3 egg rolls in heated oil and fry until golden, 1 to 2 minutes per side.

9.   Transfer to a wire rack to cool, then fry the remaining egg rolls, in batches.

10. Cool egg rolls for 2 minutes, then slice in half and serve warm with celery sticks and extra Buffalo sauce for dipping.

Traditional Smoked Thanksgiving Turkey

Servings: 8
Cooking Time: 240 Minutes

Ingredients:

- 1/2 Pound butter
- 6 Clove garlic, minced
- 8 Sprig fresh thyme
- 1 Sprig fresh rosemary

- 1 Tablespoon cracked black pepper
- 1/2 Tablespoon kosher salt
- 20 Pound Turkey, Whole Birds (18-20 lbs)

Directions:

1. Supply your smoker with wood pellets and follow the start-up procedure. Preheat the grill, with the lid closed, to 300° F.

2. In a small bowl, combine softened butter with minced garlic, thyme leaves, chopped rosemary, black pepper and kosher salt.

3. Prep the turkey by separating the skin from the breast creating a pocket to stuff the butter-herb mixture in. Cover the entire breast with 1/4" thickness of butter mixture.

4. Season the whole turkey with kosher salt and black pepper. Optional: Stuff turkey cavity with Traditional Stuffing recipe. When ready to cook, set the grill temperature to 300°F and preheat, lid closed for 15 minutes.

5. Place turkey on the grill and smoke for 3-4 hours. Check the internal temperature, the desired temperature is 175°F in the thigh next to the bone, and 160°F in the breast. Turkey will continue to cook once taken off grill to reach a final temperature of 165°F in the breast. Grill: 300 °F Probe: 160 °F

6. Let rest for 10-15 minutes before serving. Enjoy!

Smoked Chicken Vermicelli Noodles

Servings: 4 – 6
Cooking Time: 120 Minutes

Ingredients:
- 2 Cup Broccoli
- ¼ Cup Chicken Stock
- 6 - 8 Chicken Thighs, Boneless, Skinless
- 1 Tbsp Chili Flakes
- 1 Tsp Cornstarch
- 4, Chopped Garlic Cloves
- 3 Tbsp Hoisin Sauce, Divided
- Knob Of Fresh Ginger, Grated
- 1, Thin Red Bell Peppers, Sliced
- 1 Tbsp Rice Wine Vinegar
- 8 Scallions, Sliced
- 1 ½ Tbsp Sesame Oil, Divided
- 1 Tbsp, Toasted Sesame Seeds
- 3.5 Oz Shitake Mushrooms, Sliced Thin
- 8 Oz Snow Peas
- 3 Tbsp Soy Sauce
- 2 Tbsp Sweet Chili Sauce
- 3 Tbsp Vegetable Oil
- 1 Lb Vermicelli Noodles, Or Linguini, Cooked And Drained

Directions:

1. In a large bowl, whisk together rice wine vinegar, 1 tablespoon of Hoisin sauce, and 1 tablespoon of sesame oil. Toss chicken to coat and allow to marinate for 1 hour.

2. Supply your smoker with wood pellets and follow the start-up procedure. Preheat the grill, with the lid open, to 225° F. If using a gas or charcoal grill, set it for low, indirect heat. Place chicken directly on the grill grate and smoke for 1 ½ to 2 hours, or until the internal temperature reaches 165° F. Remove it from the smoker, cover with foil, and rest for 10 minutes, then slice thin and set aside.

3. In a glass measuring cup whisk together 2 tablespoons of Hoisin sauce, soy sauce, sweet chili sauce, chicken stock, ½ tablespoon of sesame oil, and cornstarch. Set aside.

4. Preheat griddle to medium flame, then add oil. Working quickly, sauté ginger and garlic for 15 seconds, then add bell pepper and mushrooms and continue cooking for another minute, then add in snow peas and slaw. Toss in cooked pasta, chicken, scallions, and pour sauce over. Cook for one minute until sauce thickens and is well incorporated.

5. Transfer to platter and serve hot. Sprinkle with chili flakes and sesame seeds, if desired.

Smoke Roasted Chicken With Herb Butter

Servings: 4
Cooking Time: 60 Minutes

Ingredients:
- 8 Tablespoon butter, room temperature

- 1 Scallions, minced
- 1 Clove garlic, minced
- 2 Tablespoon Fresh Herbs (Thyme, Rosemary, Oregano, Basil, Sage or Parsley, Minced)
- 1 1/2 Tablespoon Chicken Rub
- 1/2 Tablespoon fresh lemon juice
- 1 (4 to 4-1/2 lb) chicken
- Chicken Rub

Directions:

1. In a small bowl, combine butter, scallions, garlic, minced fresh herbs, Traeger Chicken Rub and lemon juice. Blend well with a wooden spoon.

2. Remove any giblets from the cavity of the chicken. Wash the chicken inside and out with cold running water. Dry thoroughly with paper towels.

3. Sprinkle a generous amount of Traeger Chicken Rub into the cavity of the chicken.

4. Gently loosen the skin around the chicken breast and slide in a few tablespoons of the herb butter and cover evenly. Smear the outside of the chicken with the remaining herb butter.

5. Tuck the chicken wings behind the back. Tie the legs together with butcher's twine.

6. Sprinkle the outside of the chicken with more Traeger Chicken Rub and insert sprigs of fresh herbs into the cavity of the chicken if desired.

7. Supply your smoker with wood pellets and follow the start-up procedure. Preheat the grill, with the lid closed, to 400° F.

8. When grill is hot, place chicken directly on the grill grate, breast side up. Cook for 1 to 1-1/4 hours or until the internal temperature registers 165°F. If the chicken is browning too quickly, loosely cover the breast and legs with foil and continue to cook. Grill: 400 °F Probe: 165 °F

9. Remove from the grill and let rest 15 minutes at room temperature before carving. Serve. Enjoy!

Savory Grilled Chicken Burrito Bowls

Servings: 4
Cooking Time: 20 Minutes

Ingredients:

- 1 Avocado
- 1 Can Black Beans, Rinsed And Drained
- 1 ½ Pounds Boneless Skinless Chicken Strips
- 1 Tablespoon Cilantro, Chopped
- 1 Can Corn Kernels, Drained
- Juice From 1 Lime
- ½ Lime Lime Juice
- 1 ½ Cups Long Grain White Rice
- 2 Tablespoons Olive Oil
- 2 Tablespoons Sweet Heat Rub
- ¼ Cup Salsa
- 1 Teaspoon Salt
- ½ Cup Shredded Mexican Blend Cheese
- ¼ Cup Sour Cream

Directions:

1. Supply your smoker with wood pellets and follow the start-up procedure. Preheat the grill, with the lid open, to 350° F. If using a gas or charcoal grill, set it up for medium heat.

2. Place the rice in a fine mesh sieve and rinse under cold water for 2-5 minutes, or until the water runs clear. Add the rice to a pot with 2 cups of water and 1 teaspoon of salt and bring to a boil on the stove top. Once the rice boils, drop the temperature to a simmer, place the pot lid on top securely, and let the rice cook for 20-25 minutes.

3. Once the time is up, remove the rice from the heat, and allow it to steam with the lid on for a further 10 minutes. Remove the lid from the rice, add the lime juice and cilantro, and fluff the rice with a fork. Set aside.

4. Grill the chicken for 5-7 minutes, or until the chicken reaches an internal temperature of 165°F and is golden and charred in some spots. Remove the chicken from the grill and allow it to rest for 5 minutes before slicing into bite sized pieces.

5. To assemble the burrito bowls: place a large scoop of cilantro lime rice into a bowl. Top with slices of grilled chicken, a scoop of black beans, a scoop of corn, salsa, cheese, sour cream, and avocado. Serve immediately.

Cheese Chicken Cordon Bleu

Servings: 8
Cooking Time: 75 Minutes

Ingredients:

- 8 Chicken, Boneless/Skinless
- 1 Cup Mozzarella Cheese, Shredded
- Lemon Pepper Garlic Seasoning
- 8 Prosciutto, Sliced

Directions:

1. Supply your smoker with wood pellets and follow the start-up procedure. Preheat the grill, with the lid closed, to 250° F.
2. Pound each chicken breast with a mallet or cast iron pan so that it's about ½ inch thick.
3. On a piece of prosciutto, sprinkle mozzarella cheese and roll up. Place in the middle of a chicken breast and wrap the chicken around the prosciutto roll. Sprinkle with Lemon Pepper seasoning.
4. Smoke for an hour to 75 minutes, or until internal temperature reaches 165 degrees F.

Buffalo Wings

Servings: 2-3
Cooking Time: 35 Minutes

Ingredients:

- 1 pound chicken wings
- 1 batch Chicken Rub
- 1 cup Frank's Red-Hot Sauce, Buffalo wing sauce, or similar

Directions:

1. Supply your smoker with wood pellets and follow the start-up procedure. Preheat the grill, with the lid closed, to 300°F.
2. Season the chicken wings with the rub. Using your hands, work the rub into the meat.
3. Place the wings directly on the grill grate and smoke until their internal temperature reaches 160°F.
4. Baste the wings with the sauce and continue to smoke until the wings' internal temperature reaches 170°F.

Bbq Spatchcocked Chicken

Servings: 2
Cooking Time: 45 Minutes

Ingredients:

- 1 whole chicken
- 1/4 Cup Chicken Rub
- olive oil
- 1/2 Cup Sweet & Heat BBQ Sauce

Directions:

1. Supply your smoker with wood pellets and follow the start-up procedure. Preheat the grill, with the lid closed, to 375° F.
2. With a large knife or shears, cut the bird open along the backbone on both sides, through the ribs, and remove the backbone.
3. Brush chicken with olive oil and season both sides with Traeger Chicken rub.
4. Place the poultry on the Traeger, breast side up and cook for 35 to 40 minutes or until a thermometer inserted into the breast registers 160°F. Grill: 375 °F Probe: 160 °F
5. Remove from the grill and let rest 5 minutes before slicing. Enjoy!

Spatchcocked Turkey

Servings: 10-14
Cooking Time: 120 Minutes

Ingredients:

- 1 whole turkey
- 2 tablespoons olive oil
- 1 batch Chicken Rub

Directions:

1. Supply your smoker with wood pellets and follow the start-up procedure. Preheat the grill, with the lid closed, to 350°F.
2. To remove the turkey's backbone, place the turkey on a work surface, on its breast. Using kitchen shears, cut along one side of the turkey's backbone and then the other. Pull out the bone.
3. Once the backbone is removed, turn the turkey breast-side up and flatten it.

4. Coat the turkey with olive oil and season it on both sides with the rub. Using your hands, work the rub into the meat and skin.

5. Place the turkey directly on the grill grate, breast-side up, and cook until its internal temperature reaches 170°F.

6. Remove the turkey from the grill and let it rest for 10 minutes, before carving and serving.

Beer Chicken

Servings: 4
Cooking Time: 75 Minutes

Ingredients:
- 1 Beer, Can
- 1 Chicken, Whole
- Lemon Pepper Garlic Seasoning

Directions:
1. Supply your smoker with wood pellets and follow the start-up procedure. Preheat the grill, with the lid open, to 400° F.

2. Season the chicken all over with spices. Open the can of your favorite pop/beer and place the opening of the chicken over the can. Make sure that the chicken can stand upright without falling over. Place on your Grill and barbecue until the internal temperature reaching 165 degrees F (about an hour).

3. Remove from grill, slice and serve hot.

Smoked Beer Brine Hens

Servings: 4
Cooking Time: 150 Minutes

Ingredients:
- 2 Tbsp Ales Pepper
- 12 Cups Beer Brine
- 2 Cornish Game Hens
- 2 Lemons
- 6 Rosemary Sprigs
- Salt & Freshly Ground Black Pepper
- 12 Thyme Sprigs

Directions:
1. Supply your smoker with wood pellets and follow the start-up procedure. Preheat the grill, with the lid open, to 300° F. (I have found the setting the grill at 300 will keep the top smoker temp between 200°F and 215°F, this could vary depending on the air temp and general weather conditions. You want to keep the upper smoking cabinet between 200°F and 215°F) If you're using a vertical smoker, set temp to 200°F.

2. Stuff your hens with the rosemary, thyme, and lemons. Coat the skin with the ales pepper and freshly ground black pepper.

3. Truss your hens and tie a small loop at the legs so you can hang your birds. Hang them in the smoker and insert a probe thermometer, cook to an internal temp of 155°F.

4. Remove the hens to rest. Final temp should be 160°F.

5. Serve these with some great creamed kale or charred asparagus.

Chicken Cordon Bleu Rollups

Servings: 8
Cooking Time: 30 Minutes

Ingredients:
- 4 boneless, skinless chicken breasts, each about 6 to 8oz (170 to 225g)
- garlic salt
- freshly ground black pepper
- 8 thin slices of Swiss cheese
- 8 thin slices of deli ham or prosciutto
- 4 tbsp unsalted butter, melted
- minced fresh parsley or chives

Directions:
1. Supply your smoker with wood pellets and follow the start-up procedure. Preheat the grill, with the lid closed, to 400° F.

2. Place each chicken breast between two sheets of plastic wrap and pound with a meat mallet or a rolling pin until each breast is ¼ inch (.5cm) thick. Place the breasts smooth side down on a workspace and lightly season with garlic salt and pepper. Top each breast with 2 slices of cheese and 2 slices of ham. Roll up the breasts and secure them with toothpicks that have been coated

with vegetable oil. Brush the outside of the breasts with butter and lightly season with garlic salt and pepper.

3. Place the chicken rollups on the grate at an angle to the bars. Smoke for 25 to 30 minutes.

4. Transfer the rollups to a platter and let rest for 3 minutes. Remove the toothpicks. Scatter parsley over the top before serving.

Cranberry Turkey Breast

Servings: 6
Cooking Time: 90 Minutes

Ingredients:
- 1 Bay Leaf
- 1/2 Tsp Black Pepper
- 3 Tbsp Butter, Divided
- 1 Celery Rib, Chopped
- To Taste, Cracked Black Pepper
- 4 Oz Cremini Mushrooms
- 1/2 Cup Dried Cranberries
- 2 Garlic Cloves, Minced
- 1 Package, Approx 2Lbs Honeysuckle White Turkey Breast, Boneless
- 1/2 Cup Marsala Wine
- 1 Tbsp Olive Oil
- 1 Rosemary Sprigs
- 1/2 Tsp Rubbed Sage
- 1/2 Tsp Salt
- To Taste, Sea Salt
- 6 Oz Stuffing Mix
- 1 1/4 Cup Turkey Stock, Divided
- 1 Yellow Onion, Chopped

Directions:
1. Supply your smoker with wood pellets and follow the start-up procedure. Preheat the grill, with the lid closed, to 325° F. If using a gas or charcoal grill, set it up for medium-low heat.

2. Melt the butter 1 tablespoon of butter and olive oil in a large skillet over medium heat. Add the onions and celery and cook, stirring frequently, until soft, 3 minutes.

3. Add the garlic and mushrooms and continue to cook for 5 minutes, until the mushrooms are slightly browned.

4. Deglaze with marsala wine, using a wooden spoon to scrape up any browned bits from the bottom of the pan.

5. Add the dried cranberries, black pepper, sage, and salt and simmer for 2 minutes, then remove from the heat.

6. Fold the stuffing into the vegetable mixture, then slowly pour over turkey stock, until stuffing is moistened.

7. Place the Honeysuckle White® Turkey Breast on a large cutting board, skin-side down, then butterfly it. Season with salt and pepper, then spoon over ⅓ of the stuffing, leaving an inch border.

8. Roll the turkey breast, starting at the side with less skin. Use butcher's twine to truss the turkey breast and secure the stuffing. Place in a cast iron skillet, top remaining butter, season with salt and pepper. Place a sprig of rosemary on top, add remaining ¼ cup of stock around the turkey, along with 1 bay leaf. Transfer to the grill.

9. Cook the turkey for 1 to 1 ½ hours, until an internal temperature of 165°F is reached.

10. Remove stuffed turkey breast from the grill, rest for 15 minutes, then slice and serve warm, with remaining stuffing.

Whole Smoked Honey Chicken

Servings: 4
Cooking Time: 40 Minutes

Ingredients:
- 1 Tablespoon Honey
- 1 ½ Lemon
- 4 Tablespoons Champion Chicken Seasoning
- 4 Tablespoons Unsalted Butter
- 1, 4 Pound Chicken, Giblets Removed And Patted Dry

Directions:
1. Supply your smoker with wood pellets and follow the start-up procedure. Preheat the grill, with the lid open, to 225° F.

2. In a small saucepan, melt together the butter and honey over low heat. Squeeze ½ lemon into the honey mixture and remove from the heat.

3.   Smoke the chicken, skin side down until the chicken is lightly browned and the skin releases from the grate without ripping, about 6-8 minutes.

4.   Turn the chicken over and baste with the honey butter mixture.

5.   Continue to smoke the chicken, basting every 45 minutes, until the thickest part of the chicken reaches 160°F.

Cajun Brined Maple Smoked Turkey Breast

Servings: 4
Cooking Time: 180 Minutes

Ingredients:
- 1 Gallon water
- 3/4 Cup canning and pickling salt
- 3 Tablespoon minced garlic
- 3 Tablespoon dark brown sugar
- 2 Tablespoon Worcestershire sauce
- 2 Tablespoon Cajun seasoning
- 1 (5-6 lb) bone-in turkey breast
- 3 Tablespoon extra-virgin olive oil
- 2 Tablespoon Cajun seasoning

Directions:
1.   In a large food safe container or bucket, combine all of the ingredients for the brine with 1 gallon water. Stir until the salt is dissolved.

2.   Place the turkey breast in the brine and weigh it down to ensure it is fully submerged. Cover and brine in a refrigerator for 1 to 2 days.

3.   Remove the turkey breast from the brine and pat dry. Drizzle with the olive oil using your hands to cover all areas of the bird. Season liberally with Cajun seasoning. Probe: 165 °F

4.   Supply your smoker with wood pellets and follow the start-up procedure. Preheat the grill, with the lid closed, to 225° F.

5.   Place the turkey breast directly on the grill grate, close the lid and cook for 3 hours. After 3 hours, increase the temperature to 425°F and continue to cook for another 30 minutes or until the internal temperature reads 165°F when a thermometer is inserted into the thickest part of the breast. Grill: 225 °F Probe: 165 °F

6.   Remove the turkey breast from the grill and allow to rest for at least 15 minutes before slicing. Slice and serve. Enjoy!

Lemon Chicken Breast

Servings: 6
Cooking Time: 15 Minutes

Ingredients:
- 1 Clove garlic, coarsely chopped
- 2 Teaspoon honey
- 2 Teaspoon kosher salt
- 1 Teaspoon freshly ground black pepper
- 2 Sprig fresh thyme leaves
- 1 lemon, zest and juice
- 1/2 Cup high-quality olive oil or vegetable oil
- 6 (6 oz) boneless, skinless chicken breasts
- 1 lemon, cut into wedges, for serving

Directions:
1.   To make the marinade, add the garlic, honey, salt, pepper, thyme, lemon juice and zest to a small mixing bowl. Whisk until the salt crystals and honey dissolve. Slowly whisk in the olive oil.

2.   Place the chicken breast in a large resealable plastic bag and pour the marinade over them, massaging the bag to distribute the marinade evenly.

3.   Refrigerate for 4 hours.

4.   Supply your smoker with wood pellets and follow the start-up procedure. Preheat the grill, with the lid closed, to 400° F.

5.   Drain the chicken breasts and discard the marinade.

6.   Arrange the chicken breasts directly on the grill grate and cook until the internal temperature reaches 165°F. Grill: 400 °F Probe: 165 °F

7.   If desired, grill the reserved lemon wedges alongside the chicken, cut sides down, for 15 minutes.

8.   Serve the chicken on a platter or plates with the lemon wedges.

Chile Cilantro Lime Chicken Wings

Servings: 4

Cooking Time: 20 Minutes

Ingredients:

- 1 Tsp Ancho Chili Powder
- 2 Tsp Blackened Sriracha Rub Seasoning
- 2 Lbs Chicken Wings, Split
- 2 Tbsp Cilantro, Chopped, Divided
- 1 Tsp Cumin
- 1 Lime, Zest & Juice
- 1 1/2 Tbsp Olive Oil

Directions:

1. In a medium bowl, combine 1 tablespoon of cilantro, lime juice and zest, olive oil, Blackened Sriracha, ancho chili powder, and cumin.

2. Place chicken wings in a resealable gallon bag and add cilantro mixture. Transfer to the refrigerator and marinate for 1 hour, turning occasionally.

3. Supply your smoker with wood pellets and follow the start-up procedure. Preheat the grill, with the lid closed, to 350° F. If using a gas or charcoal grill, set it up for medium heat.

4. Remove chicken wings from the marinade and place on the grill over indirect heat. Grill for 15 to 18 minutes, turning and rotating every 3 to 5 minutes.

5. Remove chicken wings from the grill, garnish with remaining cilantro, and serve warm.

Smoked Avocado Turkey Tamale Pie

Servings: 6

Cooking Time: 240 Minutes

Ingredients:

- 1 Avocado, Diced (For Topping)
- 15 Oz Black Beans, Drained (For Filling)
- To Taste, Blackened Sriracha Rub Seasoning
- 2 Tsp Blackened Sriracha Rub Seasoning (For Filling)
- To Taste, Blackened Sriracha Rub Seasoning (For Polenta)
- 2 Tbsp Butter (For Polenta)
- 2 Tbsp Cilantro, Chopped (For Topping)
- 1 Cup Corn Kernels (For Filling)
- 2 Cups Enchilada Sauce (For Filling)
- 1/2 Jalapeño, Minced (For Topping)
- 2 Cups Milk Or Water (For Polenta)
- 1 Cup Polenta, Or Fine Cornmeal (For Polenta)
- 2 Scallions, Sliced (For Topping)
- 2 Cups Smoked Turkey Breast, Shredded (For Filling)
- 2 1/2 Lbs Split Turkey Breast , Bone-In
- 2 Cups Turkey Stock (For Polenta)
- 4 Oz White Cheddar, Shredded (For Polenta)
- 4 Oz White Cheddar, Shredded (For Topping)

Directions:

1. Supply your smoker with wood pellets and follow the start-up procedure. Preheat the grill, with the lid closed, to 225° F. If using a gas or charcoal grill, set it up for low, indirect heat.

2. Season the turkey breast with Blackened Sriracha, then transfer to the grill, on a rack, over indirect heat.

3. Smoke the turkey breast for 2 ½ to 3 hours, until an internal temperature of 160° F. Remove the turkey from the grill, allow to rest for 20 minutes, then shred with 2 forks.

4. While the turkey is resting, prepare the polenta:

5. Place a deep, cast iron skillet on the grill, then increase the temperature to 375° F. Add chicken broth and milk to a skillet and bring to a boil.

6. Whisk in the polenta, then reduce the heat to a simmer, stirring often for 5 minutes. Season with Blackened Sriracha, then stir in cheese and butter. Remove the skillet from the grill and smooth out the polenta in an even layer.

7. In a large glass measuring cup or mixing bowl, combine the turkey, enchilada sauce, black beans, corn and Blackened Sriracha.

8. Spoon the turkey mixture over the polenta, then top with 4 ounces of shredded cheese. Place on the grill, over indirect heat and bake for 20 to 25 minutes, until the filling is bubbling along the edge and the cheese is melted.

9. Remove the skillet from the grill and allow it to rest for 10 minutes. Serve warm, garnished with avocado, scallions, jalapeño, and fresh cilantro.

Buffalo Chicken

Servings: 6
Cooking Time: 90 Minutes

Ingredients:

- 1 1/2 Tbsp Apple Cider Vinegar
- 3 Tbsp Bleu Cheese, Crumbled
- 1/4 Cup Buffalo Sauce
- 1/2 Cup Butter, Unsalted, Cubed
- 1/4 Tsp Cayenne Pepper
- 3 Celery Stalks, Cut Into Sticks
- 1 Cup Cheddar Jack Cheese, Shredded
- 1 Lb Chicken Breast, Boneless, Skinless
- 3 Oz Cream Cheese, Softened
- 1/8 Tsp Garlic, Granulated
- 2/3 Cup Hot Pepper Sauce
- 12 Jalapeno Peppers
- Mason Jar(S)
- 1/4 Red Bell Pepper, Chopped
- 2 Scallions, Sliced Thin
- Shredded Chicken
- 3 Tbsp Sour Cream
- To Taste, Sweet Heat Rub
- 1/2 Tsp Sweet Heat Rub (For Sauce)
- 1/4 Tsp Worcestershire Sauce

Directions:

1. Supply your smoker with wood pellets and follow the start-up procedure. Preheat the grill, with the lid open, to 200° F. If using a gas or charcoal grill, set it up for low, indirect heat.
2. Season chicken breasts with Sweet Heat, then place on the grill. Smoke for 1 hour, then remove from the grill, and set aside to rest.
3. While the chicken is resting, prepare the Buffalo sauce: Set a small cast iron pan or saucepan on the grill. Open the sear slide and increase the grill temperature to 350° F. Add the hot pepper sauce, apple cider vinegar, Worcestershire sauce, Sweet Heat, cayenne, and granulated garlic to the skillet, and whisk to combine. When the sauce begins to bubble, remove the skillet from the grill and whisk in butter. Transfer the sauce to a mason jar.
4. Shred the chicken with 2 forks in the sauce skillet. Set aside.
5. Prepare the filling: In a mixing bowl, use a hand mixer to blend cream cheese, bleu cheese, Buffalo sauce and sour cream. Fold in scallions, red bell pepper, and shredded chicken.
6. Prepare the peppers: Cut each jalapeño in half, lengthwise. Use a paring knife or teaspoon to scrape out the seeds and membrane, then place in a cast iron skillet (might need to divide between 2 skillets). Stuff the mixture into the jalapeño halves, then top with shredded cheese.
7. Transfer peppers to the grill, with the sear slide closed. Close the lid and cook for 15 to 20 minutes, until peppers begin to soften and cheese has melted.
8. Remove the peppers from the grill, transfer to a serving board or platter, and serve warm with extra Buffalo sauce.

Flavoured Hibachi Chicken

Servings: 4
Cooking Time: 10 Minutes

Ingredients:

- To Taste, Blackened Sriracha Rub Seasoning
- To Taste, Blackened Sriracha Rub Seasoning (For Vegetables)
- 2 Cups Broccoli Florets, Blanched
- 1 Tbsp Brown Sugar
- 1 Tbsp Butter, Unsalted
- 1 1/2 Lbs Chicken Breast, Boneless, Skinless, Sliced Thin
- 1 Tbsp Cilantro, Chopped
- 3 Garlic Cloves, Minced
- 2 Garlic Cloves, Minced (For Vegetables)
- 1 Tsp Ginger, Grated
- 1 Tsp Ginger, Grated (For Vegetables)
- 1/2 Lime, Juiced
- 1/2 Red Bell Pepper, Sliced Thin
- For Serving, Rice Noodles, Cooked
- 2 Scallions, Chopped
- 1 Tbsp Sesame Oil
- 2 Tbsp Sesame Oil, Divided

- 1 Cup Snap Peas, Blanched
- 1/4 Cup Tamari
- For Serving, Toasted Sesame Seeds
- 1 Tbsp Vegetable Oil
- 1 Tbsp Vegetable Oil (For Vegetables)
- For Serving, Yum-Yum Sauce

Directions:

1. Supply your smoker with wood pellets and follow the start-up procedure. Preheat the grill, with the lid open, to medium-high heat. When hot, add 1 tablespoon of sesame oil and vegetable oil. Immediately add the chicken and season with Blackened Sriracha. When the chicken starts to brown, flip it over to brown the other side.

2. Add the garlic, ginger, soy sauce, brown sugar, butter, and the remaining tablespoon of sesame oil and stir. Turn the heat down to medium-low and let the mixture simmer for 3 minutes, until it thickens and adheres to the chicken. Add lime juice, cilantro, and scallions, then remove the mixture from the griddle.

3. After starting the sauce for the chicken, sauté the vegetables: Add sesame oil and vegetable oil to the other side of the griddle. Quickly sauté broccoli, snap peas, and red bell pepper with garlic and ginger. Season with Blackened Sriracha. Remove from the griddle after 2 minutes.

4. Serve hibachi chicken warm with sautéed vegetables, toasted sesame seeds, rice noodles, and Yum-Yum sauce if desired.

Carrot Celery Chicken Drumsticks

Servings: 4
Cooking Time: 30 Minutes

Ingredients:

- Buffalo Style Dry Rub
- Carrot, Stick
- Celery, Stick
- 12 Chicken, Drumsticks

Directions:

1. Supply your smoker with wood pellets and follow the start-up procedure. Preheat the grill, with the lid closed, to 350° F.

2. Generously sprinkle the Buffalo Wing Rub all over the drumsticks. Hang each drumstick by the bone on the Wing Rack. Place in the for about 30 minutes.

3. Serve hot with celery and carrot sticks. Enjoy!

Delicious Asian Bbq Wings

Servings: 6
Cooking Time: 60 Minutes

Ingredients:

- 2 Lbs Chicken, Wing
- 1 Tsp Garlic, Minced
- 1 Tsp Ginger, Fresh
- 1 Tsp Chopped Green Onion
- 1/2 Cup Hoisin Sauce
- 1 Tsp Honey
- 2 Tsp Rice Vinegar
- 2 Tsp Sesame Oil
- 1 Tsp Sesame Seeds
- 1 Tsp Soy Sauce
- 1 Cup Water, Boiling

Directions:

1. Add all ingredients except wings and sesame seeds to a mixing bowl and whisk to incorporate. Add wings to a resealable plastic bag and pour marinade over. Allow marinating for at least 2 hours up to overnight. Remove wings from bag, reserving marinade.

2. Supply your smoker with wood pellets and follow the start-up procedure. Preheat the grill, with the lid closed, to 300° F. Place wings in a grilling basket and cook for 1 hour or until they reach an internal temperature of 165°F.

3. While wings are cooking, pour reserved marinade into a small saucepan and add rice wine vinegar. Over high heat, bring to a boil while whisking often, and reduce by 1/3, or about 10 minutes. Set aside.

4. Brush wings with reduced sauce and allow to cook for 5-10 more minutes or until glaze has set. Remove from smoker, sprinkle with sesame seeds, allow to rest for 5 minutes, and serve.

Smoked Honey Chicken Drumsticks

Servings: 4

Cooking Time: 30 Minutes

Ingredients:

- 1/2 Cup Apple Cider Vinegar
- 12 Chicken Drumsticks
- 2 Tablespoons Dijon Mustard
- 1/4 Cup Honey
- 1/4 Cup Ketchup
- 1 Tablespoon Sweet Heat Rub
- 1/2 Cup Soy Sauce

Directions:

1. Supply your smoker with wood pellets and follow the start-up procedure. Preheat the grill, with the lid open, to 225° F. Remove the wings from the marinade and place the drumsticks into the Buffalo Wing Rack.

2. Smoke for 60 minutes, or until a thermometer inserted into the thickest part of the drumstick registers at 170°F.

3. Turn the heat up to 350°F and cook for 5 to 10 minutes to make the skin crisp.

4. Remove from the smoker, serve immediately and enjoy!

Bbq Chicken Wings With Spicy Honey Glaze

Servings: 4

Cooking Time: 30 Minutes

Ingredients:

- 4 Pound chicken wings
- 6 Ounce Chicken Rub
- 2 Tablespoon corn starch
- 1 Cup honey
- 1 Cup Sriracha
- 1/2 Cup soy sauce
- 2 Tablespoon sesame oil
- 3 Tablespoon unsalted butter
- 2 Tablespoon sesame seeds

Directions:

1. Supply your smoker with wood pellets and follow the start-up procedure. Preheat the grill, with the lid closed, to 375° F.

2. While grill is preheating, dry off chicken wings with a paper towel. Mix the Traeger Chicken rub with the cornstarch and coat both sides of the chicken wings.

3. When the grill is heated, place the wings on the grill for 35 minutes flipping half way through. Grill: 375 ˚F

4. While the wings are cooking, mix the honey, Sriracha, soy sauce, sesame seed oil, and unsalted butter and heat on a stove top.

5. After the wings have cooked for 35 minutes, check the temperature. The minimum temperature must reach an internal temperature of 165 degrees F. An internal temperature between 175 to 180 degrees F may yield a better texture. Grill: 375 ˚F Probe: 177 ˚F

6. When wings are done, place in large bowl and toss with the warmed sauce.

7. Place wings on platter and sprinkle the sesame seeds. Enjoy!

Lemon & Herb Chicken

Servings: 3-4

Cooking Time: 75 Minutes

Ingredients:

- 1 roaster chicken, about 4lb (1.8kg), preferably organic
- 1 large sweet onion, peeled and sliced lengthwise into 8 wedges
- ½ cup chicken stock or broth
- sprigs of fresh rosemary, thyme, parsley, tarragon, or chives (or a mix)
- lemon wedges
- for the butter
- 4 tbsp unsalted butter, at room temperature
- 1 garlic clove, peeled and finely minced
- 2 tbsp chopped fresh herbs, such as rosemary, thyme, parsley, tarragon, or chives (or a mix)
- 2 tsp lemon zest
- 2 tsp freshly squeezed lemon juice
- ½ tsp coarse salt
- ½ tsp freshly ground black pepper

Directions:

1.   Supply your smoker with wood pellets and follow the start-up procedure. Preheat the grill, with the lid closed, to 400° F.

2.   In a small bowl, make the herb butter by combining the ingredients.

3.   Place the chicken on a rimmed sheet pan and tuck the lemon rinds from the butter into the main cavity. Rub the outside of the chicken with the herb butter. (Reserve any remainder.) Tuck the wings behind the back and tie the legs together with butcher's twine. Place the onion wedges in a shallow roasting pan to help form a natural rack for the chicken. (Alternatively, place several large carrots, trimmed and peeled, on the bottom of the pan.) Place the chicken on the onion rack. Add the chicken stock and any remaining herbed butter and lemon juice.

4.   Place the roasting pan on the grate, roast the chicken for 30 minutes, and then baste with the juices from the bottom of the pan. Baste every 15 minutes until the chicken is golden brown and the internal temperature reaches 165°F (74°C), about 45 minutes more.

5.   Transfer the chicken to a cutting board and let rest for 10 minutes. Carve the chicken and place the slices on a platter with a deep well. Spoon some of the juices over the chicken. Scatter fresh herbs over the top. Serve with the lemon wedges.

Chicken Nachos

Servings: 6-8
Cooking Time: 10 Minutes

Ingredients:
- 1 Can Black Beans, Rinsed And Drained
- 1 Cup Cheddar Cheese, Shredded
- 2 Cups Chicken, Diced
- (If Desired) Cilantro
- 1 Can Corn Kernels, Drained
- (If Desired) Pickled Jalapeno Peppers
- 1/2 Tablespoon   Champion Chicken Seasoning
- 1/2 Red Onion, Diced
- 1/2 Cup Salsa
- 1/4 Cup Sour Cream

Directions:

1.   On a large sheet pan, spread out half the tortilla chips, then cover with half the shredded cheese and one cup of chicken. Sprinkle with half of Champion Chicken seasoning. Top with the rest of the tortilla chips, cheese, chicken and remaining seasoning.

2.   Supply your smoker with wood pellets and follow the start-up procedure. Preheat the grill, with the lid closed, to 350° F. Grill for 5-7 minutes, or until the cheese is melted and bubbly and everything is warmed all the way through. Remove the pan from the grill.

3.   Top the nachos with the black beans, corn, diced red onion, sour cream, cilantro and pickled jalapenos. Serve and enjoy!

Cornish Game Hens

Servings: 4
Cooking Time: 60 Minutes

Ingredients:
- 4 Cornish game hens
- 4 Tablespoon butter, melted
- Chicken Rub
- 4 Sprig rosemary or sage, plus more for garnish

Directions:

1.   Rinse the Cornish game hens under cold running water, inside and out. (Game hens do not usually come with giblets, but check the cavity for them before rinsing. If you find giblets, freeze them for chicken stock, if desired.)

2.   Dry thoroughly with paper towels. Tuck the wings behind the backs and tie the legs together with butcher's string.

3.   Rub the outside of each hen with the melted butter. Season with Traeger Chicken Rub. Slip a sprig of rosemary into the main cavity of each hen.

4.   Supply your smoker with wood pellets and follow the start-up procedure. Preheat the grill, with the lid closed, to 375° F.

5.   Roast the hens for 50 to 60 minutes, or until the juices run clear and the internal temperature of the thigh, when read on an instant-read meat thermometer, is 165°F. Grill: 375 °F Probe: 165 °F

6.   Transfer the hens to a platter or plates and let rest for 5 minutes.

7.   Garnish with a sprig of rosemary before serving. Enjoy!

Bbq Chicken Drumsticks

Servings: 4

Cooking Time: 120 Minutes

Ingredients:

- 8 chicken drumsticks
- 2 Tablespoon Chicken Rub
- 1/2 Cup 'Que BBQ Sauce

Directions:

1. Season each drumstick and let rest for 20 minutes.

2. Supply your smoker with wood pellets and follow the start-up procedure. Preheat the grill, with the lid closed, to 275° F.

3. Hang the drumsticks on the leg hanger (alternatively, place directly on the grill grate flipping halfway through) and cook for 1 hour. Grill: 275 ˚F

4. Remove the drumsticks from the hanger (or grate) and place in a pan. Grill: 275 ˚F Probe: 190 ˚F

5. Cover with foil and cook for 45 more minutes or until meat reaches an internal temperature of 190 degrees F. Grill: 275 ˚F Probe: 190 ˚F

6. Remove the foil and sauce all drumsticks in the pan.

7. Cook for an additional 15 minutes so sauce can set. Grill: 275 ˚F

8. Remove from Traeger and let rest for 15 minutes before serving. Enjoy!

Roasted Duck With Cherry Salsa

Servings: 2-3

Cooking Time: 180 Minutes

Ingredients:

- 1 whole Long Island (Pekin) duck, about 5 to 6lb (2.3 to 2.7kg), thawed if frozen
- coarse salt
- freshly ground black pepper
- 1 white onion, peeled and quartered
- 1 orange, quartered
- 4 garlic cloves, peeled and quartered
- 3 sprigs of fresh thyme or fresh rosemary, plus more
- for the salsa
- 2 cups dark red cherries, washed, destemmed, pitted, and coarsely chopped
- 1 scallion, trimmed, white and green parts sliced crosswise
- 1 jalapeño, destemmed, deseeded, and finely diced
- 1 tbsp granulated sugar, plus more
- 1 tbsp port wine (optional)
- 2 tsp freshly squeezed lime juice
- 2 tsp freshly squeezed orange juice
- 1½ tsp finely chopped orange zest

Directions:

1. Supply your smoker with wood pellets and follow the start-up procedure. Preheat the grill, with the lid closed, to 350° F.

2. In a small bowl, make the salsa by combining the ingredients. Slightly bruise some of the cherries to release their juices. Set aside.

3. Use kitchen shears to cut off the wing tips and trim any excessive neck skin from the duck. Use a sharp knife to score the skin of the breasts in the classic diamond pattern, making the cuts about 1 inch (2.5cm) apart, but don't penetrate the meat. Use a fork with sharp tines to prick the skin on the thighs. Rinse the bird inside and out with cold running water and pat dry with paper towels.

4. Season the duck inside and out with the salt and pepper. Tuck the onion, orange, garlic, and thyme in the cavity. Pull the excess skin over the opening and tie the legs together with butcher's twine.

5. Place a wire rack in a shallow roasting pan and place the duck breast side up on top of the rack. Place the roasting pan on the grate and roast the duck for 1 hour. Use tongs to turn the bird breast side down. Roast for 1 hour more and then turn again, finishing breast side up. Roast until the skin is nicely browned and the internal temperature in the thickest part of a breast reaches 170°F (77°C), about 30 minutes to 1 hour more. (There should also be quite a bit of duck fat in the bottom of the pan. Save in a covered container and refrigerate or freeze for another use.)

6. Remove the pan from the grill and let the duck rest for 15 minutes. Transfer the duck to a cutting board and carve.

7. Place the duck meat on a platter and scatter the fresh thyme over the top. Serve with the cherry salsa.

Teriyaki Apple Cider Turkey

Servings: 8-10

Cooking Time: 180 Minutes

Ingredients:

- 1/2 Cup Apple Cider
- 1/4 Cup Melted Butter, Unsalted
- 1 Teaspoon Cornstarch
- 2 Finely Chopped Garlic, Cloves
- 1/2 Teaspoon Ginger, Ground
- 2 Tablespoon Honey
- 2 Tablespoon Champion Chicken Seasoning
- 1 Shady Brook Farms® Whole Turkey, Thawed
- 2 Tablespoon Soy Sauce
- 1 Tablespoon Water, Cold

Directions:

1. Supply your smoker with wood pellets and follow the start-up procedure. Preheat the grill, with the lid closed, to 300° F.

2. In a saucepan, whisk together melted butter, garlic, soy sauce, apple cider, ground ginger, and honey. Bring to a boil then reduce to a simmer.

3. Place the turkey in an aluminum roasting pan.

4. With a marinade injector, fill with the mixture and pierce the meat with the needle while pushing on the plunger, injecting the flavor. You want to inject into the thickest part of the breast, thigh, and wings.

5. Next, rub entire turkey with your favorite poultry seasoning or the   Champion Chicken seasoning. For added flavor, throw some extra garlic gloves into the cavity and apple cider in the aluminum pan.

6. Place the turkey in the grill and cook until the internal temperature reaches 165-170°F.

7. In a separate bowl, mix cornstarch and cold water together and add to the leftover original mixture to create a glaze. Glaze the turkey with the remaining mixture with approximately 15-20 minutes left. Skin will darken because of the sugar in the glaze.

8. Let the turkey rest 20-25 minutes before carving and enjoy!

Fig Glazed Chicken Stuffed Cornbread

Servings: 10

Cooking Time: 120 Minutes

Ingredients:

- Black Pepper
- 6 Tablespoons (For The Chicken) Butter, Unsalted
- 3 Chicken, Whole
- 2 1/5 Cups (Replace With Craisins For A Different Flavor) Dried Figs, Chopped
- 1 Egg
- 2 Tablespoon Extra-Virgin Olive Oil
- 1/2 Cup Heavy Cream
- 1/2 Cup Honey
- Kosher Salt
- 4 Tablespoon Lemon, Juice
- 1/2 Onion, Chopped
- Champion Chicken Seasoning
- 1 1/2 Teaspoon Finely Chopped Rosemary, Fresh
- 1 Pound Sweet Italian Sausage
- 3 Cups Water, Warm

Directions:

1. Mix figs, honey, lemon juice, and warm water. Cover with plastic wrap and let figs soften for 30 minutes. Strain the figs and reserve the liquid for glaze.

2. Heat olive oil over medium heat and sauté the onions with rosemary. Add the sausage. Cook until browned. Place into a large bowl, add the cornbread and figs. Season with   Champion Chicken Seasoning. Stir. In a separate bowl, Stir together egg, heavy whipping cream, and chicken stock. Pour over the cornbread/fig mix and stir together. Set aside.

3. Rinse chickens and pat dry. Season liberally with Champion Chicken Seasoning, kosher salt and black pepper. Don't forget the cavity! Stuff cavities with Stuffing. Top each Chicken with 2 tablespoons butter.

4. Supply your smoker with wood pellets and follow the start-up procedure. Preheat the grill, with the lid closed, to 300° F. Place in a roasting tray and cook until internal temp reads 165°F.

5. While chickens cook, place the fig liquid, balsamic vinegar and butter over. Reduce to thicken and baste chickens with about 160°F or 10 minutes before finished. Rest for 10 minutes. Carve and serve!

Italian Grilled Chicken Saltimbocca

Servings: 4

Cooking Time: 30 Minutes

Ingredients:

- 6 Chicken Breast
- olive oil
- Pork & Poultry Rub
- 6 Slices Prosciutto Slices
- 10 Sage, Leaves
- 1 Cup Parmesan cheese

Directions:

1. Supply your smoker with wood pellets and follow the start-up procedure. Preheat the grill, with the lid closed, to 350° F.

2. Using a sharp knife, carefully butterfly each chicken breast.

3. Oil the outside of each breast and season lightly with Traeger Pork and Poultry rub.

4. Wrap with a slice of prosciutto. Top with fresh sage and Parmesan cheese.

5. Arrange the chicken on a baking sheet or directly on the grill grate at an angle to the bars.

6. Roast until the chicken is cooked through, about 25 to 30 minutes or until it reaches an internal temperature of 165°F (75 C). Grill: 350 °F Probe: 165 °F

7. Let rest for 2 minutes before serving. Top with more fresh sage and parmesan. Enjoy!

Italian Grilled Barbecue Chicken Wings

Servings: 4

Cooking Time: 18 Minutes

Ingredients:

- 1 cup KRAFT Zesty Italian Dressing
- 2 pounds chicken wings/drummettes
- 1/2 cup barbecue sauce

Directions:

1. Pour dressing over chicken in large bowl; toss to coat.
2. Refrigerate at least 30 minutes to marinate.

3. Supply your smoker with wood pellets and follow the start-up procedure. Preheat the grill, with the lid closed, to 400° F. Drain chicken; discard marinade.

4. Grill chicken 8 minutes on each side or until done.

5. Brush with barbecue sauce; grill for another 2 minutes.

6. Remove from grill and serve.

Smoked Drumsticks

Servings: 2-4

Cooking Time: 25 Minutes

Ingredients:

- 1 pound chicken drumsticks
- 2 tablespoons olive oil
- 1 batch Sweet and Spicy Cinnamon Rub

Directions:

1. Supply your smoker with wood pellets and follow the start-up procedure. Preheat the grill, with the lid closed, to 350°F.

2. Coat the drumsticks all over with olive oil and season with the rub. Using your hands, work the rub into the meat.

3. Place the drumsticks directly on the grill grate and smoke until their internal temperature reaches 170°F. Remove the drumsticks from the grill and serve immediately.

Savory Cajun Bbq Chicken

Servings: 4

Cooking Time: 25 Minutes

Ingredients:

- ½ Cup Barbecue Sauce
- ¼ Cup Beer, Any Brand
- 1 Tablespoon Butter
- 1 Pound Boneless, Skinless Chicken Breasts
- 2 Cloves Garlic Clove, Minced
- ¼ Teaspoon Ground Thyme
- 1 Teaspoon Hot Sauce
- Juice Of 1 Lime
- 1 Tablespoon Olive Oil
- ½ Teaspoon Oregano
- 2 Tablespoons Sweet Heat Rub

* 1 Tablespoon Worcestershire Sauce

Directions:

1. In a small mixing bowl, mix together the Sweet Heat Rub, oregano, and ground thyme.

2. Rub the chicken breasts all over with olive oil, making sure to completely coat the meat. Generously season the chicken breasts on all sides with the Sweet Heat mixture.

3. Supply your smoker with wood pellets and follow the start-up procedure. Preheat the grill, with the lid closed, to 350° F. If you're using a gas or charcoal grill, set it up for medium heat. Insert a temperature probe into the thickest part of one of the chicken breasts and place the meat on the grill. Grill the meat on one side for 10-12 minutes, then flip and grill for another 5-7 minutes, or until the chicken breasts are golden brown and juicy and reaches an internal temperature of 165°F.

4. Remove the chicken from the grill and allow to rest for 10 minutes.

5. While the chicken rests, make the sauce. Combine the butter, barbecue sauce, beer, Worcestershire sauce, lime juice, and minced garlic in a heat proof saucepan and place on the grill. Bring the sauce to a boil. Once it boils, remove it from the heat, whisk it and serve with the chicken.

Chicken Tenders

Servings: 2-4
Cooking Time: 80 Minutes

Ingredients:

* 1 pound boneless, skinless chicken breast tenders
* 1 batch Chicken Rub

Directions:

1. Supply your smoker with wood pellets and follow the start-up procedure. Preheat the grill, with the lid closed, to 180°F.

2. Season the chicken tenders with the rub. Using your hands, work the rub into the meat.

3. Place the tenders directly on the grill grate and smoke for 1 hour.

4. Increase the grill's temperature to 300°F and continue to cook until the tenders' internal temperature reaches 170°F. Remove the tenders from the grill and serve immediately.

Grilled Honey Garlic Wings

Servings: 4
Cooking Time: 60 Minutes

Ingredients:

* 2 1/2 Pound chicken wings
* Pork & Poultry Rub
* 4 Tablespoon butter
* 3 Clove garlic, minced
* 1/4 Cup honey
* 1/2 Cup hot sauce
* 1 1/2 Cup blue cheese or ranch dressing

Directions:

1. Start by segmenting the wings into three pieces, cutting through the joints. Discard the wing tips or save them to make a stock.

2. Lay out the remaining pieces on a rimmed baking sheet lined with nonstick foil or parchment paper. Season well with Traeger Pork & Poultry Rub.

3. Supply your smoker with wood pellets and follow the start-up procedure. Preheat the grill, with the lid closed, to 350° F.

4. Place the baking sheet with wings directly on the grill grate and cook for 45 to 50 minutes or until they are no longer pink at the bone. Grill: 350 °F

5. To make the sauce: Melt butter in a small saucepan. Add the garlic and sauté for 2 to 3 minutes. Add in the honey and hot sauce and cook for a few minutes until completely combined. Keep sauce warm while the wings are cooking.

6. After 45 minutes, pour the spicy honey-garlic sauce over the wings, turning with tongs to coat.

7. Place wings back on the grill and cook for an additional 10 to 15 minutes to set the sauce. Grill: 350 °F

8. Serve with ranch or blue cheese dressing. Enjoy!

Spiced Bbq Turkey

Servings: 8
Cooking Time: 120 Minutes

Ingredients:

- 1 Bay Leaf
- 1/2 Tsp Black Peppercorns, Ground
- Pinch Chili Flakes
- 4 Garlic Cloves, Peeled And Smashed
- 1/4 Cup Honey
- 3/4 Cup Honey Chipotle Bbq Sauce
- 1 Honeysuckle White® Turkey, Thawed
- 1 Tsp Kosher Salt
- 1/4 Cup Olive Oil
- 3 Thyme Sprigs
- 1 Cup Turkey Stock
- 3 Cups Water
- 2 Tbsp Worcestershire Sauce

Directions:

1. Rinse Honeysuckle White® turkey thoroughly under cold water, then blot dry with paper towels. Place on a greased rack of a roasting pan. Set aside.

2. Prepare the injection solution: in a saucepot, whisk together the turkey stock, honey, olive oil, smashed garlic, Worcestershire sauce, salt, pepper, and chili flakes. Add in the thyme sprigs and bay leaf. Bring mixture to a boil, then simmer for 5 minutes. Remove from heat, cool for 30 minutes, then strain.

3. Using an injection needle, inject the solution throughout the turkey. Rub 1 tablespoon of solution over the top of the turkey. Add water to the bottom of the roasting pan. Set aside.

4. Supply your smoker with wood pellets and follow the start-up procedure. Preheat the grill, with the lid closed, to 450° F. If using a gas or charcoal grill, set it up for high heat.

5. Transfer the turkey to the grill and roast for 100 to 120 minutes, until an internal temperature of 165° F is reached, rotating every 30 minutes. Tent with foil after 30 minutes, then brush all over with BBQ sauce during the final 10 minutes of roasting time.

6. Remove from the grill, and allow the turkey to rest for 30 minutes, then carve and serve warm.

Smoked Chicken Legs

Servings: 6
Cooking Time: 110 Minutes

Ingredients:

- 1/4 Cup Brown Sugar
- 1/2 Tsp Or To Taste Cayenne Pepper
- 6 Chicken, Drumsticks
- 1 Cup Of Your Favorite Cola
- 2 Tbs Competition Chicken Seasoning
- 1 Tbs Honey
- 1/2 Tsp To Taste Hot Sauce
- 1 Cup Ketchup
- 2 Tbs   Hot Wing Sauce

Directions:

1. For the chicken: Supply your smoker with wood pellets and follow the start-up procedure. Preheat the grill, with the lid closed, to 300° F.

2. In a small bowl,Pour hot sauce over legs and toss to coat.

3. Sprinkle legs with Competition Chicken Seasoning and Hot Wing Seasoning.

4. Toss to evenly distribute seasoning.

5. Place legs in Grills Wing Rack or lay on grill.

6. Cook for 1 hour 45 minutes, or until legs reach an internal temperature of 170 degrees.

7. Brush legs with sauce and return to grill for 5- 10 minutes to allow sauce to cook onto meat.

8. Serve with extra sauce on the side.Place all ingredients into a small sauce pan and whisk.

9. Bring to a boil then immediately reduce to a simmer, whisking often

10. Allow to simmer for 15 minutes or until sauce is beginning to thicken

11. Remove from heat and allow to cool

12. Pork or Beef, chicken does not have as much intramuscular fats that need to render out to result in tender meat

13. You can cook chicken at a hotter temperature to ensure you get tender, moist chicken every time

14. Use a meat thermometer to know exactly when to pull the chicken off the grill

15. I pull white meat at 165 degrees, and dark meat, such as these legs, at 175 degrees

Texas Style Black Pepper Turkey

Servings: 6
Cooking Time: 240 Minutes

Ingredients:

- 1/2 Cup Coarse Black Pepper
- 1Lb Butter
- 1/2 Cup Salt, Kosher
- 1 Brined Turkey

Directions:

1. Supply your smoker with wood pellets and follow the start-up procedure. Preheat the grill, with the lid closed, to 300° F.
2. Liberally season Turkey with equal parts kosher salt and coarse black pepper.
3. Cook on grill until Internal temp reaches approximately 145°F or the skin has darkened to your liking.
4. Place turkey in a roasting pan topped with a pound of chopped butter and cover.
5. Return to the grill until internal temp of the thigh and breast reaches 165°F
6. Let rest for 30 minutes, carve and serve.

Lemon Parmesan Chicken Wings

Servings: 4 -8
Cooking Time: 30 Minutes

Ingredients:

- 2 Tablespoons Unsalted Butter, Melted
- 2 Lbs Chicken Wings, Trimmed And Patted Dry
- 3 Cloves Garlic, Minced
- Juice Of 1 Lemon
- 2 Tablespoons Mustard, Dijon
- ¼ Cup Olive Oil
- ¼ Cup Shredded Parmesan Cheese
- 2 Tablespoons Parsley, Chopped
- 2 Tablespoons Champion Chicken Seasoning

Directions:

1. Supply your smoker with wood pellets and follow the start-up procedure. Preheat the grill, with the lid open, to 350° F. If you are using a charcoal or gas grill, set the temperature to medium high heat.
2. In a large resealable bag, combine the olive oil, minced garlic, lemon zest, lemon juice, Dijon mustard, Champion Chicken Seasoning, and chopped parsley. Seal the resealable bag and give it a good shake to mix the ingredients.
3. Once the chicken has finished marinating, remove the chicken from the marinade and drain. Place the chicken wings on the wing rack.
4. Place the wing rack on the grill and insert a temperature probe into the thickest part of one of the wings. Grill the wings for 5 minutes, then rotate, and grill for another 5-10 minutes, or until the internal temperature of the wings reaches 165°F.
5. Toss the wings in the large bowl with the melted butter and shredded Parmesan until well coated. Serve immediately.

Roasted Whole Chicken

Servings: 6-8
Cooking Time: 120 Minutes

Ingredients:

- 1 whole chicken
- 2 tablespoons olive oil
- 1 batch Chicken Rub

Directions:

1. Supply your smoker with wood pellets and follow the start-up procedure. Preheat the grill, with the lid closed, to 375°F.
2. Coat the chicken all over with olive oil and season it with the rub. Using your hands, work the rub into the meat.
3. Place the chicken directly on the grill grate and smoke until its internal temperature reaches 170°F.
4. Remove the chicken from the grill and let it rest for 10 minutes, before carving and serving.

Easy Grilled Chicken Shawarma

Servings:
Cooking Time: 16 Minutes

Ingredients:

- 2 lbs to 2 ¼ lb chicken thighs
- Shawarma Marinade

- 2 tablespoons ground cumin
- 2 tablespoons ground coriander
- 8 garlic cloves, minced
- 2 teaspoons kosher salt
- 6 tablespoons olive oil
- 1/4 teaspoon cayenne pepper
- 2 teaspoon turmeric
- 1 teaspoon ground ginger
- 1 teaspoon ground black pepper
- 2 teaspoon allspice

Directions:

1. Supply your smoker with wood pellets and follow the start-up procedure. Preheat the grill, with the lid closed, to medium-high heat. Place all marinade ingredients in a bowl and mix, or pulse in a food processor to make a paste.

2. Rub chicken on all sides with the marinade and let sit 20 minutes.

3. Place the chicken on the grill racks, closing the lid to the BBQ, until all sides have nice grill marks, about 8 minutes each side. Move to the warming rack until cooked all the way through, about 10 minutes.

4. Enjoy the chicken shawarma over Israeli salad, or with rice and veggies, or with pita bread and tzatziki.

Smoked Wings

Servings: 6
Cooking Time: 50 Minutes

Ingredients:

- 24 chicken wings, flats and drumettes separated
- 12 Ounce Italian dressing
- 3 Ounce Chicken Rub
- 5 Ounce 'Que BBQ Sauce
- 3 Ounce chili sauce

Directions:

1. Wash all wings and place into resealable bag. Add Italian dressing to the resealable bag containing the wings. Place in refrigerator and allow to marinate for 6 to 12 hours.

2. Supply your smoker with wood pellets and follow the start-up procedure. Preheat the grill, with the lid closed, to 225° F.

3. Remove wings from marinade and shake off excess marinade. Season all sides of the wings with Traeger Chicken Rub and let sit for 15 minutes before putting wings on the Traeger.

4. In a small bowl, combine the BBQ and chili sauces. Set aside.

5. Cook wings to an internal temperature of 160°F. Remove the wings and toss in chili barbecue sauce. Grill: 225 °F Probe: 160 °F

6. Increase the grill temperature to 375°F and preheat. Once at temperature, place the wings on the Traeger and sear both sides until the internal temperature reaches 165°F. Grill: 375 °F Probe: 165 °F

7. Remove the wings from grill and let rest for 5 minutes. Serve with your favorite side wing dressing or sauce. Enjoy!

Roasted Tin Foil Dinners

Servings: 4
Cooking Time: 25 Minutes

Ingredients:

- 4 boneless, skinless chicken breast
- Chicken Rub
- 1/2 Pound new potatoes, quartered
- 8 Ounce cremini mushrooms, cleaned and quartered
- salt and pepper
- 1/2 Pound green beans, ends trimmed
- 1 Medium lemon, cut into 3/4 inch slices

Directions:

1. Supply your smoker with wood pellets and follow the start-up procedure. Preheat the grill, with the lid closed, to 400° F.

2. Season chicken breast with salt, pepper and Traeger Chicken Rub. Place the potatoes, mushrooms and chicken in the middle of a large sheet of foil, season with more salt and pepper as needed, and wrap up tightly.

3. Place foil pack directly on the grill grate and cook for 15 minutes. Grill: 400 °F

4. Open up the foil pack and add green beans, lemon and additional salt and pepper, if needed. Wrap back up and return to the Traeger for an additional 10 minutes. Grill: 400 °F

5. Remove from the Traeger, open packet and enjoy!

Bacon-wrapped Chicken Breasts

Servings: 4 - 6

Cooking Time: 270 Minutes

Ingredients:

- 5 Oz Frozen Spinach, Thawed, Strained
- 8 Bacon Slices
- 1 Tbsp Butter
- 4 Chicken Breasts, Boneless, Skinless, Butterflied
- 2 Garlic Clove, Minced
- 1 Cup Italian Cheese Blend, Shredded
- 8 Oz Mushrooms, Sliced Thin
- 1 Tbsp Olive Oil
- 1 Tbsp   Hickory Bacon Rub
- 1 Yellow Onion, Chopped

Directions:

1. Supply your smoker with wood pellets and follow the start-up procedure. Preheat the grill, with the lid open, to 375° F. If using a gas or charcoal grill, set heat to medium heat. For all other grills, preheat cast iron skillet on grill grates.

2. Heat olive oil and butter on griddle, then add mushrooms and cook for about 3 minutes, stirring frequently. Add chopped onion and garlic and cook for 2 minutes. Add spinach and sauté another minute, then transfer vegetables to a heat-safe bowl to cool slightly.

3. Season the butterflied chicken breasts with Hickory Bacon, coating both sides. Sprinkle half of cheese over each butterflied chicken breast, followed by the sautéed vegetables, and the remaining half of the cheese.

4. On a metal sheet tray, lay out two bacon slices. Gently fold chicken breast halves together and place on top of bacon slices, then wrap tightly with bacon. To secure, tuck ends of bacon underneath, or insert a toothpick to hold it together. Repeat with remaining breasts.

5. Arrange the chicken breasts, bacon seam down, directly on the grill grate and grill, turning once or twice, until the bacon is crisp and golden brown, about 25 to 30 minutes, or until internal temperature reaches 165°F.

6. Remove from grill, allow to rest for 5 minutes, remove any toothpicks, then serve hot.

Smoke-roasted Chicken Thighs

Servings: 12-15

Cooking Time: 120 Minutes

Ingredients:

- 3 pounds chicken thighs
- 2 teaspoons salt
- 2 teaspoons freshly ground black pepper
- 2 teaspoons garlic powder
- 2 teaspoons onion powder
- 2 cups prepared Italian dressing

Directions:

1. Place the chicken thighs in a shallow dish and sprinkle with the salt, pepper, garlic powder, and onion powder, being sure to get under the skin.

2. Cover with the Italian dressing, coating all sides, and refrigerate for 1 hour.

3. Supply your smoker with wood pellets and follow the start-up procedure. Preheat, with the lid closed, to 250°F.

4. Remove the chicken thighs from the marinade and place directly on the grill, skin-side down. Discard the marinade.

5. Close the lid and roast the chicken for 1 hour 30 minutes to 2 hours, or until a meat thermometer inserted in the thickest part of the thighs reads 165°F. Do not turn the thighs during the smoking process.

Savory Jerk Chicken Wings

Servings: 4

Cooking Time: 20 Minutes

Ingredients:

- 1 Tsp Allspice, Ground
- 3 Lbs Chicken Wings, Split
- 1/2 Tsp Cinnamon, Ground
- 4 Garlic Cloves, Smashed
- 2 Tsp Ginger, Grated
- 1 Habanero Pepper, Chopped
- 2 Tbsp Honey
- 2 Tbsp Lemon Juice
- 1/3 Cup Lime Juice
- 1/2 Tsp Nutmeg, Ground
- 1/2 Cup Olive Oil

- 1/4 Cup Poblano Pepper, Chopped
- 1 Tbsp Tamari
- 2 Tsp Thyme, Dried
- 1/2 Cup Yellow Onion, Chopped

Directions:

1. Add chicken to a large resealable plastic bag.

2. In the bowl of a food processor, add the garlic, onion, ginger, peppers, tamari, honey, lime juice, lemon juice, thyme, allspice, cinnamon, nutmeg, and oil. Process on low for 1 minute, then transfer marinade to the bag. Seal the bag and place in the refrigerator for at least 2 hours, up to overnight.

3. Supply your smoker with wood pellets and follow the start-up procedure. Preheat the grill, with the lid open, to 425° F. If using a gas or charcoal grill, set it up for medium-high heat.

4. Remove wings from the marinade, and discard remaining marinade. Place wings on the grill and cook for 15 to 20 minutes, flipping every 5 minutes, until an internal temperature of 165 F is reached.

5. Remove wings from the grill and serve warm.

Smoking Duck With Mandarin Glaze

Servings: 4

Cooking Time: 240 Minutes

Ingredients:

- 1 quart buttermilk
- 1 (5-pound) whole duck
- ¾ cup soy sauce
- ½ cup hoisin sauce
- ½ cup rice wine vinegar
- 2 tablespoons sesame oil
- 1 tablespoon freshly ground black pepper
- 1 tablespoon minced garlic
- Mandarin Glaze, for drizzling

Directions:

1. With a very sharp knife, remove as much fat from the duck as you can. Refrigerate or freeze the fat for later use.

2. Pour the buttermilk into a large container with a lid and submerge the whole duck in it. Cover and let brine in the refrigerator for 4 to 6 hours.

3. Supply your smoker with wood pellets and follow the start-up procedure. Preheat, with the lid closed, to 250°F.

4. Remove the duck from the buttermilk brine, then rinse it and pat dry with paper towels.

5. In a bowl, combine the soy sauce, hoisin sauce, vinegar, sesame oil, pepper, and garlic to form a paste. Reserve ¼ cup for basting.

6. Poke holes in the skin of the duck and rub the remaining paste all over and inside the cavity.

7. Place the duck on the grill breast-side down, close the lid, and smoke for about 4 hours, basting every hour with the reserved paste, until a meat thermometer inserted in the thickest part of the meat reads 165°F. Use aluminum foil to tent the duck in the last 30 minutes or so if it starts to brown too quickly.

8. To finish, drizzle with glaze.

Oktoberfest Pretzel Mustard Chicken

Servings: 4

Cooking Time: 25 Minutes

Ingredients:

- 1/4 Pound pretzel sticks
- 3 Tablespoon Dijon mustard
- 3 Tablespoon apple cider or brown ale
- 1 Tablespoon honey
- 1 1/2 Teaspoon fresh thyme, plus more for garnish
- 4 boneless, skinless chicken breasts

Directions:

1. Pulse the pretzel sticks in a food processor or crush by hand in a resealable bag until they've turned into a powder the texture of panko breadcrumbs.

2. Transfer the crumbs to a wide, shallow bowl.

3. In separate shallow bowl, whisk mustard, beer or cider, honey and thyme together.

4. Spray a wire rack with cooking spray and place atop a sheet tray. Dip each chicken breast in the mustard mixture, then dredge in the pretzel crumbs to coat evenly and place on the wire rack. Spray the top of each chicken breast lightly with cooking spray.

5. Supply your smoker with wood pellets and follow the start-up procedure. Preheat the grill, with the lid closed, to 375° F.

6. Place the pan on the Traeger and bake for about 20 to 25 minutes, until the chicken breasts are fully cooked and register 165°F on an instant-read thermometer. Grill: 375 °F Probe: 165 °F

7. Let chicken rest for 5 minutes. Garnish with fresh thyme if desired. Enjoy!

Traeger Bbq Half Chickens

Servings: 2
Cooking Time: 60 Minutes

Ingredients:
- 1 (3 to 3-1/2 lb) fresh young chicken
- Leinenkugel's Summer Shandy Rub
- Apricot BBQ Sauce

Directions:
1. Place the chicken breast side down, on a cutting board with the neck pointing away from you. Cut along one side of the backbone, staying as close to the bone as possible, from the neck to the tail. Repeat on the other side of the backbone then remove it.

2. Open the chicken and slice through the white cartilage at the tip of the breastbone to pop it open. Cut down either side of the breast bone then use your fingers to pull it out. Flip the chicken over so it is skin side up and cut down the center splitting the chicken in half. Tuck the wings back on each chicken half.

3. Season on both sides with Traeger Leinenkugel's Summer Shandy Rub.

4. Supply your smoker with wood pellets and follow the start-up procedure. Preheat the grill, with the lid closed, to 375° F.

5. Place chicken directly on the grill grate skin side up and cook until the internal temperature reaches 160°F, about 60-90 minutes. Grill: 375 °F Probe: 160 °F

6. Brush the BBQ sauce all over the chicken skin and cook for an additional 10 minutes. Remove from grill and let rest 5 minutes before serving. Enjoy! Grill: 375 °F

Chicken Corn Fritters

Servings: 8
Cooking Time: 45 Minutes

Ingredients:
- 2 Tsp Baking Powder
- 1 Cup Cheddar Jack Cheese, Shredded
- 1 1/2 Lbs Chicken Breast, Bone-In
- 3/4 Cup Corn Kernels, Drained
- 2 Eggs
- 3/4 Cup Flour
- 1 1/2 Tsp Lemon Juice
- 3 Tbsp Mayonnaise
- Olive Oil
- 2 Tbsp Parsley, Chopped
- 2 Tsp Champion Chicken Seasoning, Divided
- 1 Tbsp Scallions, Chopped
- 2 Tbsp Sour Cream
- 1 Yellow Onion, Chopped
- 1/3 Cup Milk

Directions:
1. Supply your smoker with wood pellets and follow the start-up procedure. Preheat the grill, with the lid open, to 425° F. If using a gas or charcoal grill, set it up for medium-high heat.

2. Remove skin from chicken breast. Drizzle chicken with olive oil, then season with 1 teaspoon of Champion Chicken. Place directly on grill grate, over indirect heat and grill for 25 minutes, until internal temperature is 165° F. Remove from the grill and rest for 10 minutes, then pull chicken.

3. In a mixing bowl combine onion, corn, eggs, parsley, milk, cheese, and pulled chicken.

4. In a separate mixing bowl, whisk together remaining teaspoon of Champion Chicken, flour and baking powder. Combine with the wet ingredients, then cover with plastic wrap and refrigerate for 2 hours.

5. Prepare dip: whisk together mayonnaise, sour cream, scallions, parsley, and lemon juice. Refrigerate until fritters are ready to serve.

6. Preheat griddle over medium-low flame.

7. Drizzle vegetable oil on the griddle, then add ¼ cup of fritter mixture to the griddle and cook 3 to 4 minutes per side, adding additional oil if needed.

8. Transfer fritters to a wire rack lined sheet tray. Allow to cool for 2 minutes, then serve warm with dip.

Skinny Smoked Chicken Breasts

Servings: 4-6
Cooking Time: 85 Minutes

Ingredients:
- 2½ pounds boneless, skinless chicken breasts
- Salt
- Freshly ground black pepper

Directions:
1. Supply your smoker with wood pellets and follow the start-up procedure. Preheat the grill, with the lid closed, to 180°F.
2. Season the chicken breasts all over with salt and pepper.
3. Place the breasts directly on the grill grate and smoke for 1 hour.
4. Increase the grill's temperature to 325°F and continue to cook until the chicken's internal temperature reaches 170°F. Remove the breasts from the grill and serve immediately.

Glazed Bbq Half Chicken

Servings: 6
Cooking Time: 120 Minutes

Ingredients:
- Meat Church Bird Bath Poultry Brine
- 1/2 Gallon water or chicken stock
- 1 Whole chicken
- 1 Whole whole chicken
- Meat Church Holy Gospel BBQ Rub
- 1 Stick butter
- Cup favorite BBQ sauce
- 2 Teaspoon blackberry jelly, pepper jelly or your favorite jelly

Directions:
1. Mix the Meat Church Bird Bath Poultry Brine thoroughly in a 1/2 gallon of water or chicken stock. Feel free to be creative and add ingredients to enhance the flavor profile to your liking. Completely submerge the chicken in the brine mixture and place in the refrigerator overnight. We recommend 12 to 24 hours for this brine.
2. Remove the bird from the brine. Rinse off and pat dry with a paper towel.
3. Supply your smoker with wood pellets and follow the start-up procedure. Preheat the grill, with the lid closed, to 275° F.
4. Using a pair of chicken shears or a very sharp knife, remove the backbone. Do this by trimming along one side of the backbone from one end of the chicken to the other. Then repeat the process on the other side of the backbone and remove it completely. Open the chicken once the backbone is removed. At this point you can remove the breastbone if you like. Slice the bird in half using a sharp knife. Now you have 2 half chickens.
5. Apply Meat Church Holy Gospel BBQ Rub to all sides of the chicken; underneath and on top of the skin. We also recommend working your hands underneath the chicken skin and applying rub directly on the meat. This will ensure a really flavorful bite even if they don't get any skin.
6. Place the chicken halves and butter in a half steam pan and put the pan on the Traeger. Baste the chicken with the butter periodically throughout the cook.
7. Using an instant-read thermometer, remove the chicken from the grill when they reach an internal temperature of at least 165°F in the deepest part of the breast, about 1-1/2 to 2 hours. Grill: 275 °F Probe: 165 °F
8. For the glaze, mix the BBQ sauce, honey and jelly and heat in a small sauce pan.

Turkey & Bacon Kebabs With Ranch-style Dressing

Servings: 8
Cooking Time: 25 Minutes

Ingredients:
- 1½lb (680g) skinless turkey tenders or boneless, skinless turkey breasts, cut into 1-inch (2.5cm) chunks
- 8 strips of thick-cut bacon

- 12 fresh bay leaves (optional)
- for the dressing
- 1 cup reduced-fat mayo
- 1 cup light sour cream
- ½ cup buttermilk or whole milk, plus more
- 2 tbsp minced fresh parsley
- 2 tbsp minced fresh chives
- 1 tbsp minced fresh dill
- 2 tsp freshly squeezed lemon juice
- 1 tsp Worcestershire sauce
- 1 tsp garlic salt
- 1 tsp onion powder
- ½ tsp coarse salt, plus more
- ½ tsp freshly ground black pepper, plus more

Directions:

1. In a large bowl, make the dressing by whisking together the mayo, sour cream, and buttermilk until smooth. Whisk in the remaining ingredients. Pour half the mixture into a small bowl. Cover and refrigerate.

2. Add the turkey to the mixture remaining in the bowl and toss to coat thoroughly. If the dressing seems too thick (dip-like), add more buttermilk 1 tablespoon at a time. Cover and refrigerate for 2 to 4 hours.

3. Supply your smoker with wood pellets and follow the start-up procedure. Preheat the grill, with the lid closed, to 375° F.

4. Place the bacon on the grate and cook until some of the fat has rendered and the bacon begins to brown, about 15 minutes. Remove the bacon from the grill to cool. Cut the bacon into 1-inch (2.5cm) squares. Set aside.

5. Drain the tenders and discard any excess dressing. Alternate threading the turkey, bacon pieces, and 3 bay leaves on a bamboo skewer. Repeat the threading with 3 more skewers.

6. Place the kebabs on the grate and grill until the turkey is cooked through, about 4 to 5 minutes per side, turning as needed.

7. Transfer the skewers to a platter. Serve with the reserved dressing.

Mandarin Chicken Breast

Servings: 4
Cooking Time: 25 Minutes

Ingredients:

- 1/2 Cup kosher salt
- 1/4 Cup brown sugar
- 1/2 Cup soy sauce
- 8 (6 oz) boneless, skinless chicken breasts
- sweet chili sauce
- steamed rice, for serving
- thinly sliced scallions, for garnish

Directions:

1. Pour 2 quarts water into a large mixing bowl, then add salt, brown sugar, and soy sauce. Stir until sugar and salt dissolve. Grill: 350 °F Probe: 170 °F

2. Submerge chicken breasts in the brine, cover and refrigerate for 2 hours.

3. Drain the chicken, rinse and pat dry with paper towels. Discard the brine.

4. Supply your smoker with wood pellets and follow the start-up procedure. Preheat the grill, with the lid closed, to 350° F.

5. Arrange the chicken breasts on the grill grate and cook for 25 to 30 minutes or until the internal temperature on an instant-read thermometer is 170°F. Turn chicken breasts once halfway through the cooking time. Grill: 350 °F Probe: 170 °F

6. Brush chicken breasts with the sweet chili sauce during the last few minutes of cooking.

7. Remove to a platter or plates and serve with steamed rice. Sprinkle the chicken breasts with thinly sliced scallions for garnish. Enjoy!

Thai Chicken Satays

Servings: 4
Cooking Time: 10 Minutes

Ingredients:

- 1½lb (680g) boneless, skinless chicken breasts
- for the marinade
- ½ cup unsweetened canned light coconut milk
- 2 garlic cloves, peeled and coarsely chopped
- ¼ cup loosely packed fresh cilantro leaves

- 1-inch (2.5cm) piece of fresh ginger, peeled and coarsely chopped
- 2 tbsp light soy sauce
- 1 tbsp Asian fish sauce
- 1 tbsp light brown sugar or low-carb substitute
- 2 tsp sambal oelek (optional)
- 1 tsp Thai-style curry powder
- 1 tsp ground cumin
- 1 tsp ground turmeric
- 1 tsp coarse salt
- 2 tbsp vegetable oil
- for serving
- butter lettuce leaves, washed and dried
- cherry tomatoes
- Peanut Sauce

Directions:

1. Use a sharp knife to slice the chicken breasts lengthwise into strips, each about 1 inch (2.5cm) wide. (If the chicken breasts are unusually thick, butterfly them before cutting them into strips.) Place the breasts in a resealable plastic bag.

2. In a blender, make the marinade by combining the ingredients. Blend until fairly smooth. Pour the marinade over the chicken, turning and massaging the bag to thoroughly coat the chicken. Refrigerate for 2 hours.

3. Supply your smoker with wood pellets and follow the start-up procedure. Preheat the grill, with the lid closed, to 450° F.

4. Remove the chicken from the marinade and let any excess drip off. (Discard the marinade.) Thread each chicken strip on a bamboo skewer, pushing the point in one side of the chicken and out the other as if sewing. Leave very little of the tip exposed because it will burn easily.

5. Place the skewers on the grate perpendicular to the bars. Grill until the chicken has grill marks and is fully cooked, about 3 to 5 minutes per side.

6. Remove the skewers from the grill. Place the lettuce leaves on a platter. Place the satays atop the leaves. Scatter cherry tomatoes over the top. Serve with the peanut sauce.

Traeger Mandarin Wings

Servings: 2
Cooking Time: 30 Minutes

Ingredients:

- 1 Bottle (12 oz) mandarin orange sauce
- Beef Rub
- Chicken Rub
- 2 Pound chicken wings, flats and drumettes separated

Directions:

1. Coat chicken wings with mandarin sauce. Sprinkle Traeger Beef Rub and Traeger Chicken Rub onto wings. Marinate for at least 30 minutes.

2. Supply your smoker with wood pellets and follow the start-up procedure. Preheat the grill, with the lid closed, to 350° F.

3. Place wings directly on the grill grate and cook for 30 minutes. Enjoy! Grill: 350 °F Probe: 165 °F

Whole Roasted Chicken

Servings: 4
Cooking Time: 60 Minutes

Ingredients:

- 1 Whole fresh young chicken
- 1 Bottle Chicken Rub
- water
- 1/2 Tablespoon kosher salt
- 1 Tablespoon chopped sage
- 1 Tablespoon chopped thyme
- 1/2 Cup butter, softened
- 1/2 Tablespoon coarse ground black pepper

Directions:

1. Remove whole chicken from packaging and wipe dry with a paper towel.

2. Mix water and chicken rub to create a brine. Place the chicken and brine in a container that's large enough to submerge the entire chicken.

3. Set in fridge for 4-12 hours.

4. Supply your smoker with wood pellets and follow the start-up procedure. Preheat the grill, with the lid closed, to 375° F.

5. Take chicken out of brine, do not rinse.

6. Mix together thyme, sage, salt, pepper and butter. Smear the outside of the chicken with the butter mixture. Put any of the remaining butter in the cavity of the chicken.

7. Place chicken directly on the grill grate. Cook chicken until it reaches an internal temperature of 165 degrees F (about 60 mins) with an instant-read thermometer between the leg and thigh joint. Grill: 375 °F Probe: 165 °F

8. Also check the internal temperature of the breast to ensure it registers at least 165 degrees F. Once chicken is done, let it rest for 15-20 minutes. Enjoy!

Savory Smoked Turkey Legs

Servings: 4
Cooking Time: 150 Minutes

Ingredients:
- 1 Cup Chicken Stock
- 2 Tbsp Blackened Sriracha Rub
- 4 Turkey Legs (Drumsticks)

Directions:
1. Fire up your pellet grill on SMOKE mode. With the lid open, let it run for 10 minutes.

2. Supply your smoker with wood pellets and follow the start-up procedure. Preheat the grill, with the lid closed, to 225° F. If using a gas or charcoal grill, set it up for low, indirect heat.

3. Combine turkey stock with 2 teaspoons of Blackened Sriracha Rub.

4. Place turkey legs on a sheet tray, then inject each with seasoned stock. Season the outside of the legs with remaining Blackened Sriracha.

5. Place turkey legs directly on the grate of the smoking cabinet, and cook for 1 ½ hours.

6. Increase temperature to 325°F, then transfer turkey legs to the bottom grill and cook for another 45 to 60 minutes, until the internal temperature reaches 170°F.

7. Remove turkey from the grill, allow to rest for 10 minutes, then serve warm.

Green Chile Chicken Enchiladas

Servings: 6
Cooking Time: 45 Minutes

Ingredients:
- 2 Cups Chicken, Shredded
- 1 (12 Oz) Package Colby Jack Cheese, Shredded
- 1 Enchilada Sauce, Can
- 1 Can Green Chile, Drained
- 1 Onion, Diced
- 1 Tablespoon Sweet Rib Rub
- 1 Cup Sour Cream
- 1 Package Flour Tortilla

Directions:
1. Supply your smoker with wood pellets and follow the start-up procedure. Preheat the grill, with the lid open, to 300° F.

2. In a bowl, mix - the chicken, green chiles, Sweet Heat seasoning, sour cream, diced onion, and half the bag of shredded cheese.

3. Place a large spoonful of the chicken mixture in the center of a tortilla and roll it up. Repeat with the remaining tortillas, then place in the baking pan, and pour the enchilada sauce over the tortilla pans. Top with the remainder of the shredded cheese.

4. Wrap the top of the pan tightly in aluminum foil and grill for 45 minutes or until the enchilada sauce is bubbly. Remove from the grill and serve.

Smoked Whole Chicken

Servings: 6-8
Cooking Time: 240 Minutes

Ingredients:
- 1 whole chicken
- 2 cups Tea Injectable (using Not-Just-for-Pork Rub)
- 2 tablespoons olive oil
- 1 batch Chicken Rub
- 2 tablespoons butter, melted

Directions:
1. Supply your smoker with wood pellets and follow the start-up procedure. Preheat the grill, with the lid closed, to 180°F.

2. Inject the chicken throughout with the tea injectable.

3. Coat the chicken all over with olive oil and season it with the rub. Using your hands, work the rub into the meat.

4. Place the chicken directly on the grill grate and smoke for 3 hours.

5. Baste the chicken with the butter and increase the grill's temperature to 375°F. Continue to cook the chicken until its internal temperature reaches 170°F.

6. Remove the chicken from the grill and let it rest for 10 minutes, before carving and serving.

Bbq Chicken Legs

Servings: 6
Cooking Time: 60 Minutes

Ingredients:
- 8 chicken drumsticks
- 2 Tablespoon Chicken Rub
- 1 Cup Apricot BBQ Sauce
- 1 Cup 'Que BBQ Sauce
- 1 Cup apple jelly, melted

Directions:
1. Pat drumsticks dry with a paper towel and season generously Traeger Chicken Rub.

2. Supply your smoker with wood pellets and follow the start-up procedure. Preheat the grill, with the lid closed, to 180° F.

3. Arrange the chicken legs on the grill grate and smoke for 30 minutes. Grill: 180 °F

4. Increase the grill temperature to 350 degrees F and cook for an additional 30 minutes. Grill: 350 °F

5. While the drumsticks are cooking, combine the two BBQ sauces and the jelly in a small sauce pan. Bring to a simmer over medium heat then set aside until ready to use.

6. Brush the BBQ sauce on the chicken legs. Cook for an additional 10 minutes, or until an instant-read meat thermometer inserted into the thickest part of the leg (but not touching the bone) reaches 165 degrees F. Enjoy! Grill: 350 °F Probe: 165 °F

Bbq Chicken Thighs

Servings: 4
Cooking Time: 35 Minutes

Ingredients:
- 6 bone-in, skin-on chicken thighs
- salt and ground black pepper
- Big Game Rub

Directions:
1. Supply your smoker with wood pellets and follow the start-up procedure. Preheat the grill, with the lid closed, to 350° F.

2. While grill is heating, trim excess fat and skin from chicken thighs. Season with a light layer of salt and pepper then a layer of Traeger Big Game Rub.

3. Place chicken thighs on the grill grate and cook for 35 minutes. Check internal temperature, chicken is done at 165°F, but there is enough fat that they will stay moist at an internal temperature of 180°F and the texture is better. Grill: 350 °F Probe: 165 °F

4. Remove from the grill and let rest for 5 minutes before serving. Enjoy!

Peanut Butter Chicken Wings

Servings: 4
Cooking Time: 35 Minutes

Ingredients:
- 1 Tsp Black Peppercorns, Ground
- 2 Tbsp Brown Sugar
- 4 Lbs Chicken Wings, Trimmed And Patted Dry
- 2 Tbsp Honey
- 1/4 Cup Peanut Butter
- 10 Oz Peanuts, Whole
- 2 Tsp Sweet Rib Rub
- 1/2 Red Onion, Minced
- 1/2 Cup Strawberry Preserves
- 1 Tbsp Thai Chili Sauce
- 1/4 Cup Worcestershire Sauce

Directions:
1. Place chicken wings in a 9 x13 glass baking dish. Pour mixture over chicken, cover with plastic wrap, and refrigerate for 2 hours.

2. Supply your smoker with wood pellets and follow the start-up procedure. Preheat the grill, with the lid open, to 400° F. Preheat griddle to medium-low flame. If using a gas or charcoal grill, set it to medium-high heat.

3. Place wings directly on grill grate, over indirect heat, and cook for 20 to 25 minutes, rotating wings every 5 minutes.

4. Meanwhile, place shelled peanuts on the griddle, turning occasionally with a metal spatula for 5 to 7 minutes, to lightly roast. Remove from the griddle and set aside to cool.

5. Remove wings from grill and allow to rest for 5 minutes. While wings are resting, shell the peanuts, and transfer to a resealable plastic bag. Use a rolling pin to crush the peanuts, then scatter peanuts on top of the chicken wings. Serve warm.

Bell Pepper Chicken Sliders

Servings: 5
Cooking Time: 20 Minutes

Ingredients:
- 16 Oz Chicken, Ground
- 1 Pepper, Anaheim
- Jalapeno Brat Burger Seasoning
- 1 Red Bell Peppers
- Spinach

Directions:
1. Supply your smoker with wood pellets and follow the start-up procedure. Preheat the grill, with the lid closed, to 400° F.

2. Put the ground chicken into a bowl and generously add the Jalapeno Brat Burger seasoning to the mixture.

3. Dice the Anaheim pepper and add it to the bowl as well.

4. Mix with your hands until the meat looks evenly coated.

5. Separate the meat out into 3oz balls, disperse or toss the remnants.

6. Use the 3-in-1 Burger press to create the perfect patty! If your chicken is too sticky to use the burger press, we put the 3oz balls into a tinfoil covered pan and placed that on the grill. Allow to cook 20-25 minutes, do not flip.

7. Add the buns to the grill if you'd like them toasted!

8. Remove the chicken sliders (and the buns) from the grill, add spinach, red peppers and whatever else you enjoy!

Smoked Bourbon & Orange Brined Turkey

Servings: 8
Cooking Time: 180 Minutes

Ingredients:
- 1 Orange Brine and Turkey Rub Kit
- 4 Quart water
- 1 Cup bourbon
- 1 (12-14 lb) turkey, fresh or thawed
- 1 Tablespoon butter, melted
- 1 Tablespoon Grand Mariner or other orange-flavored liquor

Directions:
1. Mix Orange Brine seasoning (from Traeger Orange Brine & Turkey Rub Kit) with one quart of water. Boil for 5 minutes. Remove from heat, add 3 quarts of cold water and bourbon. Refrigerate until completely cooled.

2. Place turkey breast side down in a large container. Pour cooled brine mix over bird. Add cold water until bird is submerged. Refrigerate for 24 hours.

3. Remove turkey and discard brine. Blot turkey dry with paper towels.

4. Combine butter and Grand Marnier and coat outside of turkey. Season outside of turkey with Traeger Turkey Rub (from Orange Brine & Turkey Rub Kit).

5. Supply your smoker with wood pellets and follow the start-up procedure. Preheat the grill, with the lid closed, to 225° F.

6. Smoke turkey, breast up, for 2 hours. Grill: 225 °F

7. Increase grill temperature to 350°F and roast turkey until the internal temperature of the thickest part of the thigh reaches 165F, 2 to 3 hours, depending on size of turkey. Grill: 350 °F Probe: 165 °F

8. Let rest 20 to 30 minutes before serving. Enjoy!

Delicious Smoked Turketta

Servings: 6
Cooking Time: 180 Minutes

Ingredients:

- 1 Shady Brook Farms® Turketta

Directions:

1. Supply your smoker with wood pellets and follow the start-up procedure. Preheat the grill, with the lid closed, to 250° F. If using a gas or charcoal grill, set it up for low, indirect heat.

2. Place the Turketta directly on the grill grate and smoke for 2½ to 3 hours, or until an internal temperature of 165°F is reached.

Red Onion Chicken Fajita Omelet

Servings: 4
Cooking Time: 12 Minutes

Ingredients:

- 1 Cup Bell Pepper, Sliced Thin
- To Taste, Blackened Sriracha Rub Seasoning
- 2 Tbsp Butter
- 1 Cup Cheddar Jack Cheese, Shredded
- 8 Oz Chicken Breast, Boneless, Skinless, Sliced Thin
- 6 Eggs, Beaten
- 1 Tbsp Heavy Cream
- 1 Jalapeño, Minced
- 1/2 Lime
- 1 Cup Red Onion, Sliced Thinly
- 1/3 Cup Salsa Roja
- 2 Tbsp Sour Cream
- 1 Tbsp Vegetable Oil, Divided

Directions:

1. Supply your smoker with wood pellets and follow the start-up procedure. Preheat the grill, with the lid open, to medium heat. If using a gas or charcoal grill, preheat a cast iron skillet.

2. Drizzle sliced chicken breast with 1 teaspoon oil, then season with Blackened Sriracha.

3. Drizzle the remaining oil on the griddle, then add the chicken. Sauté for 2 minutes, then add the bell peppers and onions. Season with additional Blackened Sriracha and continue to sauté another 2 minutes, then deglaze with fresh squeezed lime juice. Remove mixture from the griddle, set aside.

4. Turn the griddle down to low, then whisk the eggs (3 per omelet) and heavy cream.

5. Melt 1 tablespoon of butter on the griddle. Quickly pour the eggs over the melted butter.

6. Flip the eggs, then add ¼ cup of cheese and divide all but ½ cup of the reserved filling into the middle of each egg. Add additional cheese and some minced jalapeño. Fold the egg over to shape the omelet.

7. Transfer the omelet to a plate and top with additional filling, cheese, salsa, sour cream, and jalapeño. Serve warm.

Bbq Pulled Turkey Sandwiches

Servings: 6
Cooking Time: 120 Minutes

Ingredients:

- 6 Whole Turkey Thighs
- Pork & Poultry Rub
- 1 1/2 Cup chicken broth
- 1 Cup 'Que BBQ Sauce
- 6 Whole Kaiser Buns, Split

Directions:

1. Season turkey thighs on both sides with the Traeger Pork & Poultry rub.

2. Supply your smoker with wood pellets and follow the start-up procedure. Preheat the grill, with the lid closed, to 180° F.

3. Arrange the turkey thighs directly on the grill grate and smoke for 30 minutes.

4. Transfer the thighs to a sturdy disposable aluminum foil or roasting pan. Pour the broth around the thighs. Cover the pan with foil or a lid.

5. Increase temperature to 325°F and preheat, lid closed. Roast the thighs until they reach an internal temperature of 180°F. Grill: 325 °F Probe: 180 °F

6. Remove pan from the grill, but leave grill on. Let the turkey thighs cool slightly until they can be comfortably handled.

7. Pour off the drippings and reserve. Remove the skin and discard.

8. Pull the turkey meat into shreds with your fingers and return the meat to the roasting pan.

9. Add 1 cup or more of your favorite Traeger BBQ Sauce along with some of the drippings.

10. Recover the pan with foil and reheat the BBQ turkey on the Traeger for 20 to 30 minutes.

11. Serve with toasted buns if desired. Enjoy!

Spiced Cornish Hens With Cilantro Chutney

Servings: 2

Cooking Time: 60 Minutes

Ingredients:

- 2 Cornish game hens, each about 1 to 1¼lb (450 to 565g), thawed if frozen
- 1 small white onion, peeled and halved
- 4 slices of fresh ginger
- 4 garlic cloves, peeled
- 3 tbsp vegetable oil
- 2 tsp garam masala
- for the brine
- ½ gallon (1.9 liters) distilled water
- ½ cup kosher salt
- for the chutney
- 1 bunch of cilantro, washed and roughly chopped
- 4 scallions, trimmed and roughly chopped
- 2 garlic cloves, peeled and roughly chopped
- 2 small green chili peppers, deseeded and minced
- 1-inch (2.5cm) piece of fresh ginger, peeled and minced
- 1 tbsp dry-roasted peanuts
- 1 tsp coarse salt
- 1 tsp ground cumin
- ½ tsp ground coriander
- 3 tbsp freshly squeezed lemon juice
- ¼ cup extra virgin olive oil

Directions:

1. In a stockpot on the stovetop over medium-high heat, make the brine by bringing the water and salt to a boil. Stir until the salt dissolves. Remove the pot from the stovetop and let the brine cool to room temperature. Cover and refrigerate until cool.

2. Submerge the hens in the brine. If they float, place a resealable bag of ice on top. Cover and refrigerate for 4 hours or as long as 8 hours.

3. Supply your smoker with wood pellets and follow the start-up procedure. Preheat the grill, with the lid closed, to 350° F.

4. In a blender, make the chutney by combining all the ingredients except the olive oil. Blend until the ingredients begin to move, adding 1 tablespoon of water if they need help. When a paste has formed, add the olive oil in a thin stream until the chutney is smooth. If it seems too thick, add a small bit of water. If it's too thin, add a little more oil. Store in a covered container in the refrigerator until ready to use.

5. Remove the hens from the brine. Rinse inside and out under cold running water and pat dry with paper towels. Place half an onion, 2 slices of ginger, and 2 garlic cloves in the cavity of each hen. Tie the legs together with butcher's twine.

6. In a small bowl, combine the vegetable oil and garam masala. Rub the mixture thinly and evenly on the outside of the hens.

7. Place the hens on the grate and roast until they're nicely browned and the internal temperature in the thickest part of a thigh reaches 165°F (74°C), about 1 hour.

8. Transfer the hens to a platter. Serve with the chutney.

Asian Bbq Chicken

Servings: 4

Cooking Time: 60 Minutes

Ingredients:

- 1 Whole whole chicken
- Asian BBQ Rub
- 1 Whole ginger ale

Directions:

1. Rinse chicken in cold water and pat dry with paper towels. Cover the chicken all over with Traeger Asian BBQ rub; make sure to drop some in the inside too.

Place in large bag or bowl and cover and refrigerate for 12 to 24 hours.

2.   Supply your smoker with wood pellets and follow the start-up procedure. Preheat the grill, with the lid closed, to 375° F.

3.   Open your can of ginger ale and take a few big gulps. Set the can of soda on a stable surface. Take the chicken out of the fridge and place the bird over top of the soda can. The base of the can and the two legs of the chicken should form a sort of tripod to hold the chicken upright.

4.   Stand the chicken in the center of your hot grate and cook the chicken till the skin is golden brown and the internal temperature is about 165℉ on a instant-read thermometer, approximately 40 minutes to 1 hour.

5.   De-throne chicken. Enjoy!

Smoked Turkey

Servings: 6
Cooking Time: 420 Minutes

Ingredients:
•   1 (12-16 lb) fresh or frozen turkey, thawed, giblets removed
•   1 Cup Rub
•   1 1/2 Tablespoon minced garlic
•   1 Cup sugar
•   1/2 Cup Worcestershire sauce
•   2 Tablespoon canola oil

Directions:
1.   Ensure the turkey is fully thawed and remove any giblets. Pour 3 gallons of water in a 5 gallon non-metal bucket.

2.   Add Traeger rub, garlic, sugar, and Worcestershire sauce and mix until sugars are completely dissolved.

3.   Place the turkey, breast side down, into the bucket with the brine. Make sure the turkey is completely submerged.

4.   Cover bucket and place in refrigerator overnight.

5.   Remove turkey from brine and pat dry. Rub canola oil over entire outside of turkey and place breast side up into disposable aluminum roasting pan.

6.   Supply your smoker with wood pellets and follow the start-up procedure. Preheat the grill, with the lid closed, to 225° F.

7.   Place the turkey on the grill and smoke for 2 1/2 to 3 hours Grill: 180 ℉

8.   Increase grill temperature to 350℉ and cook for 3-1/2 to 4 hours, or until the internal temperature reaches 165℉ in the thickest part of the breast. Grill: 350 ℉ Probe: 165 ℉

9.   Remove from grill and allow to rest for 30 minutes before carving. Enjoy!

Grilled Honey Chicken Wings

Servings: 4 - 8
Cooking Time: 30 Minutes

Ingredients:
•   2 Chipotles Chopped In Adobo
•   1 Apple Cider Vinegar
•   2 Tablespoons Balsamic Vinegar
•   ¼ Cup Brown Sugar
•   2 ½ Lbs Chicken Wings, Trimmed And Patted Dry
•   ¼ Cup Honey
•   ½ Cup Ketchup
•   ¼ Cup Adobo Sauce
•   2 Tablespoons Sweet Rib Rub
•   2 Teaspoons Worcestershire Sauce

Directions:
1.   Supply your smoker with wood pellets and follow the start-up procedure. Preheat the grill, with the lid open, to 350° F. If you're using a charcoal or gas grill, set up the grill for medium high heat.

2.   In a large bowl, whisk together the apple cider vinegar, ketchup, brown sugar, honey, chopped chipotle peppers with adobo sauce, balsamic vinegar, Worcestershire sauce, and Sweet Rib Rub. Whisk the glaze until it's well combined.

3.   Add the wings to the glaze and place the bowl in the refrigerator. Marinade the chicken wings for up to 12 hours. Once the wings have finished marinating, remove the chicken wings from the marinade and place the chicken wings onto the wing rack.

4. Once all the wings have been placed on the wing rack, place the wing rack on the grill. Insert a temperature probe into the thickest part into one of the wings and grill the wings for 5 minutes, and then rotate the rack 180° and grill for another 5 minutes. Remove the wings once they have an internal temperature of 165°F and the juice from the chicken runs clear.

5. Remove the wings from the grill and serve immediately.

Lemon Rosemary Beer Can Chicken

Servings: 4
Cooking Time: 60 Minutes

Ingredients:

- 1 (3 to 3-1/2 lb) whole chicken
- 1 lemon, halved
- 1 Teaspoon kosher salt
- 1 Teaspoon ground black pepper
- 1 Teaspoon fresh finely chopped rosemary
- 1 (12 oz) can beer

Directions:

1. Supply your smoker with wood pellets and follow the start-up procedure. Preheat the grill, with the lid closed, to 400° F.

2. Coat the chicken inside and out with the juice from one lemon. In a small bowl, combine salt, pepper and rosemary, and sprinkle on the inside and outside of chicken.

3. Empty half of the beer from the can and place the can on a solid surface. Place the chicken atop the beer can, tucking the legs in the front.

4. Carefully place the chicken directly on the grill grate using the legs to support if needed. Alternatively, place the chicken atop the beer can on a sheet tray for a more stable surface, then place the sheet tray directly on the grill grate.

5. Cook the chicken until an instant-read thermometer reads 165°F when inserted in the thickest part of the breast, about 60 minutes. Grill: 400 °F Probe: 165 °F

6. Let the chicken rest 10 minutes before carving. Serve with Chardonnay or any of your favorite medium body red or white wines. Enjoy!

Grilled Honey Chicken Kabobs

Servings: 4
Cooking Time: 14 Minutes

Ingredients:

- 1 pound boneless skinless chicken breasts (cut into 1 inch pieces)
- 1/4 cup olive oil
- 1/3 cup soy sauce
- 1/4 cup honey
- 1 teaspoon minced garlic
- salt and pepper to taste
- 1 red bell pepper (cut into 1 inch pieces)
- 1 yellow bell pepper (cut into 1 inch pieces)
- 2 small zucchini (cut into 1 inch slices)
- 1 red onion (cut into 1 inch pieces)
- 1 tablespoon chopped parsley

Directions:

1. In a large bowl combine the olive oil, soy sauce, honey, garlic and salt and pepper, and whisk.

2. Add the chicken, bell peppers, zucchini and red onion to the bowl,tossing to thoroughly coat.

3. Cover and refrigerate for 1 to 8 hours.

4. Soak wooden skewers in cold water for at least 30 minutes. Supply your smoker with wood pellets and follow the start-up procedure. Preheat the grill, with the lid closed, to high heat.

5. Thread the chicken and vegetables onto the skewers.

6. Cook for 5-7 minutes on each side or until chicken is cooked through.

7. To serve, sprinkle with parsley. Enjoy!

BEEF LAMB AND GAME RECIPES

Traeger Bacon-wrapped Filet Mignon

Servings: 2
Cooking Time: 15 Minutes

Ingredients:

- 3 (6 oz) filet mignon steaks
- 1 Teaspoon pepper
- 1 Teaspoon salt
- 2 Clove garlic, minced
- 3 Tablespoon butter, softened
- 3 Slices bacon

Directions:

1. Filets don't have much marbling, so when selecting meat look for a rich red color.
2. In a small bowl, combine salt, pepper, garlic and softened butter. Rub on both sides of filet. Let rest 10 minutes.
3. Supply your smoker with wood pellets and follow the start-up procedure. Preheat the grill, with the lid closed, to 450° F.
4. Wrap each steak in a slice of bacon and secure with a toothpick.
5. Place steaks directly on the grill and cook for 5 to 8 minutes on each side, or until the filets reach an internal temperature of 130°F for medium-rare. Enjoy! Grill: 450 °F Probe: 130 °F

Grilled Beef Shawarma

Servings: 4
Cooking Time: 10 Minutes

Ingredients:

- arugula
- 1/2 tsp cayenne pepper
- 1/2 tsp cinnamon, ground
- 1/2 tsp cloves, ground
- 1 1/2 tsp coriander, ground
- 1 1/2 lbs flank steak
- 2 garlic cloves, minced
- 2 tsp olive oil
- 1 tsp paprika
- 4 pita
- red onion
- tt salt and pepper
- tahini
- tomatoes
- 1/2 tsp turmeric, powder

Directions:

1. Use a meat mallet to tenderize the steak, then transfer to a glass baking dish and season with salt and pepper. Drizzle with olive oil, then rub minced garlic on steak. Season with spice rub. Cover with plastic wrap and refrigerate overnight.
2. Remove steak from the refrigerator, 1 hour prior to grilling. Supply your smoker with wood pellets and follow the start-up procedure. Preheat the grill, with the lid closed, to 450° F. If using a gas or charcoal grill, set it up for medium-high heat.
3. Grill steak 3 to 5 minutes per side, then remove from grill and rest for 10 minutes. While steak is grilling, place pitas in the upper smoke cabinet of the Lockhart to warm. Slice steak thinly, against the grain and wrap in flatbread or pita with arugula, tomatoes, onion, and tahini.

Crusted Prime Rib With Rosemary

Servings: 4-6
Cooking Time: 180 Minutes

Ingredients:

- 4-6 garlic, cloves
- 1/3 cup olive oil
- chop house steak seasoning
- 7 pound, boned tied and rolled prime rib roast
- 3 tablespoon rosemary, fresh
- 3 tablespoon thyme, fresh sprigs

Directions:

1. In a food processor, blend together the garlic, rosemary, thyme, sage, and oil until a rough paste forms. Place the prime rib on a sheet pan over a wire rack and rub the prime rib generously with the herb paste on all sides.

2. Season the prime rib with   Chop House Steak Seasoning generously on all sides, then chill uncovered in the refrigerator overnight, or for 12 hours.

3. Once the prime rib has chilled for 12 hours, supply your smoker with wood pellets and follow the start-up procedure. Preheat the grill, with the lid closed, to 250° F, and grill for 2 hours or until the internal temperature of the roast reaches 110°F, then increase the temperature to 400 and grill for an additional 15-30 minutes, or until the internal temperature reaches 125 - 140°F.

4. Remove the prime rib from the grill, cover tightly in foil and allow to rest for 30 minutes. The final temperature of the prime rib should be 125 - 140°F after resting. Serve and enjoy!

Smoked Black Pepper Beef Back Ribs

Servings: 2 – 4
Cooking Time: 260 Minutes

Ingredients:
- 2 racks beef back ribs
- ½ tbsp black pepper
- ⅓ cup   chop house steak seasoning

Directions:

1. Supply your smoker with wood pellets and follow the start-up procedure. Preheat the grill, with the lid closed, to 250° F. If using a gas or charcoal grill, set it up for low heat.

2. Place the ribs on a sheet tray, then remove the membrane from the back of the ribs: Take a butter knife and wedge it just underneath the membrane to loosen it. Using your hands, or a paper towel to grip, pull the membrane up and off the bone. Rub each rack generously with Chop House Steak seasoning and black pepper.

3. Place the ribs on the grill and smoke for 2 hours. Increase the temperature to 300°F and cook an additional 45 to 60 minutes, or until the ribs reach an internal temperature of 205° F. Be sure and flip the ribs halfway to achieve good bark.

4. Remove ribs from the grill and wrap in butcher paper. Allow ribs to rest for 20 minutes, then slice and serve hot.

Dry Brined Texas Beef Ribs By Doug Scheiding

Servings: 8
Cooking Time: 360 Minutes

Ingredients:
- 2 (9-12 Lb) Uncut Prime Or Choice Beef Short Ribs
- Kosher Salt
- Worcestershire Sauce
- Prime Rib Rub
- Blackened Saskatchewan Rub
- 8 Ounce Apple Juice, For Spritzing
- 8 Ounce Beef Broth

Directions:

1. Purchase a package of uncut short ribs from your favorite grocer or butcher store – recommended Prime or Choice quality. Usually 9-12 lbs for 2 racks of 4 bones each for 8 total.

2. Trim as much fat as possible from the top of the ribs with a sharp knife. Remove the membrane from the bottom of each rack of 4 bones.

3. Sprinkle with kosher salt for the dry brine and wrap in plastic wrap for at least 6 hours or overnight in your refrigerator.

4. Supply your smoker with wood pellets and follow the start-up procedure. Preheat the grill, with the lid closed, to 275° F.

5. Wipe the excess salt mixture from the top of the ribs. Coat with a light amount of Worcestershire sauce before putting on a medium coat of Traeger Prime Rib.

6. Follow with a lighter coat of Traeger Saskatchewan rub. Spritz with apple juice and let set for 15-20 minutes.

7. Place on the Traeger with the thicker portion of the ribs (if applicable) to the back of the grill.

8. Smoke the ribs for 4-5 hours with a light spritz every 30 minutes to keep moist until internal temperature reaches approximately 180°F or the color has a nice deep char. Grill: 275 °F Probe: 180 °F

9. Like a brisket, take the ribs off the grill and wrap in 2 sheet of heavy duty foil along with 4 oz of broth for each rack of ribs.

10. Place back on the smoker for another 1 to 1-1/2 hours until internal temperature of the meat is around 203°F. Remove and cut. Serve immediately. Enjoy! Grill: 275 °F Probe: 203 °F

Grilled Double Burgers With Texas Spicy Bbq Sauce

Servings: 4
Cooking Time: 30 Minutes

Ingredients:

- 3 Pound ground beef
- 4 Tablespoon Beef Rub
- 1/2 Pound bacon
- 8 Slices cheddar cheese
- 4 Whole burger buns, for serving
- 1 Cup Texas Spicy BBQ Sauce
- sliced pickles, for serving

Directions:

1. Form ground beef into eight 1/3 pound patties. Season each patty on both sides with Traeger Beef Rub.

2. Supply your smoker with wood pellets and follow the start-up procedure. Preheat the grill, with the lid closed, to 350° F.

3. For the Bacon: Place bacon slices directly on grill grate and cook for 15 to 20 minutes, or until crispy. Grill: 350 ℉

4. Increase the Traeger temperature to 450℉ and preheat. Grill: 450 ℉

5. Place burger patties directly on grill grate and cook for 4 minutes on each side, or to desired doneness. Grill: 450 ℉

6. Top each patty with a slice of cheddar cheese and cook, lid closed, until cheese melts.

7. To serve, spread the Traeger Texas Spicy BBQ Sauce onto each bottom bun and top with the pickles and patty, then repeat with BBQ sauce, pickles, patty, BBQ sauce, and finally the bacon. Top with top bun. Enjoy!

Beer Barbecue Burgers

Servings: 4
Cooking Time: 60 Minutes

Ingredients:

- 8 bacon slices
- beer, can
- 1/2 lb cheddar jack, cubed

- 2 1/2 lbs ground beef
- 1 jalapeno pepper, minced
- kansas city barbecue rub
- 1 white onion, caramelized

Directions:

1. Supply your smoker with wood pellets and follow the start-up procedure. Preheat the grill, with the lid closed, to 300° F. If using a gas or charcoal grill, set it up for medium-low heat.

2. Place ground beef in a mixing bowl, season with Kansas City Barbecue Rub, then mix by hand. Form 4, 10 ounce balls, then use a can (any 12 ounce aluminum can will work), and press the can down the center of each ball, creating a small beef bowl. Press along the sides and roll to create a beef bowl, approximately 3 ½ inches tall.

3. Wrap beef with 2 pieces of bacon, then fill with cheese, caramelized onion, and minced jalapeño. Set filled burgers in a large cast iron skillet, then transfer to the grill. Cook for 25 minutes in the skillet, then transfer burgers to the top rack. Increase the temperature to 325°F, and cook an additional 25 to 30 minutes, rotating halfway. Remove from the grill, top with extra jalapeño, rest for 5 minutes, then serve warm.

Texas Smoked Brisket

Servings: 12-15
Cooking Time: 960 Minutes

Ingredients:

- 1 (12-pound) full packer brisket
- 2 tablespoons yellow mustard
- 1 batch Espresso Brisket Rub
- Worcestershire Mop and Spritz, for spritzing

Directions:

1. Supply your smoker with wood pellets and follow the start-up procedure. Preheat the grill, with the lid closed, to 225°F.

2. Using a boning knife, carefully remove all but about ½ inch of the large layer of fat covering one side of your brisket.

3. Coat the brisket all over with mustard and season it with the rub. Using your hands, work the rub into the meat. Pour the mop into a spray bottle.

4. Place the brisket directly on the grill grate and smoke until its internal temperature reaches 195°F, spritzing it every hour with the mop.

5. Pull the brisket from the grill and wrap it completely in aluminum foil or butcher paper. Place the wrapped brisket in a cooler, cover the cooler, and let it rest for 1 or 2 hours.

6. Remove the brisket from the cooler and unwrap it.

7. Separate the brisket point from the flat by cutting along the fat layer and slice the flat. The point can be saved for burnt ends (see Sweet Heat Burnt Ends), or sliced and served as well.

Reuben Sandwich

Servings: 4
Cooking Time: 10 Minutes

Ingredients:
- 2 Cup mayonnaise
- 1/2 Cup ketchup
- 1/4 Cup pickle relish
- 2 Tablespoon Chicken Rub
- 4 Pound leftover corned beef, thinly sliced
- 2 1/2 Cup sauerkraut
- 10 Slices Swiss cheese
- 10 Slices marble rye bread
- 6 Tablespoon butter, room temperature

Directions:
1. See Traeger Smoked Corned Beef Brisket recipe for corned beef instructions.

2. Supply your smoker with wood pellets and follow the start-up procedure. Preheat the grill, with the lid closed, to 350° F.

3. Place a large griddle directly on the grill grate to heat up while the sandwiches are being assembled.

4. Combine the mayonnaise, ketchup, relish and Traeger Chicken Rub in a bowl and stir until well mixed.

5. Butter the outsides of the bread (the side that goes on the grill). Place a layer of sauce on the other side of the bread and top with the corned beef, sauerkraut and 2 Swiss cheese slices. Top with another slice of sauced bread.

6. Place sandwiches on the hot griddle in the Traeger and cook for 5 minutes. Using a spatula, flip the sandwiches and cook for an additional 5 minutes, or until toasted with melty cheese and warm meat. Grill: 350 °F

7. Remove sandwiches from the Traeger. Enjoy!

Tomahawk Steaks With Garlic Herb Butter

Servings: 8
Cooking Time: 68 Minutes

Ingredients:
- 2 bone-in ribeye steaks, each about 1½ to 2lb (680g to 1kg)
- coarse salt
- fresh coarsely ground black pepper
- for the butter
- 1 stick unsalted butter, at room temperature
- 1 to 2 garlic cloves, peeled and minced
- 1 tbsp minced fresh chives or scallion greens
- 1 tbsp minced fresh parsley
- 1 tsp freshly squeezed lemon juice
- ½ tsp coarse salt
- ½ tsp freshly ground black pepper

Directions:
1. Supply your smoker with wood pellets and follow the start-up procedure. Preheat the grill, with the lid closed, to 225° F.

2. In a small bowl, make the herb butter by blending together the ingredients with a fork. Use wax paper, parchment paper, or plastic wrap as an aid to form the butter into a log and twist the ends of the wrapping. Chill in the refrigerator or freezer until ready to use.

3. Generously season the steaks with salt and pepper. Place them on the cast iron pan and grill until the internal temperature reaches 115°F (46°C), about 50 to 60 minutes. (Insert the probe through the side of a steak toward the center. Don't let the probe touch bone or you'll get an elevated reading.) Transfer the steaks to a rimmed baking sheet and cover loosely with aluminum foil.

4. Place a ridged cast iron grill pan or a set of Grill Grates on the grate. Raise the temperature to 450°F (232°C). Place the steaks on the cast iron pan and sear until the internal temperature reaches 130°F (54°C), about 3 to 4 minutes per side, turning once.

5. Transfer the steaks to a cutting board. Cut the butter into discs and place 3 or 4 atop each steak. Let the steaks rest for 3 minutes. If desired, cut the ribeyes off their bones and slice the meat. Reassemble the meat and bones on a platter before serving.

London Broil

Servings: 4
Cooking Time: 16 Minutes

Ingredients:

- 1 (1½- to 2-pound) London broil or top round steak
- ¼ cup soy sauce
- 2 tablespoons white wine
- 2 tablespoons extra-virgin olive oil
- ¼ cup chopped scallions
- 2 tablespoons packed brown sugar
- 2 garlic cloves, minced
- 2 teaspoons red pepper flakes
- 1 teaspoon freshly ground black pepper

Directions:

1. Using a meat mallet, pound the steak lightly all over on both sides to break down its fibers and tenderize. You are not trying to pound down the thickness

2. In a medium bowl, make the marinade by combining the soy sauce, white wine, olive oil, scallions, brown sugar, garlic, red pepper flakes, and black pepper

3. Put the steak in a shallow plastic container with a lid and pour the marinade over the meat. Cover and refrigerate for at least 4 hours.

4. Remove the steak from the marinade, shaking off any excess, and discard the marinade

5. Supply your smoker with wood pellets and follow the start-up procedure. Preheat, with the lid closed, to 350°F6. Place the steak directly on the grill, close the lid, and smoke for 6 minutes. Flip, then smoke with the lid closed for 6 to 10 minutes more, or until a meat thermometer inserted in the meat reads 130°F for medium-rare

6. Let the steak rest for about 10 minutes before slicing and serving. The meat's temperature will rise by about 5 degrees while it rests

Teriyaki Deer Jerky

Servings: 4
Cooking Time: 240 Minutes

Ingredients:

- 1/2 Cup soy sauce
- 1/4 Cup mirin
- 2 Tablespoon sugar
- 3 coins fresh ginger, each ¼ inch thick
- 1 Clove garlic, crushed
- 1/2 Teaspoon onion powder
- 1/2 Teaspoon black pepper
- 2 Pound venison, trimmed

Directions:

1. In a mixing bowl, combine the soy sauce, mirin, sugar, ginger, garlic, onion powder and pepper.

2. With a sharp knife, slice the venison into 1/4 inch thick slices. Trim any fat or connective tissue.

3. Put the meat slices in a large resealable plastic bag. Pour the marinade mixture over the venison and massage the bag so that all the slices get coated with the marinade. Seal the bag and refrigerate for several hours, or overnight.

4. Supply your smoker with wood pellets and follow the start-up procedure. Preheat the grill, with the lid closed, to 180° F. Remove the venison from the marinade; discard marinade. Dry the meat slices between paper towels.

5. Arrange the meat in a single layer directly on the grill grate. Smoke for 3 hours or until the jerky is dry but still chewy and somewhat pliant when you bend a piece. Grill: 180 °F

6. Transfer to a resealable plastic bag while the jerky is still warm leaving the top open. Let the jerky rest for an hour at room temperature.

7. Squeeze any air from the bag and refrigerate the jerky. It will keep for several weeks. Enjoy!

Kalbi-style Steak Wraps

Servings: 4

Cooking Time: 8 Minutes

Ingredients:

- 1 flat iron steak, about 1½lb (680g)
- 1 tbsp toasted sesame seeds
- 2 scallions, trimmed, white and green parts thinly sliced on a sharp diagonal
- for the marinade
- 1 small white onion, peeled and coarsely grated
- 4 garlic cloves, peeled and smashed with a chef's knife
- ½ Asian pear, decored and coarsely grated
- ½ cup light soy sauce
- ½ cup low-carb beer or distilled water
- 2 tbsp light brown sugar or low-carb substitute
- 2 tbsp rice vinegar or apple cider vinegar
- 2 tbsp toasted sesame oil
- 1 tbsp peeled and grated fresh ginger
- 1 tsp freshly ground black pepper

Directions:

1. In a large bowl, make the marinade by combining the ingredients. Stir until the sugar dissolves. Place the steaks in a resealable plastic bag and add the marinade, massaging the bag to thoroughly coat the meat. Refrigerate for 8 hours or overnight, turning the bag once or twice.

2. Supply your smoker with wood pellets and follow the start-up procedure. Preheat the grill, with the lid closed, to 450° F.

3. Remove the steaks from the marinade and remove any solids. (Discard the marinade.) Pat dry with paper towels. Place the steaks on the cast iron pan and grill until the internal temperature reaches 125 to 130°F (52 to 54°C), about 3 to 4 minutes per side, turning once.

4. Transfer the steaks to a cutting board and let rest for 2 minutes. Thinly slice each steak on a sharp diagonal and place on a platter. Scatter the sesame seeds and scallions over the top.

5. Place leaf lettuce, thinly sliced jalapeños, fresh cilantro leaves, kimchi (optional), and thinly sliced garlic on a separate platter. Place gochujang (Korean chili paste) in a small ramekin and add that to the platter.

6. Place the two platters on the table. Advise each diner to assemble the lettuce wraps to their desire. Serve with Asian beer, sake, or Korean soju.

Bacon-swiss Cheesesteak Meatloaf

Servings: 4

Cooking Time: 120 Minutes

Ingredients:

- 1 tablespoon canola oil
- 2 garlic cloves, finely chopped
- 1 medium onion, finely chopped
- 1 poblano chile, stemmed, seeded, and finely chopped
- 2 pounds extra-lean ground beef
- 2 tablespoons Montreal steak seasoning
- 1 tablespoon A.1. Steak Sauce
- ½ pound bacon, cooked and crumbled
- 2 cups shredded Swiss cheese
- 1 egg, beaten
- 2 cups breadcrumbs
- ½ cup Tiger Sauce

Directions:

1. On your stove top, heat the canola oil in a medium sauté pan over medium-high heat. Add the garlic, onion, and poblano, and sauté for 3 to 5 minutes, or until the onion is just barely translucent

2. Supply your smoker with wood pellets and follow the start-up procedure. Preheat, with the lid closed, to 225°F.

3. In a large bowl, combine the sautéed vegetables, ground beef, steak seasoning, steak sauce, bacon, Swiss cheese, egg, and breadcrumbs. Mix with your hands until well incorporated, then shape into a loaf.

4. Put the meatloaf in a cast iron skillet and place it on the grill. Close the lid and smoke for 2 hours, or until a meat thermometer inserted in the loaf reads 165°F.

5. Top with the meatloaf with the Tiger Sauce, remove from the grill, and let rest for about 10 minutes before serving.

Grilled Garlic Tomahawk Steak

Servings: 1 - 2
Cooking Time: 60 Minutes

Ingredients:

- 3 Tablespoons Unsalted Butter
- 2 Tablespoons Chophouse Steak Seasoning
- 2 Garlic, Cloves
- Kosher Salt
- 1 Sprig Rosemary, Fresh
- 1, 2-Inch Thick Bone-In Tomahawk Ribeye

Directions:

1. Supply your smoker with wood pellets and follow the start-up procedure. Preheat the grill, with the lid closed, to 225° F.

2. Generously coat the tomahawk steak with kosher salt on all sides.

3. Allow the steak to sit at room temperature for one hour. After an hour, wipe off the salt and pat the steak dry.

4. Season the tomahawk steak with Chophouse Steak on both sides.

5. Place the steak on the grill grates, insert a temperature probe, and grill, undisturbed, for 45 minutes, or until the steak reaches an internal temperature of 120°F.

6. Remove the steak from the grill, tent with aluminum foil and allow it to rest for 10 minutes.

7. Place a cast iron skillet on the grill and increase the temperature of the   to 450°F. Allow the pan to get as hot as possible.

8. Place the steak in the cast iron pan with the butter, garlic cloves, and rosemary sprig. Immediately begin spooning the butter over the steak as it melts.

9. Sear on one side for 1 minute.

10. Flip the steak, place the garlic and rosemary on top of the steak, and continue to baste the steak with the butter for another minute.

11. Pull the steak off the grill and allow it to rest for 10 minutes until the temperature rises to 130-135°F.

12. Pour the melted butter from the pan over the steak, slice, and serve immediately.

Easy Breakfast Cheeseburger

Servings: 2
Cooking Time: 10 Minutes

Ingredients:

- 4 Bacon, Strip
- 6 Ounce Lean Beef, Ground
- 2 Burger Buns
- 2 Cheese, Sliced
- 2 Egg
- Pepper
- Salt

Directions:

1. Supply your smoker with wood pellets and follow the start-up procedure. Preheat the grill, with the lid closed, to 400° F.

2. Take the ground beef and divide it into two thin patties. Brush the grate with oil, then add the patties and grill them on about 2-5 minutes on each side, or until the desired doneness, pressing down to get a good sear.

3. Remove the burgers from the grill, then build your burger. Starting with the bottom bun or bread slice, add the patty, then a slice of American cheese, top with bacon, hash browns, an egg over easy, and finish with the top bun or bread slice. Now it's ready to serve!

Salt-crusted Prime Rib

Servings: 8
Cooking Time: 180 Minutes

Ingredients:

- 1 1/2 Cup Jacobsen Salt Co. Pure Kosher Sea Salt
- 3/4 Cup coarse ground black pepper
- 1 Head garlic, peeled
- 1/2 Cup rosemary
- 2 Tablespoon chile powder
- 3/4 Cup extra-virgin olive oil
- 1 (15-16 lb) 6-bone prime rib roast

Directions:

1. In a food processor, combine salt, pepper, garlic cloves, rosemary and chile powder and process until fine. Add the olive oil and pulse to form a paste.

2.   Place the prime rib roast on a cutting board, bone-side up and rub with 1 tablespoon of the salt paste.

3.   Transfer the meat to a large roasting pan and place bone-side down. Pack the salt paste all over the fatty surface, pressing to help it adhere. Let the prime rib stand at room temperature for 1 hour.

4.   Supply your smoker with wood pellets and follow the start-up procedure. Preheat the grill, with the lid closed, to 450° F.

5.   Roast the prime rib for 1 hour, or until the crust is slightly darkened. Lower the Traeger temperature to 300°F and roast for about 2 hours and 15 minutes longer, or until an instant-read thermometer inserted into the center of the roast (not touching the bone) registers 125°F for medium-rare. Grill: 450 °F

6.   Transfer the roast to a large carving board and let the meat rest for 30 minutes. Grill: 300 °F Probe: 135 °F

7.   Carefully lift the salt crust off the meat and transfer to a bowl. Brush away any excess salt.

8.   To remove the roast in one piece while keeping the rib rack intact, run a long sharp carving knife along the bones, using them as your guide. Leave on 1/2 inch of meat, or more if reserving for leftovers.

9.   Carve the prime rib roast 1/2 inch thick and serve, using some of the crumbled salt crust as a condiment.

Spiced Cowboy Steak

Servings: x
Cooking Time: 53 Minutes

Ingredients:

*   2 cowboy steaks about 1 3/4 inches to 2 inches thick
*   Rub:
*   1 1/2 tablespoon olive oil
*   2 cloves garlic minced
*   1 tablespoon coarse salt kosher or sea salt
*   1 teaspoon black pepper
*   1 teaspoon dried thyme
*   1/2 teaspoon onion powder
*   1/2 teaspoon marjoram
*   1/4 teaspoon smoked paprika

Directions:

1.   Combine all the rub ingredients and slather onto both sides of the cowboy steaks.

2.   Supply your smoker with wood pellets and follow the start-up procedure. Preheat the grill, with the lid closed, to 225 °F.

3.   Place steaks on the cooking grate and cook until the internal temperature reaches 120 degrees F (about 45 minutes).

4.   Remove steaks from grill, cover it and set aside. Turn pellet grill to the HIGH setting.

5.   Place steaks back on the hot grill. After 4 minutes, rotate 45 degrees to create a diamond pattern of sear marks. After 4 minutes turn it over and repeat on the other side.

6.   Once seared to perfection, remove steaks from grill and place onto a clean cutting board. Let rest for 5-7 minutes and serve with a dollop of flavored butter on top, or carve and share.

Smoked Teriyaki Jerky

Servings: 6
Cooking Time: 240 Minutes

Ingredients:

*   1/2 Cup soy sauce
*   1/4 Cup mirin or sweet cooking wine
*   2 Tablespoon sugar
*   3 coins fresh ginger, each ¼ inch thick
*   1 Clove garlic, crushed
*   1/2 Teaspoon onion powder
*   1/2 Teaspoon black pepper
*   2 Pound trimmed beef top or bottom round, sirloin tip, flank steak or wild game

Directions:

1.   In a mixing bowl, combine soy sauce, mirin, sugar, ginger, garlic, onion powder and black pepper.

2.   With a sharp knife, slice the beef into 1/4 inch thick slices with the grain. This is much easier to do if the meat is partially frozen. Trim off any fat or connective tissue.

3.   Put the beef slices in a large resealable plastic bag and pour the marinade over the beef. Massage the bag so

all the slices get coated with the marinade. Seal the bag and refrigerate for several hours or overnight.

4. Supply your smoker with wood pellets and follow the start-up procedure. Preheat the grill, with the lid closed, to 180° F.

5. Remove the beef from the marinade and discard the marinade.

6. Dry the beef slices between paper towels and arrange the meat in a single layer on the grill grate.

7. Smoke on the Traeger for 4 to 5 hours or until the jerky is dry but still pliant when bent. Grill: 180 ˚F

8. Immediately transfer the jerky to a resealable plastic bag and let it rest for an hour at room temperature.

9. Squeeze the air out of the bag and keep the jerky in the refrigerator. Enjoy!

Duck Fat Fries (confit)

Servings: 6
Cooking Time: 180 Minutes

Ingredients:

- 1/4 Cup sea salt
- 12 Whole black peppercorn
- 2 Sprig thyme sprigs
- 2 Clove garlic, crushed
- 1 Whole bay leaves
- 6 Whole Duck Leg Quarters, (leg with thigh attached), preferallb moulard
- olive oil

Directions:

1. Combine the salt and the water in a large resealable plastic bag (or a large bowl) and stir until the salt crystals dissolve.

2. Add the peppercorns, thyme, garlic, bay leaf, coriander, if using, and duck leg quarters. Seal the bag, put in a pan or bowl (to contain any potential leaks) and refrigerate for 24 hours.

3. Drain the duck leg quarters (discard the brine) and rinse under cold running water. Pat dry with paper towels. Prick the skin all over with a darning needle or sharp fork, being careful not to nick the meat. (It helps if you go in at an angle.) This creates channels for the fat to escape, making for crispier skin.

4. Supply your smoker with wood pellets and follow the start-up procedure. Preheat the grill, with the lid closed, to 400° F.

5. Meanwhile add enough olive oil to a large cast iron skillet or roasting pan to film the bottom. Arrange the duck leg quarters in the skillet or roasting pan in a single layer, skin-side down.

6. Put the skillet or roasting pan on the grill grate. Roast the duck for 30 minutes, or until the duck fat begins to render. Reduce the temperature to 300F (150C). Turn the duck legs so they are skin-side up. Cover the skillet or roasting pan tightly with foil. Grill: 300 ˚F

7. Continue to roast the duck for 2 hours. Uncover the duck and roast for an additional hour, or until the skin is crisp and golden brown. Remove the duck, shred, and serve immediately. (Alternatively, you can refrigerate the duck for up to a week. Re-crisp the skin by grilling the duck, skin-side down, in a hot cast iron skillet or on your Traeger.) Serve with brown butter french fries.

8. Strain the remaining duck fat through cheesecloth or a fine-mesh kitchen strainer and transfer to a covered container; refrigerate for up to 6 months. Use the flavorful fat to saut potatoes or sturdy greens.

Brined Smoked Brisket

Servings: 4
Cooking Time: 420 Minutes

Ingredients:

- 1 (5-7 lb) flat cut brisket
- 1 Cup brown sugar
- 1/2 Cup kosher salt
- 1/4 Cup Beef Rub

Directions:

1. Dissolve salt and sugar in 6 quarts boiling water. Add 6 cups ice then let it cool. Place the brisket in the brine and cover. Leave brine in the refrigerator overnight.

2. Remove the brisket from the brine and pat it dry with a paper towel. Sprinkle evenly with Traeger Beef Rub.

3. Supply your smoker with wood pellets and follow the start-up procedure. Preheat the grill, with the lid closed, to 250° F.

4. Place the brisket on the Traeger, fat cap down and smoke for 3 hours. Grill: 250 ˚F

5. After 3 hours, double wrap the brisket in foil and turn the temperature up to 275˚F. Cook meat until internal temperature reaches 204˚F, about 3 to 4 hours. Grill: 275 ˚F Probe: 204 ˚F

6. Unwrap the brisket and place it unwrapped on the grill for 30 more minutes. Grill: 275 ˚F

7. Remove the brisket from the grill and let it rest for 15 minutes before slicing against the grain. Enjoy!

Smoked Beef Plate Ribs

Servings: 4

Cooking Time: 480 Minutes

Ingredients:

- 1 1/3 cup apple cider vinegar
- 4 lbs beef plate ribs
- 1/3 cup beef stock
- 1/2 tsp black pepper
- 1/4 tsp cayenne pepper
- 4 garlic cloves, peeled and smashed
- 2 tbsp honey
- 1/2 tsp kosher salt
- 1/4 cup molasses
- tbsp olive oil
- 2 tsp paprika
- beef and brisket rub
- 1 tbsp spicy brown mustard
- 2 lbs tomato, cubed
- 1 white onion, quartered

Directions:

1. Fire up your Grill and set it to Smoke. If using a gas or charcoal grill, set it up for low, indirect heat.

2. Prep ribs: remove the top portion of the fat cap from the rib rack. Rub with mustard, then season with Beef Brisket rub. Inject beef stock in meat, in between bones, and along sides.

3. Place the rib rack in the center of the grill, making sure the sear slide is closed. Supply your smoker with wood pellets and follow the start-up procedure. Preheat the grill, with the lid closed, to 250° F. Smoke ribs for 3 hours.

4. Meanwhile, prepare the BBQ sauce: line a sheet tray with foil and place tomatoes, onion, and garlic on top. Drizzle with olive oil, then season with 1/4 teaspoon of salt and 1/4 teaspoon of black pepper. Transfer to the smoke cabinet for 2 hours.

5. Place a quart mixture of apple cider vinegar and water in a grill-safe pan. Move the rib rack to the right side of the grill, then place the other pan in the middle. Increase temperature to 275°F.

6. Remove tomatoes for the smoke cabinet and place in a blender. Add paprika, cayenne, 1/4 teaspoon of salt, 1/4 teaspoon of black pepper, 1/3 cup apple cider vinegar, molasses, and honey. Blend until smooth and no lumps remain. Transfer sauce to a cast iron pan and place on grill. Simmer sauce for 1 hour, stirring occasionally, while the ribs continue to cook. When sauce is done, spoon sauce over ribs, then remove remaining sauce to serve when ribs are done.

7. Continue to cook ribs an additional 2-3 hours, or until internal temperature reaches 204°F, and a metal skewer goes through like butter.

Smoked Beef Ribs

Servings: 4-8

Cooking Time: 360 Minutes

Ingredients:

- 2 (2- or 3-pound) racks beef ribs
- 2 tablespoons yellow mustard
- 1 batch Sweet and Spicy Cinnamon Rub

Directions:

1. Supply your smoker with wood pellets and follow the start-up procedure. Preheat the grill, with the lid closed, to 225°F.

2. Remove the membrane from the backside of the ribs. This can be done by cutting just through the membrane in an X pattern and working a paper towel between the membrane and the ribs to pull it off.

3.   Coat the ribs all over with mustard and season them with the rub. Using your hands, work the rub into the meat.

4.   Place the ribs directly on the grill grate and smoke until their internal temperature reaches between 190°F and 200°F.

5.   Remove the racks from the grill and cut them into individual ribs. Serve immediately.

Cheesy Nachos

Servings: 8
Cooking Time: 20 Minutes

Ingredients:
- Cilantro
- Olive Oil
- Pepper
- 1 Red Bell Peppers, Sliced
- 2 Rib-Eye Steaks
- Salsa
- Salt
- 1 Cup Shredded Cheddar Cheese
- Sour Cream
- 1 Yellow Bell Pepper, Sliced
- 1 Zucchini, Sliced

Directions:
1.   Supply your smoker with wood pellets and follow the start-up procedure. Preheat the grill, with the lid closed, to 400° F.

2.   Coat both sides of the steak with olive oil and season with sea salt and pepper. Place the steak on the grates and grill for about 4 to 5 minutes per side.

3.   Remove the steak off the grill and let rest for about 10 minutes before cutting into bite-sized strips.

4.   Brush with barbecue sauce if desired.

5.   Empty a large bag of nacho chips evenly into a cast iron pan. Start loading up with toppings - steak, cheddar cheese, sautéed vegetables.

6.   These are just suggested toppings, so feel free to add anything you like!

7.   Place your loaded nachos on the grill and let the hot smoke melt your toppings into one hearty creation.

8.   Cook for about 10 minutes, or until the cheese has fully melted.

9.   Remove and serve with sour cream and salsa.

Bistro Steaks With Avocado Relish

Servings: 4
Cooking Time: 34 Minutes

Ingredients:
- 2lb (1kg) bistro steaks
- extra virgin olive oil
- liquid aminos
- for the rub
- 2 tsp coarse salt
- 2 tsp fresh coarsely ground black pepper
- 2 tsp light brown sugar or low-carb substitute
- 2 tsp chili powder
- 2 tsp ground cumin
- 2 tsp granulated garlic
- 2 tsp sweet or smoked paprika
- for the relish
- 2 avocados
- 1½ tbsp freshly squeezed lime juice, plus more
- 2 garlic cloves, peeled and finely minced
- 1 Roma tomato, decored, deseeded, and diced
- 1 jalapeño, destemmed, deseeded, and finely diced
- ¼ cup coarsely chopped fresh cilantro leaves
- 2 tbsp diced red onion
- 1 tbsp mayo
- 1 tsp hot sauce
- coarse salt

Directions:
1.   Supply your smoker with wood pellets and follow the start-up procedure. Preheat the grill, with the lid closed, to 180° F.

2.   In a small bowl, make the rub by combining the ingredients.

3.   Trim any silver skin from the steaks and place them on a rimmed sheet pan. Coat with olive oil. Dust with the rub, patting it on with your fingertips.

4.   Place the steaks on the grate and grill until the internal temperature reaches 110 to 115°F (43 to 46°C), about 30 minutes. Pour some liquid aminos into a small

spray bottle and spritz the steaks before wrapping them in heavy-duty aluminum foil. Let the steaks rest.

5. Cut the avocados in half and then pit, peel, and dice them. In a medium bowl, make the relish by combining the avocado and lime juice. Add the remaining ingredients and season with salt to taste. Use a rubber spatula to gently mix. Transfer to an attractive serving bowl. Cover and refrigerate. (The relish is best if not made more than 1 hour ahead.)

6. Raise the temperature to 450°F (232°C). Remove the steaks from the foil and place them on the grate. Sear until they're browned and the internal temperature reaches 130 to 135°F (54 to 57°C), about 2 minutes per side, turning with tongs.

7. Transfer the steaks to a cutting board and let rest for 3 minutes. Slice them crosswise on a diagonal into 3/8-inch (1cm) slices. Shingle the slices on a platter and pour any juices remaining on the cutting board over the meat. Serve with the avocado relish.

Bbq Brisket Breakfast Tacos

Servings: 6
Cooking Time: 30 Minutes

Ingredients:
- 4 Pound leftover beef brisket
- 1/2 Teaspoon extra-virgin olive oil
- 1 green bell pepper, diced
- 1 Yellow Bell Pepper, diced
- 10 eggs
- 1/2 Cup milk
- salt and pepper
- 2 Cup shredded cheddar cheese
- flour tortillas

Directions:
1. Supply your smoker with wood pellets and follow the start-up procedure. Preheat the grill, with the lid closed, to 375° F.

2. Place leftover brisket in a double layer of foil and warm in grill. Grill: 375 °F

3. Coat the inside of a cast iron skillet with oil and preheat the skillet in the grill for 10 minutes. When skillet is hot, sauté diced peppers, stirring every few minutes until desired doneness.

4. While peppers are cooking, whisk together the eggs, milk, salt and pepper to taste. Add the beaten eggs to the skillet and scramble. Add cheese to the skillet when the eggs are almost done.

5. Remove eggs and heated brisket from grill. Serve eggs in a tortilla topped with brisket. Top with salsa or guacamole if desired. Enjoy!

Garlic Parmesan Grilled Filet Mignon

Servings: 2
Cooking Time: 10 Minutes

Ingredients:
- 4 filet mignon steaks
- 1 Teaspoon salt
- 1 Teaspoon black pepper
- 1 Teaspoon garlic salt
- 1 Cup Parmesan cheese
- 4 garlic
- 1 Tablespoon Dijon mustard

Directions:
1. Supply your smoker with wood pellets and follow the start-up procedure. Preheat the grill, with the lid closed, to High heat.

2. While the grill is heating up, season the filets with salt, pepper, and garlic salt. Also mince your garlic and chop your Parmesan so it's fine, and combine.

3. When the grill reaches temperature, place filets on the grill and cook for 4 minutes on each side. After 8 minutes total, spread the filets with the Dijon mustard and dip in the minced garlic and Parmesan cheese mixture and place back on the grill for another 1-2 minutes or until the cheese is melted.

4. Let rest for 5 minutes and serve. Enjoy!

Italian Meatballs

Servings: 6
Cooking Time: 90 Minutes

Ingredients:
- 1lb (450g) ground beef (85/15), well chilled
- ½lb (225g) Italian sausage, well chilled

- 1 large egg, beaten
- ½ cup finely grated Parmesan, Asiago, or Romano cheese
- ½ cup panko or other breadcrumbs
- 1 tsp Italian seasoning
- 1 tsp coarse salt
- ½ tsp freshly ground black pepper
- 1lb (450g) thin-sliced bacon, halved crosswise
- low-carb barbecue sauce, (optional)

Directions:

1. Supply your smoker with wood pellets and follow the start-up procedure. Preheat the grill, with the lid closed, to 250° F.

2. Place the ground beef, Italian sausage, egg, cheese, breadcrumbs, Italian seasoning, and salt and pepper in a large bowl. Wet your hands with cold water. Form your hands into claw shapes and combine the ingredients using a light touch.

3. Form the mixture into 24 equal-sized balls. Wrap each with a half strip of bacon and secure the ends with a toothpick.

4. Place the meatballs on the grate and smoke until the bacon has rendered its fat and the internal temperature reaches 160°F (71°C), about 1 to 1½ hours. Brush the meatballs with barbecue sauce (if using) during the last 10 minutes of smoking.

5. Transfer the meatballs to a platter. Let rest for 5 minutes before serving.

Herb Grilled Venison Stew

Servings: 4 - 6
Cooking Time: 210 Minutes

Ingredients:
- 2 Bay Leaves
- 2 Cups Beef Stock
- 3 Carrots, Chopped
- 2 Cups Cauliflower Florets
- ¼ Tsp Cayenne Pepper
- 2 Celery Stalks, Chopped
- 4 Garlic Cloves, Minced
- 1 Tbsp Italian Parsley
- ¼ Tsp Marjoram, Dried
- 2 Tbsp Olive Oil
- 1 Onion, Chopped
- 1 Tsp Pulled Pork Rub
- 1 Cup Red Wine
- 1 Tsp Chopped Rosemary, Fresh
- (To Taste) Salt And Pepper
- 2 Cups Chopped Spinach
- 2 Sweet Potatoes, Diced
- 2 Tbs Tomato Paste
- ½ Cup Tomatoes, Canned And Diced
- 2 Lbs. Venison Stew Meat, Cut Into 1" Cubes
- 1 Cup Zucchini, Largely Diced

Directions:

1. Supply your smoker with wood pellets and follow the start-up procedure. Preheat the grill, with the lid open, to 400° F. If using a gas or charcoal grill, set heat to medium-high heat.

2. Place cast iron Dutch oven directly on grill grates and heat olive oil until shimmering. Add onion, celery, carrot, and garlic and cook, stirring constantly, for about 5-10 minutes or until onion is translucent.

3. Increase heat on the grill to 500° F. Add venison to the pot and cook until browned on all sides. Add the red wine and allow to simmer for 2 minutes.

4. Add tomato paste, beef stock, mushrooms, sweet potato, tomatoes, rosemary, Pulled Pork Rub, sage, marjoram, cayenne, salt, pepper and bay leaves and mix well to combine. Cover pot, reduce temperature to 300° F and let the stew simmer for at least 2.5 to 3 hours.

5. Remove lid and stir in the cauliflower, spinach, and zucchini. Return cover to pot and simmer an additional 15 minutes. Stir in parsley and serve hot.

Bbq Burnt End Sandwich

Servings: 2
Cooking Time: 480 Minutes

Ingredients:
- 1 point cut brisket
- Beef Rub
- 1/2 Cup beef broth
- 1 Cup Texas Spicy BBQ Sauce
- 4 Slices Monterey Jack cheese

- 4 burger buns

Directions:

1. Supply your smoker with wood pellets and follow the start-up procedure. Preheat the grill, with the lid closed, to 250° F.

2. Trim excess fat off brisket point. Season brisket point liberally with Traeger Beef rub.

3. Place brisket point directly on the grill grate. Cook until it reaches an internal temperature of 170°F, approximately 4 to 5 hours. Grill: 250 °F

4. Remove brisket from grill and cut into 1-inch cubes. Add the beef broth to the pan with the cubed brisket. Cover pan with aluminum foil.

5. Place pan in grill and cook for 90 minutes. Grill: 250 °F

6. Remove the foil and add Traeger Texas Spicy BBQ sauce. Stir and put back on the grill, uncovered, for an additional 45 minutes. Remove from grill. Grill: 250 °F

7. Top each bun with the burnt ends, cheese, and additional BBQ sauce. Enjoy!

Bacon-wrapped Elk Steaks

Servings: 2
Cooking Time: 15 Minutes

Ingredients:
- 1/4 Cup red wine
- 2 Tablespoon soy sauce
- 2 Tablespoon honey
- 2 Clove garlic, minced
- 1/4 Teaspoon freshly cracked black pepper
- 2 Tablespoon rosemary, chopped
- 1/8 Teaspoon red pepper flakes
- 2 Pound Elk Steak
- 1/2 Pound thick-cut bacon

Directions:

1. Make the marinade by whisking together the wine, soy sauce, honey, minced garlic cloves, black pepper, chopped rosemary and red pepper flakes. Slowly drizzle in the olive oil while whisking

2. Add the elk steaks into the marinade and marinate overnight, up to a day or two.

3. Supply your smoker with wood pellets and follow the start-up procedure. Preheat the grill, with the lid closed, to 450° F.

4. Take the steaks out of the marinade; wrap each steak with several pieces of bacon and secure with toothpicks.

5. Place the bacon-wrapped elk steaks directly on the grill grate and cook for 10 to 15 minutes, or until it has reached an internal temperature of 135 degrees F. Rotate halfway through for a good caramelized exterior. Enjoy!

Garlic Pigs In A Blanket

Servings: 10
Cooking Time: 15 Minutes

Ingredients:
- 1 Crescent Dough, Can
- 1 Egg
- 1 Tsp Garlic, Minced
- 20 Hot Dog, Mini
- 1/4 Cup Mustard, Dijon
- 1 Tbsp Onion, Diced
- 2 Tbsp Poppy Seeds
- 1 Tsp Salt, Coarse

Directions:

1. Supply your smoker with wood pellets and follow the start-up procedure. Preheat the grill, with the lid closed, to 350° F. Combine the poppy seeds, dried minced onion, minced garlic, and salt in a bowl.

2. Unroll the crescent roll dough, pull apart the triangles and slice each segment into three little triangle pieces. Try to get 3 strips for each roll for the mini hot dogs.

3. After the strips are cut, spread some Dijon mustard on each piece of dough. Roll the dough around mini hot dogs. Lay the pigs in a blanket on a greased cookie sheet. Brush with egg wash and sprinkle with the prepared seasoning.

4. Bake for 15 minutes, serve hot and enjoy!

Baked Venison Tater Tot Casserole

Servings: 4

Cooking Time: 40 Minutes

Ingredients:

- 2 Pound Venison, ground
- 2 Can Peas, canned
- 2 Can cream of mushroom soup
- 28 Ounce frozen tater tots

Directions:

1. Cook ground venison in a medium sauté pan over medium high until browned. Drain off excess fat and set venison aside.

2. In a 13x9 pan, combine venison, peas and soup. Top with tater tots.

3. Supply your smoker with wood pellets and follow the start-up procedure. Preheat the grill, with the lid closed, to 350° F.

4. Place casserole dish directly on grill grate and cook for 30 minutes. Serve hot, enjoy!

Bbq Sweet Pepper Meatloaf

Servings: 8

Cooking Time: 180 Minutes

Ingredients:

- 5 Pound ground beef, 80% lean
- 2 eggs
- 1 Cup plain panko breadcrumbs
- 1 Tablespoon kosher salt
- 1 Tablespoon black pepper
- 2 Tablespoon Rub
- 1 Cup diced sweet red peppers
- 1 Cup green onion, finely chopped
- 1 Cup ketchup

Directions:

1. Thoroughly mix together the ground beef, eggs, plain panko bread crumbs, kosher salt, black pepper, Traeger Rub, red sweet peppers and green onion.

2. Supply your smoker with wood pellets and follow the start-up procedure. Preheat the grill, with the lid closed, to 225° F.

3. Mold the meat mixture into a loaf and season exterior with the Traeger Rub.

4. Place meatloaf directly on the grill grate and cook for 2 hours and 15 minutes. Grill: 225 ˚F

5. Increase the grill temperature to 375°F and cook until an internal temperature of 155°F. Grill: 375 ˚F Probe: 155 ˚F

6. Glaze the meatloaf with ketchup and cook an additional 15 minutes. Grill: 375 ˚F

7. Allow to rest for 15 minutes before slicing. Enjoy!

Rosemary Prime Rib

Servings: 8

Cooking Time: 60 Minutes

Ingredients:

- 1 (8 Lb) Prime Rib Roast
- 4 Tablespoon olive oil
- 4 Tablespoon tri-color peppercorns
- 3 Whole rosemary sprigs
- 3 Whole thyme sprigs
- 1/2 Cup garlic, minced
- 1/2 Cup Jacobsen Salt Co. Cherrywood Smoked Salt
- 4 Tablespoon Olive Oil

Directions:

1. Supply your smoker with wood pellets and follow the start-up procedure. Preheat the grill, with the lid closed, to 450° F.

2. Cut rib loin in half (roast halves separately for more controlled/even cooking.) Sear both halves in olive oil over very high heat until nice dark golden color.

3. Place tricolor peppercorns into a bag, crush pepper corns with a rolling pin.

4. Strip the leaves from the rosemary and thyme springs. Mix salt, crushed peppercorns, rosemary leaves, thyme leaves and garlic.

5. Pour olive oil over the rib loin and pour on the rub mix. Pat slightly to get it to stick to the meat.

6. Roast for 20-30 minutes on HIGH setting, then reduce heat to 300°F and roast for another 30 to 40 minutes or until a meat thermometer registers 125

degrees F for rare/medium rare (roast will continue to cook slightly after removing from the grill). Grill: 300 °F

7. Remove from the Traeger and let rest at least 20 minutes before slicing. Enjoy!

Smoked Prime Rib

Servings: 8
Cooking Time: 180 Minutes

Ingredients:

* 1 (8-10 lb) boneless rib-eye roast, choice grade or higher
* kosher salt
* Meat Church Holy Cow BBQ Rub
* Meat Church Gourmet Garlic and Herb Seasoning
* Worcestershire sauce
* beef stock or water, optional
* 3 Tablespoon butter

Directions:

1. Supply your smoker with wood pellets and follow the start-up procedure. Preheat the grill, with the lid closed, to 275° F.

2. Truss your prime rib, since using the boneless option. This will help keep its shape and cook evenly.

3. Apply a very heavy coat of salt to the entire roast. Let the salt sit for one hour, then wash it off and pat it dry. Apply Meat Church Holy Cow BBQ Rub liberally on all sides of the meat. It's hard to put too much on as we want to form a great bark. Remember, this cut is so big that there will not be much crust in many bites.

4. Next, come back over the entire rib roast with a heavy coat of Meat Church Gourmet Garlic and Herb seasoning. Let these two rubs sit and adhere for 15 to 20 minutes.

5. Place your rib roast on the Traeger. Grill: 275 °F

6. If you'd like, you can baste it every 45 minutes with Worcestershire sauce, beef stock or even water.

7. We are targeting a medium-rare cook in the middle which is 130°F to 135°F. Therefore, continue to cook your rib roast until you reach an internal temperature of 125°F in the middle. Keep in mind the outer edges will be further along. The ends will be closer to medium.

Remove the meat from the grill when that temperature is obtained. Grill: 275 °F Probe: 125 °F

8. Tent the meat with aluminum foil and allow it to rest for at least 10 to 15 minutes. I prefer to top the rib roast with a high-quality butter. Let this butter melt down over your prime rib as it rests. The meat will continue to rise another 5°F to a final temperature of 130°F.

Spiced Lamb Burgers With Tzatziki

Servings: 4
Cooking Time: 10 Minutes

Ingredients:

* 1½lb (680g) ground lamb or a mixture of lamb and beef, well chilled
* 1/3 cup grated red onion
* 1 to 2 garlic cloves, peeled and minced
* 2 tbsp chopped fresh dill or fresh mint
* 1 tsp ground cumin
* ½ tsp ground cinnamon
* ½ tsp crushed red pepper flakes (optional)
* extra virgin olive oil
* coarse salt
* freshly ground black pepper
* for the tzatziki
* 1/3 hothouse cucumber, unpeeled and coarsely grated
* coarse salt
* 1½ cups plain Greek yogurt, drained
* 1 to 2 garlic cloves, peeled
* 1 tbsp freshly squeezed lemon juice or white distilled vinegar
* 1½ tbsp extra virgin olive oil
* 1 tbsp chopped fresh dill or fresh mint

Directions:

1. Supply your smoker with wood pellets and follow the start-up procedure. Preheat the grill, with the lid closed, to 450° F.

2. Make the tzatziki by placing the cucumber in a sieve and lightly sprinkle with salt. After 15 minutes, rinse with cold running water. Drain and then squeeze the cucumber dry with paper towels. Transfer the cucumber to a large bowl. Add the yogurt, garlic, and lemon juice.

Stir to mix. Season with salt to taste. Transfer to a serving bowl. Set aside. Just before serving, drizzle with the olive oil and scatter the fresh dill over the top.

3. In a large bowl, combine the lamb, red onion, garlic, dill, cumin, cinnamon, and red pepper flakes (if using). Wet your hands with cold water and mix thoroughly but gently. (Try not to overhandle the meat.) Form the meat into 4 patties of equal size, each about ¾ inch (2cm) thick. Use your thumbs to make a shallow depression in the top of each burger. Lightly oil the outsides of the burgers with olive oil. Season with salt and pepper.

4. Place the burgers on the grate and grill until the internal temperature reaches 160°F (71°C), about 4 to 5 minutes per side, turning once.

5. Transfer the burgers to a platter. On a separate platter, place thinly sliced red onions, thinly sliced tomatoes, thinly sliced cucumbers, crumbled feta, and Kalamata olives. Serve with the tzatziki and pita bread.

Leftover Tri Tip Sandwich

Servings: 4
Cooking Time: 10 Minutes

Ingredients:
- 4 Slices Cooked And Sliced In Half Bacon
- 4 Cheddar Cheese, Slices
- 4 Eggs
- 4 Split And Toasted English Muffins
- 1 Cup Cook Thinly Sliced Tri-Tip Roast

Directions:
1. Supply your smoker with wood pellets and follow the start-up procedure. Preheat the grill, with the lid closed, to 350° F.

2. In a heavy saucepan, bring water to a bare simmer. Using a spoon, stir the water to form a whirlpool and crack an egg into the water. Poach the egg for 5-7 minutes, or until the white is set but the yolk is still runny. Repeat with the remaining eggs.

3. Assemble the sandwiches: top each sandwich with a slice of cheddar cheese, two halves of a bacon slice, tri-tip, and a poached egg.

4. Grill for 5 minutes, or until everything is warmed through and the cheese is melted. Serve immediately.

Bbq Burnt Ends

Servings: 6
Cooking Time: 540 Minutes

Ingredients:
- 1 (4-6 lb) point cut brisket
- 2 Cup beef broth
- 12 Ounce Texas Spicy BBQ Sauce
- Beef Rub

Directions:
1. Supply your smoker with wood pellets and follow the start-up procedure. Preheat the grill, with the lid closed, to 250° F.

2. Combine broth and sauce in small bowl and set aside. Trim excess fat off brisket point and rub brisket with Traeger Beef Rub.

3. Place brisket on the grill grate and cook until the internal temperature reaches 190°F (approximately 6 to 7 hours). Remove brisket from grill and cut into 1 inch cubes. Grill: 250 °F Probe: 190 °F

4. Toss brisket cubes with sauce mixture in a pan and cover the pan with aluminum foil. Place pan in grill and cook for 1 hour. Grill: 250 °F

5. Stir the burnt ends and cook for an additional hour. Enjoy!

Bbq Elk Shoulder

Servings: 4
Cooking Time: 240 Minutes

Ingredients:
- 6 Pound Elk, shoulder
- 12 Fluid Ounce beef broth
- 1 Whole meat injector
- 1 Tablespoon kosher salt
- 1 Tablespoon ground black pepper

Directions:
1. Take elk roast out of the fridge and allow to sit on counter for 30-60 minutes before cooking.

2. Supply your smoker with wood pellets and follow the start-up procedure. Preheat the grill, with the lid closed, to 225° F.

3. Inject the elk all over with beef broth. Combine salt and pepper and rub over entire roast.

4. Place on preheated grill and cook for 4 to 5 hours or until an instant read thermometer inserted in the thickest part of the meat registers 145°F. Remove from grill and allow to rest for 30 minutes before slicing. Grill: 225°F Probe: 145°F

5. Serve with baked beans, potato salad, coleslaw, white bread, Traeger BBQ sauce or your favorite BBQ sides and sauces. Enjoy!

Easy Tri Tip Shepherd's Pie

Servings: 4
Cooking Time: 30 Minutes

Ingredients:
- 1 Cup Beef Broth
- 2 Tablespoons Unsalted Butter
- 2 Tablespoons Chophouse Steak Seasoning
- 2 Tablespoons Flour
- 1 Cup Mashed Potatoes, Prepared
- 2 Cups Tri-Tip, Diced
- 2 Cups Mixed Frozen Vegetables, Thawed

Directions:
1. Supply your smoker with wood pellets and follow the start-up procedure. Preheat the grill, with the lid closed, to 350° F.

2. In the sauce pan, add the butter and flour over medium low heat. Cook the flour and butter for about 1 minute, or until the flour smells toasty. Slowly add in the beef broth, whisking constantly. Cook for 5 minutes, or until the gravy is thick, and then add the Chophouse Steak. Set aside.

3. Toss the vegetables and tri-tip with the gravy and divide equally into the ramekins. Top the ramekins with mashed potatoes and grill the shepherd's pies for 10-15 minutes, or until warm all the way through and the filling is bubbling. Remove from the grill and serve immediately.

Grilled Bison Rib Eye Kabobs

Servings: 4
Cooking Time: 20 Minutes

Ingredients:
- 3 Tablespoon Prime Rib Rub
- 3 Tablespoon Rosemary, finely chopped
- 2 Teaspoon salt
- 2 Tablespoon pepper
- 4 Clove garlic, minced
- 3 Pound Bison, Rib Eye, Trimmed and Cut into 1.25" Cubes

Directions:
1. In a small bowl, mix together Traeger Prime Rib Rub, rosemary, garlic, black pepper, and salt. Place bison cubes in a large Ziploc bag and pour in marinade.

2. Toss bison in marinade to coat the meat well and transfer to the refrigerator for 45 minutes to an hour. Remove bison from marinade draining any excess liquid that has gathered.

3. Thread bison pieces on a skewer and set aside.

4. Supply your smoker with wood pellets and follow the start-up procedure. Preheat the grill, with the lid closed, to 375° F.

5. Place kabobs directly on the grill grate and cook for 8-10 minutes per side or until internal temperature reaches 135°F for medium-rare. Grill: 375°F Probe: 135°F

6. Remove from grill and let rest 5 minutes before serving. Finish with additional chopped herbs if desired. Enjoy

Smoked Moink Burger By Scott Thomas

Servings: 4
Cooking Time: 60 Minutes

Ingredients:
- 1 Pound Ground Sirloin
- 1/2 Pound ground pork
- 1/4 Cup Worcestershire sauce
- 1 Teaspoon garlic, minced
- salt
- black pepper

Directions:
1. Combine all the ingredients in a bowl and mix together. Form into six patties.

2. Supply your smoker with wood pellets and follow the start-up procedure. Preheat the grill, with the lid closed, to 350° F.

3. Cook until the burgers reach an internal temperature of 160 degrees F (about an hour depending on the size of the patties and the heat of the grill).

4. Top with your favorite cheese to melt a few minutes before burgers are done and serve with your favorite toppings.

Chorizo Cheese Stuffed Burgers

Servings: 2
Cooking Time: 45 Minutes

Ingredients:

- 2 Pound ground beef, 80% lean
- 4 Ounce Prime Rib Rub
- 12 Ounce Chorizo
- 2 Slices cheddar cheese
- 4 Whole Brioche Bun
- Tomatoes, sliced
- red onion, sliced
- lettuce, sliced

Directions:

1. Mix 2 lb of 80/20 ground beef in mixing bowl with Traeger Prime Rib Rub.

2. Divide the ground beef into eight 1/4 lb patties. Make one patty the base, lay down 1/4 of a cheese slice, add 3 oz. of chorizo and top with another 1/4 cheese slice. Apply another patty on top and pinch the ends all the way around the burger to seal together the two patties.

3. Repeat until all 4 patties are done.

4. Supply your smoker with wood pellets and follow the start-up procedure. Preheat the grill, with the lid closed, to 325° F.

5. Place burgers on the Traeger for 15 minutes on each side. If desired, top each burger with slice of Cheddar cheese, let melt. Remove from Traeger and let rest for 10 minutes tented with foil.

6. While burgers are resting, brush the brioche buns with melted better and toast for 30-45 seconds on the grill.

7. Remove buns from grill and assemble burger with toppings. Enjoy!

Reverse-seared Elk Tenderloin With Green Peppercorn Sauce

Servings: 8
Cooking Time: 66 Minutes

Ingredients:

- 1 whole elk tenderloin, about 2½lb (1.2kg)
- extra virgin olive oil
- coarse salt
- fresh coarsely ground black pepper
- granulated garlic
- for the sauce
- 3 tbsp unsalted butter, divided
- 2 large shallots, peeled and finely diced
- 2 cups low-salt beef stock
- ½ cup Cognac or brandy
- 1 cup heavy whipping cream
- 1 tbsp Dijon mustard
- ¼ brined green peppercorns, drained
- 2 tbsp fresh coarsely ground dried green peppercorns
- coarse salt
- freshly ground black pepper

Directions:

1. Supply your smoker with wood pellets and follow the start-up procedure. Preheat the grill, with the lid closed, to 225° F.

2. Tie the tenderloin at 2-inch (5cm) intervals with butcher's twine. Tuck the tail under the thicker portion of the tenderloin and secure with twine. Trim any loose strings close to the knots. Place the tenderloin on a rimmed sheet pan and use your hands to coat all the sides with olive oil. Generously season with salt and pepper and granulated garlic.

3. In a skillet on the stovetop over medium heat, make the sauce by melting 2 tablespoons of butter. Add the shallots and cook until softened but not browned, about 2 to 3 minutes. Add the beef stock and raise the heat to medium high. Bring the mixture to a boil and reduce to ½ cup, about 10 minutes. Add the Cognac and cream and then whisk in the mustard.

4.   Crush some of the brined peppercorns with the side of a knife. Stir all the brined and dried peppercorns into the sauce. Cook until the sauce is thick enough to coat a spoon, about 3 minutes. Whisk in the remaining 1 tablespoon of butter. Season with salt and pepper to taste. Keep warm.

5.   Place the tenderloin on the grate at an angle to the bars. Smoke until the internal temperature in the thickest part of the meat reaches 110 to 115°F (43 to 46°C), about 1 hour. Transfer the tenderloin to a rimmed sheet pan lined with aluminum foil.

6.   Raise the temperature to 500°F (260°C). Place the tenderloin on the grate at an angle to the bars. Sear until the internal temperature reaches 135°F (57°C), about 2 to 3 minutes per side.

7.   Transfer the meat to a cutting board. Remove the butcher's twine and slice the tenderloin into steaks. Place the slices on a platter. Rewarm and rewhisk the sauce if necessary. Spoon over the steaks before serving.

Blackened Saskatchewan Tomahawk Steaks

Servings: 4
Cooking Time: 45 Minutes

Ingredients:
*   2 Whole tomahawk steaks
*   4 Tablespoon Blackened Saskatchewan Rub
*   2 Tablespoon butter

Directions:
1.   Supply your smoker with wood pellets and follow the start-up procedure. Preheat the grill, with the lid closed, to 225° F.

2.   Cover cold steaks in the Blackened Saskatchewan Rub. Let rest 10 minutes for the seasoning to adhere.

3.   Place steaks directly on grill grates and smoke for about 40 minutes, or until an internal temp reaches 119°F. Remove from grill and wrap tightly in foil to rest.

4.   Turn up temperature on the grill to 400°F - with a cast iron pan or griddle inside. When the pan is hot, add 2 Tbsp of butter and sear the first steak, about 2-4 minutes per side, or until the internal temperature reads 125°F - 130°F. Repeat with the other Tomahawk. Rest, slice, serve. Enjoy!

Flavour Smoked Corned Beef Brisket Hash

Servings: 4
Cooking Time: 195 Minutes

Ingredients:
*   6 slices, chopped bacon
*   1 tsp black pepper
*   2 cups chicken stock
*   1, 2 lb. corned beef brisket
*   2 tbsp Italian parsley
*   1 ½ tsp hickory bacon rub
*   1, chopped red bell pepper
*   1 tsp thyme, fresh, chopped
*   1, chopped yellow onion
*   1 ½ lbs yukon gold potatoes

Directions:
1.   Remove corned beef brisket from packaging, rinse under cold water, and pat dry with paper towel.

2.   Season brisket with included seasoning packet and coarse black pepper, then rest for 30 minutes.

3.   Supply your smoker with wood pellets and follow the start-up procedure. Preheat the grill, with the lid closed, to 225° F. If using a gas or charcoal grill, set it up for low indirect heat.

4.   Lay brisket directly on the grill grate and smoke for 2 ½ to 3 hours or until the internal temperature reaches 165°F.

5.   Once this temperature is achieved, place the brisket in a 9 x 13 metal pan with potatoes and chicken stock.

6.   Cover with foil and cook until brisket reaches an internal temperature of 202°F.

7.   Remove brisket from grill and refrigerate overnight or until brisket and potatoes have fully cooled.

8.   When ready to cook, peel and dice potatoes then chop up 1 lb. of brisket, reserving the remainder for future use.

9.   Place a cast-iron skillet on the pellet grill and preheat to 400°F.

10. Once skillet is heated, add bacon and sauté for 8 to 10 minutes, until brown.

11. Remove with slotted spoon and place on paper towel-lined tray.

12. Add onion and red bell pepper to skillet with rendered bacon fat and sauté for 3 minutes, then add cooked brisket.

13. Add Hickory Bacon Rub, parsley and thyme and sauté another 3 minutes.

14. Add diced potatoes. Gently stir to incorporate and serve hot.

Bbq Beef Short Ribs

Servings: 8
Cooking Time: 600 Minutes

Ingredients:

- 4 (4 bone) beef short rib racks
- 1/2 Cup Beef Rub
- 1 Cup apple juice

Directions:

1. If your butcher has not already done so, remove the thin papery membrane from the bone-side of the ribs by working the tip of a butter knife underneath the membrane over a middle bone. Use paper towels to get a firm grip, then tear the membrane off.

2. Season both sides of ribs with Traeger Beef Rub.

3. Supply your smoker with wood pellets and follow the start-up procedure. Preheat the grill, with the lid closed, to 225° F.

4. Arrange the ribs on the grill grate, bone-side down. Grill: 225 °F

5. Cook for 8 to 10 hours, spritzing or mopping with apple juice every 60 minutes until internal temperature reaches 205°F. Grill: 225 °F Probe: 205 °F

6. Slice between ribs and serve immediately. Enjoy!

Chuck Roast Burnt Ends

Servings: 4
Cooking Time: 480 Minutes

Ingredients:

- 1 chuck roast, about 3 to 4lb (1.4 to 1.8kg)
- 2 tbsp Worcestershire sauce, plus more
- coarse salt, plus more
- freshly ground black pepper, plus more
- granulated garlic, plus more
- 1 cup low-carb barbecue sauce
- ¼ cup sugar-free dark-colored soda, plus more

Directions:

1. Supply your smoker with wood pellets and follow the start-up procedure. Preheat the grill, with the lid closed, to 250° F.

2. Place the roast on a rimmed sheet pan and brush with the Worcestershire sauce. Lightly season with salt, pepper, and granulated garlic. Place the roast on the grate and smoke until the internal temperature reaches 170°F (77°C), about 5 to 6 hours.

3. Transfer the roast to a cutting board and let rest for 10 minutes. (Leave the grill going.) Use a sharp knife to slice the meat into bite-size cubes, trimming any excess fat if necessary. Place the meat in an aluminum foil roasting pan. Lightly season with more salt, pepper, and granulated garlic and toss the cubes with your hands to distribute the seasonings. Add the barbecue sauce and soda. Toss again to coat.

4. Place the pan on the grate and smoke until the meat is tender and somewhat sticky with sauce, about 1 to 2 hours, stirring occasionally. (Don't let the sauce scorch.) Add another splash of soda if needed.

5. Remove the pan from the grill and stir the meat again before serving.

Carrot Elk Burgers

Servings: 4
Cooking Time: 15 Minutes

Ingredients:

- To Taste, Blackened Sriracha Rub Seasoning
- 1/2 Tbsp Butter
- To Taste, Cilantro Mayonnaise
- 4 Pieces Green Leaf Lettuce
- 2 Lbs Ground Elk
- 4 Hamburger Buns
- 1 Jalepeno, Sliced
- 4 Pickled Carrots

Directions:

1. Place ground elk in a mixing bowl and season with Blackened Sriracha. Divide into 4 portions, then form into large patties.

2. Supply your smoker with wood pellets and follow the start-up procedure. Preheat the grill, with the lid open, to medium heat. If using a gas or charcoal grill, set it up for medium heat and use a cast iron skillet.

3. Place butter on the left side of the griddle and let melt. Place buns on the left side (on melted butter), and burger patties on the right side.

4. Toast the buns, then turn off the burner, keeping the buns in place to keep warm. Cook the burgers 2 to 3 minutes per side, then remove from the griddle and allow to rest for 5 minutes.

5. Assemble burger: bottom bun, cilantro mayonnaise, lettuce, burger, pickled carrots, sliced jalapeño, cilantro mayonnaise on top bun.

Smoked Beer Corned Beef

Servings: 6
Cooking Time: 240 Minutes

Ingredients:
- 6 lb corned beef brisket raw
- 2 tbsp black pepper
- 8 oz light beer

Directions:

1. Supply your smoker with wood pellets and follow the start-up procedure. Preheat the grill, with the lid closed, to 275 °F.

2. Cut open packaging of corned beef and drain off liquid. Be sure to grab the spice packet included with the brisket. Gently rinse off corned beef and then pat dry with a paper towel.

3. Open the spice packet included with your corned beef and sprinkle contents over the brisket, then sprinkle a light dusting of black pepper according to your preference.

4. Once pellet grill has reached temperature, insert probes into corned beef brisket pieces. If you only have a single probe, insert that probe in the center of the smallest piece because it will cook the fastest.

5. Smoke for 3 to 4 hours until corned beef reaches an internal temperature of 175 degrees F. Next transfer briskets to an aluminum pan and pour just enough beer in to cover the bottom of the pan. Cover with foil leaving one corner open to let out steam.

6. Continue cooking for another 2-3 hours until internal temperature reaches about 205 degrees F. Use an instant read thermometer and poke different parts of the brisket checking for tenderness. If probe goes into the meat with very little tension than it is done. If not, continue cooking until it becomes tender.

7. Once meat is tender and fully cooked, remove pan from pellet grill and let the corned beef rest for about 30 minutes still covered with one corner open to prevent overcooking.

8. Slice corned beef into 1/8 inch slices cutting against the grains of the brisket. If brisket crumbles make slices a little thicker.

Pulled Beef

Servings: 5-8
Cooking Time: 840 Minutes

Ingredients:
- 1 (4-pound) top round roast
- 2 tablespoons yellow mustard
- 1 batch Espresso Brisket Rub
- ½ cup beef broth

Directions:

1. Supply your smoker with wood pellets and follow the start-up procedure. Preheat the grill, with the lid closed, to 225°F.

2. Coat the top round roast all over with mustard and season it with the rub. Using your hands, work the rub into the meat.

3. Place the roast directly on the grill grate and smoke until its internal temperature reaches 160°F and a dark bark has formed.

4. Pull the roast from the grill and place it on enough aluminum foil to wrap it completely.

5. Increase the grill's temperature to 350°F.

6. Fold in three sides of the foil around the roast and add the beef broth. Fold in the last side, completely

enclosing the roast and liquid. Return the wrapped roast to the grill and cook until its internal temperature reaches 195°F.

7.   Pull the roast from the grill and place it in a cooler. Cover the cooler and let the roast rest for 1 or 2 hours.

8.   Remove the roast from the cooler and unwrap it. Pull apart the beef using just your fingers. Serve immediately.

Korean Style Bbq Prime Ribs

Servings: 5
Cooking Time: 480 Minutes

Ingredients:

- 3 lbs beef short ribs
- 2 tbsp sugar
- 3/4 cup water
- 1 tbsp ground black pepper
- 3 tbsp white vinegar
- 2 tbsp sesame oil
- 3 tbsp soy sauce
- 6 cloves garlic, minced
- 1/3 cup light brown sugar
- 1/2 yellow onion, finely chopped

Directions:

1.   Combine soy sauce, water, and vinegar in a bowl. Mix and whisk in brown sugar, white sugar, pepper, sesame oil, garlic, and onion. Whisk until the sugars have completely dissolved

2.   Pour marinade into large bowl or baking pan with high sides. Dunk the short ribs in the marinade, coating completely. Cover marinaded short ribs with plastic wrap and refrigerate for 6 to 12 hours3. Preheat pellet grill to 225°F.

3.   Remove plastic wrap from ribs and pull ribs out of marinade. Shake off any excess marinade and dispose of the contents left in the bowl.

4.   Place ribs on grill and cook for about 6-8 hours, until ribs reach an internal temperature of 203°F. Measure using a probe meat thermometer

5.   Once ribs reach temperature, remove from grill and allow to rest for about 20 minutes. Slice, serve, and enjoy!

Santa Maria Tri-tip With Pico De Gallo

Servings: 4
Cooking Time: 68 Minutes

Ingredients:

- 1 tri-tip roast, about 2 to 2½lb (1 to 1.2kg)
- coarse salt
- freshly ground black pepper
- granulated garlic or garlic powder
- for the pico de gallo
- 8 Roma tomatoes, decored, deseeded, and diced
- 1 white onion, peeled and diced
- 1 serrano pepper, destemmed, deseeded, and minced, plus more
- 1 garlic clove, peeled and minced
- juice of 1 lime
- ½ cup loosely packed cilantro leaves, chopped
- 1 tsp coarse salt

Directions:

1.   In a medium bowl, make the pico de gallo by combining the tomatoes, onion, serrano, garlic, lime juice, and cilantro. Stir gently with a rubber spatula and season with salt to taste. Cover and refrigerate for 2 hours.

2.   Approximately 45 minutes before you're ready to cook, season the roast on all sides with salt and pepper and granulated garlic.

3.   Supply your smoker with wood pellets and follow the start-up procedure. Preheat the grill, with the lid closed, to 180° F.

4.   Place the roast on the grate and smoke until the internal temperature in the thickest part of the roast reaches 115°F (46°C), about 45 minutes to 1 hour. Transfer the roast to a plate.

5.   Raise the temperature to 450°F (232°C). Place the roast on the grate and sear until the internal temperature in the thickest part of the roast reaches 130 to 135°F (54 to 57°C), about 3 to 4 minutes per side. For best results, don't cook beyond medium rare. (The thinner tail should satisfy any diner who prefers beef to be more well done.)

6.   Remove the roast from the grill and thinly slice on a sharp diagonal against the grain. Serve with the pico de gallo.

Lime Carne Asada Tacos

Servings: 4

Cooking Time: 10 Minutes

Ingredients:

- 1/2 Tsp Black Pepper
- 1 Tsp Garlic Powder
- 2 Lime, Juiced
- 1 Tsp Salt
- 1 1/2 Lbs Steak, Skirt
- 8 Tortilla

Directions:

1. Supply your smoker with wood pellets and follow the start-up procedure. Preheat the grill, with the lid closed, to 400° F. Place the steaks on the grill, and grill them for 4-8 minutes, then flip the steaks and grill for an additional 4-8 minutes.

2. Remove steaks from the grill, loosely cover them with foil, and let them sit for 5-10 minutes. Next chop the steaks into pieces and serve with tortillas and any desired toppings.

Smoked Longhorn Brisket

Servings: 8

Cooking Time: 420 Minutes

Ingredients:

- 1 (12-14 lb) whole packer brisket, trimmed
- 1/4 Cup Prime Rib Rub
- 2 Tablespoon coffee grounds

Directions:

1. Supply your smoker with wood pellets and follow the start-up procedure. Preheat the grill, with the lid closed, to 250° F.

2. Rub brisket with Traeger Prime Rib Rub and coffee grounds.

3. Place brisket on the grill grate fat-side down and smoke until it reaches an internal temperature of 160°F, this should take about 4 to 5 hours. Grill: 250 °F Probe: 160 °F

4. Remove brisket from grill and double wrap in foil. Return wrapped brisket to grill and cook until brisket reaches an internal temperature of 204°F, about 2-1/2 to 3 hours. Grill: 250 °F Probe: 204 °F

5. Once finished, remove from grill, unwrap and let rest for 15 minutes. Slice against the grain and serve. Enjoy!

Savory Cheese Steak Rolls With Puff Pastry

Servings: 4

Cooking Time: 25 Minutes

Ingredients:

- 4 oz american or jack cheese, shredded, divided
- 2 tbsp butter
- to taste, chop house steak rub
- to taste, chop house steak rub (for sauce)
- 3 oz cream cheese
- 1 egg, beaten
- 1 tbsp flour
- 1 tbsp flour (for sauce)
- 1 puff pastry sheet, thawed
- 1 lb sandwich steak, shaved/sliced thin
- 1 tbsp vegetable oil
- 1 cup yellow onion, sliced thin
- 2/3 cup milk

Directions:

1. Supply your smoker with wood pellets and follow the start-up procedure. Preheat the grill, with the lid closed, to 400° F. If using a gas or charcoal grill, set it up for medium-high heat. Preheat the griddle to medium flame.

2. Add oil to the griddle, then cook steak for 2 to 3 minutes, turning with a spatula. Add onions, season with Chop House and cook another minute to soften. Transfer steak and onions to a bowl, then set aside to cool.

3. Meanwhile, melt butter in a sauté pan on the griddle. Stir in flour, then cook for 1 minute. Whisk in milk, then add cream cheese, and 2 ounces of shredded cheese. Whisk until smooth, then remove from the griddle to cool slightly. Use half of the sauce in the pastry, and the other half for serving/dipping once baked.

4.   Flour your rolling surface, then set the pastry sheet on top of the flour. Roll the pastry sheet into a 10 to 12 inch square, then cut into 4 squares.

5.   Spoon cheese sauce on each pastry square, then divide the steak and onion mixture among the pastries. Top each with remaining shredded cheese, brush sides with beaten egg, then fold pastries over, corner to corner. Secure the seams by pressing down with a fork. Brush the top with beaten egg, then place on a sheet tray.

6.   Place the sheet tray on the grill and bake for 18 to 20 minutes, until golden. Remove from the grill, cool for 5 minutes, then cut in half and serve warm with cheese sauce.

Savory Teriyaki Smoked Steak Bites

Servings: 2
Cooking Time: 90 Minutes

Ingredients:
- Sirloin steak
- Teriyaki sauce
- Light brown sugar
- Garlic powder
- Garlic salt
- Soy sauce
- Apple cider vinegar
- Pepper

Directions:
1.   Mix all ingredients for the marinade.
2.   Trim steak and cut into 2 inches pieces.
3.   Place in a zip lock bag and pour marinade over the steak. Squeeze as much air out as possible and tightly seal the bag.
4.   Freeze the steak for at least 8 hours or overnight.
5.   Supply your smoker with wood pellets and follow the start-up procedure. Preheat the grill, with the lid closed, to 225 °F.
6.   Place the steak bites directly on the rack. Discard remaining marinade.
7.   Smoke for 1 hour and 30 minutes or until the internal temp is 135-140 degrees F.

Asian Steak Skewers

Servings: 6
Cooking Time: 80 Minutes

Ingredients:
- 1 1/2 lbs top sirloin steak
- 6 garlic cloves, minced
- 1 red onion
- 1/3 cup sugar
- 3/4 cup soy sauce
- 1 tbsp ground ginger
- 1/4 cup sesame oil
- 3 tbsp sesame seeds
- 1/4 cup vegetable oil
- Bamboo skewers

Directions:
1.   Cut sirloin steak into cubes, about 1 inch.
2.   Cut red onion into chunks similar in size to the sirloin steak cubes.
3.   In a bowl, combine and whisk soy sauce, sesame oil, vegetable oil, minced garlic, sugar, ginger, and sesame seeds.
4.   Add steak to sauce bowl and toss to coat until steak is covered in the sauce.
5.   Marinate for at least 1 hour in a refrigerator (if you are in a rush it's ok to skip this part, but you'll sacrifice a little bit of flavor).
6.   Preheat pellet grill to 350°F.
7.   Thread marinated beef and red onion pieces onto bamboo skewers.
8.   Grill the skewers, turning after about 4 minutes. Cook for 8 minutes total or until meat reaches your desired doneness.

Mesquite Smoked Brisket

Servings: 8-12
Cooking Time: 720 Minutes

Ingredients:
- 1 (12-pound) full packer brisket
- 2 tablespoons yellow mustard (you can also use soy sauce)
- Salt
- Freshly ground black pepper

Directions:

1. Supply your smoker with wood pellets and follow the start-up procedure. Preheat the grill, with the lid closed, to 225°F.

2. Using a boning knife, carefully remove all but about ½ inch of the large layer of fat covering one side of your brisket.

3. Coat the brisket all over with mustard and season it with salt and pepper.

4. Place the brisket directly on the grill grate and smoke until its internal temperature reaches 160°F and the brisket has formed a dark bark.

5. Pull the brisket from the grill and wrap it completely in aluminum foil or butcher paper.

6. Increase the grill's temperature to 350°F and return the wrapped brisket to it. Continue to cook until its internal temperature reaches 190°F.

7. Transfer the wrapped brisket to a cooler, cover the cooler, and let the brisket rest for 1 or 2 hours.

8. Remove the brisket from the cooler and unwrap it.

9. Separate the brisket point from the flat by cutting along the fat layer, and slice the flat. The point can be saved for burnt ends (see Sweet Heat Burnt Ends), or sliced and served as well.

Zucchini Onion Meatloaf

Servings: 8
Cooking Time: 180 Minutes

Ingredients:

- 3 Pounds Ground Beef
- 1 Pound Italian Sausage
- 1/2 Cup Diced Onion
- 1/2 Cup Diced Green Pepper
- 1 Cup Shredded Fresh Zucchini
- 1 Egg
- 3/4 Cup Ketchup
- 1 Sleeve Crackers, Crushed (Buttery Or Saltine)
- 4 Slices Bread, Cubed
- 1/3 Cup Grated Parmesan Cheese
- 1/4 Teaspoon Each Salt and Pepper to Taste
- Garnish:
- Onion Slices, For Eyes

- 1 Pound Thick Sliced Bacon, for Bandages
- Green Pepper Slices, Nose and Teeth
- Sweet Ketchup Sauce:
- 2 Cups Ketchup
- 1/3 Cup Brown Sugar
- 1 Tablespoon Worcestershire Sauce
- 1/2 Teaspoon Onion Powder
- 1/2 Teaspoon Garlic Powder

Directions:

1. Supply your smoker with wood pellets and follow the start-up procedure. Preheat the grill, with the lid closed, to 350 °F.

2. In a large bowl mix together all ingredients.

3. Place mixture into a 13 x 9 inch baking dish and shape into a skull.

4. Place onion slices on meatloaf where the eyes should beand green pepper slices for teeth.

5. Randomly place bacon slices on meatloaf skull to look like bandages.

6. Bake meatloaf in your grill, covered with foil for 2 hours (drain excess grease if necessary).

7. Remove foil, and continue baking for another hour (drain excess grease if necessary).

8. Meanwhile, in a small saucepan, stir together ketchup, brown sugar, Worcestershire sauce, onion powder,and garlic powder. Put in the grill grate and simmer on low until warm. Baste meatloaf with sauce every 15 minutes during last hour of baking.

9. Serve with remaining sauce.

Smoked Garlic Meatloaf

Servings: 8
Cooking Time: 180 Minutes

Ingredients:

- 2 Tsp Apple Cider Vinegar
- 2 Lbs Beef, Ground
- 1/2 Tsp Chipotle Pepper Flakes
- 3 Cups Crushed Chips Corn Tortillas
- 2 Grated Garlic, Cloves
- 2/3 Cup Ketchup
- 1 Small Grated Onion, Chopped
- 4 Oz Into Sticks Pepper Jack Cheese, Sliced

- 2 Tbsp Competition Smoked Rub
- 1 Lbs Pork, Ground
- 1/4 Cup Tomato Paste
- 1 Tsp Worcestershire Sauce

Directions:

1. Supply your smoker with wood pellets and follow the start-up procedure. Preheat the grill, with the lid closed, to 250° F.

2. First make the glaze: in a bowl, combine the ketchup, tomato paste, vinegar, Worcestershire, chipotle flakes and Competition Smoked Seasoning. Whisk well to combine and set aside.

3. In a large bowl, mix together the crushed corn chips, eggs, onion and garlic. Add 2/3rds of the glaze to this mixture, reserving the rest for glazing the meatloaf. Mix well to combine and allow to sit until the corn chips have hydrated.

4. Add the ground beef and pork to the corn chip mixture and mix until everything is well distributed.

5. Form the meatloaf into a log and push the sticks of pepper jack cheese into the center of the meatloaf and cover with the meat mixture. Loosely wrap in tin foil and poke holes in the foil with a knife to allow smoke to penetrate.

6. Grill for 1 ½ hours covered, then remove the top half of the tin foil, glaze with reserved glaze, and grill for another 1 ½ hours or until the internal temperature is 165F.

Reverse Grilled Potato Bacon Wrapped Steaks

Servings: 2
Cooking Time: 60 Minutes

Ingredients:
- 1 Bunch Asparagus
- 4 Bacon, Strip
- BBQ Sauce
- 2 Tbsp Olive Oil
- 1 Bag Potato, Baby
- 2 - 1" Thick Steak, Bone-In Ribeye

Directions:

1. Supply your smoker with wood pellets and follow the start-up procedure. Preheat the grill, with the lid open, to 250° F.

2. Wrap two pieces of bacon around each steak. Place on the grates of your preheated Grill. You'll want to cook the steaks until the internal temperature reaches 130°F (for medium-rare). Follow these internal temperatures if you'd like to cook your steak more/less done:

3. Rare: 125°F

4. Medium Rare: 130°F

5. Medium: 140°F

6. Well Done: 160°F

7. If you're cooking your steaks medium rare, it will take around 45 minutes. Put your baby potatoes in a cast iron pan, drizzle with oil and place on grill with the steaks. When your steaks reach the desired internal temperature, remove steaks from the grill and let them rest for 15 minutes. In the meantime, open up your Flame Broiler Plate and crank up the grill to HIGH, keeping your potatoes on the grill. Add the asparagus to the top of the potatoes and cook. When the grill is preheated to HIGH, sear each side of the steak for about 1 minute each. Serve immediately with or without BBQ Sauce.

Delicious Barbecue Beef Brisket

Servings: 12
Cooking Time: 480 Minutes

Ingredients:
- 1 Beef Soup, Campbells Can
- 1 - 12 To 14 Lb Packer Beef, Brisket

Directions:

1. The night before you plan on cooking the brisket, trim the surface fat off the brisket with your sharp boning knife. Trim to leave about 1/8 to ¼ in fat.

2. Place the brisket in an unscented trash bag or on a sheet pan fat side up and season the meat side liberally with your favorite Rub. Let rest on the counter for 30 minutes until the rub is all soaked up. Flip the brisket over and season the fat side liberally. Cover or wrap up the brisket and put in the fridge overnight.

3. Prep your Grill by cleaning the grates, grease tray and firepot is clean. Supply your smoker with wood pellets and follow the start-up procedure. Preheat the grill, with the lid closed, to 250° F.

4. When grill has settled to 250°F place brisket in center of grill fat side down and cook for 4 hours.

5. After 4 hours, insert the meat probe into the fat seam between the point and flat so the end of the meat probe is in the center of the fat seam and continue to cook for about 2 more hours.

6. Prep aluminum foil to wrap the brisket in by tearing off 4 sheets of foil at least twice as large as the brisket. Plus one more piece about the same size as the brisket.

7. When the meat thermometer reads 150°F to 160°F wrap the brisket in foil by placing the brisket fat side down on 2 sheets of foil. The cover with the other 2 sheets of foil and tightly roll/fold 3 sides up to seal – leaving one side open. Leave the meat probe in place in the brisket and lay the probe wire between the bottom and top foil sheets. Roll/fold the meat probe wire between the foil sheets as you are closing the foil. Dump the can of Campbell's Beef Consume into the foil through the open end and roll/fold that end closed.

8. Place the small foil sheet on the grill grate and place the foil-wrapped brisket on the small foil sheet on the grate. The small foil sheet will prevent the foil from sticking to the grate to prevent the foil from ripping and losing the foil juice that you can use later.

9. Continue to cook until the meat thermometer reads 200°F. Then unwrap one or two sides of the foil being careful not to lose any of the liquid in the foil. Insert a dinner fork into the flat portion of the brisket – if it goes in and out like a hot knife through butter it is done, if it has very much resistance, seal the sides of the foil and place back in grill and cook until the meat thermometer reads 205°F and test for tenderness again.

10. When the brisket is done, remove from grill, wrap in a clean towel and place in a small clean cooler to rest for at least 2 hours.

11. When ready to slice, remove brisket from foil. Separate the point end from the flat end by running your slicing knife down the fat seam. Slice the brisket across the grain into slices just thick enough to hold together.

12. Cube the point section into ½ in sq cubes by slicing ½ in slices across the grain first and then ½ in slices with the grain.

13. Place all slices and cubes into a pan and pour some of the liquid from the foil over the brisket.

14. Serve with your favorite BBQ Sauce on the side.

Flavour Bbq Brisket Burnt Ends

Servings: 6-8
Cooking Time: 420 Minutes

Ingredients:
- 1 Brisket Point
- Georgia Style BBQ Sauce (Mustard Base)
- As Needed Chop House Steak Rub

Directions:
1. Supply your smoker with wood pellets and follow the start-up procedure. Preheat the grill, with the lid closed, to 250° F.

2. Place your brisket on the grates, cook for 6 to 7 hours or until the internal temperature reaches 190°F

3. Remove from the grill and cut into 1-inch cubes. Toss brisket cubes with seasoning and your favorite BBQ sauce into a pan.

4. Place the pan in the grill for 2 hours, stirring half-way through.

3-2-1 Bbq Beef Cheeks

Servings: 8
Cooking Time: 480 Minutes

Ingredients:
- 2 (2 lb) beef cheeks, silverskin trimmed
- Beef Rub
- 1/4 Cup liquid of choice (beef stock, dark beer, etc.)
- 2 Tablespoon honey, brown sugar or other sweetener

Directions:
1. Make sure the beef cheeks are trimmed of all silverskin. Season liberally with Traeger Beef rub.

2. Supply your smoker with wood pellets and follow the start-up procedure. Preheat the grill, with the lid closed, to 180° F.

3. Place beef cheeks directly on the grill grate and cook until they reach an internal temperature of 165°F, about

3 hours. Remove from grill and place the cheeks in a small rimmed baking dish. Grill: 180 °F Probe: 165 °F

4.   Increase grill temperature to 225°F.

5.   In a small bowl, combine liquid and sweetener and stir until sweetener is dissolved. Pour mixture into the baking dish and return the cheeks to the grill to cook for an additional two hours. Grill: 225 °F

6.   Remove cheeks from the grill and cover with foil. Return to the grill to cook for an additional hour or until the internal temperature reaches 205°F. Grill: 225 °F Probe: 205 °F

7.   Remove from the grill and allow the steam to escape. Wrap with foil again and let rest for 30 minutes before shredding or slicing. Enjoy!

Smoked Spiced Rump Roast

Servings: 8
Cooking Time: 60 Minutes

Ingredients:

- 3 pounds rump roast (or bottom round roast)
- 1 ½ teaspoons coarse ground pepper
- 1 teaspoon kosher salt
- ¼ teaspoon garlic powder
- ¼ teaspoon onion powder

Directions:

1.   Supply your smoker with wood pellets and follow the start-up procedure. Preheat the grill, with the lid closed, to 250 °F.

2.   Combine the seasonings in a small bowl and coat the rump roast evenly with seasonings on all sides.

3.   Place roast into the smoker.

4.   Cook for 1 hour and 45 minutes, or until the internal temperature reaches 135 degrees (or your desired level of doneness; rare: 135 °F, medium rare: 145 °F, medium: 155 °F, well done: 170 °F)

5.   Remove rump roast from the smoker and let it rest for 10 minutesbefore slicing.

6.   Slice thinly and serve.

Savory Whiskey Grilled Elk Steaks

Servings: 4
Cooking Time: 10 Minutes

Ingredients:

- ¼ Cup Brown Sugar
- 1 Tbsp Chop House Steak Seasoning
- 1 Tbsp Coarse Ground Pepper
- 4 Elk Steaks
- ½ Cup Olive Oil
- ½ Cup Soy Sauce
- ½ Cup Whiskey, Such As Jack Daniel'S
- ¼ Cup Yellow Mustard

Directions:

1.   In a large mixing bowl, add the whiskey, soy sauce, olive oil, brown sugar, yellow mustard, and Chophouse Steak seasoning to a large mixing bowl and whisk until everything is well combined. Pour the marinade into a large, resealable plastic bag or glass baking dish, then add the elk steaks. Seal the bag and turn the steaks once to coat. Place the bag in the refrigerator and marinate for 4-12 hours.

2.   Supply your smoker with wood pellets and follow the start-up procedure. Preheat the grill, with the lid open, to 425° F. If you're using a gas or charcoal grill, set it up for medium heat. Remove the elk steaks from the bag and discard the excess marinade. Insert a temperature probe into one of the elk steaks and place on the grill.

3.   Grill the steaks for 7-10 minutes per side, or until the steaks reach an internal temperature of 135°F. Remove the steaks from the grill and allow the steaks to rest for 10 minutes before serving.

Venison Sausage Sandwiches

Servings: 6
Cooking Time: 330 Minutes

Ingredients:

- 1 Tsp Black Pepper, Ground
- 1 Tbsp Butter
- 1 Tbsp Competition Smoked Rub
- 1/4 Cup Distilled Ice Water
- 1 Tsp Fennel Seed, Cracked
- To Taste, Fresh Basil
- 6 Hoagie Rolls, Sliced Lengthwise
- 32-35 Mm Hog Casings

- 1 Cup Marinara Sauce
- 1 Tbsp Olive Oil
- 1 Tsp Oregano, Dried
- 1/2 Tsp Paprika
- 1 Tsp Parsley, Dried
- 1 Lb Pork, Ground
- 12 Slices Provolone Cheese
- 1 Red Bell Pepper, Sliced Thin
- 2 Red Onions, Sliced Thin
- 1/2 Tsp Red Pepper Flakes, Crushed
- 1 Lb Venison, Ground

Directions:

1. In a glass bowl or measuring cup, cover hog casings in warm water and let soak for 1 hour.

2. In a small bowl, whisk together Competition Smoked, parsley, black pepper, red pepper flakes, oregano, fennel, and paprika.

3. In a large bowl, combine ground venison and ground pork. Mix together by hand, then add seasoning and distilled ice water. Mix mixture by hand for 1 minute, until seasoning is incorporated throughout.

4. Prepare the sausage stuffer and fit one hog casing over a 1 to 1 ¼ inch horn. Place a sheet tray, with a bit of water on it, underneath the nozzle of the stuffer and start filling the casing.

5. Once the casing is filled, twist off into desired lengths, prick to rid of any air bubbles, wrap and refrigerate overnight.

6. Supply your smoker with wood pellets and follow the start-up procedure. Preheat the grill, with the lid open, to 200° F. If using a gas or charcoal grill, set it up for low, indirect heat.

7. Pull open both side handles to increase the level of smoke and temperature in the smoking cabinet. Goal is to maintain a temperature between 150 and 160° F.

8. Hang the linked sausage with S-hooks from the top rack, being careful to not have links touching for even smoking. Smoke for 3 hours, then increase grill temperature to 225° F, which will raise the temperature of the smoking cabinet to 170° F and continue smoking the sausage for another 1 to 2 hours, until the internal temperature of the sausage reaches 155° F.

9. Set hoagie rolls in the upper cabinet to keep warm, then remove sausage from the smoking cabinet. Portion cut with scissors, then set aside.

10. Meanwhile, place a cast iron skillet on the gill. Open the sear slide. Add olive oil and butter, then sauté peppers and onion for 3 minutes. Slide the skillet to the left then sear sausages over open flame for 1 minute.

11. While peppers and onion are on the grill, place 2 slices of provolone in each roll, then keep warm in the cabinet.

12. Enjoy sausage sandwiches hot with marinara, provolone cheese, sautéed bell peppers and onion, and fresh basil. Alternatively, place sausages in an ice water bath for 15 minutes, dry at room temperature and refrigerate or freeze for future use.

Flavour Memphis Bbq Beef Brisket

Servings: 10
Cooking Time: 600 Minutes

Ingredients:
- 1 Cup Beef Broth
- 1, 10-12 Pound Brisket
- 1 Bottle Sweet Rib Rub

Directions:

1. Cut away any silver skin or excess fat from the flat muscle and discard. Next, there will be a large, crescent shaped fat section on the flat of the meat.

2. Trim that fat until it is smooth against the meat so that it looks like a seamless transition between the point and flat. Flip the brisket over and trim the fat cap to ¼ inch thick. Slice between the point and the flat and save the flat for later.

3. Generously season the trimmed brisket point on all sides with the Sweet Rib Rub. Allow the brisket to sit for 30 minutes to marinate.

4. Pour the beef broth in the spray bottle and set aside.

5. Supply your smoker with wood pellets and follow the start-up procedure. Preheat the grill, with the lid closed, to 225° F. Place the brisket in the smoker, insert the smoker's attached temperature probe, if you have one, and set the brisket to cook for about 6-8 hours or until

the internal temperature reaches 165°F. Spray the brisket with the beef broth every 2 hours to keep it moist.

6. Once the brisket reaches 165°F, remove from the smoker, wrap in peach butcher paper, folding the edges over to form a leakproof seal, and return to the smoker seam-side down for another 3-4 hours, or until the brisket reaches 200°F.

7. Remove the brisket from the smoker and allow it to rest for at least one hour before serving.

Naked Juicy Lucy Burgers With Special Sauce

Servings: 4
Cooking Time: 40 Minutes

Ingredients:

- 2lb (1kg) ground beef (80/20), preferably chuck, well chilled
- 1 tbsp Worcestershire sauce or liquid aminos
- 6oz (170g) grated Cheddar, pepper Jack, or another melting cheese
- coarse salt
- freshly ground black pepper
- for the sauce
- ¼ cup reduced-fat mayo
- ¼ cup yellow mustard
- ¼ cup ketchup
- ¼ cup Heinz 57 sauce
- 2 tbsp sweet pickle relish
- for serving
- sliced tomatoes
- sliced sweet onions
- lettuce leaves
- cooked bacon strips
- Pickles

Directions:

1. Supply your smoker with wood pellets and follow the start-up procedure. Preheat the grill, with the lid closed, to 225° F.

2. In a small bowl, make the sauce by combining the ingredients. Transfer the sauce to a serving bowl. Cover and refrigerate until ready to use. (Leftover sauce will keep for several weeks.)

3. Place the ground beef in a large bowl and add the Worcestershire sauce. Wet your hands with cold water and lightly mix. Divide the mixture into 8 equal-sized balls. Flatten each ball into a round patty.

4. Place 4 patties on a rimmed sheet pan. Mound an equal amount of cheese in the middle of each patty, leaving a meat border. Place a patty on top of each cheese mound. Rewet your hands with cold water and press and pinch the edges of patties together to form a tight seal. (You don't want the cheese to leak out.) Season on both sides with salt and pepper.

5. Place the patties on the grate and smoke for 30 minutes. Transfer the burgers to a clean plate.

6. Raise the temperature to 450°F (232°C). Return the burgers to the grate and sear them until the burgers reach an internal temperature of 160°F (71°C), about 3 to 4 minutes per side, turning once.

7. Transfer the burgers to a platter and let rest for 3 minutes. Serve with the special sauce and the suggested accompaniments.

Smoked Peppered Beef Tenderloin

Servings: 4
Cooking Time: 60 Minutes

Ingredients:

- 1 (2 to 2-1/2 lb) Snake River Farms Beef Tenderloin Roast, trimmed
- 1/2 Cup Dijon mustard
- 2 Clove garlic, minced to a paste
- 2 Tablespoon bourbon or strong cold coffee
- Jacobsen Salt Co. Pure Kosher Sea Salt
- coarse ground black and green peppercorns

Directions:

1. Lay the tenderloin on a large piece of plastic wrap.

2. Combine the mustard, garlic and bourbon in a small bowl. Slather the mixture evenly all over the tenderloin. Wrap in plastic and allow to sit at room temperature for 1 hour.

3. Unwrap the plastic wrap and generously season the tenderloin on all sides with the salt and ground black and green peppercorns.

4. Supply your smoker with wood pellets and follow the start-up procedure. Preheat the grill, with the lid closed, to 180° F.

5. Place the tenderloin directly on the grill grate and smoke for 60 minutes. Grill: 180 ˚F

6. Remove the tenderloin from the grill and set aside. Increase the grill temperature to 400˚F. Once the grill is hot, place the tenderloin back on the grill. Roast until the internal temperature reaches 130˚F, about 20 to 30 minutes depending on the thickness of the tenderloin. Do not overcook. Grill: 400 ˚F Probe: 130 ˚F

7. Let rest for 10 minutes before slicing. Enjoy!

Smoked Beer Brisket

Servings: 16
Cooking Time: 420 Minutes

Ingredients:
- 1 15 lb brisket
- Brisket Baste:
- 1 cup beer
- 1/4 cup apple cider vinegar
- 1/4 cup beef stock
- 5 tbsp butter, melted
- Brisket Rub:
- 2 tbsp garlic powder
- 2 tbsp onion powder
- 2 tbsp paprika
- 2 tbsp chili powder
- 2 tbsp kosher salt
- 2 tbsp coarse ground black pepper
- 1 tbsp brown sugar

Directions:
1. Supply your smoker with wood pellets and follow the start-up procedure. Preheat the grill, with the lid closed, to 225 ˚F.

2. In a small bowl, mix together garlic powder, onion powder, paprika, chili pepper, kosher salt, and pepper.

3. Rub the seasonings on all sides of the brisket.

4. Place the brisket on the grill grate, fat side down.

5. Cook the brisket until it reaches an internal temperature of 160 ˚F(about 3 to 4 hours).

6. When brisket reaches an internal temperature of 160 ˚F, remove it from the grill.

7. Double wrap the meat in aluminum foil and add the beef broth to the foil packet.

8. Return brisket to the grill grate and cook until it reaches an internal temperature of 204 ˚F(about 3 hours more).

9. Once finished, remove the brisket from the grill, unwrap from foil and let it rest for 15 minutes.

10. Cut against the grain and serve. Enjoy!

Grilled Tomahawk Steak

Servings: 4
Cooking Time: 60 Minutes

Ingredients:
- 2 Large tomahawk steaks
- 2 Tablespoon kosher salt
- 2 Tablespoon ground black pepper
- 1 Tablespoon paprika
- 1/2 Tablespoon garlic powder
- 1/2 Tablespoon onion powder
- 1/2 Tablespoon brown sugar
- 1 Teaspoon ground mustard
- 1/4 Teaspoon cayenne pepper

Directions:
1. In a small bowl, combine all ingredients for the rub. Season the steaks liberally with the rub and set steaks aside while the grill preheats.

2. Supply your smoker with wood pellets and follow the start-up procedure. Preheat the grill, with the lid closed, to 225° F.

3. Place the steaks directly on the grill grate and smoke for 45 minutes to 1 hour, until the internal temperature reaches 120°F. Grill: 225 ˚F

4. Remove steaks from the grill and set aside to rest.

5. Increase the grill temperature to 450°F. Grill: 450 ˚F

6. Place the steaks directly on the grill grate and cook 7 to 10 minutes per side, or until the internal temperature reaches 130°F. Grill: 450 ˚F Probe: 130 ˚F

7. Remove from grill and let rest 5 minutes before serving. Enjoy!

Reverse Seared Rib-eye Steaks

Servings: 2

Cooking Time: 50 Minutes

Ingredients:

- 2 (1-1/2 inch thick) rib-eye steaks
- Meat Church Holy Cow BBQ Rub
- Meat Church Gourmet Garlic and Herb Seasoning
- butter, preferably high-quality

Directions:

1. Supply your smoker with wood pellets and follow the start-up procedure. Preheat the grill, with the lid closed, to 225° F.

2. Season both sides of steak with Meat Church Holy Cow BBQ Rub, and Meat Church Garlic and Herb Seasoning. Place steaks on grill and cook for 30 to 45 minutes or until an instant read thermometer inserted in the thickest part of the meat reads 120°F for medium-rare. Grill: 225 ˚F Probe: 120 ˚F

3. Remove steaks from grill and increase grill temperature to 500°F. Allow steaks to rest while grill preheats.

4. Place steaks back on grill and sear on both sides for 3 minutes.

5. Remove from grill, top with butter and lightly tent with foil to allow the butter to melt and the steaks to rest before slicing, about 5 minutes. Enjoy!

Beef Brisket With Chophouse Steak Rub

Servings: 12

Cooking Time: 480 Minutes

Ingredients:

- As Needed, Chop House Steak Rub
- 1, 10 To 12 Lb Whole Beef Brisket

Directions:

1. Supply your smoker with wood pellets and follow the start-up procedure. Preheat the grill, with the lid closed, to 250° F.

2. While the grill is heating up, trim your brisket of excess fat, score the meat against the grain and season with Chop House Steak Rub or your favorite seasoning.

3. Place your brisket on the grates, fat side up and cook for 7-8 hours or until the internal temperature reaches 190°F. If the meat is not probe tender, keep cooking until your temperature probe can easily slide into the meat with little to no resistance.

4. Remove from the grill and allow to rest for 20-30 minutes.

5. Slice against the grain and enjoy!

Grilled Rosemary Rack Of Lamb

Servings: 8

Cooking Time: 30 Minutes

Ingredients:

- 2 Tablespoons Dijon Mustard
- 1 Tablespoon Fresh Parsley, Chopped
- Chop House Steak Rub
- 2 Chine Bones Removed, And Excess Fat Trimmed Racks Of Lamb
- 1 Teaspoon Rosemary, Finely Chopped

Directions:

1. Place the racks of lamb on a flat work surface, then generously brush the lamb all over with Dijon mustard.

2. Season the meat on all sides with Chophouse Steak seasoning and sprinkle with parsley and rosemary.

3. Supply your smoker with wood pellets and follow the start-up procedure. Preheat the grill, with the lid closed, to 400° F.

4. If you're using a gas or charcoal grill, set it up for high heat.

5. Insert a temperature probe into the thickest part of the rack of lamb and sear the rack, meaty side down for about 6 minutes.

6. Remove the lamb from the grill and turn the temperature down to 300°F.

7. Return the lamb to the grill and lean the two racks against each other so that they stand up, and grill for another 20 minutes, or until the internal temperature reaches 130°F.

8. Remove the racks from the grill and allow to rest for 10 minutes before carving and serving.

Whiskey Bourbon Bbq Cheeseburger

Servings: 4

Cooking Time: 45 Minutes

Ingredients:

- 3 Pound ground beef
- Rub
- 1/2 Cup brown sugar
- 1 To Taste hot sauce
- 1/2 Cup bourbon whiskey
- 1 Pound bacon
- 4 Slices cheddar cheese

Directions:

1. In a medium bowl, combine ground beef and Traeger Rub and mix well using caution not to overwork or allow the beef to get too warm.

2. Divide the ground beef in quarters and put each quarter in a 6" cake ring. Press down and form the beef into a patty.

3. With a skewer, poke about 40 holes about ¾" of the way through each patty. Spread brown sugar all over the top of the patties then drizzle with hot sauce. Pour whiskey over each burger, transfer to the fridge and let sit for about a half hour.

4. Supply your smoker with wood pellets and follow the start-up procedure. Preheat the grill, with the lid closed, to 225° F.

5. Remove burgers from the cake rings. When the grill is to temp, place bacon and burgers directly on the grill grate and cook until burgers internal temperature reaches 165 °F. In the last ten minutes of cooking, top with cheddar cheese to melt. Grill: 225 °F Probe: 165 °F

6. Remove burgers and bacon from the grill and build your burger to your liking. Enjoy!

Bourbon Beef And Pork Meatballs

Servings: 4

Cooking Time: 25 Minutes

Ingredients:

- 1 cup cubed stuffing, unseasoned
- 2 , beaten eggs
- 3 garlic cloves, minced
- 1 lb ground beef
- 1 lb. ground pork
- 2.5 cups maple bourbon glaze
- 1 tbsp sweet heat rub
- 1, grated yellow onion
- 2 tbsp milk

Directions:

1. Supply your smoker with wood pellets and follow the start-up procedure. Preheat the grill, with the lid closed, to 350° F. If using a gas or charcoal grill, set it up for medium heat.

2. Put the stuffing in a food processor and pulse to process into small crumbs. Pour the crumbs out into a mixing bowl, then add the onion, garlic, eggs, milk, and Sweet Heat. Let the mixture sit for 10 minutes, then add the ground meat. Using your hands, combine the mixture together until fully incorporated.

3. Form mixture into 2 ounce balls and place on cast iron skillet, evenly spaced apart.

4. Transfer skillet to preheated grill and cook for 15 minutes, then generously glaze with sauce. Cook an additional 5 minutes, then glaze again and cook for 2 more minutes.

5. Remove meatballs from grill and serve hot with remaining sauce (about ⅓ cup).

Sweetheart Steak With Lobster Ceviche

Servings: 2

Cooking Time: 15 Minutes

Ingredients:

- 1 (20 Oz) Boneless Strip Steak Or Rib Steak, Butterflied Into Heart Shape
- 2 Teaspoon Jacobsen Salt Co. Pure Kosher Sea Salt
- 2 Teaspoon black pepper
- 2 Tablespoon Raw Dark Chocolate, finely chopped
- 1/2 Tablespoon olive oil
- 1 1/2 Pound Lobster Tail
- 1 Cup lemon juice
- 1/3 Cup lime juice
- 1/2 jalapeño, diced

Directions:

1. For the Sweetheart Steak, draw a large heart on a piece of cardboard, shape to size of meat selected. Cut out cardboard heart shape, then trim meat into heart shape.

2. Combine Jacobsen Salt, pepper, chocolate, and olive oil in a small bowl. Place on top of cut steak.

3. Cut raw lobster tail, remove meat, and chop. In a separate medium bowl, combine the lemon juice, lime juice, and jalapeno.

4. Toss in the lobster meat; ensure it is completely submerged in the liquid. Let lobster soak for 30 minutes. The citric acid actually cooks the lobster meat. If you prefer to have fully-cooked meat, grill lobster in shell for 3-5 minutes at 350 degrees F. Grill: 350 °F

5. Remove from grill, then toss with lemon juice, lime juice, and jalapeno.

6. Supply your smoker with wood pellets and follow the start-up procedure. Preheat the grill, with the lid closed, to 450° F.

7. Place the steak directly on the grill grate and cook for 5 to 7 minutes per side, or until you've reached desired doneness. Remove from grill. Let rest for 5 minutes. Grill: 450 °F

8. Serve lobster ceviche over steak. Enjoy!

APPETIZERS AND SNACKS

Chicken Wings With Teriyaki Glaze

Servings: 4
Cooking Time: 50 Minutes

Ingredients:

- 16 large chicken wings, about 3lb (1.4kg) total
- 1 to 1½ tbsp toasted sesame oil
- for the glaze
- ½ cup light soy sauce or tamari
- ¼ cup sake or sugar-free dark-colored soda
- ¼ cup light brown sugar or low-carb substitute
- 2 tbsp mirin or 1 tbsp honey
- 1 garlic clove, peeled, minced or grated
- 2 tsp minced fresh ginger
- 1 tsp cornstarch mixed with 1 tbsp distilled water (optional)
- for serving
- 1 tbsp toasted sesame seeds
- 2 scallions, trimmed, white and green parts sliced sharply diagonally

Directions:

1. Supply your smoker with wood pellets and follow the start-up procedure. Preheat the grill, with the lid closed, to 350° F.

2. Place the chicken wings in a large bowl, add the sesame oil, and turn the wings to coat thoroughly.

3. Place the wings on the grate at an angle to the bars. Grill for 20 minutes and then turn. Continue to cook until the wings are nicely browned and the meat is no longer pink at the bone, about 20 minutes more.

4. To make the glaze, in a saucepan on the stovetop over medium-high heat, combine the ingredients and bring the mixture to a boil. Reduce the glaze by 1/3, about 6 to 8 minutes. If you prefer your glaze to be glossy and thick, add the cornstarch and water mixture to the glaze and cook until it coats the back of a spoon, about 1 to 2 minutes more.

5. Transfer the wings to an aluminum foil roasting pan. Pour the glaze over them, turning to coat thoroughly.

Place the pan on the grate and cook the wings until the glaze sets, about 5 to 10 minutes.

6. Transfer the wings to a platter. Scatter the sesame seeds and scallions over the top. Serve with plenty of napkins.

Bacon-wrapped Jalapeño Poppers

Servings: 12
Cooking Time: 30 Minutes

Ingredients:

- 8 ounces cream cheese, softened
- ½ cup shredded Cheddar cheese
- ¼ cup chopped scallions
- 1 teaspoon chipotle chile powder or regular chili powder
- 1 teaspoon garlic powder
- 1 teaspoon salt
- 18 large jalapeño peppers, stemmed, seeded, and halved lengthwise
- 1 pound bacon (precooked works well)

Directions:

1. Supply your smoker with wood pellets and follow the start-up procedure. Preheat, with the lid closed, to 350°F. Line a baking sheet with aluminum foil.

2. In a small bowl, combine the cream cheese, Cheddar cheese, scallions, chipotle powder, garlic powder, and salt.

3. Stuff the jalapeño halves with the cheese mixture.

4. Cut the bacon into pieces big enough to wrap around the stuffed pepper halves.

5. Wrap the bacon around the peppers and place on the prepared baking sheet.

6. Put the baking sheet on the grill grate, close the lid, and smoke the peppers for 30 minutes, or until the cheese is melted and the bacon is cooked through and crisp.

7. Let the jalapeño poppers cool for 3 to 5 minutes. Serve warm.

Bacon Pork Pinwheels (kansas Lollipops)

Servings: 4-6
Cooking Time: 20 Minutes

Ingredients:
- 1 Whole Pork Loin, boneless
- To Taste salt and pepper
- To Taste Greek Seasoning
- 4 Slices bacon
- To Taste The Ultimate BBQ Sauce

Directions:
1. When ready to cook, start the smoker and set temperature to 500F. Preheat, lid closed, for 10 to 15 minutes.
2. Trim pork loin of any unwanted silver skin or fat. Using a sharp knife, cut pork loin length wise, into 4 long strips.
3. Lay pork flat, then season with salt, pepper and Cavender's Greek Seasoning.
4. Flip the pork strips over and layer bacon on unseasoned side. Begin tightly rolling the pork strips, with bacon being rolled up on the inside.
5. Secure a skewer all the way through each pork roll to secure it in place. Set the pork rolls down on grill and cook for 15 minutes.
6. Brush BBQ Sauce over the pork. Turn each skewer over, then coat the other side. Let pork cook for another 5-10 minutes, depending on thickness of your pork. Enjoy!

Bayou Wings With Cajun Rémoulade

Servings: 8
Cooking Time: 40 Minutes

Ingredients:
- 16 large whole chicken wings or 32 drumettes and flats, about 3lb (1.4kg) total
- for the rub
- 1 tbsp kosher salt
- 1 tsp freshly ground black pepper
- 1 tsp paprika
- ½ tsp ground cayenne, plus more
- ½ tsp garlic powder
- ½ tsp celery salt
- ½ tsp dried thyme
- 2 tbsp vegetable oil
- for the rémoulade
- 1¼ cups reduced-fat mayo
- ¼ cup Creole-style or whole grain mustard
- 2 tbsp horseradish
- 2 tbsp pickle relish
- 1 tbsp freshly squeezed lemon juice
- 1 tsp paprika, plus more
- 1 tsp hot sauce, plus more
- 1 tsp Worcestershire sauce
- coarse salt
- for serving
- lemon wedges
- pickled okra (optional)

Directions:
1. Supply your smoker with wood pellets and follow the start-up procedure. Preheat the grill, with the lid closed, to 350° F.
2. If using whole wings, cut through the two joints, separating them into drumettes, flats, and wing tips. (Discard the wing tips or save them for chicken stock.) Alternatively, leave the wings whole. Place the chicken in a resealable plastic bag.
3. In a small bowl, make the rub by combining the ingredients. Mix well. Pour the rub over the wings and toss them to thoroughly coat. Refrigerate for 2 hours.
4. In a small bowl, make the Cajun rémoulade by whisking together the mayo, mustard, horseradish, pickle relish, lemon juice, paprika, hot sauce, and Worcestershire. Season with salt to taste. The mixture should be highly seasoned. Transfer to a serving bowl and lightly dust with paprika. Cover and refrigerate until ready to serve.
5. Remove the wings from the refrigerator and allow the excess marinade to drip off. Place the wings on the grate at an angle to the bars. Grill for 20 minutes and then turn. (They'll brown more evenly but will also have less of a tendency to stick.) Continue to cook until the wings are nicely browned and the meat is no longer pink at the bone, about 20 minutes more.
6. Remove the wings from the grill and pile them on a platter. Serve with the Cajun rémoulade, lemon wedges, and pickled okra (if using).

Pulled Pork Loaded Nachos

Servings: 4
Cooking Time: 10 Minutes

Ingredients:

- 2 cups leftover smoked pulled pork
- 1 small sweet onion, diced
- 1 medium tomato, diced
- 1 jalapeño pepper, seeded and diced
- 1 garlic clove, minced
- 1 teaspoon salt
- 1 teaspoon freshly ground black pepper
- 1 bag tortilla chips
- 1 cup shredded Cheddar cheese
- ½ cup The Ultimate BBQ Sauce, divided
- ½ cup shredded jalapeño Monterey Jack cheese
- Juice of ½ lime
- 1 avocado, halved, pitted, and sliced
- 2 tablespoons sour cream
- 1 tablespoon chopped fresh cilantro

Directions:

1. Supply your smoker with wood pellets and follow the start-up procedure. Preheat, with the lid closed, to 375°F.
2. Heat the pulled pork in the microwave.
3. In a medium bowl, combine the onion, tomato, jalapeño, garlic, salt, and pepper, and set aside.
4. Arrange half of the tortilla chips in a large cast iron skillet. Spread half of the warmed pork on top and cover with the Cheddar cheese. Top with half of the onion-jalapeño mixture, then drizzle with ¼ cup of barbecue sauce.
5. Layer on the remaining tortilla chips, then the remaining pork and the Monterey Jack cheese. Top with the remaining onion-jalapeño mixture and drizzle with the remaining ¼ cup of barbecue sauce.
6. Place the skillet on the grill, close the lid, and smoke for about 10 minutes, or until the cheese is melted and bubbly. (Watch to make sure your chips don't burn!)
7. Squeeze the lime juice over the nachos, top with the avocado slices and sour cream, and garnish with the cilantro before serving hot.

Citrus-infused Marinated Olives

Servings: 6
Cooking Time: 30 Minutes

Ingredients:

- 1½ cups mixed brined olives, with pits
- ½ cup extra virgin olive oil
- 1 tbsp freshly squeezed lemon juice
- 1 garlic clove, peeled and thinly sliced
- 1 tsp smoked Spanish paprika
- 2 sprigs of fresh rosemary
- 2 sprigs of fresh thyme
- 2 bay leaves, fresh or dried
- 1 small dried red chili pepper, deseeded and flesh crumbled, or ¼ tsp crushed red pepper flakes
- 3 strips of orange zest
- 3 strips of lemon zest

Directions:

1. Supply your smoker with wood pellets and follow the start-up procedure. Preheat the grill, with the lid closed, to 180° F.
2. Drain the olives, reserving 1 tablespoon of brine. Spread the olives in a single layer in an aluminum foil roasting pan. Place the pan on the grate and cook the olives for 30 minutes, stirring the olives or shaking the pan once or twice.
3. In a small saucepan on the stovetop over low heat, warm the olive oil. Whisk in the lemon juice and the reserved 1 tablespoon of brine. Stir in the garlic and paprika. Add the rosemary, thyme, bay leaves, chili pepper, and orange and lemon zests. Warm over low heat for 10 minutes. Remove the saucepan from the heat.
4. Transfer the olives and olive oil mixture to a pint jar. Tuck the aromatics around the sides of the jar. Let cool and then cover and refrigerate for up to 5 days. Let the olives come to room temperature before serving.

Chorizo Queso Fundido

Servings: 4-6
Cooking Time: 20 Minutes

Ingredients:

- 1 poblano chile
- 1 cup chopped queso quesadilla or queso Oaxaca

- 1 cup shredded Monterey Jack cheese
- ¼ cup milk
- 1 tablespoon all-purpose flour
- 2 (4-ounce) links Mexican chorizo sausage, casings removed
- ⅓ cup beer
- 1 tablespoon unsalted butter
- 1 small red onion, chopped
- ½ cup whole kernel corn
- 2 serrano chiles or jalapeño peppers, stemmed, seeded, and coarsely chopped
- 1 tablespoon minced garlic
- 1 tablespoon freshly squeezed lime juice
- 1 teaspoon ground cumin
- 1 teaspoon salt
- 1 teaspoon freshly ground black pepper
- 1 tablespoon chopped fresh cilantro
- 1 tablespoon chopped scallions
- Tortilla chips, for serving

Directions:

1. Supply your smoker with wood pellets and follow the start-up procedure. Preheat, with the lid closed, to 350°F.

2. On the smoker or over medium-high heat on the stove top, place the poblano directly on the grate (or burner) to char for 1 to 2 minutes, turning as needed. Remove from heat and place in a closed-up lunch-size paper bag for 2 minutes to sweat and further loosen the skin.

3. Remove the skin and coarsely chop the poblano, removing the seeds; set aside.

4. In a bowl, combine the queso quesadilla, Monterey Jack, milk, and flour; set aside.

5. On the stove top, in a cast iron skillet over medium heat, cook and crumble the chorizo for about 2 minutes.

6. Transfer the cooked chorizo to a small, grill-safe pan and place over indirect heat on the smoker.

7. Place the cast iron skillet on the preheated grill grate. Pour in the beer and simmer for a few minutes, loosening and stirring in any remaining sausage bits from the pan.

8. Add the butter to the pan, then add the cheese mixture a little at a time, stirring constantly.

9. When the cheese is smooth, stir in the onion, corn, serrano chiles, garlic, lime juice, cuvmin, salt, and pepper. Stir in the reserved chopped charred poblano.

10. Close the lid and smoke for 15 to 20 minutes to infuse the queso with smoke flavor and further cook the vegetables.

11. When the cheese is bubbly, top with the chorizo mixture and garnish with the cilantro and scallions.

12. Serve the chorizo queso fundido hot with tortilla chips.

Grilled Guacamole

Servings: 6
Cooking Time: 30 Minutes

Ingredients:

- 3 large avocados, halved and pitted
- 1 lime, halved
- ½ jalapeño, deseeded and deveined
- ½ small white or red onion, peeled
- 2 garlic cloves, peeled and skewered on a toothpick
- 1 tsp coarse salt, plus more
- 1½ tbsp reduced-fat mayo
- 2 tbsp chopped fresh cilantro
- 2 tbsp crumbled queso fresco (optional)
- tortilla chips

Directions:

1. Supply your smoker with wood pellets and follow the start-up procedure. Preheat the grill, with the lid closed, to 225° F.

2. Place the avocados, lime, jalapeño, and onion cut sides down on the grate. Use the toothpicks to balance the garlic cloves between the bars. Smoke for 30 minutes. (You want the vegetables to retain most of their rawness.)

3. Transfer everything to a cutting board. Remove the garlic cloves from the toothpick and roughly chop. Sprinkle with the salt and continue to mince the garlic until it begins to form a paste. Scrape the garlic and salt into a large bowl.

4. Scoop the avocado flesh from the peels into the bowl. Squeeze the juice of ½ lime over the avocado. Mash the avocados but leave them somewhat chunky. Finely dice the jalapeño. Dice 2 tablespoons of onion. (Reserve the

remaining onion for another use.) Add the jalapeño, onion, mayo, and cilantro to the bowl. Stir gently to combine. Taste for seasoning, adding more salt, lime juice, and jalapeño as desired.

5.   Transfer the guacamole to a serving bowl. Top with the queso fresco (if using). Serve with tortilla chips.

Pigs In A Blanket

Servings: 4-6
Cooking Time: 15 Minutes

Ingredients:
*   2 Tablespoon Poppy Seeds
*   1 Tablespoon Dried Minced Onion
*   2 Teaspoon garlic, minced
*   2 Tablespoon Sesame Seeds
*   1 Teaspoon salt
*   8 Ounce Original Crescent Dough
*   1/4 Cup Dijon mustard
*   1 Large egg, beaten

Directions:
1.   When ready to cook, start your smoker at 350 degrees F, and preheat with lid closed, 10 to 15 minutes.
2.   Mix together poppy seeds, dried minced onion, dried minced garlic, salt and sesame seeds. Set aside.
3.   Cut each triangle of crescent roll dough into thirds lengthwise, making 3 small strips from each roll.
4.   Brush the dough strips lightly with Dijon mustard. Put the mini hot dogs on 1 end of the dough and roll up.
5.   Arrange them, seam side down, on a greased baking pan. Brush with egg wash and sprinkle with seasoning mixture.
6.   Bake in smoker until golden brown, about 12 to 15 minutes.
7.   Serve with mustard or dipping sauce of your choice. Enjoy!

Simple Cream Cheese Sausage Balls

Servings: 5
Cooking Time: 30 Minutes

Ingredients:
*   1 pound ground hot sausage, uncooked
*   8 ounces cream cheese, softened

*   1 package mini filo dough shells

Directions:
1.   Supply your smoker with wood pellets and follow the start-up procedure. Preheat, with the lid closed, to 350°F.
2.   In a large bowl, using your hands, thoroughly mix together the sausage and cream cheese until well blended.
3.   Place the filo dough shells on a rimmed perforated pizza pan or into a mini muffin tin.
4.   Roll the sausage and cheese mixture into 1-inch balls and place into the filo shells.
5.   Place the pizza pan or mini muffin tin on the grill, close the lid, and smoke the sausage balls for 30 minutes, or until cooked through and the sausage is no longer pink.
6.   Plate and serve warm.

Deviled Eggs With Smoked Paprika

Servings: 6
Cooking Time: 30 Minutes

Ingredients:
*   6 large eggs
*   3 tbsp reduced-fat mayo, plus more
*   1 tsp Dijon or yellow mustard
*   ½ tsp Spanish smoked paprika or regular paprika, plus more
*   dash of hot sauce
*   coarse salt
*   freshly ground black pepper
*   for garnishing
*   small sprigs of fresh parsley, dill, tarragon, or cilantro
*   chopped chives
*   minced scallions
*   Mustard Caviar
*   sliced green or black olives
*   celery leaves
*   sliced radishes
*   diced bell peppers
*   sliced cherry tomatoes
*   fresh or pickled jalapeños
*   sliced or diced pickles

- slivers of sun-dried tomatoes
- bacon crumbles
- smoked salmon
- Hawaiian black salt
- Caviar

Directions:

1. Supply your smoker with wood pellets and follow the start-up procedure. Preheat the grill, with the lid closed, to 180° F.

2. On the stovetop over medium-high heat, bring a saucepan of water to a boil. (Make sure there's enough water in the saucepan to cover the eggs by 1 inch [5cm].) Use a slotted spoon to gently lower the eggs into the water. Lower the heat to maintain a simmer. Set a timer for 13 minutes.

3. Prepare an ice bath by combining ice and cold water in a large bowl. Carefully transfer the eggs to the ice bath when the timer goes off.

4. When the eggs are cool enough to handle, gently tap them all over to crack the shell. Carefully peel the eggs. Rinse under cold running water to remove any clinging bits of shell, but don't dry the eggs. (A damp surface will help the smoke adhere to the egg whites.)

5. Place the eggs on the grate and smoke until the eggs take on a light brown patina from the smoke, about 25 minutes. Transfer the eggs to a cutting board, handling them as little as possible.

6. Slice each egg in half lengthwise with a sharp knife. Wipe any yolk off the blade before slicing the next egg. Gently remove the yolks and place them in a food processor. Pulse to break up the yolks. Add the mayo, mustard, paprika, and hot sauce. Season with salt and pepper to taste. Pulse until the filling is smooth. Add additional mayo 1 teaspoon at a time if the mixture is a little dry. (It shouldn't be too loose either.)

7. Spoon the filling into each egg half or pipe it in using a small resealable plastic bag. You can also use a pastry bag fitted with a fluted tip.

8. Place the eggs on a platter and lightly dust with paprika. Accompany with one or more of the suggested garnishes.

Smoked Cashews

Servings: 6
Cooking Time: 60 Minutes

Ingredients:

- 1 pound roasted, salted cashews

Directions:

1. Supply your smoker with wood pellets and follow the start-up procedure. Preheat the grill, with the lid closed, to 120°F.

2. Pour the cashews onto a rimmed baking sheet and smoke for 1 hour, stirring once about halfway through the smoking time.

3. Remove the cashews from the grill, let cool, and store in an airtight container for as long as you can resist.

Pig Pops (sweet-hot Bacon On A Stick)

Servings: 24
Cooking Time: 30 Minutes

Ingredients:

- Nonstick cooking spray, oil, or butter, for greasing
- 2 pounds thick-cut bacon (24 slices)
- 24 metal skewers
- 1 cup packed light brown sugar
- 2 to 3 teaspoons cayenne pepper
- ½ cup maple syrup, divided

Directions:

1. Supply your smoker with wood pellets and follow the start-up procedure. Preheat, with the lid closed, to 350°F.

2. Coat a disposable aluminum foil baking sheet with cooking spray, oil, or butter.

3. Thread each bacon slice onto a metal skewer and place on the prepared baking sheet.

4. In a medium bowl, stir together the brown sugar and cayenne.

5. Baste the top sides of the bacon with ¼ cup of maple syrup.

6. Sprinkle half of the brown sugar mixture over the bacon.

7. Place the baking sheet on the grill, close the lid, and smoke for 15 to 30 minutes.

8. Using tongs, flip the bacon skewers. Baste with the remaining ¼ cup of maple syrup and top with the remaining brown sugar mixture.

9. Continue smoking with the lid closed for 10 to 15 minutes, or until crispy. You can eyeball the bacon and smoke to your desired doneness, but the actual ideal internal temperature for bacon is 155°F

10. Using tongs, carefully remove the bacon skewers from the grill. Let cool completely before handling.

Chuckwagon Beef Jerky

Servings: 6
Cooking Time: 300 Minutes

Ingredients:

- 2½lb (1.2kg) boneless top or bottom round steak, sirloin tip, flank steak, or venison
- 1 cup sugar-free dark-colored soda
- 1 cup cold brewed coffee
- ½ cup light soy sauce
- ¼ cup Worcestershire sauce
- 2 tbsp whiskey (optional)
- 2 tsp chili powder
- 1½ tsp garlic salt
- 1 tsp onion powder
- 1 tsp pink curing salt

Directions:

1. Slice the meat into ¼-inch-thick (.5cm) strips, trimming off any visible fat or gristle. (Slice against the grain for more tender jerky and with the grain for chewier jerky.) Place the meat in a large resealable plastic bag.

2. In a small bowl, whisk together the soda, coffee, soy sauce, Worcestershire sauce, whiskey (if using), chili powder, garlic salt, onion powder, and curing salt (if using). Whisk until the salt dissolves. Pour the mixture over the meat and reseal the bag. Refrigerate for 24 to 48 hours, turning the bag several times to redistribute the brine.

3. Supply your smoker with wood pellets and follow the start-up procedure. Preheat the grill, with the lid closed, to 150° F.

4. Drain the meat and discard the brine. Place the strips of meat in a single layer on paper towels and blot any excess moisture.

5. Place the meat in a single layer on the grate and smoke for 4 to 5 hours, turning once or twice. (If you're aware of hot spots on your grate, rotate the strips so they smoke evenly.) To test for doneness, bend one or two pieces in the middle. They should be dry but still somewhat pliant. Or simply eat a piece to see if it's done to your liking.

6. For the best texture, when you remove the meat from the grill, place the still-warm jerky in a resealable plastic bag and let rest for 30 minutes. (You might see condensation form on the inside of the bag, but the moisture will be reabsorbed by the meat.) Or let the meat cool completely and then store in a resealable plastic bag or covered container. The jerky will last a few days at room temperature but will last longer (up to 2 weeks) if refrigerated.

Smoked Cheese

Servings: 4
Cooking Time: 150 Minutes

Ingredients:

- 1 (2-pound) block medium Cheddar cheese, or your favorite cheese, quartered lengthwise

Directions:

1. Supply your smoker with wood pellets and follow the start-up procedure. Preheat the grill, with the lid closed, to 90°F.

2. Place the cheese directly on the grill grate and smoke for 2 hours, 30 minutes, checking frequently to be sure it's not melting. If the cheese begins to melt, try flipping it. If that doesn't help, remove it from the grill and refrigerate for about 1 hour and then return it to the cold smoker.

3. Remove the cheese, place it in a zip-top bag, and refrigerate overnight.

4. Slice the cheese and serve with crackers, or grate it and use for making a smoked mac and cheese.

Roasted Red Pepper Dip

Servings: 8
Cooking Time: 45 Minutes

Ingredients:
- 4 red bell peppers, halved, destemmed, and deseeded
- 1 cup English walnuts, divided
- 1 small white onion, peeled and coarsely chopped
- 2 garlic cloves, peeled and smashed with a chef's knife
- ¼ cup extra virgin olive oil, plus more
- 1 tbsp balsamic vinegar or balsamic glaze
- 1 tsp honey (eliminate if using balsamic glaze)
- 1 tsp coarse salt, plus more
- 1 tsp ground cumin
- 1 tsp smoked paprika
- ½ to 1 tsp Aleppo red pepper flakes, plus more
- ¼ cup fresh white breadcrumbs (optional)
- distilled water (optional)
- assorted crudités or wedges of pita bread

Directions:
1. Supply your smoker with wood pellets and follow the start-up procedure. Preheat the grill, with the lid closed, to 400° F.
2. Place the peppers skin side down on the grate and grill until the skins blister and the flesh softens, about 30 minutes. Transfer the peppers to a bowl and cover with plastic wrap. Let cool to room temperature. Remove the skins with a paring knife or your fingers. Coarsely chop or tear the peppers.
3. Place ¾ cup of walnuts in an aluminum foil roasting pan. Place the pan on the grate and toast for 10 to 15 minutes, stirring twice. Remove the pan from the grill and let the walnuts cool.
4. Place the peppers, onion, garlic, and walnuts in a food processor fitted with the chopping blade. Pulse several times. Add the olive oil, balsamic vinegar, honey, salt, cumin, paprika, and red pepper flakes. Process until the mixture is fairly smooth. Taste for seasoning, adding more salt or red pepper flakes (if desired). (If the mixture is too loose, add breadcrumbs until the texture is to your liking. If it's too thick, add olive oil or water 1 tablespoon at a time.)
5. Transfer the dip to a serving bowl. Use the back of a spoon to make a shallow depression in the center. Top with the remaining ¼ cup of walnuts and drizzle olive oil in the depression. Serve with crudités or pita bread.

Delicious Deviled Crab Appetizer

Servings: 30
Cooking Time: 10 Minutes

Ingredients:
- Nonstick cooking spray, oil, or butter, for greasing
- 1 cup panko breadcrumbs, divided
- 1 cup canned corn, drained
- ½ cup chopped scallions, divided
- ½ red bell pepper, finely chopped
- 16 ounces jumbo lump crabmeat
- ¾ cup mayonnaise, divided
- 1 egg, beaten
- 1 teaspoon salt
- 1 teaspoon freshly ground black pepper
- 2 teaspoons cayenne pepper, divided
- Juice of 1 lemon

Directions:
1. Supply your smoker with wood pellets and follow the start-up procedure. Preheat, with the lid closed, to 425°F.
2. Spray three 12-cup mini muffin pans with cooking spray and divide ½ cup of the panko between 30 of the muffin cups, pressing into the bottoms and up the sides. (Work in batches, if necessary, depending on the number of pans you have.)
3. In a medium bowl, combine the corn, ¼ cup of scallions, the bell pepper, crabmeat, half of the mayonnaise, the egg, salt, pepper, and 1 teaspoon of cayenne pepper.
4. Gently fold in the remaining ½ cup of breadcrumbs and divide the mixture between the prepared mini muffin cups.
5. Place the pans on the grill grate, close the lid, and smoke for 10 minutes, or until golden brown.
6. In a small bowl, combine the lemon juice and the remaining mayonnaise, scallions, and cayenne pepper to make a sauce.
7. Brush the tops of the mini crab cakes with the sauce and serve hot.

Smoked Turkey Sandwich

Servings: 1

Cooking Time: 15 Minutes

Ingredients:

- 2 slices sourdough bread
- 2 tablespoons butter, at room temperature
- 2 (1-ounce) slices Swiss cheese
- 4 ounces leftover Smoked Turkey
- 1 teaspoon garlic salt

Directions:

1. Supply your smoker with wood pellets and follow the start-up procedure. Preheat the grill, with the lid closed, to 375°F.

2. Coat one side of each bread slice with 1 tablespoon of butter and sprinkle the buttered sides with garlic salt.

3. Place 1 slice of cheese on each unbuttered side of the bread, and then put the turkey on the cheese.

4. Close the sandwich, buttered sides out, and place it directly on the grill grate. Cook for 5 minutes. Flip the sandwich and cook for 5 minutes more. Remove the sandwich from the grill, cut it in half, and serve.

Sriracha & Maple Cashews

Servings: 10

Cooking Time: 60 Minutes

Ingredients:

- 2 tbsp unsalted butter
- 3 tbsp pure maple syrup
- 1 tbsp sriracha
- 1 tsp coarse salt (use only if nuts are unsalted)
- 2½ cups unsalted cashews

Directions:

1. Supply your smoker with wood pellets and follow the start-up procedure. Preheat the grill, with the lid closed, to 250° F.

2. In a small saucepan on the stovetop over low heat, melt the butter. Add the maple syrup, sriracha, and salt (if using). Stir until combined. Add the nuts and stir gently to coat thoroughly.

3. Spread the nuts in a single layer in an aluminum foil roasting pan coated with cooking spray. Place the pan on the grate and smoke the nuts until they're lightly toasted, about 1 hour, stirring once or twice.

4. Remove the pan from the grill and let the nuts cool for 15 minutes. They'll be sticky at first but will crisp up. Break them up with your fingers and store at room temperature in an airtight container, such as a lidded glass jar.

Jalapeño Poppers With Chipotle Sour Cream

Servings: 8

Cooking Time: 45 Minutes

Ingredients:

- 3 strips of thin-sliced bacon
- 12 large jalapeños, red, green, or a mix
- 8oz (225g) light cream cheese, at room temperature
- 1 cup shredded pepper Jack, Monterey Jack, or Cheddar cheese
- 1 tsp chili powder
- ½ tsp garlic salt
- smoked paprika
- for the sour cream
- 1¼ cups light sour cream
- juice of ½ lime
- ½ to 1 canned chipotle peppers in adobo sauce, finely minced, plus 1 tsp of sauce, plus more
- 1 tbsp minced fresh cilantro leaves
- ½ tsp coarse salt, plus more

Directions:

1. Supply your smoker with wood pellets and follow the start-up procedure. Preheat the grill, with the lid closed, to 375° F.

2. Line a rimmed sheet pan with aluminum foil and place a wire rack on top. Place the bacon in a single layer on the wire rack. Place the pan on the grate and grill until the bacon is crisp and golden brown, about 20 minutes. Transfer the bacon to paper towels to cool and then crumble. Set aside.

3. In a small bowl, make the chipotle sour cream by whisking together the ingredients. Add more salt, chipotle peppers, or adobe sauce to taste. Cover and refrigerate.

4. Slice the jalapeños lengthwise through their stems. Scrape out the veins and seeds with the edge of a small metal spoon.

5. In a small bowl, beat together the cream cheese, shredded cheese, chili powder, and garlic salt. Stir in the crumbled bacon. Mound the cream cheese mixture in the jalapeño halves. Line another rimmed sheet pan with aluminum foil and place a wire rack on top. Place the jalapeños filled side up in a single layer on the wire rack.

6. Place the sheet pan on the grate and roast the jalapeños until the filling has melted and the peppers have softened, about 20 to 25 minutes. (They should no longer look bright in color.) Remove the pan from the grill and let the peppers rest for 5 minutes.

7. Transfer the poppers to a platter and lightly dust with paprika. Serve with the chipotle sour cream.

Cold-smoked Cheese

Servings: 6

Cooking Time: 180 Minutes

Ingredients:

- 2lb (1kg) well-chilled hard or semi-hard cheese, such as:
- Edam
- Gouda
- Cheddar
- Monterey Jack
- pepper Jack
- goat cheese
- fresh mozzarella
- Muenster
- aged Parmigiano-Reggiano
- Gruyère
- blue cheese

Directions:

1. Unwrap the cheese and remove any protective wax or coating. Cut into 4-ounce (110g) portions to increase the surface area.

2. If possible, move your smoker to a shady area. Place 1 resealable plastic bag filled with ice on top of the drip pan. This is especially important on a warm day because you want to keep the interior temperature of the grill between 70 and 90°F (21 and 32°C) or below.

3. Place a grill mat on one side of the grate. Place the cheese on the mat and allow space between each piece.

4. Fill your smoking tube or pellet maze (see Cast Iron Skillets and Grill Pans) with pellets or sawdust and light according to the manufacturer's instructions. Place the smoking tube on the grate near—but not on—the grill mat. When the tube is smoking consistently, close the grill lid.

5. Smoke the cheese for 1 to 3 hours, replacing the pellets or sawdust and ice if necessary. Monitor the temperature and make sure the cheese isn't beginning to melt. Carefully lift the mat with the cheese to a rimmed baking sheet and let the cheese cool completely before handling.

6. Package the smoked cheese in cheese storage paper or bags or vacuum-seal the cheese, labeling each. (While you can wrap the cheese tightly in plastic wrap, the cheese will spoil faster.) Let the cheese rest for at least 2 to 3 days before eating. It will be even better after 2 weeks.

COCKTAILS RECIPES

Smoked Berry Cocktail

Servings: 2

Cooking Time: 15 Minutes

Ingredients:

- 1/2 Cup strawberries, stemmed
- 1/2 Cup blackberries
- 1/2 Cup blueberries
- 8 Ounce bourbon or iced tea
- 2 Ounce lime juice
- 3 Ounce simple syrup
- soda water
- fresh mint, for garnish

Directions:

1. Supply your smoker with wood pellets and follow the start-up procedure. Preheat the grill, with the lid closed, to 180° F.

2. Wash berries well, spread them on a clean cookie sheet and place on the grill. Smoke berries for 15 minutes. Grill: 180 °F

3. Remove berries from grill and transfer to a blender. Puree berries until smooth then pass through a fine mesh strainer to remove seeds.

4. To create a layered cocktail, pour 2 ounces of berry puree in the bottom of a glass. Next, pour 2 ounces of bourbon or iced tea over the back of a spoon into the glass, then 1/2 ounce lime juice and 1/2 ounce simple syrup, top with soda water and ice. Finish with mint or extra berries for garnish.

5. Repeat the same process for 3 more servings. Enjoy!

Smoking Gun Cocktail

Servings: 2

Cooking Time: 45 Minutes

Ingredients:

- 2 Jar vermouth soaked cocktail onions
- 3 Ounce vodka
- 1 Ounce dry vermouth

Directions:

1. Supply your smoker with wood pellets and follow the start-up procedure. Preheat the grill, with the lid closed, to 180° F.

2. To make the smoked onion vermouth: Pour jar of vermouth soaked cocktail onions onto a shallow sheet pan. Smoke for 45 minutes. Remove from grill and set aside to chill. Grill: 180 °F

3. To make the cocktail: Add vodka, 1 teaspoon liquid from the smoked onions and dry vermouth to a mixing glass. Shake and strain into a chilled martini glass.

4. Garnish with smoked cocktail onions on a skewer. Enjoy!

Traeger Smoked Daiquiri

Servings: 2

Cooking Time: 25 Minutes

Ingredients:

- 2 limes, sliced
- 2 Tablespoon granulated sugar
- 3 Ounce Rum
- 1 Ounce Smoked Simple Syrup
- 1 1/2 Ounce lime juice

Directions:

1. Supply your smoker with wood pellets and follow the start-up procedure. Preheat the grill, with the lid closed, to 350° F.

2. Toss the lime slices with granulated sugar and place directly on the grill grate. Cook 20-25 minutes or until grill marks form. Remove from grill and cool. Grill: 350 °F

3. In a mixing glass add rum, Traeger Simple Syrup, and fresh lime juice. Add ice to the mixing glass and shake. Strain contents into a chilled glass.

4. Garnish with a grilled lime wheel. Enjoy!

In Traeger Fashion Cocktail

Servings: 2

Cooking Time: 20 Minutes

Ingredients:

- 2 Whole orange peel

- 2 Whole lemon peel
- 3 Ounce bourbon
- 1 Ounce Smoked Simple Syrup
- 6 Dash Bitters Lab Charred Cedar & Currant Bitters

Directions:

1.   Supply your smoker with wood pellets and follow the start-up procedure. Preheat the grill, with the lid closed, to 350° F.

2.   Place the lemon and orange peel directly on the grill grate and cook 20 to 25 minutes or until lightly browned. Grill: 350 ˚F

3.   Add bourbon, Traeger Smoked Simple Syrup and bitters to a mixing glass and stir over ice. Stir until glass is chilled and contents are well diluted.

4.   Strain into a new glass over fresh ice and garnish with grilled lemon and orange peel. Enjoy!

Smoked Apple Cider

Servings: 2

Cooking Time: 30 Minutes

Ingredients:

- 32 Ounce apple cider
- 2 cinnamon sticks
- 4 whole cloves
- 3 star anise
- 2 Pieces orange peel
- 2 Pieces lemon peel

Directions:

1.   Supply your smoker with wood pellets and follow the start-up procedure. Preheat the grill, with the lid closed, to 225° F.

2.   Combine the cider, cinnamon stick, star anise, clove, lemon and orange peel in a shallow baking dish.

3.   Place directly on the grill grate and smoke for 30 minutes. Remove from grill, strain and transfer to four mugs. Grill: 225 ˚F

4.   Finish with a slice of apple and a cinnamon stick to serve. Enjoy!

Grilled Blood Orange Mimosa

Servings: 4

Cooking Time: 15 Minutes

Ingredients:

- 3 blood orange, halved
- 2 Tablespoon granulated sugar
- 1 Bottle sparkling wine
- thyme sprigs, for garnish

Directions:

1.   Supply your smoker with wood pellets and follow the start-up procedure. Preheat the grill, with the lid closed, to 375° F.

2.   When the grill is hot, dip the cut side of the orange halves in sugar and place cut side down directly on the grill grate. Grill: 375 ˚F

3.   Grill the oranges for 10-15 minutes or until grill marks develop. Grill: 375 ˚F

4.   Remove from the grill and let cool at room temperature.

5.   When cool enough to handle, juice the oranges and strain through a fine strainer removing any pulp.

6.   Pour 5 oz of sparkling wine into each glass and top with 1 oz blood orange juice.

7.   Garnish with a sprig of thyme. Enjoy!

Sunset Margarita

Servings: 2

Cooking Time: 55 Minutes

Ingredients:

- 4 oranges
- 2 Cup plus 1 teaspoon agave
- 1/2 Cup water
- 1 Ounce burnt orange agave
- 3 Ounce reposado tequila
- 1 1/2 Ounce fresh squeezed lime juice
- Jacobsen Salt Co. Cherrywood Smoked Salt

Directions:

1.   Supply your smoker with wood pellets and follow the start-up procedure. Preheat the grill, with the lid closed, to 350° F.

2.   For the Burnt Orange Agave Syrup: Cut one orange in half and brush cut side with agave. Place cut side down directly on the grill grate and grill for 15 minutes or until grill marks develop. Grill: 350 ˚F

3. While the orange halves are grilling, slice the other orange and brush both sides of the slices with agave. Place slices directly on the grill grate next to the halves and cook for 15 minutes or until grill marks develop. Grill: 350 °F

4. Remove orange halves from grill grate and let cool. After they have cooled, juice halves and strain. Set aside.

5. Combine 1/4 cup water and agave in a shallow dish and mix well. Remove orange slices from the grill and place in the agave mixture, reserving a few for garnish.

6. Reduce the grill temperature to 180 degrees F and place the shallow dish with agave and oranges directly on the grill grate. Smoke for 40 minutes. Remove from heat and strain. Set aside. Grill: 180 °F

7. To Mix Drink: Rim glass with Jacobsen Smoked Salt. Combine tequila, fresh lime juice, grilled orange juice and burnt orange agave syrup in a glass. Add ice and shake well.

8. Strain into a rimmed glass over clean ice. Garnish with a grilled orange slice. Enjoy!

Ryes And Shine Cocktail

Servings: 2
Cooking Time: 30 Minutes

Ingredients:
- 2 lemon, cut into wheels for garnish
- 6 Tablespoon granulated sugar
- 2 Ounce rye
- 1 Ounce bourbon
- 3 Ounce lemon juice
- 1 Ounce Smoked Simple Syrup
- 6 Dash Fernet-Branca

Directions:
1. Supply your smoker with wood pellets and follow the start-up procedure. Preheat the grill, with the lid closed, to 325° F.

2. Toss lemon wheels with granulated sugar to coat on both sides. Place wheels directly on the grill grate and cook for 15 minutes on each side or until grill marks form. Grill: 325 °F

3. Add rye, bourbon, lemon juice, Traeger Smoked Simple Syrup and Fernet-Branca to a shaker and shake until slightly diluted (about 10 to 15 seconds).

4. Pour into a fresh glass, serve neat and garnish with a grilled lemon wheel. Enjoy!

Grilled Peach Sour Cocktail

Servings: 2
Cooking Time: 15 Minutes

Ingredients:
- 2 peach, sliced
- 2 Tablespoon sugar
- 1 1/2 Ounce Smoked Simple Syrup
- 4 Ounce bourbon
- 6 Dash Bitters Lab Apricot Vanilla Bitters
- 2 Sprig fresh thyme, for garnish

Directions:
1. Supply your smoker with wood pellets and follow the start-up procedure. Preheat the grill, with the lid closed, to 325° F.

2. Toss peach slices with granulated sugar and place directly on grill grate. Cook for 20 minutes or until grill marks form. Remove from grill and let cool. Grill: 325 °F

3. Place peaches and Traeger Smoked Simple Syrup into tin and muddle. Peaches should form about an ounce of juice during the muddling. Once completed, add remaining ingredients and shake.

4. Pour contents into glass over fresh ice and garnish with fresh thyme. Enjoy!

Zombie Cocktail Recipe

Servings: 2
Cooking Time: 45 Minutes

Ingredients:
- fresh squeezed orange juice
- pineapple juice
- 2 Ounce light rum
- 2 Ounce dark rum
- 2 Ounce lime juice
- 1 Ounce Smoked Simple Syrup
- 6 Ounce smoked orange and pineapple juice
- 2 grilled orange peel, for garnish

- 2 grilled pineapple chunks, for garnish

Directions:

1. Supply your smoker with wood pellets and follow the start-up procedure. Preheat the grill, with the lid closed, to 180° F.

2. Smoked Orange and Pineapple Juice: Pour equal parts fresh squeezed orange juice and pineapple juice into a shallow sheet pan and smoke for 45 minutes. Remove and let cool. Measure out 3 ounces of juice and reserve any remaining juice in the refrigerator for future use. Grill: 180 °F

3. Add dark and light rums, 3 ounces smoked orange and pineapple juice, lime juice and Traeger Smoked Simple Syrup to a mixing glass.

4. Add ice, shake and strain over clean ice into a Tiki glass.

5. Garnish with a grilled orange peel and grilled pineapple. Enjoy!

Smoked Hot Buttered Rum

Servings: 4
Cooking Time: 30 Minutes

Ingredients:

- 2 Cup water
- 1/4 Cup brown sugar
- 1/2 Stick butter, melted
- 1 Teaspoon ground cinnamon
- 1/4 Teaspoon ground nutmeg
- ground cloves
- salt
- 6 Ounce Rum

Directions:

1. Supply your smoker with wood pellets and follow the start-up procedure. Preheat the grill, with the lid closed, to 180° F.

2. In a shallow baking dish, combine 2 cups water with all ingredients except for the rum and place directly on the grill grate. Smoke for 30 minutes. Grill: 180 °F

3. Remove from the grill and pour into the pitcher of a blender. Process until somewhat frothy.

4. Pour 1.5 ounces of rum each into 4 glasses. Split hot butter mixture evenly between the four glasses.

5. Garnish with a cinnamon stick and freshly grated nutmeg. Enjoy!

Strawberry Mule Cocktail

Servings: 2
Cooking Time: 15 Minutes

Ingredients:

- 8 grilled strawberries, plus more for serving
- 3 Ounce vodka
- 1 Ounce Smoked Simple Syrup
- 1 Ounce lemon juice
- 6 Ounce ginger beer
- fresh mint leaves

Directions:

1. Supply your smoker with wood pellets and follow the start-up procedure. Preheat the grill, with the lid closed, to 400° F.

2. Place strawberries directly on the grill grate and cook 15 minutes or until grill marks appear. Grill: 400 °F

3. For the cocktail: Add vodka, grilled strawberries, Traeger Smoked Simple Syrup and lemon juice to a shaker. Shake vigorously.

4. Double strain into a fresh glass or copper mug with crushed ice.

5. Top with ginger beer and garnish with extra grilled strawberries and fresh mint. Enjoy!

Garden Gimlet Cocktail

Servings: 2
Cooking Time: 45 Minutes

Ingredients:

- 2 Cup honey
- 4 lemons, zested
- 4 Sprig rosemary, plus more for garnish
- 1/2 Cup water
- 4 Slices cucumber
- 1 1/2 Ounce lime juice
- 3 Ounce vodka

Directions:

1. Supply your smoker with wood pellets and follow the start-up procedure. Preheat the grill, with the lid closed, to 180° F.

2. To make smoked lemon and rosemary honey syrup, thin 1 cup honey by adding 1/4 cup water to a shallow pan. Add lemon zest and 2 sprigs rosemary.

3. Place the pan directly on the grill grate and smoke 45 minutes to an hour. Remove from heat, strain and cool. Grill: 180 °F

4. In a cocktail shaker, muddle the cucumbers and 1oz of the smoked lemon and rosemary honey syrup.

5. After muddling, add lime juice, vodka, and ice. Shake and double strain into a coup glass.

6. Garnish with a sprig of rosemary. Enjoy!

Grilled Hawaiian Sour

Servings: 2
Cooking Time: 15 Minutes

Ingredients:

- 2 Whole pineapple, trimmed and sliced
- 1/2 Cup palm sugar
- 3 Ounce bourbon
- 2 Ounce grilled pineapple juice
- 2 Ounce Smoked Simple Syrup
- 10 Ounce lemon juice
- 2 grilled pineapple chunk, for garnish
- 2 pineapple leaf, for garnish

Directions:

1. Supply your smoker with wood pellets and follow the start-up procedure. Preheat the grill, with the lid closed, to 350° F.

2. For the Grilled Pineapple Juice: Dust pineapple slices with palm sugar. Place directly on the grill grate and cook for 8 minutes per side. Grill: 350 °F

3. Remove from grill and let cool. Reserve a few pieces for garnish. Run remaining pineapple pieces through centrifugal juicer to extract juice.

4. To Make the Drink: Add bourbon, grilled pineapple juice, simple syrup and lemon juice to a cocktail strainer with ice. Shake vigorously. Double strain into a chilled coupe glass. Garnish with grilled pineapple chunk and pineapple leaf. Enjoy!

Smoked Pomegranate Lemonade Cocktail

Servings: 2
Cooking Time: 45 Minutes

Ingredients:

- 32 Ounce POM Juice
- 2 Cup pomegranate seeds
- 3 Ounce vodka
- 8 Ounce lemonade
- lemon wheel, for garnish
- fresh mint, for garnish

Directions:

1. Supply your smoker with wood pellets and follow the start-up procedure. Preheat the grill, with the lid closed, to 225° F.

2. For the Smoked Pomegranate Ice Cubes: Pour one small container of POM juice and 1 cup of pomegranate seeds into a shallow sheet pan. Smoke on the Traeger for 45 minutes. Pull off grill and let sit until cooled. Grill: 180 °F

3. Pour smoked POM juice into ice molds of your choice and put into freezer.

4. When ready to serve, place the frozen pomegranate cubes into a mason jar. Pour vodka and lemonade over the ice cubes.

5. Garnish with a lemon wheel and fresh mint. Enjoy!

Smoked Mulled Wine

Servings: 10
Cooking Time: 60 Minutes

Ingredients:

- 2 Bottle red wine
- 1/2 Cup whiskey
- 1/2 Cup white rum
- 1/2 Cup honey
- 1 cinnamon stick
- 2 pods star anise
- 4 whole cloves
- 1 (3 in) orange peel

Directions:

1. Supply your smoker with wood pellets and follow the start-up procedure. Preheat the grill, with the lid closed, to 180° F.

2. In a shallow baking dish, combine wine, whiskey, rum, honey, cinnamon stick, star anise, cloves and orange peel. Stir well until combined.

3. Place the dish directly on the grill grate and smoke for one hour until the mixture is warm. Grill: 180 °F

4. Remove from grill and ladle into mugs leaving the mulling spices behind. Garnish with fresh cinnamon sticks, anise, orange zest or a combination. Enjoy!

Batter Up Cocktail

Servings: 2

Cooking Time: 60 Minutes

Ingredients:

- 2 whole nutmeg
- 4 Ounce Michter's Bourbon
- 3 Teaspoon pumpkin puree
- 1 Ounce Smoked Simple Syrup
- 2 Large egg

Directions:

1. Supply your smoker with wood pellets and follow the start-up procedure. Preheat the grill, with the lid closed, to 180° F.

2. Place whole nutmeg on a sheet tray and place in the grill. Smoke 1 hour. Remove from grill and let cool. Grill: 180 °F

3. Add everything to a shaker and shake without ice. Add ice, then shake and strain into a chilled highball glass.

4. Garnish with grated, smoked nutmeg. Enjoy!

Smoked Ice Mojito Slurpee

Servings: 2

Cooking Time: 30 Minutes

Ingredients:

- water
- 1 Cup white rum
- 1/2 Cup lime juice
- 1/4 Cup Smoked Simple Syrup
- 12 Whole fresh mint leaves

- 4 Sprig mint
- 4 Whole lime wedge, for garnish

Directions:

1. Supply your smoker with wood pellets and follow the start-up procedure. Preheat the grill, with the lid closed, to 180° F.

2. For optimal flavor, use Super Smoke if available. Grill: 180 °F

3. Remove water from grill and pour smoked water into ice cube trays. Place in freezer until frozen.

4. Add rum, lime juice, Traeger Smoked Simple Syrup, mint and smoked ice to a blender.

5. Blend until a slushy consistency and pour into glasses.

6. Garnish with a mint sprig and lime wedge. Enjoy!

Grilled Frozen Strawberry Lemonade

Servings: 4

Cooking Time: 15 Minutes

Ingredients:

- 1 Pound fresh strawberries
- 1/2 Cup turbinado sugar
- 8 lemon, halved
- 1/4 Cup Cointreau
- 1/4 Cup simple syrup
- 2 Cup ice
- 1 Cup Titos Vodka

Directions:

1. Supply your smoker with wood pellets and follow the start-up procedure. Preheat the grill, with the lid closed, to High heat.

2. Dip the lemon halves in turbinado sugar and place directly on the grill grate. Toss the strawberries with remaining sugar and place next to the lemons.

3. Cook until grill marks develop on both, about 15 min for lemons and 10 min for strawberries.

4. Remove from heat and let cool.

5. Juice grilled lemons straining out any seeds or pulp. Pour into a blender pitcher.

6. Remove stems from grilled strawberries and place in blender pitcher with lemon juice. Add simple syrup, vodka, cointreau, and 2 cups of ice.

7. Puree until smooth and transfer to 4-6 glasses. Garnish with grilled strawberries and grilled lemon slices if desired. Enjoy!

Smoked Sangria

Servings: 6

Cooking Time: 45 Minutes

Ingredients:

- 1 (750 ml) medium-bodied red wine
- 1/4 Cup Grand Marnier
- 1/4 Cup Smoked Simple Syrup
- 1 Cup fresh cranberries
- 1 Whole apple, sliced
- 2 Whole limes, sliced
- 4 cinnamon stick
- soda water

Directions:

1. Supply your smoker with wood pellets and follow the start-up procedure. Preheat the grill, with the lid closed, to 180° F.

2. In a shallow dish, combine red wine, Grand Marnier, Traeger Smoked Simple Syrup and cranberries, and place directly on the grill grate.

3. Smoke for 30 to 45 minutes or until the liquid picks up desired amount of smoke. Remove from grill and place in the fridge to cool. Grill: 180 ˚F

4. When the mixture has cooled, place in a large pitcher. Add sliced apples, limes, cinnamon sticks and ice to pitcher.

5. Top with soda water, if desired. Enjoy!

Smoked Pumpkin Spice Latte

Servings: 4

Cooking Time: 45 Minutes

Ingredients:

- 1 Small sugar pumpkin
- olive oil
- 1 Can sweetened condensed milk
- 1 Cup whole milk
- 2 Tablespoon Smoked Simple Syrup
- 1 Teaspoon pumpkin pie spice
- pinch of salt
- cinnamon
- whipped cream
- shaved nutmeg
- 8 Ounce smoked cold brew coffee

Directions:

1. Supply your smoker with wood pellets and follow the start-up procedure. Preheat the grill, with the lid closed, to 325° F.

2. Cut the sugar pumpkin in half, scoop out the seeds and discard. Place the pumpkin halves cut side up on a baking sheet and brush lightly with olive oil.

3. Place the sheet tray directly on the grill grate and cook 45 minutes or until the flesh is tender. Remove from heat and place on the counter to cool. Grill: 325 ˚F

4. When the pumpkin is cool enough to handle, scoop out the flesh and mash until smooth.

5. Place 3 Tbsp of the pumpkin puree in a separate bowl and reserve the remaining for another use.

6. Add the sweetened condensed milk, whole milk, Traeger Smoked Simple Syrup, pumpkin pie seasoning and salt to the pumpkin puree. Whisk to combine.

7. Pour the cold brew over ice, add desired amount of pumpkin spice creamer and top with whipped cream, cinnamon, and shaved nutmeg if desired. Enjoy!

Fig Slider Cocktail

Servings: 2

Cooking Time: 15 Minutes

Ingredients:

- 2 peach, halved
- 4 oranges
- honey
- sugar
- 2 Teaspoon orange fig spread
- 1 Ounce fresh lemon juice
- 4 Ounce bourbon
- 3 Ounce honey glazed grilled orange juice

Directions:

1. Supply your smoker with wood pellets and follow the start-up procedure. Preheat the grill, with the lid closed, to 325° F.

2. Pit the peach and cut in half. Cut one of the oranges in half. Glaze the peach and orange cut sides with honey and set directly on the grill grate until the honey caramelizes and fruit has grill marks. Grill: 325 ˚F

3. Cut the second orange into wheels and coat with granulated sugar on both sides. Place directly on the grill grate and cook 15 minutes each side or until grill marks form. Grill: 325 ˚F

4. In a mixing tin, add grilled peaches, bourbon, orange fig spread, fresh lemon juice and honey glazed orange juice.

5. Shake vigorously to blend the juices and fig spread. Strain over clean ice. Garnish with grilled orange wheel. Enjoy!

Bacon Old-fashioned Cocktail

Servings: 2

Cooking Time: 20 Minutes

Ingredients:
- 16 Slices bacon
- 1/2 Cup warm water (110°F to 115°F)
- 1500 mL bourbon
- 1/2 Fluid Ounce maple syrup
- 4 Dash Angostura bitters
- 2 fresh orange peel

Directions:

1. Smoke bacon prior to making Old Fashioned using this recipe for Applewood Smoked Bacon.

2. To Make Bacon: Supply your smoker with wood pellets and follow the start-up procedure. Preheat the grill, with the lid closed, to 325° F.

3. Place bacon in a single layer on a cooling rack that fits inside a baking sheet pan. Cook in Traeger for 15-20 minutes or until bacon is browned and crispy. Reserve bacon for later. Let the fat cool slightly; you'll use the fat to infuse the bourbon. Grill: 325 ˚F

4. Combine 1/4 cup of warm (not hot) liquid bacon fat with the entire contents of a 750ml bottle of bourbon in a glass or heavy plastic container.

5. Use a fork to stir well. Let it sit on the counter for a few hours, stirring every so often.

6. After about four hours, put bourbon fat mixture into the freezer. After about an hour, the fat will congeal and you can simply scoop it out with a spoon. You can fine-strain the mixture through a sieve to remove all fat if desired.

7. Combine ingredients with ice and stir until cold. Strain over fresh ice in an Old Fashioned glass and garnish with reserved bacon and orange peel. Enjoy!

Smoked Salted Caramel White Russian

Servings: 4

Cooking Time: 20 Minutes

Ingredients:
- 16 Ounce half-and-half
- salted caramel sauce
- 6 Ounce vodka
- 6 Ounce Kahlúa

Directions:

1. Supply your smoker with wood pellets and follow the start-up procedure. Preheat the grill, with the lid closed, to 180° F.

2. Pour the half-and-half in a shallow baking dish and place directly on the grill grate. In another shallow baking dish, pour 2 to 3 cups of water and place on the grill next to the half-and-half.

3. Smoke both the half-and-half and water for 20 minutes. Remove from the grill and let cool. Grill: 180 ˚F

4. Place the half-and-half in the fridge until ready to use. Pour the smoked water into ice cube trays and transfer to the freezer until completely frozen.

5. Separate the smoked ice cubes into four glasses. Drizzle the salted caramel sauce around the inside of the glass.

6. Pour 1-1/2 ounce vodka and 1-1/2 ounce Kahlúa into each of the glasses and top with the smoked half-and-half. Enjoy!

Smoky Scotch & Ginger Cocktail

Servings: 2

Cooking Time: 60 Minutes

Ingredients:
- 1 Ounce ginger syrup
- 1/2 Ounce brandied cherry juice
- 1/2 Ounce agave nectar

* 4 Ounce scotch
* 1 1/2 Ounce lemon juice
* 2 Slices grilled lemon, for garnish
* 2 cherry, for garnish

Directions:

1. Supply your smoker with wood pellets and follow the start-up procedure. Preheat the grill, with the lid closed, to 180° F.

2. For the smoked ginger cherry syrup: Place ginger syrup, cherry juice and agave nectar in a shallow dish and place the dish directly on the grill grate.

3. Smoke for 60 minutes, or until the mixture has picked up the smoke flavor. Remove from grill and allow to cool for 30 minutes. Grill: 180 °F

4. Place smoked ginger cherry syrup, scotch and lemon juice into a shaker tin and shake with ice. Strain into a glass over fresh ice and garnish with a grilled lemon wheel and cherry. Enjoy!

A Smoking Classic Cocktail

Servings: 2

Cooking Time: 60 Minutes

Ingredients:

* 2 Bottle Angostura orange bitters
* 10 sugar cubes
* 8 Ounce Champagne
* lemon twist

Directions:

1. Supply your smoker with wood pellets and follow the start-up procedure. Preheat the grill, with the lid closed, to 180° F.

2. For the Smoked Orange Bitters: In a small skillet, combine 1 bottle of Angostura orange bitters with a splash of water and 4 sugar cubes.

3. Place skillet on the grill grate and smoke for 60 minutes. Cool the smoked bitters and put back into the bottle. Grill: 180 °F

4. Add a sugar cube to each Champagne flute and soak the sugar cubes with the smoked bitters.

5. Add champagne and a lemon twist in a flute glass. Enjoy!

Cran-apple Tequila Punch With Smoked Oranges

Servings: 2

Cooking Time: 15 Minutes

Ingredients:

* 6 Cup apple juice, chilled
* 6 Cup light cranberry cocktail
* 1 Cup cranberries, fresh or thawed
* 3 Large oranges, halved
* 1 Cup sugar, for rimming glasses
* 2 Tablespoon lemon juice
* 2 Cup reposado tequila
* 1 Cup orange-flavored liqueur, such as Grand Marnier or Cointreau
* 2 Bottle sparkling wine (such as prosecco) or sparkling water

Directions:

1. Combine 1 cup each of the apple and cranberry juices, then pour into ice cube trays. If the cube molds are big enough, place a few cranberries into each cube. Freeze for 6 hours to overnight.

2. Supply your smoker with wood pellets and follow the start-up procedure. Preheat the grill, with the lid closed, to 180° F.

3. Place the orange halves cut-side down on the grill and smoke for 15 minutes. Remove from the grill and juice oranges. Reserve smoked orange juice. Grill: 180 °F

4. When ready to serve, place the sugar on a flat plate. Pour the lemon juice into a bowl that will fit the rim of each glass.

5. Carefully dip the rim of each glass in the lemon juice, then dip in the sugar to create a 1/8" sugar rim. Turn the glass right-side up and allow to dry for a few minutes before using.

6. Just before serving, mix the remaining apple juice, cranberry cocktail and smoked orange juice with the tequila, orange liqueur, and sparkling wine in a large bowl or pitcher. Taste, adding more of any ingredient to meet your preference.

7. When ready to serve, place a few ice cubes in each glass, then pour a cup of the punch over the top. Alternatively, place all of the ice cubes in the punch bowl and allow guests to help themselves. Enjoy!

Smoked Cold Brew Coffee

Servings: 8
Cooking Time: 120 Minutes

Ingredients:

- 12 Ounce coarse ground coffee
- heavy cream or milk
- sugar

Directions:

1. Place half the coffee grounds in a plastic container and slowly pour 3-1/2 cups water over the top of the grounds. Add remaining grounds and pour another 3-1/2 cups water over the top in a circular motion.

2. Press the grounds down into the water using the back of a spoon. Cover and transfer to the refrigerator and let sit for 18 to 24 hours.

3. Remove from refrigerator and strain into a clean container through a fine mesh strainer or double layer of cheese cloth.

4. Supply your smoker with wood pellets and follow the start-up procedure. Preheat the grill, with the lid closed, to 180° F.

5. Pour cold brew into a shallow baking dish and place directly on the grill grate. Smoke for 1 to 2 hours depending on desired level of smoke. Grill: 180 °F

6. Remove from grill and place over an ice bath to cool. Drink as is over ice, with cream or sugar or use in your favorite coffee recipes. Enjoy!

Smoked Hibiscus Sparkler

Servings: 4
Cooking Time: 30 Minutes

Ingredients:

- 1/2 Cup sugar
- 2 Tablespoon dried hibiscus flowers
- 1 Bottle sparkling wine
- crystallized ginger, for garnish

Directions:

1. Supply your smoker with wood pellets and follow the start-up procedure. Preheat the grill, with the lid closed, to 180° F.

2. Place water in a shallow baking dish and place directly on the grill grate. Smoke the water for 30 minutes or until desired smoke flavor is achieved. Grill: 180 °F

3. Pour water into a small saucepan and add sugar and hibiscus flowers. Bring to a simmer over medium heat and cook until sugar is dissolved.

4. Strain out the hibiscus flowers and transfer your simple syrup to a small container and refrigerate until chilled.

5. Pour 1/2 ounce smoked hibiscus simple syrup in the bottom of a champagne glass and top with sparkling wine.

6. Drop in a few pieces of crystallized ginger to garnish. Enjoy!

Smoked Jacobsen Salt Margarita

Servings: 2
Cooking Time: 1 Day

Ingredients:

- kosher sea salt
- 3 Cup Jacobsen Co. Honey
- 6 Ounce tequila
- 4 Ounce fresh squeezed lime juice
- 1/2 Cup Jacobsen Salt Co. Cherrywood Smoked Salt or smoked kosher salt
- 2 Ounce simple syrup
- 2 Teaspoon orange liqueur

Directions:

1. If making your own smoked salt, take kosher sea salt (however much you want to smoke) and spread it out on a tray.

2. Supply your smoker with wood pellets and follow the start-up procedure. Preheat the grill, with the lid closed, to 165° F.

3. Place tray of salt directly on the grill grate and smoke for about 24 hours, stirring the salt every 8 hours. Once it has smoked for 24 hours, take off grill and use in all your favorite dishes. Note: If you want to skip the long smoke session, use Jacobsen Salt Co. Cherrywood Smoked Salt. Grill: 165 °F

4. Simple Syrup: Put the honey and 1 cup water in a small saucepan. Cook over low heat, stirring, for about 20 min.

5. Fill a cocktail shaker with ice. Add tequila, lime juice, simple syrup and orange liqueur. Cover and shake until mixed and chilled, about 30 seconds.

6. Place smoked salt on a plate. Press the rim of a chilled rocks glass into the salt to rim the edge. Strain margarita into the glass. Enjoy!

Smoked Barnburner Cocktail

Servings: 2
Cooking Time: 45 Minutes

Ingredients:
- 16 Ounce fresh raspberries
- 1/2 Cup Smoked Simple Syrup
- 1 1/2 Ounce smoked raspberry syrup
- 3 Ounce reposado tequila
- 1 Ounce lime juice
- 1 Ounce lemon juice
- 2 grilled lime wheel, for garnish

Directions:
1. Supply your smoker with wood pellets and follow the start-up procedure. Preheat the grill, with the lid closed, to 180° F.

2. For Smoked Raspberry Syrup: Place fresh raspberries on a grill mat and smoke for 30 minutes. After the raspberries have been smoked, reserve a few for garnish and place the remainder into a shallow sheet pan with Traeger Smoked Simple Syrup. Grill: 180 ˚F

3. Place sheet pan on the grill grate and smoke for 45 minutes. Remove from grill and let cool. Strain through a fine mesh sieve discarding solids. Transfer the syrup to the refrigerator until ready to use. Makes about 1/2 cup of smoked raspberry syrup. Grill: 180 ˚F

4. For cocktail: Add 3/4 ounce smoked raspberry syrup, tequila, lime juice and lemon juice with ice into a mixing glass. Shake and pour over clean ice. Garnish with smoked raspberries and a grilled lime wheel. Enjoy!

Smoked Pineapple Hotel Nacional Cocktail

Servings: 2
Cooking Time: 20 Minutes

Ingredients:
- 2 pineapple
- 1/2 Cup water
- 1/2 Cup sugar
- 3 Fluid Ounce white rum
- 1 1/2 Fluid Ounce lime juice
- 1 1/2 Fluid Ounce Pineapple Syrup
- 1 Fluid Ounce apricot brandy
- 2 Dash Angostura bitters

Directions:
1. For the Syrup: Supply your smoker with wood pellets and follow the start-up procedure. Preheat the grill, with the lid closed, to 180° F.

2. Trim both ends of the pineapple, discard the ends. Cut the pineapple into slices about 3/4" thick. Don't worry about the skin, it doesn't hurt to leave it on. Place the pineapple slices on the grill and smoke for about 15 minutes on each sideTrim both ends of the pineapple and discard the ends. Cut the pineapple into slices about 3/4 inch thick. Don't worry about the skin, it doesn't hurt to leave it on. Place the pineapple slices on the grill and smoke for about 15 minutes per side. Grill: 180 ˚F

3. While the pineapple is smoking, combine 1/4 cup water and sugar in a saucepan over low heat, stirring constantly, until sugar is dissolved. Pour syrup into a large bowl and set aside.

4. When the pineapple is done cooking, cut each slice into eight or so wedges and add the wedges to the bowl with the simple syrup, tossing to coat and cover.

5. Leave the mixture to macerate for at least 4 hours (or up to 24) in the refrigerator, stirring from time to time.

6. Strain the syrup into a clean bowl through a fine-mesh strainer and press on the pineapple with a ladle to extract as much liquid as possible. You can bottle and refrigerate the syrup for up to 4 days.

7. To make the cocktail: Combine the rum, lime juice, pineapple syrup, apricot brandy, and bitters in a cocktail

shaker or mixing glass. Fill with ice cubes and shake until cold.

8. Strain into a chilled cocktail glass. Garnish with a lime wheel and serve. Enjoy!

Dublin Delight Cocktail

Servings: 2
Cooking Time: 20 Minutes

Ingredients:

- 2 orange, sliced
- 3 Fluid Ounce Teeling Whiskey
- 1 1/2 Fluid Ounce Smoked Simple Syrup
- 6 Dash aromatic bitters
- 6 Fluid Ounce Guinness beer
- 2 Amarena cherry, for garnish

Directions:

1. Supply your smoker with wood pellets and follow the start-up procedure. Preheat the grill, with the lid closed, to 450° F.

2. Place orange slices directly on the grill grate and cook 20 to 25 minutes. Remove from grill and let cool. Grill: 450 °F

3. In a mixing glass, add whiskey, Traeger Smoked Simple Syrup and bitters. Add ice and shake. Pour over a beer glass filled with ice and top off with cold Guinness.

4. Garnish with a grilled orange slice and Amarena cherry. Enjoy!

Grilled Peach Mint Julep

Servings: 2
Cooking Time: 45 Minutes

Ingredients:

- 2 Whole peach
- 4 Ounce whiskey
- 2 Cup sugar
- 4 Tablespoon pink peppercorns
- 20 Whole fresh mint leaves, plus more for garnish
- 2 lime wedge, for garnish
- 4 Ounce bourbon

Directions:

1. For the Grilled Whiskey Peaches: cut peach into slices, then soak peach slices in whiskey in the refrigerator for 4 to 6 hours.

2. For the Pink Peppercorn Simple Syrup: In a shallow pan, combine sugar, 1 cup water and pink peppercorns.

3. Supply your smoker with wood pellets and follow the start-up procedure. Preheat the grill, with the lid closed, to 180° F.

4. Cook syrup down on the grill for 30 minutes, or until desired smoke flavor has been reached. Remove from the grill. Grill: 180 °F

5. Increase Traeger temperature to 350°F and preheat. Place the whiskey peach slices directly on the grill grate and cook 10 to 12 minutes or until peaches soften and get grill marks. Grill: 350 °F

6. To make the Julep: Muddle 1/2 ounce Pink Peppercorn Simple Syrup with 10 fresh mint leaves and 4 slices of grilled whiskey peaches.

7. Add crushed ice over the rim of the glass. Pour bourbon over the crushed ice and stir. Garnish with 1 large sprig of mint and fresh lime. Enjoy!

Smoked Irish Coffee

Servings: 2
Cooking Time: 15 Minutes

Ingredients:

- 10 Ounce hot coffee
- 1/2 Cup heavy cream
- 1 Tablespoon sugar
- 2 Ounce Irish whiskey
- freshly grated nutmeg, for garnish (optional)

Directions:

1. Supply your smoker with wood pellets and follow the start-up procedure. Preheat the grill, with the lid closed, to 180° F.

2. Place the coffee and cream in separate shallow baking dishes and place both directly on the grill grate. Smoke for 10 to 15 minutes until the liquids pick up a slight smoke flavor. Grill: 180 °F

3. Remove from the grill and cool the cream. When the cream is cool, add sugar and whip in a stand mixer or by hand to soft peaks.

4. Pour the hot coffee into two mugs then add 2 ounces of whiskey to each.

5. Top with smoked whipped cream and finish with freshly grated nutmeg, if desired. Enjoy!

Smoked Texas Ranch Water

Servings: 4
Cooking Time: 60 Minutes

Ingredients:
- 3 Whole limes
- 1 Tablespoon Blackened Saskatchewan Rub
- 12 Ounce blanco tequila
- 24 Ounce Topo Chico or other sparkling mineral water
- 8 Slices jalapeño, optional

Directions:
1. Supply your smoker with wood pellets and follow the start-up procedure. Preheat the grill, with the lid closed, to 225° F.

2. Cut two of the limes in half and sprinkle with Traeger Blackened Saskatchewan Rub. Place the four lime halves on the edge of the grill grate and smoke for 1 hour. Remove from grill and set aside to cool. Grill: 225 °F

3. Pour some of the rub onto a small plate. Cut the third lime into 1/4 wedges and use the lime to rub the rim of 4 cocktail glasses, turn the glasses upside down, and into the rub to salt the rim.

4. Place several ice cubes into your rimmed glasses and pour 3 ounces tequila, 6 ounces Topo Chico, squeeze the juice of one smoked lime (discard after squeezing), and add one fresh lime wedge to each. If using the jalapeño, add one or two slices to each glass (muddle if desired).

5. Stir to combine and enjoy!

Traeger Old Fashioned

Servings: 2
Cooking Time: 60 Minutes

Ingredients:
- 2 orange
- 2 Cup cherries
- 3 Ounce bourbon
- 1 Ounce Smoked Simple Syrup
- 8 Dash Bitters Lab Apricot Vanilla Bitters

Directions:
1. Supply your smoker with wood pellets and follow the start-up procedure. Preheat the grill, with the lid closed, to 180° F.

2. While Traeger preheats, slice whole orange into wheels.

3. Place cherries on a small sheet pan and place in the Traeger. Place orange slices directly on the grill grate.

4. Smoke cherries for 1 hour and oranges for 25 minutes, depending on taste, before removing from the grill. Let oranges and cherries cool. Grill: 180 °F

5. Pour bourbon into glass, followed by Traeger Smoked Simple Syrup and bitters. Add ice and stir for 45 seconds or until drink is well-diluted.

6. Strain contents into new glass over fresh ice. Skewer orange wheel and add cherry for garnish. Enjoy!

Traeger Boulevardier Cocktail

Servings: 2
Cooking Time: 60 Minutes

Ingredients:
- 4 oranges
- 1/2 Cup honey
- 1500 mL rye whiskey
- 1 1/2 Ounce Campari
- 1 1/2 Ounce sweet vermouth
- 2 Tablespoon granulated sugar
- 3 Ounce grilled orange infused rye

Directions:
1. Supply your smoker with wood pellets and follow the start-up procedure. Preheat the grill, with the lid closed, to 350° F.

2. Slice 2 oranges in half and coat cut side with honey. Peel remaining orange and place peels on the grill. Cook 20 to 25 minutes. Grill: 350 °F

3. Remove from grill and let cool. Place orange halves cut side down directly on the grill grate and cook 20 to 30 minutes or until dark grill marks appear. Remove orange halves and allow to cool. Grill: 350 °F

4. Place orange halves into a bottle of rye whiskey and let steep for 10 to 12 hours. The longer they steep, the sweeter and more pronounced the orange flavor will be.

5. Add all ingredients into a mixing glass and stir until diluted. Strain into a fresh coupe glass and serve neat.

6. Garnish with grilled orange peel. Enjoy!

Grilled Rabbit Tail Cocktail

Servings: 2

Cooking Time: 25 Minutes

Ingredients:
- 1 1/2 Ounce lemon juice
- 4 Ounce Apple Brandy
- 1 Ounce orange juice
- 1 Ounce Smoked Simple Syrup

Directions:

1. Supply your smoker with wood pellets and follow the start-up procedure. Preheat the grill, with the lid closed, to 350° F.

2. Place lemon halves directly on the grill grate and cook for 20-25 minutes or until grill marks appear. Remove from grill and let cool. Once cool enough to handle, juice the lemons then chill and reserve the juice. Grill: 350 ˚F

3. Using the proportions listed above and considering the size and consumption rate of your tailgate crew or party, mix all the above ingredients in a large thermos and top with a bit of ice.

4. Using 6-8 oz glasses or cups, guests can serve themselves from the thermos and garnish each drink with a grilled apple slice. Enjoy!

Traeger Paloma Cocktail

Servings: 2

Cooking Time: 25 Minutes

Ingredients:
- 4 grapefruit, halved
- Smoked Simple Syrup
- 10 Stick cinnamon
- 3 Ounce reposado tequila
- 1 Ounce lime juice
- 1 Ounce Smoked Simple Syrup

- grilled lime, for garnish
- cinnamon stick, for garnish

Directions:

1. Supply your smoker with wood pellets and follow the start-up procedure. Preheat the grill, with the lid closed, to 350° F.

2. Grilled Grapefruit Juice: Cut 2 grapefruits in half. Place a cinnamon stick in each grapefruit half and glaze with Traeger Smoked Simple Syrup. Place on grill grate and cook for 20 minutes or until edges start to burn and it acquires grill marks. Remove from heat and let cool. Grill: 350 ˚F

3. After grapefruits have cooled, squeeze and strain juice. It should yield 10 to 12 ounces of juice.

4. In a mixing glass, add tequila, lime juice, Traeger Smoked Simple Syrup and 2 ounces of the grilled grapefruit juice.

5. Add ice and shake. Strain over ice in an old fashioned glass.

6. Add a grilled lime slice and cinnamon stick to garnish. Enjoy!

Smoked Grape Lime Rickey

Servings: 4

Cooking Time: 45 Minutes

Ingredients:
- 1/2 Pound red grapes
- 1/2 Cup plus 1 tablespoon sugar
- 1/2 Cup water
- 1 limes, sliced
- 2 limes, halved
- 1 Tablespoon sugar
- 1 L lemon lime soda

Directions:

1. Supply your smoker with wood pellets and follow the start-up procedure. Preheat the grill, with the lid closed, to 180° F.

2. Rinse grapes well and place in a shallow baking dish. Combine 1/2 cup sugar and water and stir until sugar dissolves. Pour over grapes.

3. Place the baking dish directly on the grill grate and smoke for 30 to 40 minutes until grapes are tender. Grill: 180 ˚F

4. Remove from the grill and pour entire contents of the baking dish in a blender. Puree on high until smooth then pass the mixture through a fine mesh strainer.

5. Increase Traeger temperature to 350˚F . Grill: 350 ˚F

6. Toss the lime slices and lime halves with 1 tablespoon sugar and place directly on the grill grate. Cook for 15 to 20 minutes or until grill marks develop. Remove from grill and set slices aside. When cool enough to handle, juice grilled lime halves. Grill: 350 ˚F

7. To build the drink, fill a pint glass with ice. Pour in 1-1/2 ounce grilled lime juice, 1-1/2 ounce smoked grape syrup and top off with soda. Garnish with grilled lime slice. Enjoy!

Honey Glazed Grapefruit Shandy Cocktail

Servings: 2
Cooking Time: 20 Minutes

Ingredients:
- 4 grapefruits
- 4 Tablespoon honey
- granulated sugar
- 2 Ounce bourbon
- 1 Ounce Smoked Simple Syrup
- 4 Ounce honey glazed grilled grapefruit, juiced
- 2 Bottle Ballast Point Grapefruit Sculpin

Directions:
1. Supply your smoker with wood pellets and follow the start-up procedure. Preheat the grill, with the lid closed, to 375° F.

2. For the honey glazed grapefruit: Slice one grapefruit in half and coat with 2 tablespoons honey.

3. Take the other grapefruit and slice into wheels. Toss the wheels in granulated sugar until well coated.

4. Place the grapefruit halves and wheels directly on the grill grate, cut side down, and cook for 20 to 30 minutes. Remove from grill and set the wheels aside. Grill: 375 ˚F

5. Squeeze the grapefruit halves into a measuring cup. It should yield about 2 oz juice.

6. Pour the grapefruit juice into a shaker and add bourbon and Traeger Smoked Simple Syrup then top with ice. Shake for 10-15 seconds.

7. Strain into glass, add ice and fill with beer. Garnish with the grilled grapefruit wheel. Enjoy!

Smoked Plum And Thyme Fizz Cocktail

Servings: 2
Cooking Time: 60 Minutes

Ingredients:
- 6 fresh plums
- 4 Fluid Ounce vodka
- 1 1/2 Fluid Ounce fresh lemon juice
- 2 Ounce smoked plum and thyme simple syrup
- 4 Fluid Ounce club soda
- 2 Slices smoked plum, for garnish
- 2 Sprig fresh thyme, for garnish
- 8 Sprig thyme
- 2 Cup Smoked Simple Syrup

Directions:
1. Supply your smoker with wood pellets and follow the start-up procedure. Preheat the grill, with the lid closed, to 180° F.

2. Cut plums in half and remove the pit. Place the plum halves directly on the grill grate and smoke for 25 minutes. Grill: 180 ˚F

3. For the Plum and Thyme Simple Syrup: After 25 minutes, remove plums from the grill and cut into quarters. Add plums and thyme sprigs to 1 cup of Traeger Smoked Simple Syrup. Smoke the mixture for 45 minutes. Remove from grill, strain and let cool. Grill: 180 ˚F

4. Add vodka, fresh lemon juice and smoked plum and thyme simple syrup to a mixing glass.

5. Add ice and shake. Strain over clean ice, top off with club soda and garnish with a piece of thyme and slice of smoked plum. Enjoy!

Grilled Peach Smash Cocktail

Servings: 2

Cooking Time: 10 Minutes

Ingredients:

- 2 peach, sliced and grilled
- 10 fresh mint leaves
- 1 1/2 Ounce Smoked Simple Syrup
- 4 Ounce bourbon
- 2 mint sprig, for garnish

Directions:

1. Supply your smoker with wood pellets and follow the start-up procedure. Preheat the grill, with the lid closed, to 375° F.

2. Cut the peach into 6 slices and brush with Traeger Smoked Simple Syrup. Place directly on the grill grate and cook 10 to 12 minutes or until peaches soften and get grill marks. Grill: 375 ˚F

3. In a mixing glass, add 3 slices of grilled peaches, 5 mint leaves and Traeger Smoked Simple Syrup.

4. Muddle ingredients to release oils of the mint and juices from the grilled peaches. Add bourbon and crushed ice.

5. Shake and pour into a stemless wine glass. Top off with more crushed ice. Garnish with a grilled peach and mint sprig. Enjoy!

Smoked Eggnog

Servings: 4

Cooking Time: 60 Minutes

Ingredients:

- 2 Cup whole milk
- 1 Cup heavy cream
- 4 egg yolk
- Cup sugar
- 3 Ounce bourbon
- 1 Teaspoon vanilla extract
- 1 Teaspoon nutmeg
- 4 egg white
- whipped cream

Directions:

1. Plan ahead, this recipe requires chill time.

2. Supply your smoker with wood pellets and follow the start-up procedure. Preheat the grill, with the lid closed, to 180° F.

3. Pour the milk and the cream into a baking pan and smoke on the Traeger for 60 minutes. Grill: 180 ˚F

4. Meanwhile, in the bowl of a stand mixer, beat the egg yolks until they lighten in color. Gradually add 1/3 cup sugar and continue to beat until sugar completely dissolves.

5. After the milk and cream have smoked, add them along with the bourbon, vanilla and nutmeg into the egg mixture and stir to combine.

6. Place the egg whites in the bowl of a stand mixer and beat to soft peaks. When you lift the beaters the whites will make a peak that slightly curls down.

7. With the mixer still running, gradually add 1 tablespoon of sugar and beat until stiff peaks form.

8. Gently fold the egg whites into the cream mixture and then whisk to thoroughly combine.

9. Chill eggnog for a couple hours to let the flavors meld. Garnish with a dash of nutmeg and whipped cream on top. Enjoy!

RECIPE INDEX

Roasted Whole Chicken 165
Rosemary Cranberry Apple Sage Stuffing 37
Rosemary Prime Rib 194
Rub-injected Pork Shoulder 103
Ryes And Shine Cocktail 227

S

Salmon Cakes With Homemade Tartar Sauce 80
Salt Crusted Baked Potatoes 126
Salt-crusted Prime Rib 186
Santa Maria Tri-tip With Pico De Gallo 202
Savory Beaver Tails 44
Savory Cajun Bbq Chicken 162
Savory Cheese Steak Rolls With Puff Pastry 203
Savory Grilled Chicken Burrito Bowls 150
Savory Jerk Chicken Wings 167
Savory Smoked Turkey Legs 173
Savory Teriyaki Smoked Steak Bites 204
Savory Whiskey Grilled Elk Steaks 208
Seared Ahi Tuna Steak With Soy Sauce 51
Seared Bluefin Tuna Steaks 72
Sicilian Stuffed Mushrooms 144
Simple Cream Cheese Sausage Balls 219
Simple Glazed Salmon Fillets 80
Simple Smoked Baby Backs 104
Skillet Potato Cake 122
Skinny Smoked Chicken Breasts 170
Smoke Roasted Chicken With Herb Butter 149
Smoked & Loaded Baked Potato 135
Smoked Apple Cider 226
Smoked Asparagus Soup 134
Smoked Avocado Turkey Tamale Pie 155
Smoked Barnburner Cocktail 235
Smoked Bbq Onion Brussels Sprout 136
Smoked Beef Plate Ribs 189
Smoked Beef Ribs 189
Smoked Beer Brine Hens 152
Smoked Beer Brisket 211
Smoked Beer Corned Beef 201
Smoked Beet-pickled Eggs 142
Smoked Berry Cocktail 225

Smoked Black Pepper Beef Back Ribs 181
Smoked Bourbon & Orange Brined Turkey 175
Smoked Cashews 220
Smoked Cedar Plank Salmon 58
Smoked Cheese 221
Smoked Chicken Legs 164
Smoked Chicken Vermicelli Noodles 149
Smoked Chorizo & Arugula Pesto 87
Smoked Cold Brew Coffee 234
Smoked Drumsticks 162
Smoked Eggnog 240
Smoked Fish Chowder 81
Smoked Garlic Meatloaf 205
Smoked Grape Lime Rickey 238
Smoked Hibiscus Sparkler 234
Smoked Honey Chicken Drumsticks 158
Smoked Honey Salmon 78
Smoked Hot Buttered Rum 228
Smoked Ice Mojito Slurpee 230
Smoked Irish Coffee 236
Smoked Jacobsen Salt Margarita 234
Smoked Jalapeño Poppers 128
Smoked Lemon Cheesecake 42
Smoked Lemon Tea 32
Smoked Lobster Scampi 68
Smoked Longhorn Brisket 203
Smoked Macaroni Salad 133
Smoked Mango Shrimp 56
Smoked Mashed Potatoes 124
Smoked Moink Burger By Scott Thomas 197
Smoked Mulled Wine 229
Smoked Parmesan Herb Popcorn 119
Smoked Peppered Beef Tenderloin 210
Smoked Pickled Green Beans 119
Smoked Pico De Gallo 145
Smoked Pineapple Hotel Nacional Cocktail 235
Smoked Plum And Thyme Fizz Cocktail 239
Smoked Pomegranate Lemonade Cocktail 229
Smoked Porchetta With Italian Salsa Verde 96
Smoked Pork Loin 87